VIENNESE SILVER

VIENNESE SILVER

MODERN DESIGN 1780–1918

EDITED FOR THE NEUE GALERIE NEW YORK
AND THE KUNSTHISTORISCHES MUSEUM VIENNA
BY MICHAEL HUEY

KUNSTHISTORISCHES MUSEUM WIEN

Hatje Cantz Publishers

This book is published on the occasion of the exhibition
Viennese Silver • Modern Design 1780–1918
at the Neue Galerie New York (October 17, 2003–February 15, 2004)
and the Kunsthistorisches Museum Vienna (November 11, 2004–March 13, 2005);
with thanks to the MAK, Vienna for scholarly support.

Curator: Christian Witt-Dörring, Curator of MAK, Vienna
Exhibition concept: Günther Stefan Asenbaum, Paul Asenbaum, Michael Huey, Christian Witt-Dörring
Direction of exhibition office: Isabella Croÿ
Consultants: Ernst Ploil and Elisabeth Schmuttermeier, Curator of MAK, Vienna
Architect: Lawrence Kenny

Transport with the kind support of:

AUSTRIAN AIRLINES ➤

Editor and translator: Michael Huey, Vienna
Copyediting: Ingrid Nina Bell, Basel
Coordinating editor: Tas Skorupa
Design and typesetting: Pandiscio Co., New York/Richard Pandiscio, Takaya Goto
Production: Christine Müller
Photography: Dirk Bakker, Detroit; Krebs und Kedro, Vienna; David Schlegel, New York; Gerhard Trummler, Vienna
Reproduction: C + S Repro, Filderstadt and Fayer & Co., Vienna
Printed by Dr. Cantz'sche Druckerei, Ostfildern-Ruit

Published by
Hatje Cantz Verlag
Senefelderstrasse 12
73760 Ostfildern-Ruit
Germany
Tel. +49 / 711 / 44 05 0
Fax +49 / 711 / 44 05 220
Internet www.hatjecantz.de

Distribution in the United States by
D.A.P., Distributed Art Publishers, Inc.
155 Avenue of the Americas, Second Floor
New York, NY 10013–1507

ISBN 3–7757–1317–4 (English edition)
ISBN 3–7757–1316–6 (German edition)

Printed in Germany

FRONTISPIECE: Günther Stefan Asenbaum, Richard Pandiscio, Christian Witt-Dörring, photo montage of Koloman Moser in his studio (gelatin silver print, ca. 1898) with silver and niello coffer designed by Moser in 1903 (cat. no. 119)
Neue Galerie New York

PAGE EIGHT: C. H. Kniep, Sir William Hamilton opening a tomb at Nola
Engraved by Clever, Naples 1791–95
The British Museum, London

LENDERS TO THE EXHIBITION

Camilo Antonio, Vienna
Günther Stefan Asenbaum, London
Inge Asenbaum, Vienna
Bauhaus-Archiv, Museum für Gestaltung, Berlin
Grassimuseum, Museum für Kunsthandwerk, Leipzig
Michael Huey, Vienna
Kunsthistorisches Museum Vienna, Kunstkammer
Manfred Ludewig, Berlin
MAK, Vienna
Museen des Mobiliendepots, Silberkammer, Vienna
The Museum of Modern Art, New York
Neue Galerie New York
Ernst Ploil, Vienna
Clarisse Praun, Vienna
Courtney Ross-Holst Collection
Sammlung der Universität für angewandte Kunst, Vienna
Schlossmuseum, Kunstsammlung zu Weimar
Ellen and William Taubman Collection
Technisches Museum, Vienna
Christian Witt-Dörring, Vienna
Marietta Witt-Dörring, Vienna

Our thanks also go to those lenders who preferred to remain anonymous.

ACKNOWLEDGMENTS

Without the assistance of the following institutions and private individuals, who made available important material and valuable advice, this project would not have been possible.

Albertina, Vienna
Alte Nationalgalerie, Berlin
Max, Binia und Jakob Bill Stiftung,
    Adligenswil
The British Museum, London
Centraal Museum, Utrecht
Sterling & Francine Clark Art Institute,
    Williamstown
Deutsches Museum, Munich
Fondation Le Corbusier, Paris
Glasgow School of Art, Glasgow
Haags Gemeentemuseum, The Hague
Norbert Hethke Verlag, Schönau
Historisches Museum der Stadt Wien
Georg Jensen, Frederiksberg
Kapuzinergruft, Vienna
Knoll Inc., New York
Kungl. Hovstaterna, Stockholm
The Library and Museum of
    Freemasonry, London
MAK, Vienna
David Mellor Design, Sheffield
The Metropolitan Museum of Art,
    New York
Museé des Arts Décoratifs, Paris
Museen des Mobiliendepots,
    Silberkammer, Vienna
Nationalmuseum, Stockholm
Österreichische Nationalbibliothek,
    Vienna
Frank Den Oudsten Associates,
    Amsterdam
Philadelphia Art Museum, Philadelphia
The Pulitzer Foundation for the Arts,
    St. Louis
Rijksmuseum, Amsterdam
Saint Louis Art Museum, St. Louis
Sammlung der Universität für
    angewandte Kunst, Vienna
Sir John Soane's Museum, London

The State Russian Museum,
    St. Petersburg
Stedelijk Museum, Amsterdam
A/S Stelton, Hellerup
Stiftung Weimarer Klassik, Weimar
Technisches Museum, Vienna
Technische Universität, Vienna
Veste Coburg, Coburg
Victoria and Albert Museum, London
Rafael Viñoly Architects, New York
Vitra AG, Birsfelden
Wilhelm Wagenfeld Stiftung, Bremen
WestLicht, Vienna
Wittgenstein Archive, Cambridge

Anthony Alofsin, Austin
Eugenie Altenburg, Vienna
Franz Josef Altenburg, Asperding
Carl Auböck, Vienna
Christian Brandstätter, Vienna
Lenneke Bueller, Amsterdam
Fausto Calderai, Florence
Diane Clements, London
Michael Conforti, Williamstown
Antonia Croÿ, Vienna
Alexander David, Vienna
Rudolf Distelberger, Vienna
Anneliese Fanto, Vienna
Irene Fuchs, Vienna
Stefan Fuhrer, Vienna
Georg Gaugusch, Vienna
Wolfgang Glück, Vienna
Takaya Goto, New York
Pater Gottfried, Vienna
Scott Gutterman, New York
Peter Hahn, Berlin
Sabine Hartmann, Berlin
Ingrid Haslinger, Vienna
Irmgard Hauser-Köchert, Vienna
Christian Hölzl, Vienna
Charles Janoray, New York
Ilse Jung, Vienna
Koji Katsuta, New York
Anthony Kersting, London
Franz Kirchweger, Vienna
Nikolaus Koliusis, Stuttgart

Sieglinde Koza, Vienna
Max Kübeck, Vienna
Elizabeth Kujawski, New York
Peter Kupelwieser, Lunz am See
Manfred Ludewig, Berlin
Heinz Lunzer, Vienna
Annita Mader, Vienna
Siegfried Mattl, Vienna
Cara McCarty, St. Louis
Michael Nedo, Cambridge
Jerry Neuner, New York
Vlasta Odell, New York
Derek Ostergard, New York
Susan Palmer, London
Richard Pandiscio, New York
Peter Parenzan, Vienna
Erika Patka, Vienna
Veronika Pfolz, Vienna
Franz Pichorner, Vienna
Ernst Ploil, Vienna
Kathrin Pokorny-Nagel, Vienna
Paulus Rainer, Vienna
Courtney Ross-Holst, New York
Leah Ross, New York
Mary Rozell, New York
Sefa Saglam, New York
Inge Scholz, Weimar
Cornelia Schörk, Vienna
Helmut Seling, Munich
Tasha Seren, New York
Cecilia Sjögren, Vienna
Janis Staggs-Flinchum, New York
Laurie Stein, St. Louis
Major John Stonborough †, Ferndown
Pierre and Françoise Stonborough,
    Vienna
Kathrin Sumereder, Vienna
William and Ellen Taubman, New York
Evelyne Trehin, Paris
Jörg Tuske, Cambridge
Simon Weber-Unger, Vienna
Hubert Weitensfelder, Vienna
Friedrich Wittgenstein, Vienna
Gabriele Zugay, Vienna

CONTENTS

10
RONALD S. LAUDER
Preface

11
RENÉE PRICE AND WILFRIED SEIPEL
Foreword

12
GÜNTHER STEFAN ASENBAUM
AND PAUL ASENBAUM
Foreword

13
CHRISTIAN WITT-DÖRRING
Introduction

NARRATIVE TEXTS BY MICHAEL HUEY
16
The Turning Point

20
Neoclassicism
The Reception of Antiquity

38
Neoclassicism
Formal Reduction

64
Neoclassicism
Geometry as Language of the Enlightenment

90
From an Ideal of Simplicity to the
Modern Commodity

146
Mobility as Maxim of Modern Society

176
Style & Self-Expression

282
Vienna's Experiment of Modernity

336
MARKUS BRÜDERLIN
Architectural Abstraction and the Vision of
the Modern

343
MICHAEL HUEY
The Aestheticized Individual
Subjects and Their Objects in Turn-of-the-Century Vienna

354
J. S. MARCUS
In All Directions
Travel and its Meanings in a Modernizing Europe

363
CHRISTOPHER WILK
Looking at the Past through Modernist Eyes

368
JOSEPH RYKWERT
Moist and Dry

372
ELISABETH SCHMUTTERMEIER
Viennese Silver
A Stylistic Survey

375
WILLIAM D. GODSEY, JR.
A "Bourgeois Century"?
Society and High Culture in Vienna 1780–1920

380
SYLVIA MATTL-WURM
Creative Density

386
DIETHER HALAMA
Biographies of Viennese
Gold- and Silversmiths

394
Selected Bibliography

396
Index

398
Photography and Copyright Credits

PREFACE

Two years ago, when I was overseeing the first installation of the collection at the Neue Galerie, I insisted that works of decorative art be placed alongside paintings, drawings, and sculpture. Some observers questioned the decision. One French journalist commented, "You cannot say that a teapot is the equal of a great painting." My answer then, as now, was yes: that in Vienna at the turn of the 20th century, the aesthetic of the era was conveyed through every means available, from the exalted to the everyday. That is part of the magic of fin-de-siècle Vienna: one can see the *Zeitgeist* even in a teapot.

With *Viennese Silver · Modern Design 1780–1918,* we are pleased to be able to look further into the history of Austrian decorative arts, and to locate some of the sources of its genius. Our curator Christian Witt-Dörring, whose brilliant Dagobert Peche exhibition set the standard for displays of decorative art at the Neue Galerie, traces the course from imperial to modern approaches, and finds astonishing affinities over a period of more than a century. He was guided in his journey by two extraordinary brothers, Stefan and Paul Asenbaum. Their unparalleled knowledge of Viennese silver, founded on generations of family research, laid the groundwork for this exhibition. To all of them, I offer my thanks and admiration.

I am also delighted that the Neue Galerie has partnered with the Kunsthistorisches Museum Vienna as a co-organizer of this endeavor. The depth of experience at that great institution is most welcome at our young museum.

Ronald S. Lauder
President, Neue Galerie New York

FOREWORD

It is indeed an honor to present *Viennese Silver · Modern Design 1780–1918.* We are pleased to be able to show the wonderful objects from this exhibition in both New York and Vienna, where viewers will have the chance to experience first-hand the sublime craftsmanship and sheer seductiveness of Viennese silver. This work is widely admired for the quality of its workmanship and for its striking combination of gracefulness and strength.

Yet it is not just the works themselves, but the ideas they represent, that make them so extraordinary. In Vienna, the desire for new forms grows out of centuries of intellectual and formal refinement. One can see in these objects their makers' search for truth as it is expressed through essential, distilled form.

Viennese Silver represents a first collaboration between the Neue Galerie New York and the Kunsthistorisches Museum Vienna, one that we hope to repeat on many occasions in the future. We are much obliged to the Jubilee Fund of the Austrian National Bank and its former president, Dr. Maria Schaumayer, for their support. We would also like to thank the Association of the Viennese Silversmith Archives for the many years of preparatory work conducted under the chairmanship of Herbert Asenbaum, as well as Günter Templ for his kind assistance. In addition, we wish to express our appreciation for the scholarly support of the MAK, Vienna, under the directorship of Peter Noever.

This catalogue is dedicated to our esteemed colleague, the late Gerwald Sonnberger, who was instrumental during the early phase of this project.

Renée Price
Director, Neue Galerie New York

Wilfried Seipel
General Director, Kunsthistorisches Museum Vienna

FOREWORD

The idea for a comprehensive exhibition on Viennese gold and silver making goes back more than forty years. At that time Wilhelm Mrazek, then director of the Österreichisches Museum für angewandte Kunst (Museum of Applied Arts) in Vienna, and our father, Herbert Asenbaum, an advisor to the museum, began to put together documentation on Viennese silver. The state of scholarship on this topic was minimal; the last major exhibition on the subject had taken place in Vienna in 1907. Our father, a renowned expert on German and Austrian silver, took it as his mission to systematically photograph Viennese silver objects and to record their hallmarks and makers' marks. In so doing he laid the cornerstone for the creation of an impressive archive, the bulk of which concerned 16th- to 19th-century objects. Upon entering this field, we rounded out his collection of materials with examples from the 20th century, in particular with silver and metal work from the Wiener Werkstätte.

Our mother, Inge Asenbaum, who was also an advisor to the Museum of Applied Arts, shared an interest in *Jugendstil* art with Wilhelm Mrazek. He was one of the first to recognize the significance of the Wiener Werkstätte and as early as 1967 he dedicated an exhibition to the topic. In the early 1960s, when our mother began to collect Viennese *Jugendstil* objects, the general interest in them was very low and they were hardly perceived as valuable. Even within our family, one can see that the highly desirable collectibles of today were regarded quite differently by our forebears. An anecdote told, remorsefully, within our family has it that, as late as the beginning of the 1950s, our grandparents had Wiener Werkstätte pieces melted down for cash when business was bad in their antiques shop.

Our mother's enthusiasm for *Jugendstil* led to our parents' acquisition, in 1967, of the atelier of the Secessionist painter Josef Engelhart in Vienna. The building, whose design had been influenced by Belgian art nouveau, stood—separated by a park—across from the compound of the Mautner Markhof family. It had been part of an artist's colony around 1900; this colony also contained the residence of the well-known stage set designer and co-founder of the Vienna Secession, Alfred Roller, and the atelier of the Wiener Werkstätte co-founder Koloman Moser.

We spent our youth in the Engelhart atelier. In its living room, which was outfitted with Wiener Werkstätte furniture, we sometimes had the good fortune of meeting, at afternoon get-togethers, the descendants of the important members of the Viennese *sacre printemps* from around 1900. We listened, over coffee and cake, with rapt attention as they told of the turn of the century and, through these personal conversations, had a living view into the exclusive society of the patrons and artists of the Wiener Werkstätte. It is hardly surprising, then, that Vienna 1900 became our passion. Our appreciation of the geometric/constructive designs of Viennese architects and artists led us to an intense study of 20th-century

design. The objects of Christopher Dresser, the Bauhaus, and the De Stijl movement and beyond, up through the designs of Arne Jacobsen—in short, functionalist and constructivist design—began to influence our aesthetic sensibilities. Our understanding of modernity took its cue from what became known as classical modernity, which evolved prior to postmodernism's critique of the Modern movement.

Our study of design history encouraged us in our belief that the avant-garde in Vienna around 1900 had been an important source for the development of modern design throughout the 20th century. It sharpened our view for the formal parallels between these objects and those from the first half of the 19th century. The first time we spied a pair of astonishingly modern-looking candlesticks from 1807 in a vitrine with other antique silver items, it was an eye-opening experience for us. In the years that followed, we learned that Viennese silversmiths had begun around 1800 and afterward, particularly during the Biedermeier period, to produce quite a few of these clear, formally reduced objects for everyday use. Even today they surprise us by their *Sachlichkeit* (objectivity), spareness, and functionality; in their reduction to the forms of basic geometry and the exclusion of ornamentation, they still appear timelessly modern.

Fascinated by this modernity, we began to consider the formal developments in the early 19th century and the early 20th century in direct relation to each other. We found that the avant-garde of 1900, which had turned against the art industry of eclecticism, saw in the everyday culture of its grandparents' generation a model. Influential authors of the sacred spring movement in Vienna wrote of Biedermeier as a locally distinct bourgeois style, which, independent of social station, had been welcomed in the interiors of all classes. Its special qualities in combining *Sachlichkeit* and comfort were stressed. Biedermeier was to become an "ideal educator" for the movement, a guide in the search for a new style befitting a new and modern age.

With our longtime friend and colleague Christian Witt-Dörring, we organized an exhibition at the Vienna Künstlerhaus in 1981 entitled *Moderne Vergangenheit: Wien 1800–1900* (Modern Past: Vienna 1800–1900), pointing out for the first time the formal and philosophical similarities between Viennese Biedermeier and Viennese *Jugendstil*. The selection of objects included all media of everyday culture, such as furniture, metalwork, ceramics, glass, and textiles.

Twenty-two years later, working again with Dr. Witt-Dörring, we have lent our collective understanding to the realization of the exhibition *Viennese Silver · Modern Design 1780–1918*. It is our honor to help introduce this viewpoint to an international audience and to share with readers and viewers the fascinating aesthetic of these objects.

Günther Stefan Asenbaum and Paul Asenbaum

INTRODUCTION

Art always has its roots in a particular age, but art is more than just an echo and a reflection of an epoch—it has a prophetic energy that reaches far and deep into the future.[1]

Vasily Kandinsky, *Essays on Art and Artists*

The broad scope of this exhibition allows the Viennese tradition of modern design to be seen in a larger context and with new associations. It bridges the period from neoclassicism to the age of the Wiener Werkstätte, and concentrates exclusively on objects made in silver and other metals. In these materials, the modern formal language is most clearly recognizable. The selection of objects does not purport to be a comprehensive overview of the stylistic variety seen in Viennese silver products during the period, but is instead a selective presentation of only those objects that can be regarded as forerunners of modern design. It does not take into account various countercurrents, such as historicism.

Over the course of six chapters, the exhibition invites the visitor to embark upon an associative journey, in both an aesthetic and an intellectual sense. The historical, art-historical, and literary texts of the catalogue authors are important contributions that illuminate the given topics from a range of different viewpoints.

Serving as both a turning and a jumping-off point is "Neoclassicism," the various aspects of which are explored in the first chapter: "The Reception of Antiquity," the "Formal Reduction" of shapes and ornamentation as a specifically Viennese play on the neoclassical canon, and "Geometry as Language of the Enlightenment." In the second chapter, "From an Ideal of Simplicity to the Modern Commodity," Viennese silver from the first half of the 19th century is compared with that of the early 20th century. In the third chapter, "Mobility as Maxim of Modern Society," traveling household sets of the 19th century, with their functionally oriented shapes, are discussed as a source of the modern aesthetic. In addition, the streamlined designs of Josef Hoffmann and Koloman Moser are considered alongside various futuristic objects. The fourth chapter, "Style & Self-Expression," describes how the close relationship between the artists of the Wiener Werkstätte and their clients served as the driving force behind the creation of a new style. In the fifth chapter, "Vienna's Experiment with Modernity," radical designs by Hoffmann and Moser from the early years of the Wiener Werkstätte are placed in close proximity to architectural models of the same era. The blurring of lines between design and art can be seen as a precursor of cubism and constructivism.

The years chosen for the title of this exhibition mark the beginning and endpoint of a social and cultural evolution. In 1780, following the death of Empress Maria Theresa, Queen of Hungary and Bohemia and Archduchess of Austria, and after fifteen years of co-regency with her, Emperor Joseph II succeeded to the throne. He pushed through a course of reforms partly begun during the reign of his mother. During his own reign, the effects of the Enlightenment, which had begun to blossom elsewhere in Europe, also came to be felt in Austria, bringing Joseph II the reputation of an enlightened absolutist. The basis was laid for an intellectual and social revision of values, one that must be seen as a prerequisite for a subsequent shift in taste that was to last into our own age. *Sachlichkeit* and spareness were raised up as virtues; the tomb of Joseph II plainly symbolizes this.

In 1918, with the end of the First World War, the Hapsburg monarchy fell apart, Austria shrank to a sixth of its former size, and the First Republic was instated. Vienna, which at its peak was a metropolis of two million people, remained the capital city; however, with the loss of the crown lands and Hungary, it not only lost the basis of its economic prosperity, but also, in many areas, its primacy as an innovative center for art and culture in the heart of Europe.

In the period from 1780 to 1918, Vienna's population increased tenfold. As the capital and imperial residence of the Hapsburgs, the city had always attracted craftsmen and artists. With the Vienna Congress of 1814–15 and the city expansion in 1858 creating one of the largest building booms of the age, this attraction continued to grow. Increased emigration from all parts of the monarchy at the end of the 19th century resulted in a bubbling melting pot of many cultures—an ideal and fertile ground for new impulses.

The 1900 movement was a short but intense fireworks in all genres of art, and remains a high point of Austrian culture. Particularly in the realm of design, Viennese architects and artists of the day took innovative and influential steps toward 20th-century modernism. In so doing, they were continuing a development begun with the aforementioned shift in taste at the end of the 18th century, which reached its first climax in the spare, objective design of Viennese Biedermeier. By considering and drawing connections between work of the early 19th and 20th centuries, one sees the flaring brilliance of Viennese design at its height.

Christian Witt-Dörring

---

1 English translation Michael Huey.

Neues
Caffehau

Johann Esaias Nilson,
Neues Caffehaus
(New Coffee House)
Copperplate engraving, Augsburg 1756
Illustration from Ernst H. Gombrich, *Ornament
und Kunst: Schmucktrieb und Ordnungssinn
in der Psychologie des dekorativen Schaffens*,
Stuttgart 1982, p. 41.

1

THE TURNING
POINT

In the 17th and throughout most of the 18th century in Vienna surfaces existed—in architecture and the decorative arts alike—for the sake of ornamentation. Clear volumes led secret lives beneath ornate dress. Questions of structure were not the questions that captured the imagination; things functioned—this was taken for granted—it was not necessary to see loads being borne, as it had been during the Renaissance and would again be during the neoclassical and Biedermeier periods. Construction techniques in Vienna still bespeak this baroque principle: the regular building method calls for covering up an underlying brick structure with stucco. Surface counts—exposed brick is usually deemed unfinished or indecorous—and sometimes it is all that counts. In 1847 the English architect Peter Hubert Desvignes, who was lavishly remodeling the Vienna town palace of Prince Liechtenstein at the time, brought his employer's censure upon himself by insisting that "it is not my fault—if such or such thing will be concealed or only brought very seldom into use—I must take care that it will bear being seen into."[1] (In a culture enamored of the performing arts, looking at something is often more important than looking into it.)

The old-fashioned (for its time) overall design of the Viennese breakfast service (cat. no. 1) tells the viewer everything he needs to know from a distance. Like palace interiors of the 17th and 18th century, or even the sarcophagus of Empress Maria Theresa[2] and her husband Francis Stephen of Lorraine, the service suggests a world in which public ostentation takes precedence over the private realm.

In the history of furniture, the "commode" (meaning, in French, literally "convenient"), or dresser type, which allowed a person to care for his own things in proximity to his living quarters, only began its popular ascent and replacement of servant-maintained cabinets during the 18th century, around the time the modern concept of privacy itself began to develop in court life. Well into the neoclassical age, plain silver and other metalwork would have had no place in aristocratic—and therefore fashionable—life. But like the commode, their star was on the rise. The body language of undecorated or slightly decorated applied arts pieces from the early 19th century declared that they might be used by anyone: cheaper to produce and maintain and easier to handle, they were private, functional and to the point, and often conveniently mobile. The ornate gold breakfast service of Maria Theresa and the plain silver chocolate pot of her son Joseph are an aesthetic generation gap made visible.

1 Peter Hubert Desvignes, letter to Prince Alois Josef II von und zu Liechtenstein from the year 1847, Prince Liechtenstein Hausarchiv K. H1853, Vienna.
2 Though not Empress in her own right, Maria Theresa, who was Queen of Hungary and Bohemia and Archduchess of Austria, became Empress when Francis Stephen of Lorraine was elected Holy Roman Emperor.

RIGHT: Tomb of Emperor Joseph II in the *Kapuzinergruft* with the double sarcophagus of Emperor Francis Stephen of Lorraine and Empress Maria Theresa, Queen of Hungary and Bohemia, Archduchess of Austria, etc., in the background
Vienna ca. 1790 and 1765

The effect of the influence of Joseph II on matters of furnishings was felt in a maximization of simplicity; this was even the case in the surface treatment of furniture. From his precise directives for the new adaptation of the living quarters of his brother Maximilian in the Hofburg in 1775, we learn that white-gold finishes were to be replaced with ones of pure white.[3]

3 Christian Witt-Dörring, "Die Farbgebung der Möbel am Wiener Hof während der Regierungszeit Maria Theresias," *alte und moderne Kunst*, Salzburg 1978, yr. 23, issue 158, p. 12. English translation Michael Huey.

KAISER   KAISERIN
FRANZ STEPHAN ✝ MARIA THERESIA
1708 - 1765   1717 - 1780
KAISER JOSEPH II. 1741-1790

1. BREAKFAST SERVICE FOR EMPRESS MARIA THERESA, QUEEN OF HUNGARY AND BOHEMIA, ARCHDUCHESS OF AUSTRIA, ETC., INCLUDING CHOCOLATE POT, TEAPOT, TEA CADDY, CHOCOLATE CUP AND SAUCER, COVERED BEAKER

Anton Matthias Joseph Domanek, Vienna ca. 1750

Gold, fruitwood, porcelain
Maker's mark DOMANEK on some pieces
H 23.4 cm/9.4 in. (chocolate pot) Weight 1,392.7 g/55.7 oz.
Kunsthistorisches Museum Vienna, Kunstkammer, inv. nos. 1260, 1207, 1220, 1205, 1206, 1213, 1197

2. CHOCOLATE POT OF EMPEROR JOSEPH II

Ignaz Sebastian Würth, Vienna ca. 1780

Silver, ebony
Vienna hallmark, maker's mark ISW, Austrian control mark (*Repunze*)
H 15 cm/6 in. Weight 625 g/27.4 oz.
Museen des Mobiliendepots, Silberkammer, Vienna, inv. no. 180368/003–006

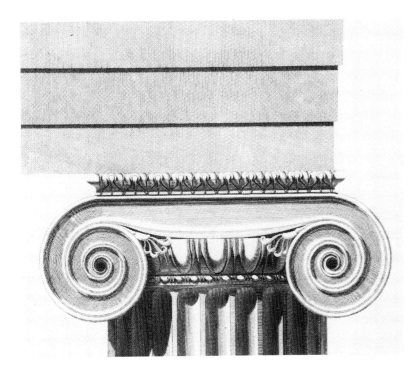

Ionic capital from the temple of Athena Polias at Priene

Copperplate engraving, London 1769
Illustration from R. Chandler, *Ionian Antiquities*.

The neoclassical sensibilities of the mid (in England and France) or later 18th century (in the Hapsburg empire) were stimulated by the excavation of classical sites throughout the antique world, Pompeii and Herculaneum in particular. Implicit in the archaeological premise—indeed, in any return to and preoccupation with an earlier time—is the idea that the essence of that time can be discovered and put to practical use in one's own age. In Vienna and elsewhere in Europe around 1800, the volute shape as taken from the capital of the Ionic column—abstracted and applied to a wide range of household items from furniture to teacups to trays for confection—functioned as a symbol for a particular approach to the world. Its use immediately circumscribed the user within a certain context, as name-dropping might. And like a dropped name, the volute became a platform to which a range of emotions, including longing and desire, could adhere themselves and find expression. The aesthetic energy of the Viennese tray derives in part from the design's allusion to the process, whether actual or idealized, of its making; the volute is not added to the body of the tray as an afterthought, but appears to grow naturally from the fashioning of its handles. Ornament here literally evolves into function. The yearbooks of the Polytechnisches Institut (Polytechnic Institute) in Vienna divulge the fact that early 19th-century silversmiths' curiosity about archeological finds also went beyond matters of style: metallurgical analysis of Roman coins was repeatedly a topic of discourse.

Painted tôle cheese cradle

Wales ca. 1820
Nationalmuseum, Stockholm

3. SMALL TRAY
Maker CG, Vienna 1807
Silver
Vienna hallmark, maker's mark CG
L 20.7 cm/8.3 in. Weight 149 g/6 oz.
Courtney Ross-Holst Collection

Henry Tresham, Grand Tour travelers
purchasing antiquities in Italy
Pen and ink and gray wash, ca. 1790
Private collection

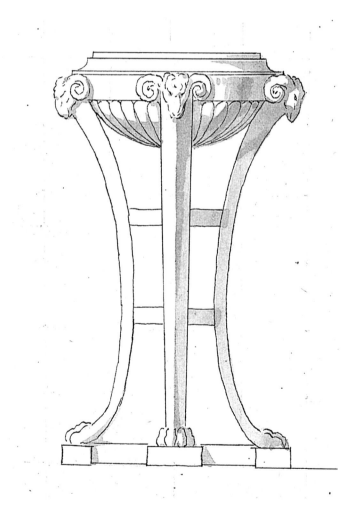

The furor over the archaeological sites of the 18th and 19th century made the idea of the Grand Tour attractive to an ever-broader segment of the population, and the grand tour may have given rise to the modern kitsch object. Souvenirs were acquired on the tour, but they were also "produced" at home: in either case according to the means of the client. The word souvenir, as a verb, means "to remember," and that is what kitsch—whether high or low in nature—helps us to do. Kitsch makes emotion material, tangible. It helps us to return to a particular sensation whenever we like, and then to replace it neatly on the shelf. The tazza depicted here is a miniature, stylized version of a three-legged table or tripod from antiquity. For some, the purchase of such an item was a substitution for actual experience and served as a vicarious act of participation and approval.

Antonio Grassi (master for the models at the Wiener Porzellan Manufaktur under Konrad von Sorgenthal), tripod drawn after classical examples in the archaeological museum at Portici near Naples.
Pen and ink and wash, 1792
MAK, Vienna

4. SMALL TAZZA
Alois Würth, Vienna 1807
Silver
Vienna hallmark, maker's mark AW
H 9.2 cm/3.7 in. Weight 142 g/5.7 oz.
Private collection

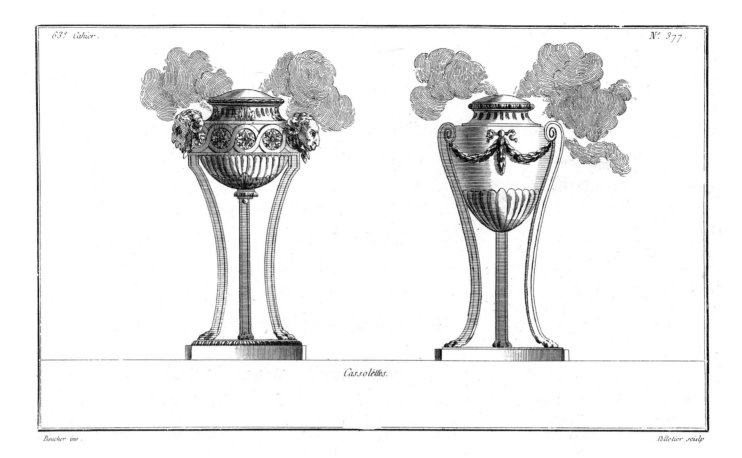

Cassolettes.

Boucher inv.

Pelletier sculp.

Juste-François Boucher, design for incense burners "*à la moderne*"
Engraved by Jean Pelletier, Paris ca. 1775
Formerly from the library of the furniture-maker Portois & Fix, Vienna

Most Viennese pieces are of thirteen-lot, but many are made also of fifteen-lot silver and distinguish themselves from foreign products chiefly by means of their solidity; as a rule, local taste favors more solid, handmade, weighty items to light hammered or pressed wares.[4]

W. C. W. Blumenbach, 1825

4 W. C. W. Blumenbach, *Wiener Kunst- und Gewerbsfreund oder der neueste Wiener Geschmack,* vol. 1, Vienna 1825. English translation Michael Huey.

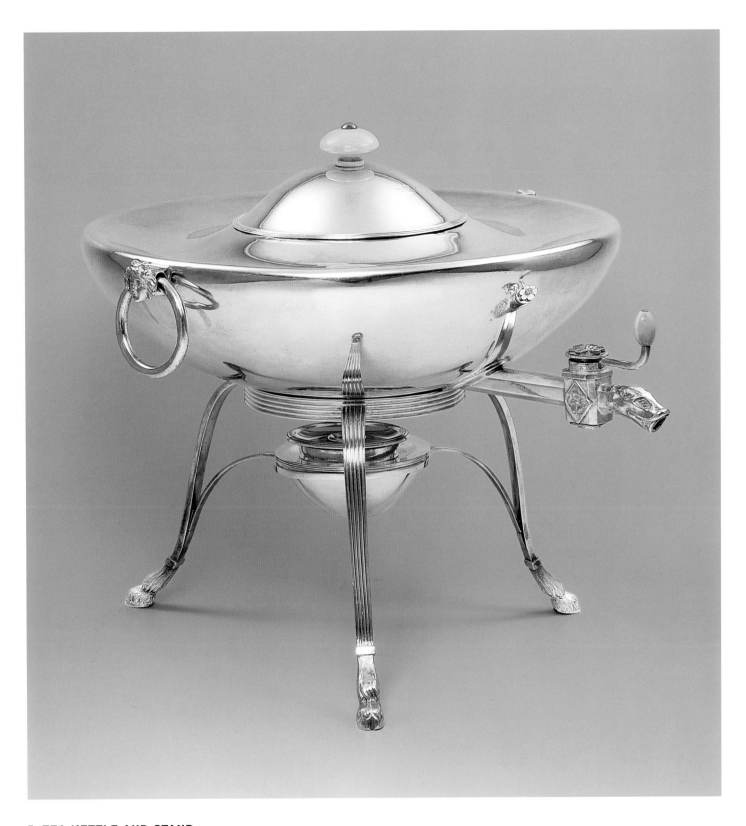

5. TEA KETTLE AND STAND

Jakob Krautauer, Vienna 1814

Silver, ivory

Vienna hallmark, maker's mark K, Austrian control mark (*Taxfreistempel*)

Monogram of Prince JT

H 25.5 cm/10 in. Weight 2,187 g/87.5 oz.

Courtney Ross-Holst Collection

No: 5.

A. Ægÿptische Basen des Cardinals Chigi.
B. Isis von Agath in gestalt eines Canopi, aus der Kaÿserl. Schatz Kammer.
C. Egÿptisches Vase Petri Bellori.
D. Anubis des Authoris.
E. Osiris wovon der Author gleichfals das original hat.
F. Ægÿptische Urne von Francesco Pichetti Napolitanischen Architecto.

A. Vases Ægyptiens du Cardinal Chigi.
B. Isis d'Agathe en forme de Canope, du Cabinet Imperial.
C. Vase Ægyptien de Pierre Bellori.
D. Anubis de l'Auteur.
E. Osiris, dont l'Auteur possede de même l'original.
F. Urne Ægyptienne de François Pichetti, Architecte Napolitain.

G. B. F. v. E. delin: Cum Privil: Sacr: Cæsar: Majest: Carl de la Haye Sculp.

Classical vases from Johann Bernhard Fischer von Erlach, *Entwurf einer historischen Architektur*
Engraved by Carl de la Haye, Vienna 1721
Michael Huey, Vienna

Stolen goods can also be a form of Grand Tour souvenir; when Napoleon returned from his Egyptian campaign the many artifacts he had taken along with him lent further impetus to a new fashion. The form of the canopic jar was popularized in Europe as early as 1771 when Wedgwood and Bentley began producing it in replica as a decorative vase or, in slightly modified form, as the base for a candlestick. While the Wedgwood interpretation visually preserved the outward appearance of the jars, faithfully reproducing a stylized version of the Egyptian decor of figures and symbols—as did similar porcelain jars from the Vienna manufactory—this later Viennese silver urn, which may also have its aesthetic roots in the canopic tradition, takes the stylization one step further, reducing the original to its essence: an unadorned assemblage of pure volumes. Like Wedgwood's version, the Viennese urn perverts the function of the canopic jar, which was first designed to hold the viscera of a deceased person, by turning it into a sugar bowl.

6. SUGAR URN

Johann Klima, Vienna 1814
Silver
Vienna hallmark, maker's mark I. K.,
Austrian control mark (*Taxfreistempel*)
H 16.5 cm/6.6 in.   Weight 339 g/13.6 oz.
Private collection

Ancient Greek black-figure drinking cup from Tanagra, third quarter of the 6th century B.C.

Albumen print, Karl Bosnjak, Vienna 1904

© Kunsthistorisches Museum Vienna, Antikensammlung, inv. no. IV 1672

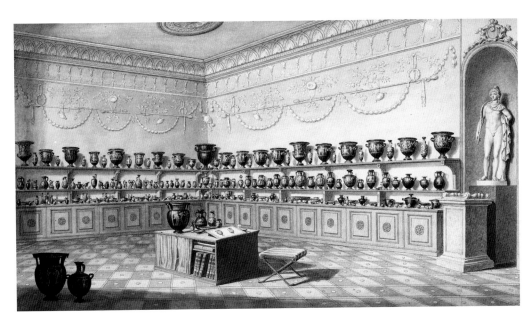

Carl Schütz, *Collection of classical vases belonging to Count Franz Anton Lamberg-Sprinzenstein*

Copperplate engraving, Vienna 1791

© Kunsthistorisches Museum Vienna

7. CONFECTION DISH

Benedikt Ranninger, Vienna 1818

Silver
Vienna hallmark, maker's mark BNR, Austrian control mark (*Vorratspunze*)
W 25.9 cm/10.2 in. Weight 512 g/20.5 oz.
Private collection

The ancient Greek drinking cup with its emphasis on grace-ful, generously-sized handles at the sides was likely an inspiration for this dish for sweets. Unlike mannerist, baroque, and some neoclassical dishes of this type, which are heav-ily decorated as though in anticipation of the bounty they were to present, this piece is reserved in its décor: a return to the clear, classical lines of Greek models, which were likewise almost completely undisturbed by three-dimensional ornamentation (their surfaces were usually painted).

Some excavated pieces, such as the one shown opposite, be-came part of the imperial collections as early as 1815, when the Antikenkabinett purchased vases and marble works from the collection of the president of the Vienna Akademie der bildenden Künste (Academy of Fine Arts), Count Franz An-ton Lamberg-Sprinzenstein, for 125,000 florins.[5] (Even prior

to that date, the Lamberg collection had been made ac-cessible for study via the copperplate engravings of Alexandre Conte de Laborde.) Artisans would have also have made use, however, of drawings turned out at the site, such as those made for the Vienna porcelain manufactory which, notably, reproduced the shapes, but not the painted decor, of classical finds.

The handles—which in French neoclassical silver, for exam-ple, are in a way secondary to whatever conveniently shaped form came to be perched in their place—are so reduced in Benedikt Ranninger's dish as to be reminiscent of stick figure drawings.

5 Alfons Lhotsky, *Die Geschichte der Sammlungen,* Festschrift des Kunsthistorischen Museums zur Feier des fünfzigjährigen Bestehens, Horn and Vienna 1941–45, part 2, pp. 503–504.

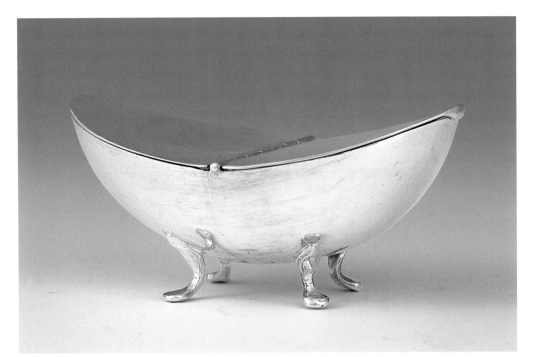

8. SPICEBOX
Benedikt Ranninger, Vienna 18[2]1
Silver
Vienna hallmark, maker's mark BNR,
Austrian control mark (*Vorratspunze*)
W 8.2 cm/3.3 in. Weight 82 g/3.3 oz.
Private collection

In 1784 and again in 1787 Emperor Joseph II put heightened trade barriers in effect forbidding—or placing prohibitive
duties on—the importation of a variety of products from abroad,
including certain decorative arts pieces in silver. (Under Maria
Theresa the importation of foreign products for retail had
already been strongly curtailed as early as 1764.) He
further imposed new requirements on craftsmen, among them
obligatory drawing instruction at the Vienna Akademie, to
make up for this deficit in available patterns and help bring
them up to date with fashionable trends from France and
England. As a result, gold-, silver-, and bronzesmiths suddenly found themselves in a protected market, as well as in
the unexpected company of textile producers and ceramists,
stonemasons, room painters, and furniture makers. Johann
Baptist Hagenauer, who was employed beginning in 1780
as a professor of sculpture at the academy (and hired not
so much for "genius, inventive spirit, or skill in his work" but
rather for his "pedagogical faculties, his modesty and
patience, as well as his theoretical knowledge of art")[6] soon
became the head of the so-called Graveurakademie
(Engravers' Academy), which oversaw this drawing instruction.
His own drawings hung in the classrooms to be copied by
students, thereby influencing a generation of craftsmen, who,
in turn, passed on their learning to others in the workshops.
It thus becomes possible to trace the genealogy of an idea—
such as that of the folding chair or footed vase excavated
at Herculaneum and displayed in the 18th century at the
Portici Museum near Naples—via Hagenauer to the craftsmen who adapted the form to their purposes for anything
from a bed to a spicebox.

Johann Thomas Hauer, various antiques
discovered at Herculaneum and preserved
in the museum at Portici near Naples
Etching, Paris 1781
MAK, Vienna

6 Claudia Boesch, *Johann Baptist Hagenauer: Die Entwürfe und Kupferstiche im
  Rahmen seiner Tätigkeit von 1780–1810 an der Graveurakademie in Wien*, M.A.
  thesis in the humanities at the University of Vienna, Vienna 1990, p. 2. English translation Michael Huey.

LEFT: Bedroom with Empire furnishings from ca. 1810 in Vranov Castle, Czech Republic
Illustration from Max von Boehn, *Das Empire–Die Zeit: Das Leben: Der Stil,* Berlin 1925.

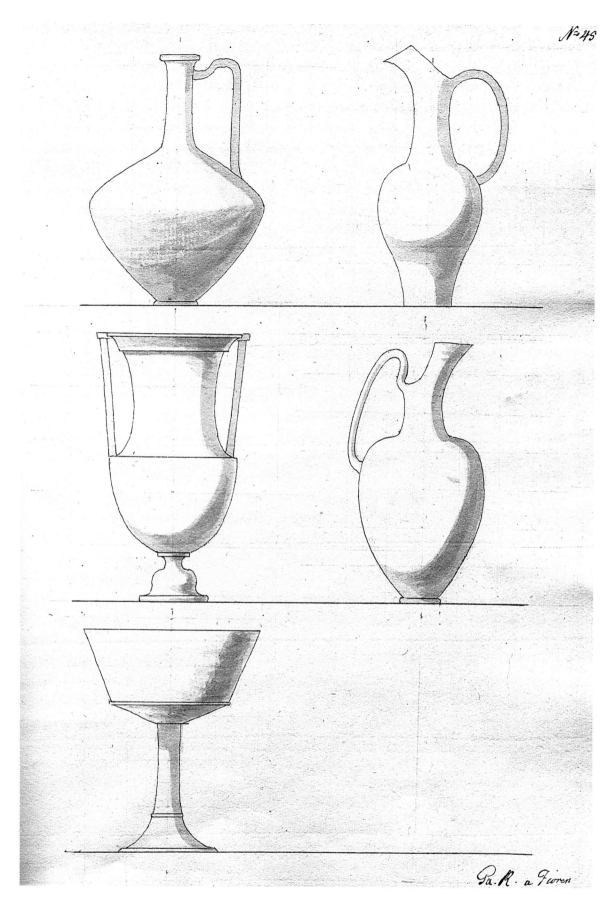

N⁰ 45

Antonio Grassi, pitchers and vases drawn after classical examples in Palazzo Pitti, Florence

Pen and ink and gray wash, 1792

MAK, Vienna

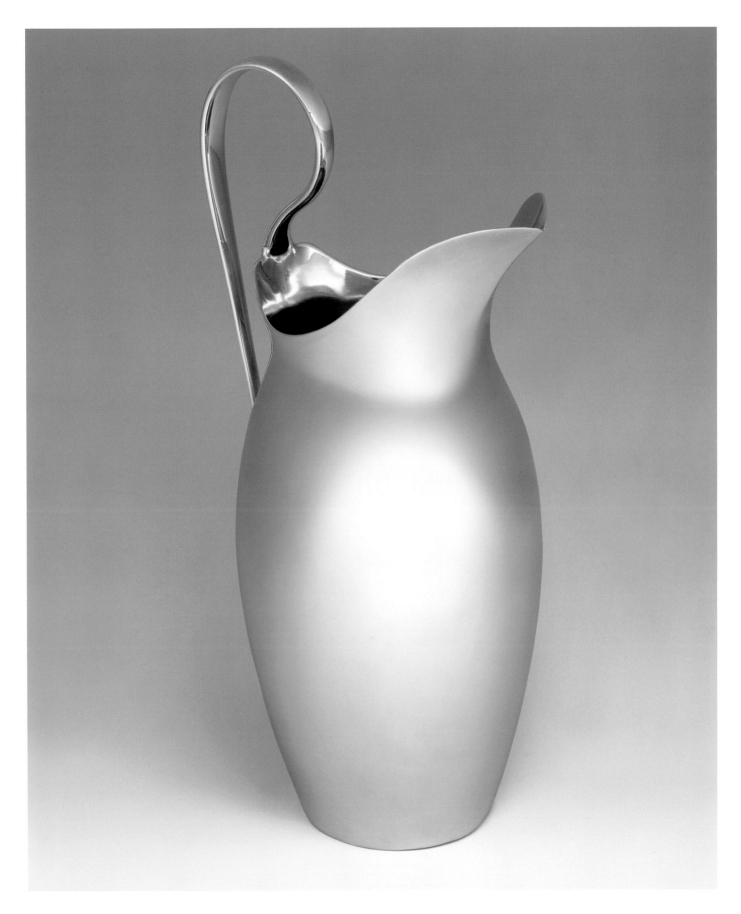

9. WATER JUG

Lorenz Wieninger, Vienna 1817

Silver

Vienna hallmark, maker's mark LW, Austrian control mark (*Vorratspunze*)

H 22 cm/8.8 in.   Weight 433 g/17.3 oz.

Courtney Ross-Holst Collection

During his term as British envoy to the Kingdom of the Two Sicilies, Sir William Hamilton famously assembled and disastrously shipped to England two highly-regarded and valuable collections of classical vases. Baron d'Hancarville (Pierre François Hughes) published the catalogue of the collections in 1766 under the title *Antiquités Etrusques,* and it sparked a fad in England and abroad that kept Wedgwood and hundreds of his imitators in business and culminated, after 1786, in a historic proliferation of Portland vases. (Hamilton is known to have lent objects from his collection directly to Wedgwood, but he had also earned £8,400 in 1771 by selling pieces to the British Museum, where they were on public view. As Jenny Uglow notes, "Wedgwood later calculated that Etruria had made three times that sum in profits from the vases Hamilton had inspired.")[7]

But other forms, too, captured the public's imagination. From London to Paris to Vienna versions of this wine jug appeared. In Vienna the type remained the standard for use as a wine decanter through the 1820s, often decorated with patterned bands, lidded, and paired with a second, matching jug for water. Few attained the rigor of form evident in this example, with the dramatic line of its handle uninterrupted from the base of the vessel to the tip of its spout. Plain bands—like citations—mark the places on the lower neck and the joint between body and foot where other versions were (often heavily) decorated.

7 Jenny Uglow, *The Lunar Men: the Friends Who Made the Future,* London 2002, p. 202.

Pitcher from Sir William Hamilton and P. H. d'Hancarville, *Collection of Etruscan, Greek and Roman Antiquities from the Cabinet of the Hon'ble William Hamilton…*
Copperplate engraving, London 1766
The British Museum

Ancient Greek red-figure oil flask, second half of the 5th century B.C.
Albumen print, Karl Bosnjak, Vienna 1904
© Kunsthistorisches Museum Vienna, Antikensammlung, inv. no. IV 383

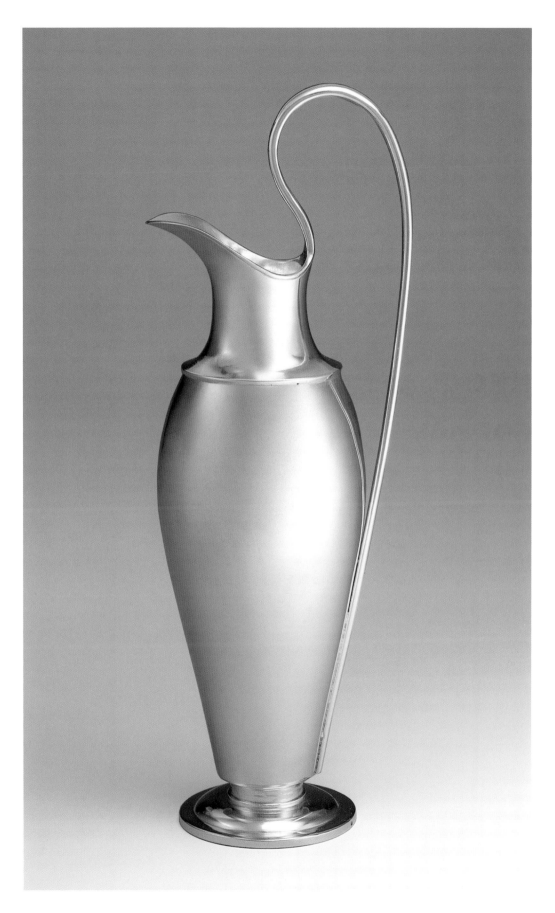

10. WINE JUG

Joseph Heinisch, Vienna 1807

Silver

Vienna hallmark, maker's mark IH, Austrian control mark (*Vorratspunze*)

H 24.5 cm/9.8 in. Weight 403 g/16.1 oz.

Private collection

Dressing table in the bedroom of Empress Maria Ludovica in the Hofburg in Vienna, detail

In a certain type of Viennese Biedermeier interior from around 1820—such as the bedroom of Empress Maria Ludovica in the Hofburg—the use of paintings or pictures on the walls seems to have been shunned. Even, as in this case, where textile swags produce a decorative effect around the perimeter of the room, notably large expanses of undecorated, unused wall (or mirror) space remain. The effect is, in fact, strikingly similar to that achieved by the engraved ornamentation on a wine or water jug from around the same period; a second contemporary wine or water jug of the same size and shape but entirely lacking ornamentation articulates—exaggerates—this emphasis on plainness even further. (That the local aesthetic was not pleasing to all eyes is made evident by the reaction of Prince de Ligne, who sniffed to Count Zinzendorf that Maria Ludovica had succeeded, in her rooms, in combining poor Italian with poor German taste.)[8]

These types of jugs were quite common in households that could afford them during the early 19th century in Vienna, and one is shown in the bedroom of Empress Maria Ludovica—on the dressing table in the background at left—in use. The type endured.

The Biedermeier predilection for bare expanse on the walls was likewise possibly an inspiration for some of the work of Josef Hoffmann around the turn of the 20th century, including the unusually plain dining room of industrialist and early Wiener Werkstätte financier Fritz Waerndorfer (see fig. p. 220).

8 Philip Mansel, *Charles-Joseph de Ligne 1735–1814: Le charmeur de l' Europe*, Paris 1992, p. 184.

Bedroom of Empress Maria Ludovica in the Hofburg in Vienna
Watercolor, ca. 1815
Illustration from Hermann Freiherr von Egloffstein, *Maria Ludovica von Österreich und Maria Paulowna*, Leipzig 1909.

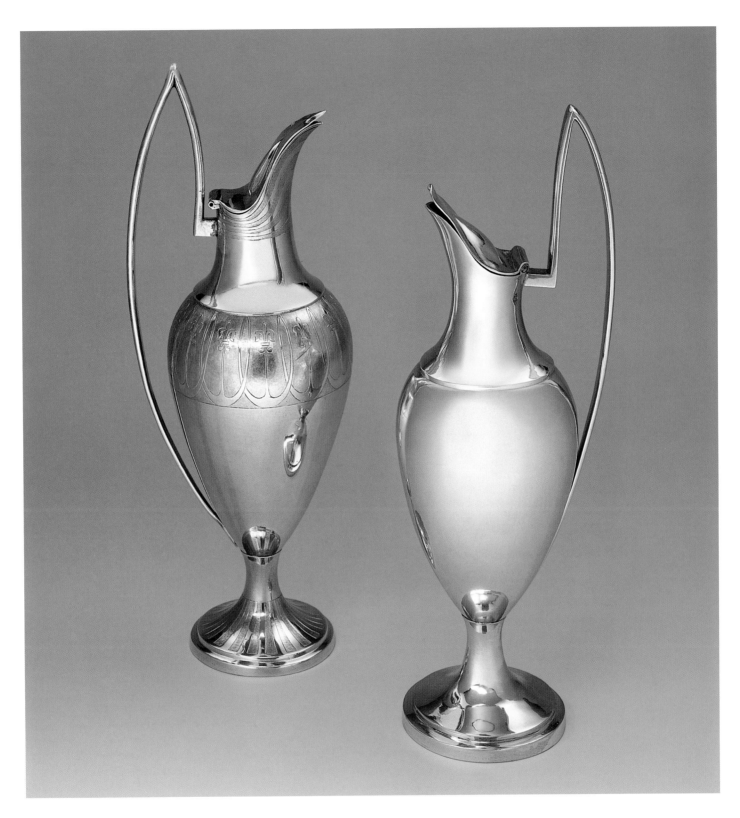

11. WINE OR WATER JUG

Jakob Krautauer, Vienna 1803

Silver

Vienna hallmark, maker's mark K,

Austrian control marks (*Repunze, Taxfreistempel*)

H 33.8 cm/13.5 in. Weight 819 g/32.8 oz.

MAK, Vienna, inv. no. Go 1840b

12. WINE OR WATER JUG

Joseph Stelzer, Vienna 1805

Silver

Vienna hallmark, maker's mark ISl

H 33 cm/13.2 in. Weight 813 g/32.5 oz.

MAK, Vienna, inv. no. Go 1364

13. COFFEE POT

Caspar Haas, Vienna 1807
Silver, fruitwood
Vienna hallmark, maker's mark CH,
Austrian control marks (*Taxfreistempel, Vorratspunze*, unknown mark)
H 20.5 cm/8.2 in. Weight 628 g/25.1 oz.
Private collection

Two nearly identical coffee pots—an undecorated one made by Joseph Heinisch in 1805 and one with Empire style detailing made by Kaspar Haas in 1807—highlight not only the range of possibilities available to consumers in early 19th-century Vienna, but also the effect of ornamentation on the character of an object. Many important questions surrounding the use of ornamentation or the complete lack of it remain unanswered. What is known is that, unsurprisingly, the addition of ornamental work to an object also raised its price. In 1830 Stephan Keesz and W. C. W. Blumenbach reported that "Plain work, such as cutlery, costs one and a half guilders per lot of thirteen-lot silver including workmanship and testing fee; services, candelabra, tea and coffee machines, pots, etc. cost one guilder thirty-nine farthings. Decorated items increase to one guilder forty-two farthings

and up to two guilders. Items in fifteen-lot silver are more expensive, as the value of the metal is greater by ten farthings per lot; in addition, slightly more is usually charged for workmanship in fine silver. The workmanship alone on a machine-made candelabrum (regardless of whether it weighs ten or twenty lot) was set at three and a half guilders some time ago."[9]

Unadorned silver was also particularly well-suited for items that were meant to travel, such as certain types of candlesticks, tea and coffee services, cutlery, beakers, and other paraphernalia such as boxes for toilet services.

In addition, it seems likely—and examination of watercolor interior depictions from 1800–50 seems to support this—

14. COFFEE POT

Joseph Heinisch, Vienna 1805
Silver, fruitwood
Vienna hallmark, maker's mark JH
H 20.5 cm/´8.2 in. Weight 632 g/25.3 oz.
Courtney Ross-Holst Collection

that plain silver was relegated a certain rank within the household. Its relationship to the highly decorated silver of the day may have been parallel to that between Empire and Biedermeier furnishings. Christian Witt-Dörring was among the first to point out that, in Austria, the Empire and Biedermeier styles were concurrent, rather than preceding/anteceding each other. In the imperial household, for example, Empire style was used for "public" spaces or those in which an emblematic, or representational, character was called for, while private apartments were furnished in Biedermeier taste. This same division may well have held true for silver household items, with "simpler" silver associated with notions of the familial or of privacy.

Unquestionably, however, and perhaps inevitably, a liking developed for the pure, undecorated form that went beyond criteria such as price and what might or might not be put to use in everyday life.

In terms of the ornamentation itself, a significant aspect is that the décor of most embellished Empire silver from Vienna is more naive or more abstract (depending on whether one views this as negative or positive), and also longer-lived (it retained its immediacy from 1800 into the 1830s), than its counterparts in France. Ornamentation is usually limited to decorative bands with vegetable- or geometric-based patterns, or the stylization of joints and extremities such as finials.

9 Steph. Ritter von Keesz and W. C. W. Blumenbach, *Systematische Darstellung der neuesten Fortschritte in den Gewerben und Manufacturen und des gegenwärtigen Zustandes derselben*, Vienna 1830, pp. 292–293. English translation Michael Huey.

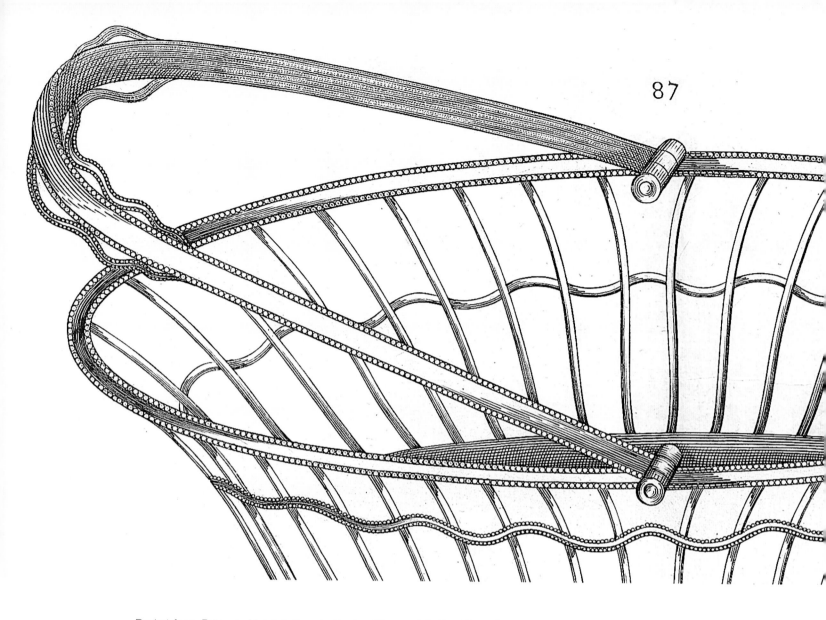

Basket from *Britannia Metal: A Sample Book of Tea- and Coffee-Plate, Salt-Boxes, Spoons, Knives, Forks, Bowls, Cups, Baskets, Mugs, Pots, Candlesticks, Consoles, etc. etc.*
Copperplate engraving, London 1790
MAK, Vienna

In the wagon at our feet lay a rush basket with two handles that aroused my interest. "I brought it with me," said Goethe, "from Marienbad, where there are baskets like it in all sizes, and I have grown so used to it that I cannot travel without having it along. You see, when it is empty it folds up and takes up little space; when filled it expands in all directions and holds more than one might imagine. It is soft and flexible and yet so tough and strong that it can be used to transport the heaviest of things."

"It looks quite picturesque and even antique," said I.

"You are correct," said Goethe, "it comes close to the classical [model], for it is not only rational and functional as can be, but it has, moreover, at the same time the most simple pleasant form, so that one can safely say: it is the pinnacle of perfection."[10]

Johann Wolfgang von Goethe in conversation with
Johann Peter Eckermann, September 24, 1827.

10 Johann Peter Eckermann, *Gespräche mit Goethe in den letzten Jahren seines Lebens,* Leipzig 1910, pp. 276–277. English translation Michael Huey.

15. SMALL BASKET WITH HANDLE
Jakob Krautauer, Vienna 1802
Silver
Vienna hallmark, maker's mark K,
Austrian control mark (*Repunze, Taxfreistempel*)
W 16.2 cm/6.5 in. Weight 137 g/5.5 oz.
Private collection

Design for a garden basin from Johann Gottfried Grohmann, ed., *Neues Ideen-Magazin für Liebhaber von Gärten, Englischen Anlagen und für Besitzer von Landgütern* (New Ideas Magazine for Enthusiasts of Gardens, English Parks and for Owners of Country Estates). Engraved by J. C. Leonhardt, Leipzig 1799

In the important matters of shawls, blonds, velvets, silks, satins, and so forth, it is quite impossible that they [the Viennese merchants] should be surpassed. The silversmiths and jewelers certainly exceed in their rich exhibitions those either of France or England, with the exception, perhaps, of the interior arcana of Rundel and Bridges [sic], and of Hamlets [sic].[11]

Frances Trollope, 1838

11 Frances Trollope, *Vienna and the Austrians*, London 1838, vol. 2. p. 108.

16. DISH

Ignaz Binder, Vienna 1819

Silver

Vienna hallmark, maker's mark JB, fifteen-lot (*fünfzehn-löthig*),

Austrian control mark (*Taxfreistempel*)

Monogram "I. v. K.," engraved dedication from the 1970s

Diameter 21.4 cm/8.6 in. Weight 413 g/16.5 oz.

Asenbaum Collection

Claude-Nicolas Ledoux, principal façade of the director's house at the Royal Saltworks in Chaux/Arc-et-Senans 1775–79

Illustration from Marcel Raval, *Claude-Nicolas Ledoux: Architecte du Roi, 1736–1806,* Paris 1945.

In architecture, rustication is a decorative treatment of stone that was first employed by the Greeks to "suggest the original strength of the natural rock" and thereby express power. Nearly every neoclassical architectural style makes use of it, and it almost always has as a result an emphasis on the horizontal. The façade of the Palazzo Pitti declares political power; Ledoux's columns of the director's house at Chaux, administrative power. Hoffmann's façade of the Primavesi country house in Winkelsdorf—a modern abstraction (in wood) of the idea of rustication—announces financial power, while Loos's planned house for Josephine Baker, which takes this abstraction a step further (there is no longer any recessing to the façade, only a single flat plane), is a hymn to creative power. Rustication does this by specifically alluding to, rather than disguising, the sheer physical strength that went into the construction. It is a constant reminder of the weight of stone or other building materials, and of gravity. This strength is not smoothed over or sculpted away, but placed on display, or, where the actual load-bearing elements are ineffectually expressive, even added on as a kind of veneer. (Here ornamentation poses as function, precisely the opposite of the rococo ideal of function posing as ornamentation.)

The Joseph Laubenbacher candelabra make similar use of this architectural vocabulary, but now its purpose is to express, perhaps, a different kind of power: energy. The horizontal lines map the surface of the object, delineating and describing its contours, and suggesting an additive constructive principle where, in fact, none exists. (In the decorative arts in Austro-Hungary such ornamentation can occasionally be found on items ranging from late 18th-century stoneware to black and white striped tin vessels designed by Dagobert Peche around 1920.) Loos's gas lamp fixtures for the office and reception area of the Goldman & Salatsch Salon from 1898—spring-coiled copper tubing with globes attached at the nether-ends—take this idea to its extreme by barring all substance that is not structure and leaving a highly decorative, purely structural form.

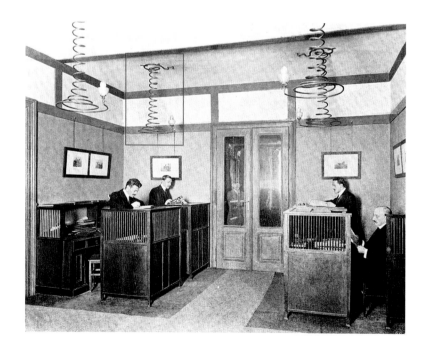

Adolf Loos, the office and reception of the haberdashery Goldman & Salatsch, 1898 with coiled gas lamps (detail at right)

Illustration from *Das Interieur* 2, p.148, Vienna 1901.

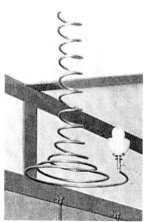

17. CANDELABRA
Joseph Laubenbacher, Vienna 1804
Silver
Vienna hallmark, maker's mark IL
H 32.5 cm/13 in. Weight 848 g/33.9 oz.
Private collection

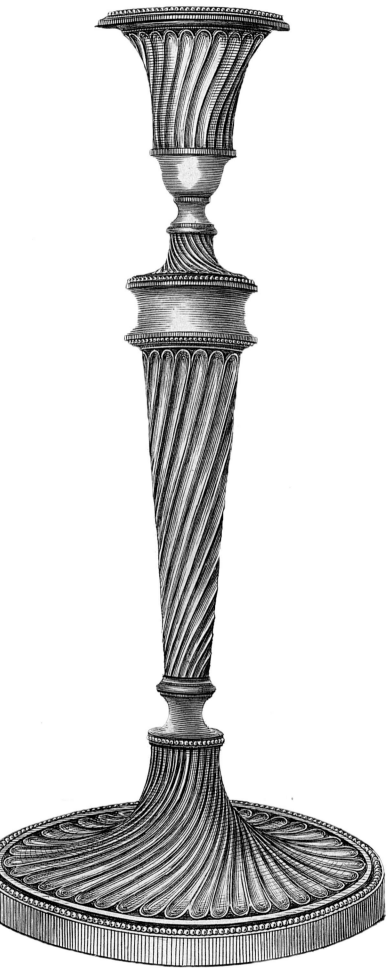

Johann Baptist Schneider, pair of silver candlesticks
Vienna 1781
Private collection

Some decorative arts items make a point of showing us how they were made; others show us how they want to be used. (Still others disguise both.) The Krautauer candlesticks from 1800 are nearly completely unornamented with the exception of the grooved foot and nodus. The latter, whose bulbous form contrasts with the smooth, shiny shaft like a gall on a plant stem, is perfectly shaped and positioned to invite the thumb and two forefingers to pick up the candlestick. The grooving prevents their leaving fingerprints—nothing to blemish the clarity of the trumpet-shaped base. Devoid of fluting or any other decor, the unbroken silhouette of the candlesticks is an abstraction of the idea of earlier English and continental models.

LEFT: Candlestick from *Britannia Metal: A Sample Book of Tea- and Coffee-Plate, Salt-Boxes, Spoons, Knives, Forks, Bowls, Cups, Baskets, Mugs, Pots, Candlesticks, Consoles, etc. etc.*
Copperplate engraving, London 1790
MAK, Vienna

18. PAIR OF CANDLESTICKS
Jakob Krautauer, Vienna 1800
Silver
Vienna hallmark, maker's mark K
H 25.8 cm/10.3 in. Weight 596 g/23.8 oz.
Private collection

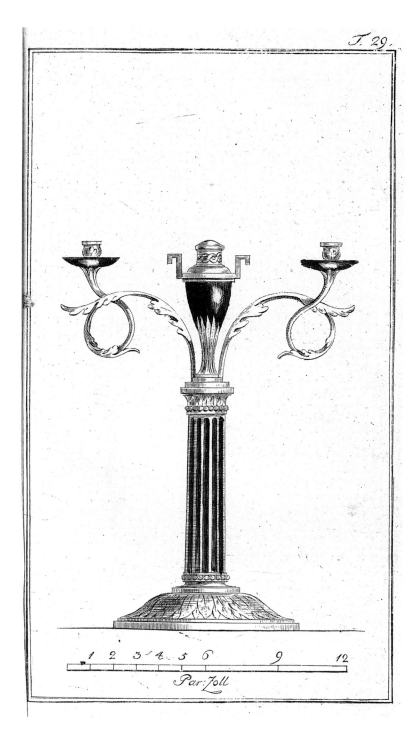

Michael Thonet, bentwood armchair
made in Boppard ca. 1835
Albumen print, Carl Daiber, Boppard ca. 1900
Michael Huey, Vienna

*Tafel-Leuchter von schöner Form und neuestem Geschmacke/
Churfürstliche Spiegelfabrik zu Dresden* (Candelabrum of pleasing Shape and
in the latest Taste/Prince-Electoral Mirror Factory in Dresden) with blue glass
and matte and shiny *argent-argé* from *Journal des Luxus und der Moden*.
Copperplate engraving, Weimar, October 1789
MAK, Vienna

The *Journal des Luxus und der Moden* (Journal of Luxury and
Fashion) and the *Magazin für Freunde des guten Geschmacks*
(Magazine for Friends of Good Taste) were important
arbiters of style in Vienna during the last two decades of the
18th century, referred to by clients and manufacturers alike.

Whether Stephan Mayerhofer was familiar with these works
or not is unknown, however a catalogue of the first
Austrian *Gewerbsprodukten-Ausstellung* (Decorative Arts
Show) in 1835 makes a point of mentioning Mayerhofer's
devotion to "the demands of fashion." Mayerhofer's interest
in new trends went beyond the aesthetic: he was among
the first to specialize in plated wares, as well as embracing
early forms of mass production. The Mayerhofer workshop
was located at Marokkanergasse 411 in Leopoldstadt,
Vienna's second district. (There was also a shop located
downtown at Kohlmarkt 253.) The exhibition catalogue
offers a short overview of the firm's history: "… [Mayerhofer]
is notorious for having been the first to undertake the tool-
ing of silver on the lathe; the first to open an establishment
for plated goods in Vienna; for introducing expensive
machinery and presses with which he and he alone was
able to produce his luxury items in factory style and thereby
keep up with the constant flow of orders; and for employ-
ing a great many workers in his firm."[12]

Michael Thonet's armchair from about 1835 similarly makes
innovative use of a bentwood technique that had been known
since the Middle Ages to efficiently reproduce the fashionable curved forms of the day.

12 *Bericht über die erste allgemeine österreichische Gewerbsprodukten-Ausstellung im
Jahre 1835*, Vienna 1835, pp. 179–180. English translation Michael Huey.

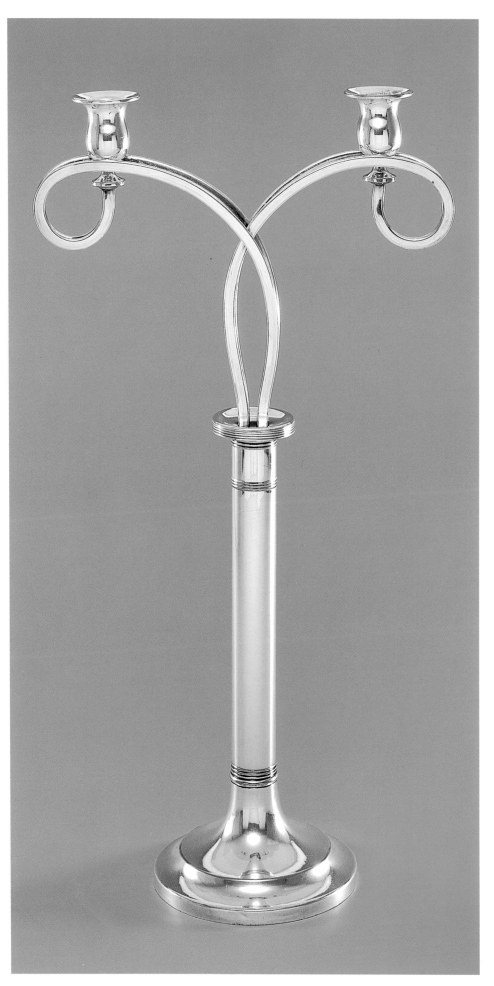

19. ONE OF A PAIR OF CANDELABRA

Stephan Mayerhofer, Vienna ca. 1820

Silver-plated copper
Maker's mark Mayerhofer,
manufacturer's privilege mark
H 47.8 cm / 19.1 in.
Christian Witt-Dörring, Vienna

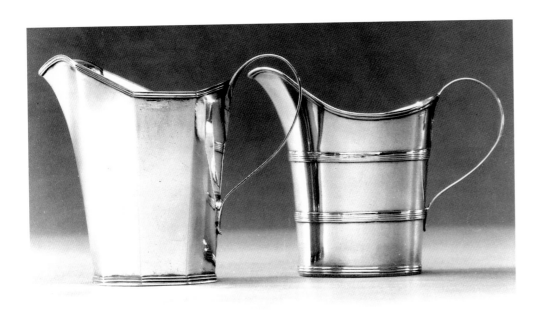

Peter Zethelius, silver creamers
Stockholm 1797
Nationalmuseum, Stockholm

An easily perceived shape devoid of ostentatious, eyesore embellishment, combined with an overall uniqueness is therefore the main characteristic of all that is aesthetically noble. In this way it presents itself to us as a pleasing entirety, as something that somehow retreats modestly within itself; but then, through that unique quality—the novelty of the whole—it effortlessly stirs our imagination from its slumber, spurring it into action and appearing to the educated taste as noble.

But just as nobility is nothing other than a modestly-retreating grandeur concealed by beauty—the naive is nothing other than, if I may express myself thus, a kind of submerged sublime.[13]

Lazarus Bendavid, 1799

13 Lazarus Bendavid, *Versuch einer Geschmackslehre*, Berlin 1799, pp. 112–113. English translation Michael Huey.

Boulton and Fothergill, silver jug
Birmingham 1775
Messrs. Lumley Collection, London

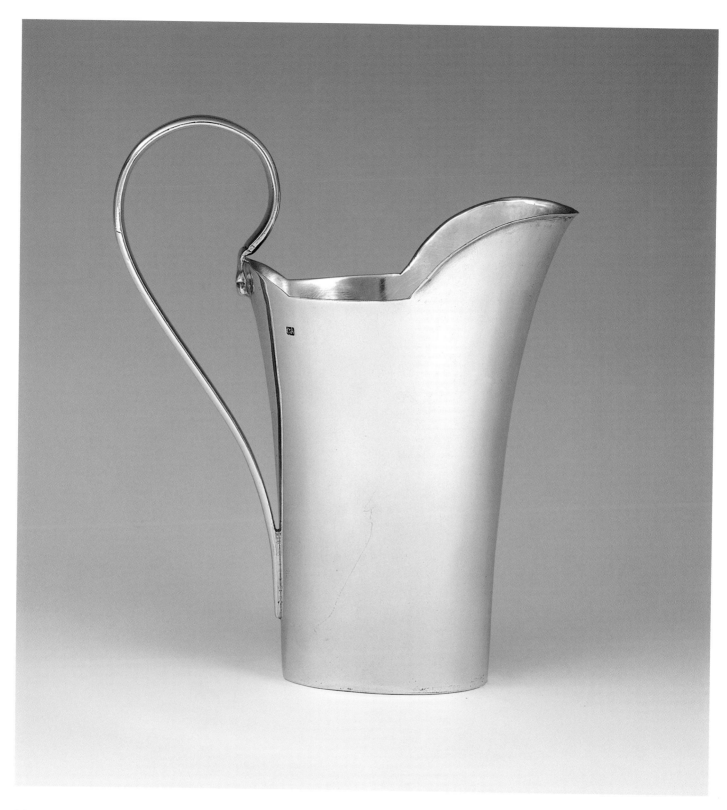

20. WATER JUG
Carl Blasius, Vienna 1814
Silver
Vienna hallmark, maker's mark CB,
Austrian control mark (*Vorratspunze*)
H 16.3 cm/6.5 in. Weight 285 g/11.4 oz.
Courtney Ross-Holst Collection

The industrial revolution seems already present in a caster made by Georg Forgatsch in 1807, whose emphasis on the negative shape that appears to have been "cut" from the positive, as well as the grooving at the foot, shoulders, and lid, calls to mind the burgeoning importance of mechanical aids like the lathe in 19th-century design. (Though the lathe existed since Graeco-Roman times, its capabilities took on a new light after the invention of the steam engine. Josiah Wedgwood also did his part by putting the process of engine-turning to use in the production of his popular ceramics.) As a type, the Forgatsch caster naturally descends from rococo and Louis XVI designs such as those shown on this page, but it is a rather distant relative, making of their lower body curves a solid volume (its sides are more or less defined by a straight line drawn from the widest part of the 1778 caster to its foot, thereby eliminating the base and its attempt at monumentality). The mind takes pleasure—although defying, by so doing, the reality of the silversmith's craft—in comparing the two and imagining the body of the earlier vision as chiseled from the solid volume of the later. What little ornamentation does exist in the Forgatsch caster is relegated to the openings of the lid. Here, too, the finial is a plain knob and not a stylization of a fruit or other product of the natural world.

Joseph Gschnadt, silver caster
Vienna 1774
Private collection

Dirk Evert Grave, silver caster
Amsterdam 1778
Rijksmuseum, Amsterdam

21. CASTER
Georg Forgatsch, Vienna 1807
Silver
Vienna hallmark, maker's mark IF
H 13.6/5.2 in. Weight 190 g/7.6 oz.
Private collection

Maker IFE and Ignaz Krautauer, pair of silver candlesticks
Vienna 1776 and Vienna 1779
Private collection

The baroque candlestick form in Vienna and elsewhere in central and northern Europe was marked by its base, which, with its upturned edge, formed a little tray around the candlestick's shaft. From the 1780s into the first decade of the 19th century in Vienna the lower part of the shaft was elongated, setting the stage for the candlestick type that was to follow—a pure cylindrical form rising uninterrupted, after a slight depression, from the top edge, rather than the bottom, of the base. In the examples shown here, grooved bands are all that remain to mark the undulations of the baroque type (other examples make use of different geometric or naturalistic patterns in place of the grooving). The widened lip of the nozzle echoes the round shape of the base and together these, along with the grooved bands, create the impression of concentric circles. The modernity of the later solution owes primarily to the simplification of the candlestick's silhouette, but also stems from its aesthetic allusion to machinery—the turbine—and technical instruments—microscopes, telescopes—of the day. This became the classic Viennese type from around 1807 through the 1850s, and was produced in a variety of materials in addition to silver including tin, brass, and even stone. Later silver versions were industrially made of pressed sheet silver and are considerably lighter; in early examples the base and nozzle were hammered from a silver core, the shaft was hand-formed from thicker sheet silver, and the grooving—solid silver bands—soldered on as a final step.

Joseph Heinisch, pair of silver candlesticks
Vienna 1787
Private collection

22. PAIR OF CANDLESTICKS
Georg Kohlmayer, Vienna 1816
Silver
Vienna hallmark, maker's mark GK,
Austrian control mark (*Taxfreistempel*)
Monogram AB with count's coronet
H 23.5 cm/9.4 in. Weight 709 g/28.36 oz.
Asenbaum Collection

23. ONE OF A PAIR OF CANDLESTICKS
Benedikt Ranninger, Vienna 1815
Silver
Vienna hallmark, maker's mark BR,
Austrian control marks (*Taxfreistempel, Vorratspunze*)
H 15.3 cm/6.1 in. Weight 415 g/16.6 oz.
Private collection

Joseph Kern, design for a silver casserole from W. C. W. Blumenbach,
Wiener Kunst- und Gewerbsfreund oder der neueste Wiener Geschmack
(Viennese Art and Applied Arts Friend or the Latest Viennese Taste).
Copperplate engraving, Vienna 1825
Wiener Stadt- und Landesbibliothek

This Viennese casserole from 1813 demonstrates an early emphasis on functionalism; in contrast to other earlier and contemporary casseroles, whose finials masquerade as a variety of stylized fruits and other decorative objects, its finial is plain and blatantly suited to its purpose. The body of the casserole has something of the unbroken surface of an expertly-glazed Sacher-Torte. (The gateau, incidentally, was invented in 1832 by Franz Sacher, who was employed by Prince Metternich at the time.) Only the rim is discreetly ornamented with a grooved pattern. The handle rings repeat the round shape of the body, lid, and finial. Their attachment to the body of the casserole by means of a cube-shaped mount plays on two basic geometrical forms: the square and the circle.

Jacques-Antoine Bonhomme, silver casserole and platter
Paris 1781–82
Musée des Arts décoratifs, Paris/Photo: Laurent Sully Jaulmes

24. CASSEROLE

Jakob Krautauer, Vienna 1813

Silver
Vienna hallmark, maker's mark K,
Austrian control marks (*Taxfreistempel, Vorratspunze*)
Diameter 21.6 cm/8.6 in. Weight 1,291 g/51.6 oz.
Private collection

You will find, in the circles of the nobility, an union of every thing delightful, with that stateliness and solidity which blend the ancient grandeur with modern taste. The picture of Austrian high life is less dazzling than the French, but it is more solid. There is less extravagance, less variety than in Paris, but infinitely more reality.[14]

Charles Sealsfield, 1828

14 Charles Sealsfield a.k.a. Karl Post, *Austria as it is: or sketches of continental courts, by an eye-witness, London 1828,* Vienna et al. 1994, p. 85.

F. Maleck, interior view of a bedroom/sitting room; note plain silver and ceramics displayed at left. Watercolor, Vienna 1836
Historisches Museum der Stadt Wien

Because we no longer pay for goods in silver coin it is perhaps impossible for us today to fully perceive the message of silver decorative arts pieces in the home during the 18th and 19th century. (New York writer Fran Lebowitz came close, however, when she was asked in an interview to characterize 1980s interior design and replied, "Can I use actual piles of cash?")[15] It was this direct connection to the currency that turned the conspicuous consumption of luxury goods made of silver into something more akin to conspicuous savings: candlesticks and beakers were like money in the bank, except that that money was transformed into shapes convenient for burning candles and drinking. (In 18th-century France, Louis XV prohibited the making of *desks* in solid silver.)[16]

This was recognized during the Napoleonic Wars by Emperor Francis I of Austria, among others, and he capitalized on it by introducing new (retroactive) taxes on silver acquired for the domestic interior. The taxes were aimed at reducing the number of "gold and silver items that have piled up in uncommonly high numbers among all the classes;"[17] these measures were heightened in 1808 when all silver goods (with the exception of cutlery, watch cases, and other small items) were confiscated unless their owner could pay the entire material value of the piece—in silver coin. As a result, much of the sacred and secular silver produced prior to the war years was destroyed. That which was kept most often belonged, according to Elisabeth Schmuttermeier, to "groups of objects considered indispensable at the time, such as candlesticks, tea and coffee pots, boxes, or tableware for daily use. Unnecessary things, i.e. objects purely for decoration, seldom survived."[18] The Emperor's own silver, incidentally, was not spared: in 1793, the first year of his reign and the year of Archduke Charles's defeat of Napoleon at Aspern, he ordered that the imperial silver be melted down, with the exception of a few pieces used for travel.[19]

The ornaments of the churches; the plate of the noblemen; the trinkets of the wealthy; the silver spoons and forks of the middle classes, all went the same way, to defray the expenses of this war [1809], without murmuring or repining.[20]

Charles Sealsfield, 1828

20 Charles Sealsfield a.k.a. Karl Post, *Austria as it is: or sketches of continental courts, by an eye-witness*, London 1828, Vienna et al. 1994, p. 61.

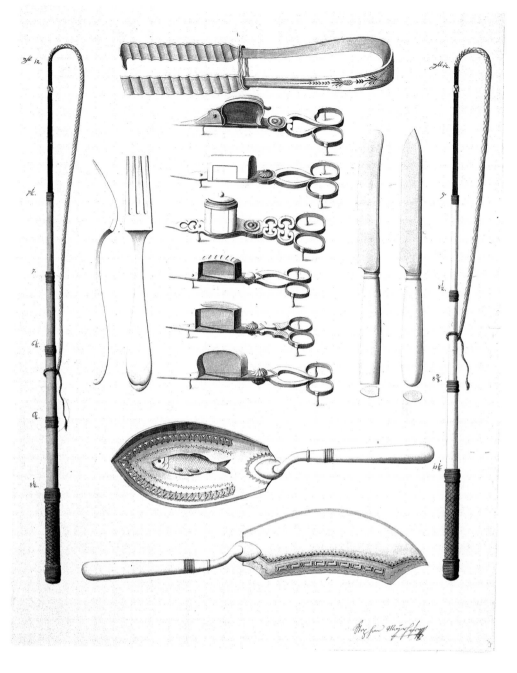

Stephan Mayerhofer, drawing of silver-plate goods included in the maker's license for the production of machine-made silver objects
Vienna 1822
Universitätsarchiv der TU, Vienna

15 Fran Lebowitz, *HG*, January 1990, p. 110.

16 Henry Havard, *Dictionnaire de l'ameublement et de la decoration depuis le XIIIme siècle jusque'á nos jours*, as cited in Siegfried Giedion, *Mechanization Takes Command*, New York 1948, p. 306.

17 Elisabeth Schmuttermeier, "*Wiener Silber und Schmuck des Biedermeier*," in *Bürgersinn und Aufbegehren: Biedermeier und Vormärz in Wien 1815–1848*, exh. cat. Historisches Museum der Stadt Wien, Vienna 1987, p. 228.

18 Schmuttermeier 1987 (see note 17), p. 229. English translation Michael Huey.

19 Hubert Chryspolitus Winkler, "Kurze Geschichte der ehem. Hofsilber- und Tafelkammer," in: Ilsebill Barta Fliedl and Peter Parenzan, eds., *Ehemalige Hofsilber- und Tafelkammer, Sammlungskatalog Band 1*, Vienna 1996, p. 18.

2.3

NEOCLASSICISM
GEOMETRY AS LANGUAGE OF THE ENLIGHTENMENT

Stein des guten Glückes (Stone of Good Fortune), one of the first non-figural sculptures in Germany, erected under the direction of Johann Wolfgang von Goethe in his garden on the Ilm
Weimar 1777
Stiftung Weimarer Klassik, Herzogin Anna Amalia Bibliothek, Fotothek, Weimar

A Free Mason,
Form'd out of the Materials of his Lodge

Behold a Master-Mason rare,
Whose mystic Portrait does declare
The Secrets of Free Masonry.
Fair for all to read and see;
But few there are to whom they're known;
Tho' they so plainly here are Shown.

A. Slade delin.

25. TEAPOT
Jakob Krautauer, Vienna 1802
Silver, fruitwood
Vienna hallmark, maker's mark K,
Austrian control marks
(*Befreiungsstempel, Repunzierung*)
H 14.8 cm/5.9 in. Weight 565 g/22.6 oz.
Asenbaum Collection

Many teapots from the late 18th and early 19th century in Vienna are striking in their similarity to, or obvious descent from, traditional English teapots. Since Austria had given up its own East India Company in 1731 in exchange for England's agreement to the so-called Pragmatic Sanction that kept Maria Theresa on her father's throne, the concept of tea and all its appurtenances remained firmly in British, or, even more remotely, Asian hands. This particular teapot, however, designed by Jakob Krautauer in 1802, is perhaps most striking in its divergence from the English canon, in both its shape and its ornamentation.

In the Viennese decorative arts from 1800–50 some of the most interesting and original shapes derive from variations on the standard geometrical repertoire: marriages of circular and rectangular or square forms that produce a curiously attractive ambivalence. The Krautauer teapot is neither spherical, nor rectangular, nor oval, exactly, and this idiosyncrasy is a significant part of its personality.

Contrasting with that equivocality, though, is the rigid pattern of its décor. Strict geometry was an important feature in the concept of neoclassicism, and it was sometimes used as the medium for a particular symbolic message. According to a

Freemason legend, the black and white checkerboard pattern goes back to the paving stones of the Temple of Solomon; the Freemasons borrowed it in the late 18th century to illustrate an idea about order and rationality that challenged both aesthetic and societal norms. (Their intent was not to do away with the norms, but merely to replace what they considered arbitrary ones with others based on science and knowledge. Rosalind Krauss, who has examined the connection between 19th-century optical experiments and the use of the grid in modern art, has described the grid as "what art looks like when it turns its back on nature.")[21] In early 19th-century Austria the square pattern increasingly came into use—perhaps partly in this same context, but also as an outgrowth of tradition—and it could be found on floors, walls, building façades, and certain decorative arts objects.

Krautauer's remarkable use of the square pattern in this example is echoed a hundred years later in a coffer designed by Koloman Moser (cat. no. 119) for the Wiener Werkstätte in 1903 which, in turn, conceptually pre-dates and foreshadows the Werkstätte's later ubiquitous use of the sawed-out grid pattern.

21 Rosalind E. Krauss, "Grids," in *The Originality of the Avant-Garde and Other Modernist Myths*, Cambridge Mass. and London 1997, p. 9.

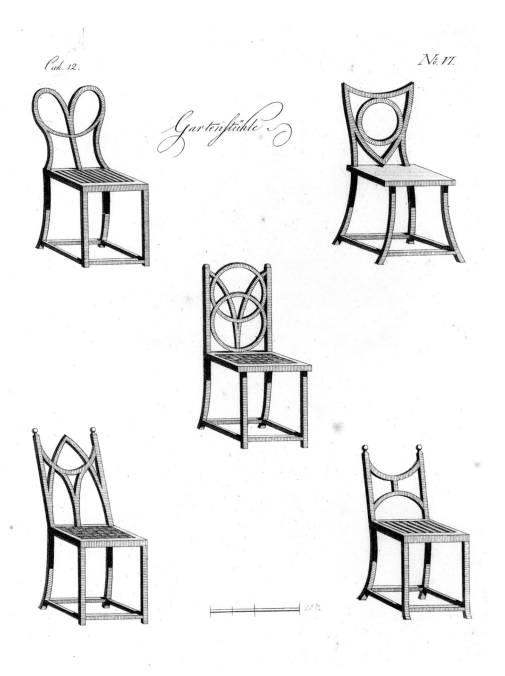

Design for *Gartenstühle* (Garden chairs) from Johann Gottfried Grohmann, ed., *Neues Ideen-Magazin für Liebhaber von Gärten, Englischen Anlagen und für Besitzer von Landgütern* (New Ideas Magazine for Enthusiasts of Gardens, English Parks and for Owners of Country Estates).

Copperplate engraving, Leipzig 1797

The parts that should appear to have been cut out are first drilled through, then cut out smoothly with jigsaws, and finally lines and points are engraved with other tools as the drawing demands. This work is done by so-called silver-cutters who, like the engravers, are assistants to the producers of silver wares. In the Austrian nation this work requires a license of its own.[22]

Stephan Keesz and W. C. W. Blumenbach, 1825

22 Stephan Ritter von Keesz and W. C. W. Blumenbach, *Systematische Darstellung der neuesten Fortschritte in den Gewerben und Manufacturen und des gegenwärtigen Zustandes derselben,* Vienna 1830, p. 286. English translation Michael Huey.

26. PAIR OF KNIFE-RESTS

Johann Kain, Vienna 1819

Silver

Vienna hallmark, maker's mark K,

Austrian control marks (*Vorratspunze, Taxfreistempel*)

W 10.7 cm/4.3 in. Weight 61 g/2.4 oz.

Private collection

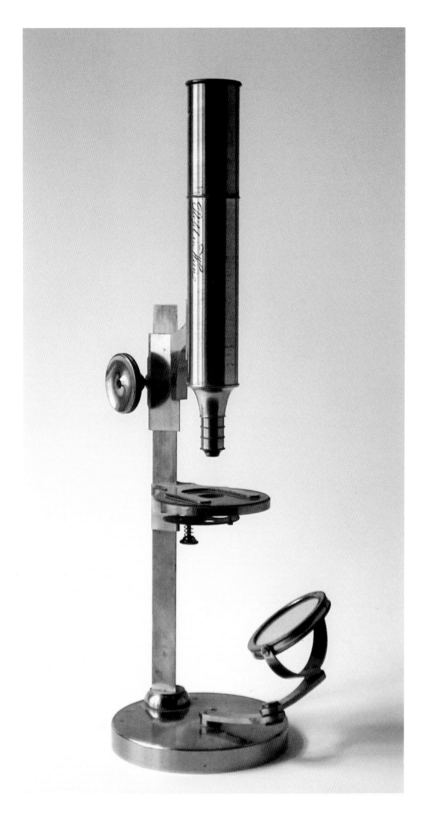

Reason and imagination thus prove themselves excellently useful in the judgment of beauty; and so we can assume, to a certain degree, that only what agrees with these qualities, allowing them to carry out their business, may be considered beautiful.[23]

Lazarus Bendavid, 1799

23 Lazarus Bendavid, *Versuch einer Geschmackslehre*, Berlin 1799, p. 21. English translation Michael Huey.

Simon Plössl, medium-sized microscope no. 2 with round base
Vienna ca. 1840
Simon Weber-Unger, Wissenschaftliches Kabinett, Vienna

27. PAIR OF CANDLESTICKS
Franz Weissenböck, Vienna 1814
Silver
Vienna hallmark, maker's mark FW, Austrian control mark (*Taxfreistempel*)
H 18.3 cm/7.3 in. Weight 366 g/14.6 oz.
Asenbaum Collection

G. SORGATO FIRENZE

Antonio Canova, Funeral monument for Archduchess Maria Christina in the Church of St. Augustine in Vienna, 1798–1805
Albumen print by C. Sorgato, Florence ca. 1885
Michael Huey, Vienna

28. CHAMBER CANDLESTICK
Maker LL, Vienna 1819

Silver
Vienna hallmark, maker's mark LL, Austrian control mark (*Taxfreistempel*)
H 7 cm/2.8 in. Weight 150 g/6 oz.
Private collection

Christopher Dresser, silver-plated white metal
chamber candlestick
Executed by Hukin & Heath, Birmingham and London 1894
Private collection

Bisque porcelain model of the Theseus Temple in the Vienna Volksgarten by Peter von Nobile, built in 1820–23 to accommodate Antonio Canova's monumental sculpture of Theseus.
Wiener Porzellan Manufaktur, 1847
MAK, Vienna

The heaping-up of adornments, or even decorations, is one of the surest signs of a small-minded style. Both are inessential to the whole...

Thus the Roman column—simply because of its many adornments—is far less pleasing to our eyes than the Doric, and the tasteful artist will surely give precedence to the latter over the former.[24]

Lazarus Bendavid, 1799

24 Lazarus Bendavid, *Versuch einer Geschmackslehre*, Berlin 1799, p. 244.

Maker M. I., pair of silver salt and pepper cellars and spoons
Vienna 1819
Private collection

29. PAIR OF CANDLESTICKS
Benedikt Ranninger, Vienna 1817
Silver
Vienna hallmark, maker's mark BNR
H 13.6 cm/5.4 in. Weight 153 g/6.1 oz.
Private collection

Jacques-Germain Soufflot, the Panthéon
Paris 1756–90
Photo: A. F. Kersting, London

Proposition 1.
**The Decorative Arts arise from, and should properly be
attendant upon, Architecture.**[25]

Owen Jones, 1856

25 Owen Jones, "General Principles in the Arrangement of Form and Colour in Architecture
and the Decorative Arts," in Isabelle Frank, ed., *The Theory of Decorative Art: An
Anthology of European & American Writings, 1750–1940*, New York, p. 271.

30. CASTER
Karl Sedelmayer, Vienna 1810
Silver
Vienna hallmark, maker's mark KS,
Austrian control mark (*Vorratsstempel*)
H 11 cm/4.4 in. Weight 148 g/5.9 oz.
Private collection

Design for a *ländliches Wirtshaus oder Gasthof* (Country tavern or inn) from Johann Gottfried Grohmann, ed., *Neues Ideen-Magazin für Liebhaber von Gärten, Englischen Anlagen und für Besitzer von Landgütern* (New Ideas Magazine for Enthusiasts of Gardens, English Parks and for Owners of Country Estates).
Copperplate engraving, Leipzig 1806

The strong emphasis on basic geometric shapes in neoclassical design illustrates a school of thought prevalent toward the end of the 18th century in which styles and shapes were relegated to gender and invested with "typical" feminine and masculine attributes. The neoclassical age was one in which qualities regarded as masculine took precedence. From its vantage point, rococo curves, exuberance, asymmetry, and unpredictability were considered weak and degenerate—a "feminine" style. Neoclassicism, on the other hand, symmetrical and "rational," was praised as "masculine." This kind of reasoning was often employed in the posturing that was done in aesthetic circles over the virtues of one style versus another; it paralleled the debate over the English landscape garden versus the French-style formal garden that had been the standard throughout Europe in the late 17th and much of the 18th century, in which the French variety was pejoratively associated with the artificial, the affected, and the weak.

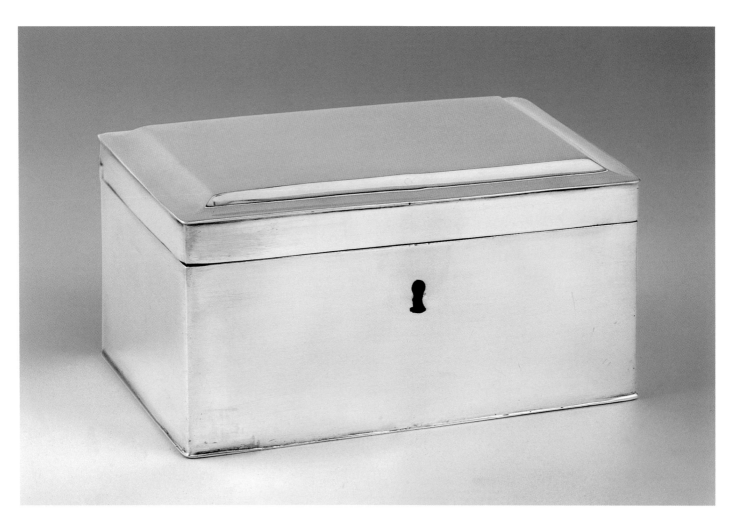

31. SUGAR BOX

Johann Georg Hann, Vienna 1810

Silver, parcel-gilt (interior)

Vienna hallmark, maker's mark GH

W 13.9 cm/5.6 in. Weight 504 g/20.2 oz.

Private collection

Joseph Kornhäusel, design for the Circus Bach in the Vienna Prater
Pen and ink and watercolor, Vienna 1807
Albertina, Vienna

32. CASSEROLE
Anton Köll, Vienna 1807

Silver
Vienna hallmark, maker's mark AK,
Austrian control mark (*Repunze*)
Diameter 19.1 cm/7.6 in. Weight 1,149 g/46 oz.
Private collection

Claude-Nicolas Ledoux, design for the *Maison du Directeur de la Loue* (House of the administrator of the Loue River), 1775–79, from Johann Gottfried Grohmann, ed., *Neues Ideen-Magazin für Liebhaber von Gärten, Englischen Anlagen und für Besitzer von Landgütern* (New Ideas Magazine for Enthusiasts of Gardens, English Parks and for Owners of Country Estates). Copperplate engraving, Leipzig 1806

Another room had a large tea-table, where, as if by magic, eternal fountains of hot and excellent tea played into every cup extended to receive it throughout the whole evening. In truth, the tea-making here [in Vienna] is brought to a degree of scientific perfection of which we dream not with us. In the first place, the finer teas which they get, sometimes as presents I believe, viâ Russie [sic], far exceed in flavor any species with which I have been hitherto acquainted; and not only is the tea-urn always kept boiling by spirits of wine, but even the tea-pots are also frequently placed on stands furnished with small flames of the same kind, so that cold or weak tea is a misery unknown.[26]

Frances Trollope, 1838

26 Frances Trollope, *Vienna and the Austrians*, London 1838, vol. 2, p. 236.

33. TEA KETTLE AND STAND

Probably Johann Guttmann Jr., Vienna 1816

Silver, fruitwood, zinc, brass

Vienna hallmark, maker's mark IG

Austrian control marks (*Vorratspunze, Taxfreistempel*)

H 26 cm/10.4 in. Weight 1,050 g/42 oz.

Asenbaum Collection

Sir John Soane, perspective design of the New Four Per Cent (later Colonial) Office, 1818–23
Pen and watercolor drawing by Joseph Michael Gandy
By courtesy of the Trustees of Sir John Soane's Museum, London

34. TEA KETTLE AND STAND

Bartholomäus Huber, Vienna ca. 1815

Silver, fruitwood
Vienna hallmark, maker's mark BH,
Austrian control mark (*Taxfreistempel*)
H 32.5 cm/13 in. Weight 2,300 g/92 oz.
Camilo Antonio, Vienna

Claude-Nicolas Ledoux, design for a *Maison des Gardes Agricoles* (House for Field Guards) at Meaupertuis
Paris ca. 1780
Illustration from Marcel Raval, *Claude-Nicolas Ledoux. Architecte du Roi (1736–1806)*, Arts et Métiers Graphiques, Paris 1945.

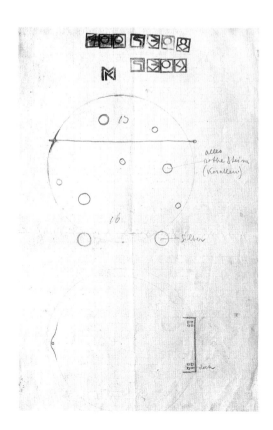

Koloman Moser, design for a silver and coral
Dose (Box) (WW model no. S 308) for the
Wiener Werkstätte
Pencil and colored pencil, Vienna 1905
MAK, Vienna

The French Revolution produced two major utopian architects—Claude-Nicolas Ledoux and Étienne-Louis Boullée—who experimented with stark geometric forms such as the sphere in radical (and usually unrealized) new ways. Just as the tremors of the revolution were felt in Vienna, so, too, was its creativity, born of the desire to rebuild the existing world and its structures. (Both the metric system and a new calendar were part of the rational redefinition.) In Ledoux's *Maison des Gardes Agricoles* (House for Field Guards at Meaupertuis) and Boullée's related design for a cenotaph for Newton, the ideal of fashioning not just a piece of architecture but one that aspired to a reconciliation of physical law, reason, and aesthetics—what became known as "revolutionary classicism"—reached its zenith. Like human cells, which contain in their DNA full plans of genetic material, a spherical house or mausoleum is a microcosm of the universe—a part of the whole that purports to express the whole. The dome of Boullée's structure was even pierced through with holes to create the effect of a starry sky. (From our present-day vantage point, we also see that such "heroic" architecture, taken to its negative extreme, is a seed that grows remarkably well in the all-encompassing and omniscient totalitarian state.)

In the first half of 19th-century Vienna it was the constructivist attitude of revolutionary classicism that was most firmly embraced. (Chancellor Metternich also clearly envied the post-revolutionary era some of its draconian measures and installed an over-powerful state apparatus as an inoculation against revolution itself.) Clear geometric volumes achieved a fixed status in the decorative arts as part of the contemporary creative vocabulary, and the sphere—as the perfect geometric form—enjoyed a particularly revered status. Spheres were intriguingly, though contradictorily, placed between tabletops and their bases; perfectly spherical chandeliers were made of perfectly unblemished alabaster or frosted glass (these related as well to round 18th-century French chandeliers that doubled as fishbowls); and a whole new type of table—the so-called *Globustisch* (globe table)—evolved in the German-speaking realm. Seen in this light, Koloman Moser's coral-studded box for the Wiener Werkstätte from 1905 (a version without stones was purchased by Karl Wittgenstein) appears perhaps slightly more embedded in the tradition than it otherwise might, as does the later 20th-century work of the constructivists and the post-modernists.

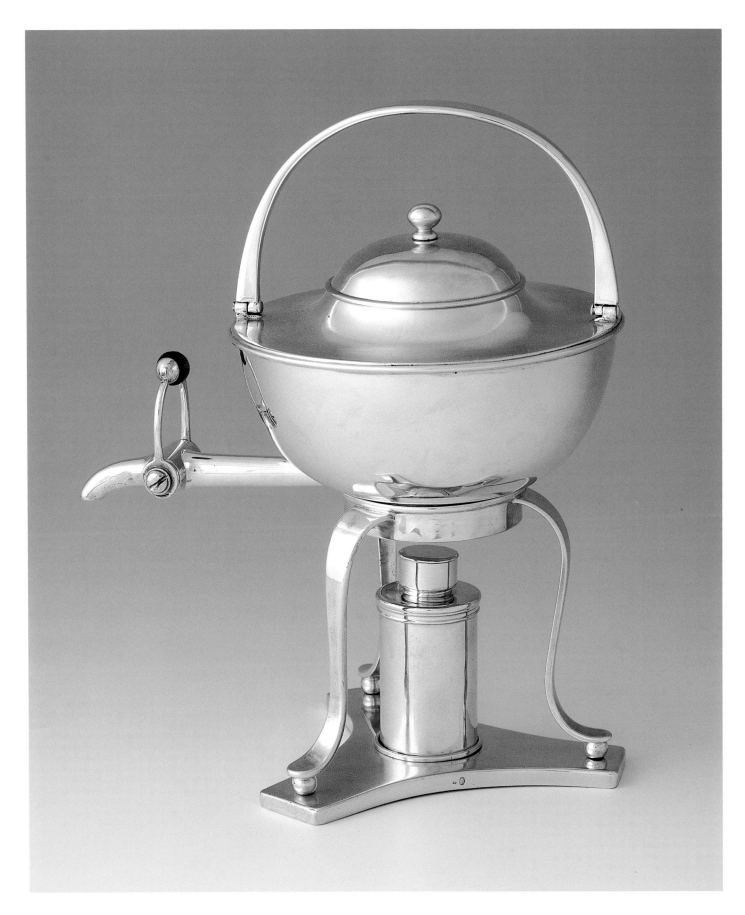

35. TEA KETTLE AND STAND

Joseph Kern, Vienna 1820

Silver

Vienna hallmark, maker's mark K, Austrian control marks (*Vorratspunze, Taxfreistempel*)

H 23.5 cm/9.4 in. Weight 919 g/36.8 oz.

Asenbaum Collection

36. COOKIE BOX

Maker AK, Vienna 1801

Silver

Vienna hallmark, maker's mark AK

Diameter 15.8 cm/6.3 in. Weight 805 g/ 32.2 oz.

Christian Witt-Dörring, Vienna

37. CAVIAR DISH (*KAVIARAUFSATZ*)

Designed by Josef Hoffmann, Vienna 1909

Executed by the Wiener Werkstätte, model no. S 1701

First made May, 1909 for 350 crowns

Four pieces produced

Silver, glass

Vienna hallmark, JH, illegible silversmith's mark, WW, rose mark

Diameter 21.1 cm/8.4 in. Weight 1,267 g/50.7 oz.

Private collection

3

FROM AN IDEAL OF SIMPLICITY TO THE MODERN COMMODITY

A thing is good and beautiful if it is what it should be.[27]

Johann Joachim Winckelmann, 1760

27 Johann Joachim Winckelmann, "Anmerkungen über die Baukunst der Alten," 1760, as cited in *Die Verborgene Vernunft: Funktionale Gestaltung im 19. Jahrhundert*, exh. cat. Neue Sammlung, Munich 1971, p. 31. English translation Michael Huey.

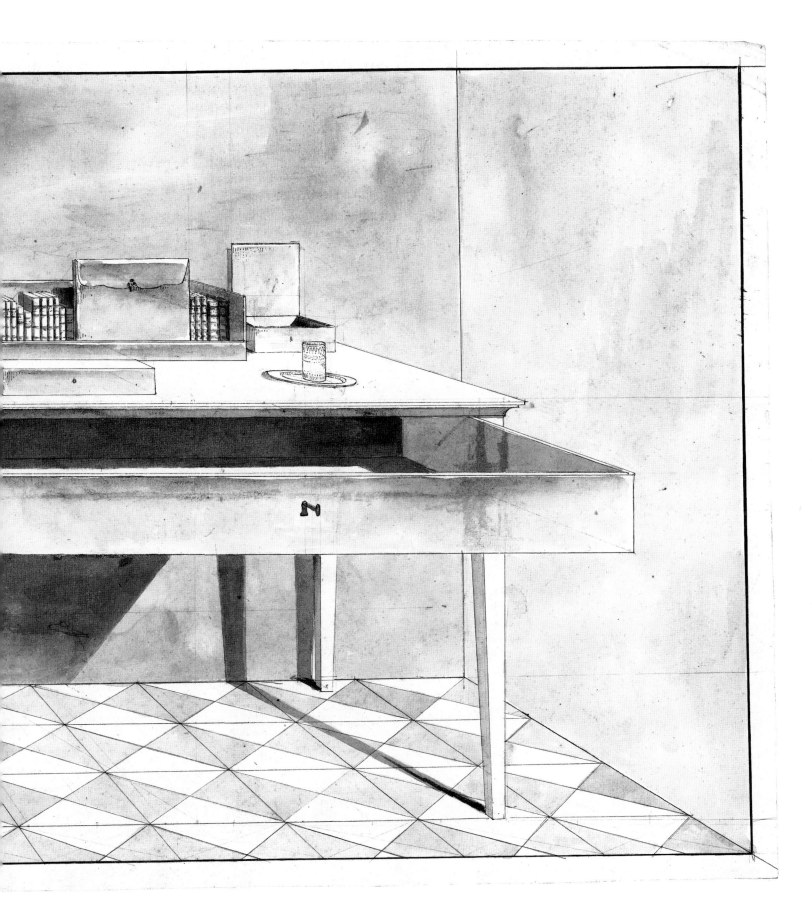

Anonymous, perspective study from drawing instruction for craftsmen

Pen and ink and gray wash, Vienna ca. 1815

Michael Huey, Vienna

38. COFFEE POT AND PERCOLATOR

Vienna, first half of the 19th century

Zinc-plated sheet iron, fruitwood
Unmarked
H 29.5 cm/11.8 in.
Christian Witt-Dörring, Vienna

A conversation between mother and daughter:

CHILD: **Mama! Why did the painter paint a garland across the middle of that beautiful mirror?**
MOTHER: **Don't you see that it is cracked and that he was trying to hide the crack?**
CHILD: **Mama! Why did the merchant use a fabric full of holes for the lovely chintz you bought me?**
MOTHER: **So that the holes would be forgotten in looking at the beauty of the colors.**
CHILD: **Mama! Are hidden cracks and holes to be found everywhere where there is excessive decoration?**
MOTHER: **Yes, my child, everywhere. Much ornament is always a sign that something somewhere is missing, be it in someone's head or in some material.**[28]

Berlin, ca. 1786

28 Justus Moeser, "Patriotische Phantasien," in *Die Durchgeistigung der deutschen Arbeit: Ein Bericht vom Deutschen Werkbund*, Berlin 1911, pp. 18–19. English translation Michael Huey.

A zinc-plated sheet iron coffee pot/percolator from the first half of the 19th century helps us to understand something about the very similar Franz Köll silver version from 1818: namely, that the material—and not the ornamentation—of the object was what gave it its allure and perceived value. It is again worth recalling that, although the Habsburg empire was slowly making the change to paper currency in the early 19th century, silver coin had been in uninterrupted circulation until its use was restricted during the Napoleonic wars.[29] (Our own belief in the "value" of silver today is an almost sentimental attachment to this earlier view and has little to do with market reality; interestingly, it is not only the craftsmanship aspect, but also the impractical aspect of silver—the necessity of cleaning it—and the labor both imply

that shape the present consciousness as to its being a luxury good.)

The coffee machine for the "simple" household is in nearly every way the close kin of the luxury version (if anything, the cheaper model is *more* highly ornamented in the ridge of its lid and the carving of its finial). Even in use they betray an unexpectedly close relationship: what would seem a class refinement in the Franz Köll model—that the percolator element can be removed and its lid placed on the lower element for serving—works precisely the same way with the tin model. The fact that both percolator elements are of the same material as the coffee pot elements, particularly in the silver version, reveals that they must nonetheless have been

**39. COFFEE POT
AND PERCOLATOR**

Franz Köll, Vienna 1818

Silver, fruitwood
Vienna hallmark, maker's mark FK,
Austrian control mark (*Taxfreistempel*)
H 29.5 cm/11.8 in. Weight 648 g/25.9 oz.
Asenbaum Collection

made to be seen and that the coffee-making process likely took place in company. In this they relate to Wilhelm Wagenfeld's Jena transparent glass teapot, which only becomes "visible" as a teapot when tea is being made in it.

There are, however, marked differences between the two as well. While their similarities would seem to tell us that "simple" things evolve out of patterns of everyday use, these differences—in particular the extreme precision with which the silver version was made, as well as the craftsman's insistence on an exact cylindrical shape—indicate that a further layer has been added to the concept of simplicity. (It should also be noted that the manufacture of the unornamented silver coffee pot/percolator in this quality was anything but easy:

as customers even in the late 17th century were aware, ornamentation often served to disguise minimal inconsistencies and errors in production. The "naked" form of the pot/percolator has no swags, garlands, or engraving to hide behind.)

Each of the coffee pots/percolators is likely missing the wicker-work braiding that would have covered the metal handles.

29 After the wars, silver coin was introduced again. Paper money, which had existed since 1762, was unloved and remained so even after the wars increased the necessity of producing it. Adelbert Schusser, "Münzwesen und Geldwirtschaft," in *Bürgersinn und Aufbegehren: Biedermeier und Vormärz in Wien 1815–1848,* exh. cat. Historisches Museum der Stadt Wien, Vienna 1987, p. 46.

40. COFFEE HOUSE TRAY FROM THE CAFÉ RIEDMÜLLER

Berndorfer Metallwaren-Fabrik Arthur Krupp A.G., Lower Austria after 1930

Silver-plated alpacca
Krupp Berndorf, Berndorf alpacca
L 26.9 cm/10.8 in.
Private collection

Similar to the Thonet chair no. 14—the quintessential coffee house chair, first made in 1859 and produced continually (and in the millions) from that time onward—this serving tray type became standard equipment for coffee houses from the 1870s until our own time. It is now still in use in almost all Viennese coffee houses, where coffee and a small glass of water are served on it, even though it is no longer in production by Berndorf.

41. SALVER

Stephan Mayerhofer, Vienna 1833

Silver

Vienna hallmark, maker's mark STM

L 21 cm/8.4 in. Weight 244 g/9.8 oz.

Private collection

Working from the constraints of use and designation, England seeks to find the form most perfectly suited to each thing. It long searched for the pot that could hold the most water while remaining easy to handle and not proving too tippy on an excessively narrow base. It developed a squat, thick-bellied form with an opening that allows fast and plentiful pouring. This shape has been reproduced for twenty years, and in another twenty years it will be no different. England has also made its teapot, its pitcher, its wash basin, its covered serving dishes, its rinsing dishes all on its own. One had a good feeling in the rooms reserved for its ceramics. A simple housewife could admire their charms just as a great artist might. In this way England has not achieved an ideal perfection of form, nor an epoch-making unity of style, but it has found forms highly suited to these things. And since man in his nature is unchanged since God placed him on this earth, he has gradually and without great effort— naturally, so to speak—and without even realizing it, reached a point of finding what the antique world once sought and found: shapes derived from usage, and ones to which the English manufacturers have skillfully adapted Greek ornamentation. Let us beware of this practical sense. It will defeat us![30]

Comte Léon de Laborde, Paris 1855

I have never yet conversed with an Austrian who, in speaking of the two countries, did not give the preference to England, over France,—to London, over Paris.[31]

Frances Trollope, 1838

30 Comte Léon de Laborde, "De l'union des arts et de l'industrie", Paris 1855, as cited in *Die Verborgene Vernunft: Funktionale Gestaltung im 19. Jahrhundert*, exh. cat. Neue Sammlung, Munich 1971, p. 31. English translation Michael Huey.

31 Frances Trollope, *Vienna and the Austrians*, London 1838, vol. 2, p. 50.

Christopher Dresser, silver-plated sugar bowl and shovel ca. 1880
Executed by A. Klein Wien Hoflieferant ca. 1880
Private collection

Christopher Dresser, electroplated white metal "claret jug"
Executed by Elkington & Co., Birmingham 1885
Illustration from the Elkington & Co. catalogue 1885

Adolf Loos once wrote that being properly dressed meant not standing out. This suggests that there is—or, at least, was previously considered to be—something universal within a culture (perhaps even between cultures) akin to good manners that could be applied as a standard. To Loos it certainly went beyond notions of cultured behavior or dress and into the realm of "good form" in all its possible connotations.

The idea of the standard, or canon, in our time has undergone fairly radical readjustment. Some of the battering it has taken has been well-deserved; still, at its best it was once understood to be *unifying,* not divisive, and to represent a positive human commonality. (Whether this was, in fact, the case or not is irrelevant in this context: people like Loos believed it to be so.) That idea of "good form" is perhaps what links objects such as the pair of pots by Georg Forgatsch and the one designed by Christopher Dresser, more than another kind of art-historical, antecedent/descendant relationship, which—in this instance—would appear to have been unlikely. And yet, there they are, seventy years before Dresser: two unadorned little barrel-shaped pots with useful scissor handles, truncated foreheads and bases, and wafer-like lids crowned by small round finials of a very basic shape, likewise descendants of a common English type.

The imperialistic aspect of the canon is an interesting one here: toward the end of the 18th century the Austrian aristocracy began to learn English in greater numbers and what followed was their seduction by the English marketplace: English goods and emulative products made in Vienna and elsewhere in the empire were all the rage. (Entire industries, such as the stoneware manufactories in Vranov and other towns in southern Bohemia, relied heavily on copying English models; especially so after the Continental Blockade—which had been imposed against England by Napoleon in 1806 and recognized by the Hapsburg Empire in 1808—was lifted in 1812.)

Anglophilia remained constant in Vienna throughout the 19th century, rejuvenated over and over again in part by the constant supply of "conveniences" the English had invented for the household. (That the inherent proposition of conveniences is to "simplify" life should not, perhaps, be forgotten in a discussion of the "simple" shapes and plainness of certain examples of Viennese Biedermeier silver.) In any event, even the progressive designs of Christopher Dresser found surprisingly broad acceptance, often among a conservative aristocratic clientele in late 19th-century Vienna—so much so that local firms in Vienna began to borrow heavily from Dresser for their metalware designs, up to the point of making identical copies. (Hukin and Heath, who worked with Dresser in England, exhibited at the 1873 World's Fair in Vienna. As a result, the silversmiths Gebrüder Frank and A. Klein both began to shape new products after Dresser designs.) The interest in these designs was more than mere fashion, as Otto Wagner and other architect-designers showed by picking up on Dresser's concern with objects that unified the ideals of usefulness, mass-production, and aesthetic truth.

42. PAIR OF SMALL POTS
Georg Forgatsch, Vienna 1807
Silver
Vienna hallmark, maker's mark GF
H 11.7 cm and 9.4 cm/4.7 in. and 3.8 in. Weight 275 g/11 oz.
Asenbaum Collection

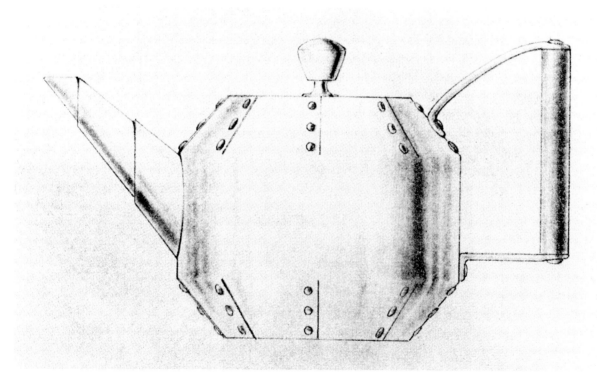

Christopher Dresser, design for a teapot for Elkington & Co., ca. 1888
Illustration from *The Studio*, vol. 15, 1899, p. 111.

43. TEAPOT

Joseph Koch, Vienna 1836

Silver, ivory
Vienna hallmark, maker's mark IK
H 7.5 cm/3 in. Weight 264 g/10.6 oz.
Private collection

For telescope see cat. no. 88

Biedermeier design has become, for better or worse, tied up with notions of blindered comfort, the familial, and the apolitical. This tea-cosy view of an era is one that was called into question around the turn of the 20th century. "What do we know of our country's own artistic and cultural past," asked the author of an article in *Hohe Warte* in 1905–06.[32] He went on to praise the "blossoming of architecture, painting, the decorative arts, and furniture" in the period from 1750 to 1850 and to bemoan the contemporary "extinguishing" of artistic energy, a circumstance Josef Hoffmann and other like-minded architect designers were actively working against at the time.

Seeking out inspiration from revolutionary, even radical, design from the 1820s—such as Josef Danhauser's imaginative sofa pictured here—was a part of reconnecting with creative roots. Actually, it was a source that had never completely dried up. Despite the eagerness of historicism to identify with older role models, its traces can still be felt in an overstuffed eclectic-style sofa—indeed, in the geometricism of fashion—as late as the 1870s. From the standpoint of historicism, Biedermeier was considered a decline in craftsmanship because it was *too* simple. Later movements saw this exactly the other way around. In 1905–06, Hoffmann designed two silver boxes (cat. nos. 142 and 147) that took up the thread of that earlier age and made it seem modern all over again.

32 "Wien und die künstlerischen Gemeinde-Aufgaben," *Hohe* Warte, issue 1, yr. 2, Vienna 1905–06.

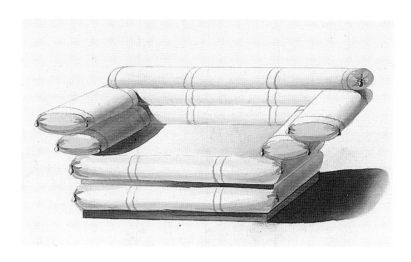

Joseph Danhauser Furniture Factory, design for "Canapé N° 60"
Pen and ink and gray wash, Vienna ca. 1825
MAK, Vienna

Amalie Haizinger, actress at the Vienna Court Theater, seated on a sofa with tufted upholstery
Albumen photo, L. Haase & Comp., Berlin, Cologne, or Breslau, ca. 1870
Michael Huey, Vienna

Josef Hoffmann, armchair with cloth covering, ca. 1910
Illustration from *Deutsche Kunst und Dekoration*, 14, p. 149, Darmstadt 1910.

44. SUGAR BOX

Thomas Dub, Vienna 1855

Silver, parcel-gilt (interior)
Vienna hallmark, maker's mark TD
W 13.3 cm/5.3 in. Weight 396 g/15.8 oz.
Private collection

45. SUGAR BOX

Joseph Wieninger, Vienna ca. 1840

Silver, parcel-gilt (interior)
Vienna hallmark, maker's mark JW
W 12.7 cm/5.5 in. Weight 366 g/14.6 oz.
Private collection

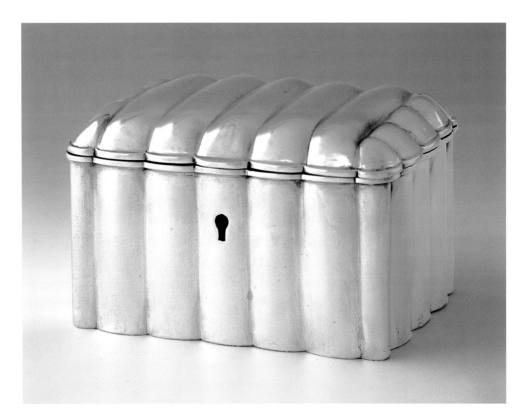

Josef Hoffmann, white-painted zinc *Blumenvase* (Cachepot) (WW model no. M 1045)
Executed by the Wiener Werkstätte, Vienna 1908
Contemporary photograph from the photo albums of the Wiener Werkstätte
MAK, Vienna

46. SUGAR BOX

Joseph Wieninger, Vienna 1833

Silver, parcel-gilt (interior)

Vienna hallmark, maker's mark JW

L 13 cm/5.2 in. Weight 533 g/21.3 oz.

Private collection

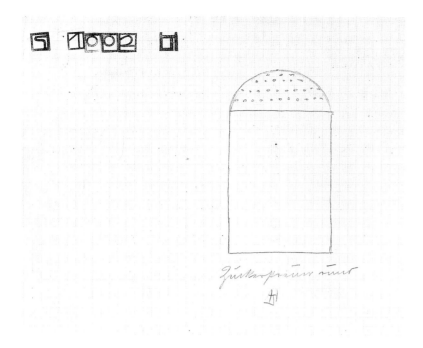

Those who copy Empire forms or any other earlier style show their character to be that of the uneducated parvenu. The part of the Wetzdorf [palace] furnishings that is far closer to our sense of functionality is that which belongs to the Biedermeier period and has sacrificed formal excess of ornamentation in favor of pure and clear constructions. Its forms are suitable to its materials. Here, too, where the pure form speaks according to human needs, the concern is for excellent workmanship and good, appropriately-worked material. This is what can be put into practice from Wetzdorf—the work process, not individual forms. These must continually be derived anew from human needs and the materials utilized.[33]

Hohe Warte, 1904–05

33 "Schloß Wetzdorf," *Hohe Warte*, yr. 1, issue 18, p. 314. English translation Michael Huey.

Josef Hoffmann, design for a silver *Zuckerstreuer* (Sugar caster) (WW model no. S 1002) for the Wiener Werkstätte
Pencil, Vienna 1907
MAK, Vienna

47. CASTER
Vienna 1807
Silver
Vienna hallmark, illegible maker's mark,
Austrian control mark (*Vorratspunze*)
Inventory marks PL, JS
H 9.7 cm/3.9 in. Weight 124 g/5 oz.
Private collection

48. BOX FROM A TOILET SERVICE

Joseph Stelzer, Vienna 1807

Silver
Vienna hallmark, maker's mark IST
Diameter 7.7 cm/3.1 in. Weight 145 g/5.8 oz.
Private collection

Josef Hoffmann, silver *Puderdose*
(Powder jar) (WW model no. S 436)
Executed by the Wiener Werkstätte, Vienna 1905
Contemporary photograph from the photo albums
of the Wiener Werkstätte
MAK, Vienna

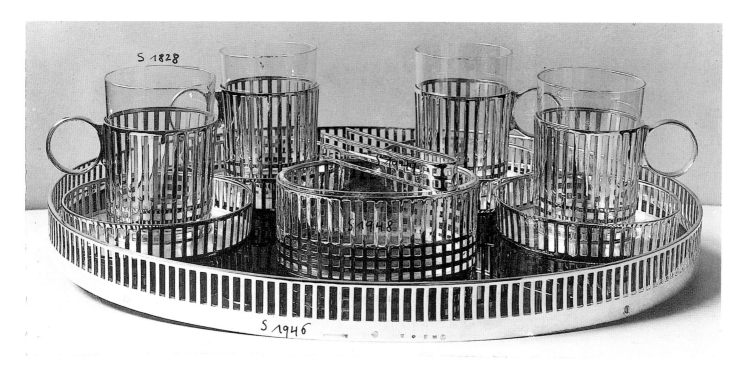

Josef Hoffmann, silver tea service (WW model nos. S 1828, S 1946, S 1948–49)
Executed by the Wiener Werkstätte, Vienna 1909–10
Contemporary photograph from the photo albums of the Wiener Werkstätte
MAK, Vienna

Josef Hoffmann, silver-plated alpacca *Zuckertasse* (Sugar bowl)
(WW model no. M 958) and tongs (WW model no. M 962)
Executed by the Wiener Werkstätte for the Kabarett Fledermaus, Vienna 1908
Contemporary photograph from the photo albums of the Wiener Werkstätte, detail
MAK, Vienna

An old style can be translated into a new language, re-introduced, so to speak, in a <u>manner</u> appropriate to our age. This is actually only reproductive, and it is what I did in building.

What I mean, however, is *not* just a new pruning of an old style. One does not take the old forms and try to fit them to the new taste. Rather, one truly speaks, perhaps unconsciously, the old language, but speaks it in a way that belongs to the new world, though not necessarily to its taste.[34]

Ludwig Wittgenstein, 1947

34 Georg Henrik von Wright, ed., *Ludwig Wittgenstein. Vermischte Bemerkungen. Eine Auswahl aus dem Nachlass*, Frankfurt am Main 1994, pp. 118–119. English translation Michael Huey.

49. WINE COASTER
Alois Würth, Vienna 1828

Silver
Vienna hallmark, maker's mark AW
Diameter 12.4 cm/5 in. Weight 116 g/4.6 oz.
Courtney Ross-Holst Collection

50. SALT CELLAR
Joseph Weirich, Vienna 1840

Silver
Vienna hallmark, maker's mark IW
L 7.4 cm/3 in. Weight 55 g/2.2 oz.
Private collection

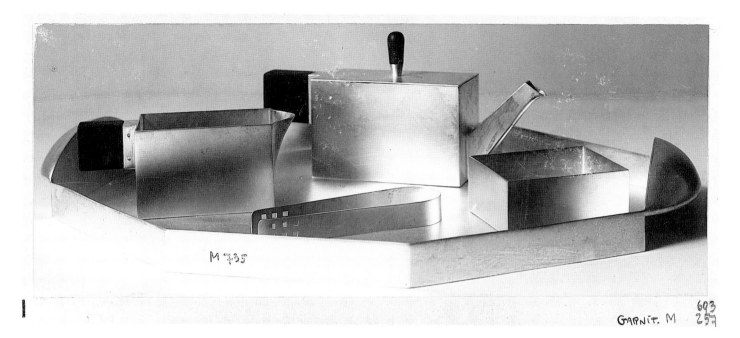

Josef Hoffmann, silver-plated alpacca *Moccaservice* (Mocha service) (WW model no. M 257)
Executed by the Wiener Werkstätte, Vienna 1904
MAK, Vienna

Marianne Brandt, bronze and German silver tea-extract pot with silver-plated interior (MT 49)
Bauhaus Weimar, 1924
Bauhaus-Archiv Berlin/Photo: Jost Schilgen

51. SMALL TRAY ACQUIRED BY THE WAERNDORFER/HELLMANN FAMILY

Designed by Josef Hoffmann, Vienna 1904

Executed by the Wiener Werkstätte, model no. M 735 (part of service M 257) (Adolf Wertnik)
First made August, 1904 for eighty crowns
Five pieces produced, in varying sizes
Silver-plated alpacca
JH, WW, AW, rose mark
L 35 cm/14 in.
Asenbaum Collection

In the 19th century, metal formed the skeleton of the industrial-age world: its bridges and glass houses, railway systems and ships. The primacy of metal went unchallenged well into the 20th century: its shininess and strength were glorified in Fritz Lang's *Metropolis*, and parodied in Charlie Chaplin's *Modern Times,* but they were still the essential requirements of modern architecture from the 1930s until the 1960s and beyond.

At the Bauhaus—as at the Wiener Werkstätte before it—the metalwork shop was the first of many workshops to be established. Intriguingly, a Viennese goldsmith who had worked at the Wiener Werkstätte, Naum Slutzky, joined this workshop early on in 1919 under Walter Gropius and Johannes Itten; eventually he became its leader.[35] There were, additionally, another six students brought by Itten from Vienna.

35 Klaus Weber, "'Vom Weinkrug zur Leuchte.' Die Metallwerkstatt am Bauhaus," in Klaus Weber, *Die Metallwerkstatt am Bauhaus,* Bauhaus-Archiv, Berlin 1992, p. 9.

Wilhelm Wagenfeld, German silver and ebony coffee and tea service (MT 40–45)
Bauhaus Weimar 1923–24
Contemporary photograph by Lucia Moholy
Bauhaus-Archiv Berlin

In Franz Würth's teapot from 1803 it is again the English late 18th-century model that speaks. The demure swags and garlands, however, that adorned most silver of a similar stature in England have not been adopted. Did they not translate well into the local vernacular? Or was what they had to say somehow not in agreement with local taste? Or was it only that silversmiths had pattern books at their disposal—such as those made for the Wiener Porzellan Manufaktur (Vienna Porcelain Manufactory) by Antonio Grassi at the Portici Museum in Naples (see cat. nos. 4 and 9)—that reproduced shapes but not ornamentation? Actual evidence is nearly impossible to come by, since none of the archives of the important Viennese silversmiths are known to have survived.

A teapot fashioned out of a plain oval cylinder with a flat lid: such very graphic contours appealed to Viennese neoclassical taste, and stood in stark contrast to the painterliness of the decorative arts during the baroque and rococo, which would have seized upon the teapot as an excuse, or a kind of stage, to discuss something other than the clarity of forms. The preoccupation with the cylinder may owe, in part, to a fascination with the pistons of the steam engine, which was perfected by James Watt between 1769 and 1784, as well as with other mechanical devices. (In both English and German, pistons are also referred to as cylinders. The fascination with basic stereometric shapes, incidentally, was revived in the early 1920s—a time in which pistons were moving faster than ever—in Bauhaus designs.) The graphic attitude of teapots such as this is, moreover, a possible direct consequence of the emphasis placed on the practice of drawing by silversmiths and other craftsmen—a two-dimensional exercise—in Vienna in the late 18th and early 19th centuries. The plain cylinder was typically used in Vienna for silver coffee- and teapots, in addition to porcelain coffee cups in the basic neoclassical shape from around 1790 until around 1830, and ceramic woodstoves of the same period.

The handle of the teapot, which appears to illustrate an abstraction of a function, likewise possesses a vivid, though much more old-fashioned, line. Its one concession to ornamentation is the carving at its base, which rather modestly repeats the form of the finial.

Touchingly, it is the handle—the point where the human hand comes into contact with the object—where the expression of the age is most evident, i.e. where the teapot seems the most dated. This is also, of course, the part of the teapot not actually made by the silversmith, although he would have been responsible for its design.

52. TEAPOT

Franz Würth, Vienna 1803

Silver, fruitwood

Vienna hallmark, maker's mark FW, Austrian control marks (*Taxfreistempel, Repunze*)

H 15.5 cm/6.1 in. Weight 831 g/33.2 oz.

Asenbaum Collection

53. TEAPOT
Carl Wallnöfer (Franz Wallnöfer & Sons), Vienna 1830

Silver, fruitwood
Vienna hallmark, maker's mark Wallnöfer
H 6.6 cm/3 in. Weight 229 g/9.2 oz.
Private collection

Christian Dell, silver and ebony teapot

Executed in the metal workshop of the Frankfurter Kunstschule, Frankfurt 1926–33
Bauhaus-Archiv Berlin/Photo: Jost Schilgen

54. SALVER
Anton Köll, Vienna 1817

Silver
Vienna hallmark, maker's mark AK, Austrian control mark
D 23.2 cm/9.3 in. Weight 460 g/18.4 oz.
Private collection

Josef Albers, chrome-plated brass fruit bowl with glass and turned-wood legs
Bauhaus Weimar 1923
Bauhaus-Archiv Berlin/Photo: Hans-Joachim Bartsch

55. BOWL

Alois Würth, Vienna 1805

Silver

Vienna hallmark, maker's mark AW

L 36.8 cm/14.7 in. Weight 819 g/32.8 oz.

Private collection

Marianne Brandt, chrome-plated brass *Frühstücksschale* (Breakfast bowl) (ME 37)

Bauhaus Dessau 1926

Contemporary photograph

Bauhaus-Archiv Berlin

56. DISH

Michael Klama, Vienna 1817
Silver
Vienna hallmark, maker's mark MK
D 13.1 cm/5.2 in. Weight 172 g/6.9 oz.
Private collection

In a letter to the Bauhaus-Archiv, Marianne Brandt explained that the "little hand-hammered ashtray was my first hand-made piece from my one of my own designs in Weimar, 1924."[36] Its striking resemblance to a Viennese dish by Michael Klama from 1817 begs the reevaluation of some of what is taken for granted about the modernity of the Modern movement.

The allusion it makes to the world of machine-made goods via its clean lines and smooth surface was achieved, somewhat perversely, through precise hand craftsmanship. Owing to financial limitations, the Bauhaus was never able to invest in the machinery that would have made its ideal of mass-production feasible. Indeed, pieces such as Brandt's ashtray were criticized at the Leipzig Fair of 1924 for "looking like cheap machine-made work but being, in reality, expensively hand-crafted."[37]

Marianne Brandt, nickel-plated brass ashtray
Bauhaus Weimar 1924
Bauhaus-Archiv Berlin/Photo: Jost Schilgen

36 Klaus Weber, "Vom Weinkrug zur Leuchte. Die Metallwerkstatt am Bauhaus," in Klaus Weber, *Die Metallwerkstatt am Bauhaus*, Bauhaus Archiv, Berlin 1992, p. 138. English translation Michael Huey.
37 Ibid., p. 23. English translation Michael Huey.

Marianne Brandt, silver-plated German silver *bonbonnière*
Bauhaus Dessau 1926–27
Bauhaus-Archiv Berlin/Photo: Walter Danz

57. BOX FROM A TOILET SERVICE

Stephan Mayerhofer, Vienna 1834

Silver

Vienna hallmark, maker's mark STM

D 8.8 cm/3.5 in. Weight 196 g/7.8 oz.

Private collection

Wilhelm Wagenfeld, *Kubus Geschirr* (*Kubus* food storage containers)
Executed by Vereinigte Lausitzer Glaswerke AG, Weisswasser 1938
© Nikolaus Koliusis, Stuttgart

58. SUGAR BOX
Jakob Schleicher, Vienna 1819
Silver, parcel-gilt (interior)
Vienna hallmark, maker's mark IS
Monogram BD
W 14.6 cm/5.7 in. Weight 588 g/23.5 oz.
Private collection

59. CASSEROLE
Ignatz Joseph Würth, Vienna 1804
Silver
Vienna hallmark, maker's mark IIW
W 23.2 cm/9.3 in. Weight 880 g/35.2 oz.
Asenbaum Collection

Wilhelm Wagenfeld, heat-resistant pressed glass
baking dish
Executed by Glaswerk Schott & Gen., Jena 1932
Wilhelm Wagenfeld Stiftung, Bremen

60. SMALL TRAY
Vienna 1819

Silver
Vienna hallmark, illegible maker's mark,
Austrian control mark (*Taxfreistempel*)
L 19.9 cm/8 in. Weight 102 g/4.1 oz.
Private collection

Wilhelm Wagenfeld, cromargan dish
Executed by Württembergische Metallwarenfabrik AG, Geislingen/Steige 1954
Wilhelm Wagenfeld Stiftung, Bremen

61. CASTER
Christian Sander, Vienna 1827

Silver
Vienna hallmark, maker's mark CS
H 6.7 cm/2.7 in. Weight 49 g/2 oz.
Private collection

Wilhelm Wagenfeld, glass and cromargan
salt and pepper shakers
Executed by Württembergische Metallwarenfabrik AG,
Geislingen/Steige 1952–53
© Nikolaus Koliusis, Stuttgart

David Mellor, silver-plated and white celluloid "Pride" cutlery
Executed by Walker & Hall, Sheffield 1954

In 1898, when the Österreichisches Museum für Kunst und Industrie (Austrian Museum for Art and Industry, today MAK, Vienna) organized the *Kongressausstellung,* Empire and Biedermeier were revived for the first time in the public consciousness after a generation of neglect, if not outright despisement. (The term "Biedermeier" was originally a derogatory one—couching the style in narrow, petit bourgeois terms—from the second half of the 19th century.) Both Josef Hoffmann and Adolf Loos saw in Biedermeier design an important source of inspiration. When Hoffmann and Koloman Moser rented the first atelier space for the Wiener Werkstätte, they outfitted it with Biedermeier furniture,[38] Hoffmann's comment was that it "seemed to us the last genuine [period of] artistic expression." Loos was also a tireless proponent of the tried and true: he used Chippendale reproductions in many of his interiors, as well as Viennese Biedermeier—his handsome design for a satinwood drawing room table for the residence of Emil Löwenbach in 1913 is a direct reinterpretation of a standard Biedermeier pedestal table.

Yet Hoffmann and Loos had strongly divergent ideas about what the Biedermeier model meant: for Hoffmann it was a source of inspiration for *new* creativity, while Loos strongly believed in leaving well enough alone where forms that had evolved over centuries were concerned. Unsurprisingly, Loos, who recommended the cultivation of a consciousness for the presence of modernity in past styles, became a sharp critic of Hoffmann's "reinvention" of what in his eyes was *already* modern. In 1908 he subtly attacked Hoffmann and the "flat" model cutlery he had made for Fritz and Lili Waerndorfer: "In order to find the style of our age, one must be a modern man. But those who seek to alter or replace with other forms things that are already in the style of our own age— I need merely mention the word 'cutlery'—show by so doing that they have not recognized the style of our age. They will search for it in vain."[39]

38 Werner J. Schweiger, *Meisterwerke der Wiener Werkstätte,* Vienna 1990, pp. 5–6. (*Stücke aus der Biedermeierzeit, die uns als letzte echte Kunstäusserung vorschwebte.*)

39 Adolf Loos, "Kulturentartung" (Cultural Degeneration) as cited in Christian Witt-Dörring, "Checklist: Viennese Decorative Arts around 1900," in Renée Price, ed., *New Worlds: German and Austrian Art 1890–1940,* Cologne 2001, p. 463.

62. THREE PIECES FROM A CUTLERY SERVICE INCLUDING FORK, KNIFE, AND SPOON

Karl Sedelmayer, Vienna 1817

Silver
Vienna hallmark, maker's mark KS, Austrian control marks (*Taxfreistempel*, *Vorratspunze*)
L 24.5 cm/9.8 in. (knife) Weight 85 g/3.4 oz.
Private collection

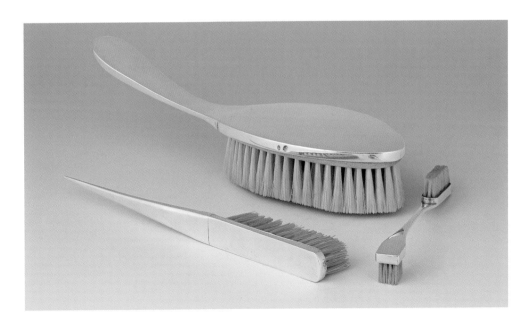

63. HAIR BRUSHES AND TOOTHBRUSH FROM A TOILET SERVICE

Ludwig Bock, Vienna 1821

Silver, bristles, bone, wood
Vienna hallmark, maker's mark LB, Austrian control mark (*Taxfreistempel*)
L 22.5 cm/9 in. (larger hair brush) Weight 166 g/6.6 oz. (larger hair brush)
Asenbaum Collection

Henning Koppel, covered silver dish
Executed by Georg Jensen, Denmark 1956
Georg Jensen Sölvsmedie A/S, Copenhagen

Lino Sabattini, silver-plated tea and coffee service "Como" (1956)
Executed by Christofle, Paris 1959–70
Private collection

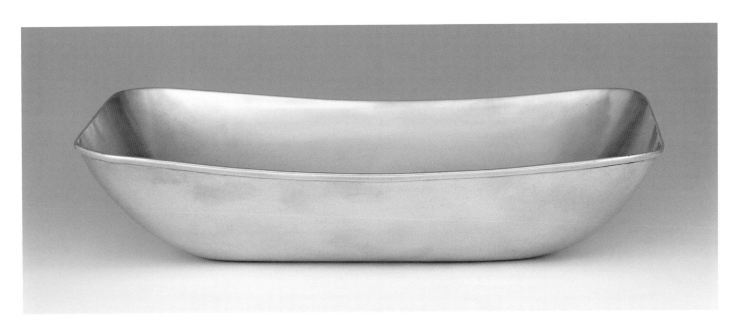

64. DISH

Carl Wallnöfer (Franz Wallnöfer & Company), Vienna 1826

Silver

Vienna hallmark, maker's mark Wallnöfer, manufacturer's privilege mark

L 31.5 cm/12.6 in. Weight 864 g/34.6 oz.

Private collection

65. PAP BOAT

Franz Schubert, Vienna 1848

Silver

Vienna hallmark, maker's mark FS

L 12.3 cm/4.9 in. Weight 75 g/3 oz.

Private collection

Arne Jacobsen, stainless steel sugar bowl and creamer "Cylinda Line"
Executed by A/S Stelton, Hellerup 1967
Philadelphia Museum of Art: Gift of A. S. Stelton, 1982/Photo: Eric Mitchell

Arne Jacobsen, stainless steel ice bucket and ashtray "Cylinda Line"
Executed by A/S Stelton, Hellerup 1967

66. COOKIE BOX

Alois Würth, Vienna 1815

Silver
Vienna hallmark, maker's mark AW
Monogram I. Sz.
Diameter 12.5 cm/5 in. Weight 470 g/18.8 oz.
Private collection

67. BOX WITH HANDLE

Joseph Kern, Vienna 1813

Silver
Vienna hallmark and maker's mark K
H 14 cm/5.6 in. Weight 435 g/17.4 oz.
Private collection

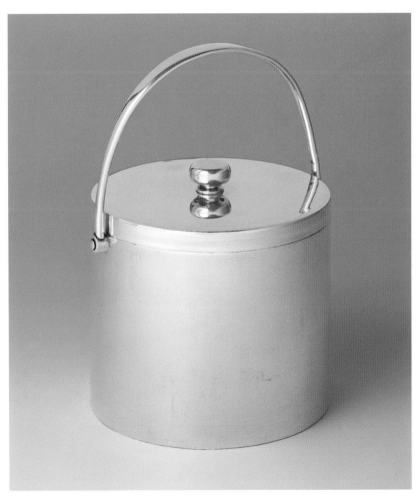

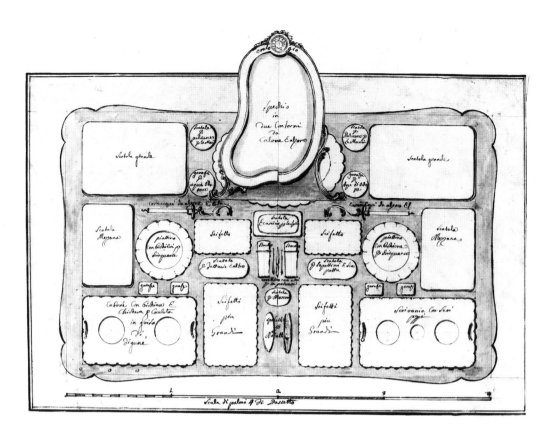

Luigi Valadier, design for a toilet service, possibly for Prince Chigi
Pen and brown ink and blue and gray wash, Rome ca. 1767
Private collection

Contemporary remote control wand and mobile telephone

During her long stay in Vienna from mid September, 1836 to early May, 1837 Frances Trollope made the following note of a visit to the home of Baron and Baroness E. on December 12, 1836: "A handsome entrance, or anteroom; a fine salle either for dancing or music, with polished walls of white stucco reflecting to advantage the multitude of bougies that hung suspended in magnificent chandeliers of or-molu from the ceiling; a suite of very well-furnished rooms, consisting, I think, of three drawing-rooms, la Baronne's bedchamber, with its elegant chintz hangings, and le Baron's dressing-room, with its rich toilet of silver, and its splendid magazine of pipes, were all, I think, that we entered; but these were quite sufficient fully to justify the reiterated compliment—*Vous êtes parfaitement bien logées—mais parfaitement!*"[40] (You are perfectly well-lodged—just perfectly!)

Her careful choice of mentionable household items is telling: the display of the baron's impressive silver toilet service had

68. BOX FROM A TOILET SERVICE

Joseph Kern, Vienna 1828
Silver, parcel-gilt (interior)
Vienna hallmark, maker's mark K
L 21.5 cm/8.6 in. Weight 553 g/22.1 oz.
Private collection

69. BOX FROM A TOILET SERVICE

Joseph Kern, Vienna 1820
Silver
Vienna hallmark, maker's mark K
L 16 cm/6.4 in. Weight 258 g/10.3 oz.
Private collection

clearly functioned according to plan. And it was to satisfy the similar needs of many hundreds of other barons, counts, princes, and archdukes that Vienna—well into the 19th century the largest city in German-speaking Europe—had accumulated an astonishing concentration of silversmiths. In the year 1820, for example, there were 123 registered silversmiths and makers[41] (the population, in roughly the same year, was 280,000).

The toilet service was a unique opportunity for conspicuous outlay. It was in equal parts an emblematic and a highly personal affair—and therein, possibly, lay its attraction. (An ink and wash drawing of a toilet service by Luigi Valadier about 1767, possibly for Prince Chigi, shows the geography of such sets to have been a matter of sober reflection, like a plan for the construction of a formal garden.)

The array of boxes and implements in these sets allegorized the importance of their user, who sat before them at a symbolic command center. (They also provide, even nowadays, a seemingly endless supply of individual items to be parsed out among descendants and eventually to land, piecemeal, on the market.) Perhaps it is not surprising, then, that the hand-friendly shape of Joseph Kern's silver boxes turned up again in our own time in the calculator, as well as in that reassuring implement of our own absolute authority: the TV remote control switch.

40 Frances Trollope, *Vienna and the Austrians*, London 1838, vol. 2, pp. 105–106.

41 With thanks to Diether Halama.

Stefano Giovannoni and Guido Venturini, stainless steel fruit basket
Executed by Alessi, Crusinallo 1994

70. TRAY

Stephan Mayerhofer, Vienna 1819

Silver
Vienna hallmark, maker's mark STM
Inscribed 10.L 7/16
Diameter 24.5 cm/9.8 in. Weight 434 g/17.4 oz.
Courtney Ross-Holst Collection

Is the use of prime stereometric shapes a sign of modernity? The agglomeration of volumes in Karl Sedelmayer's 1810 caster would seem to suggest so to early 21st-century eyes. At the same time, its conical top is hardly a pure intellectual form divorced from the tradition: apart from its pyramidal—possibly Egyptomanial—associations (which would have been even more highly emphasized in a craftsman's two-dimensional drawing), it relates back to the basic haystack shape, which was a likely source for any number of inventive, late 18th-century designs for rustic ice-houses and garden follies with acorn-like finials. Perhaps most evocatively, in this case, the cone is the shape taken by grains of sand, or salt, as they are made to fall through a restricted space.

Casters were used in the 19th century for everything from sugar to salt and other spices or sand (for the drying of ink while writing—archival materials are often full of fine sand). The small openings of this caster indicate that its use was most likely for the timid dispersion of a substance such as salt.

So the question, slightly rephrased, is this: was Sedelmayer attempting to add a dimension of sentimentality or remembrance to daily life—or to strip one away? The grooving, the collar, and the acorn finial are obstacles to a modern interpretation of studied disattachment, and yet—for 1810! (or for what we thought we knew about 1810)—what calculated reserve. Successive generations inevitably, blamelessly, buried Sedelmayer's intentions in their various contemporary understandings and definitions like so many sedimentary layers until the Bauhaus and the Modern movement finally invested these shapes with the meanings that still manage to lay claim to validity today.

Ironically, the "ultimate" modernist take on the vocabulary of plain forms is undermined by designs such as Aldo Rossi's postmodern coffee pot for Alessi (1980–83), a familiar icon from our own age. Through whimsy, it transmogrifies the idea of a spotless, remote formal vocabulary and expands the idea of function to include emotion.

Aldo Rossi, stainless steel coffee pot "Conic"
Executed by Alessi, Crusinallo 1980–83

71. CASTER

Karl Sedelmayer, Vienna 1810

Silver
Vienna hallmark, maker's mark KS, Austrian control mark (*Taxfreistempel*)
H 9.8 cm/3.9 in. Weight 80 g/3.2 oz.
Asenbaum Collection

Josef Hoffmann, items from a silver-plated
alpacca service
Executed by the Wiener Werkstätte for the Kabarett
Fledermaus, Vienna 1908
Contemporary photograph from the photo albums of
the Wiener Werkstätte
MAK, Vienna

72. DINNER-BELL

Mayerhofer & Klinkosch, Vienna 1864

Silver
Vienna hallmark, maker's mark M&K
H 7.7 cm/3.1 in. Weight 108 g/4.3 oz.
Private collection

73. GOULASH DISH (*GULASCHSCHÜSSEL*)
FOR THE KABARETT FLEDERMAUS

Designed by Josef Hoffmann, Vienna 1907

Executed by Wenzel Bachmann & Co. for the Wiener Werkstätte, model no. M 832
First made December, 1907 for seventy-five crowns
Eighteen pieces produced
Silver-plated alpacca
JH, WIENER/WERK/STÄTTE, rose mark, 2, 3
W 22.5 cm/9 in.
Private collection

74. COVERED PLATTER (*SCHÜSSELGLOCKE OVAL*) FOR THE KABARETT FLEDERMAUS

Designed by Josef Hoffmann, Vienna 1907

Executed by Wenzel Bachmann & Co. for the Wiener Werkstätte,
model no. M 830
First made December, 1907 for 145 crowns
Two pieces produced
Silver-plated alpacca
WW
L 29 cm/11.6 in.
Ernst Ploil Collection

75. SOUP TUREEN WITH LID (*SUPPENTOPF MIT DECKEL*) FOR THE KABARETT FLEDERMAUS

Designed by Josef Hoffmann, Vienna 1908

Executed by Wenzel Bachmann & Co. for the Wiener Werkstätte, model no. M 956

First made August, 1908 for seventy-five crowns

Eight pieces produced

Silver-plated alpacca

JH, WIENER/WERK/STÄTTE, rose mark, 4

H 15.8 cm/6.3 in.

Asenbaum Collection

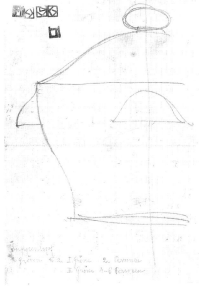

Josef Hoffmann, design for a silver-plated alpacca *Suppentopf* (Soup tureen) (WW model no. M 956) for the Wiener Werkstätte and the Kabarett Fledermaus

Pencil, Vienna 1908

MAK, Vienna

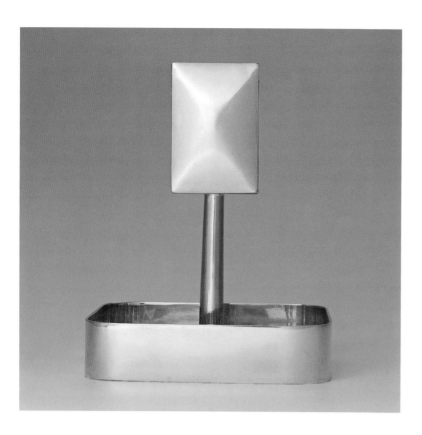

76. ASHTRAY (*FEUERZEUG*)
FOR THE KABARETT FLEDERMAUS

Designed by Josef Hoffmann, Vienna 1907

Executed by Wenzel Bachmann & Co. for the Wiener Werkstätte,
model no. M 780

First made December, 1907 for twenty-five crowns

Eighty-five pieces produced

Silver-plated alpacca

WW

H 13.3 cm/5.3 in.

Ernst Ploil Collection

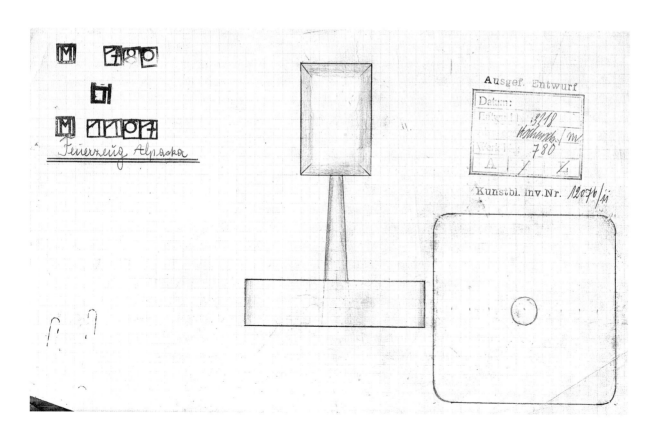

Josef Hoffmann, design for a silver-plated alpacca *Feuerzeug* (Ashtray) (WW model no. M 780)
for the Wiener Werkstätte and the Kabarett Fledermaus

Pencil, Vienna 1907

MAK, Vienna

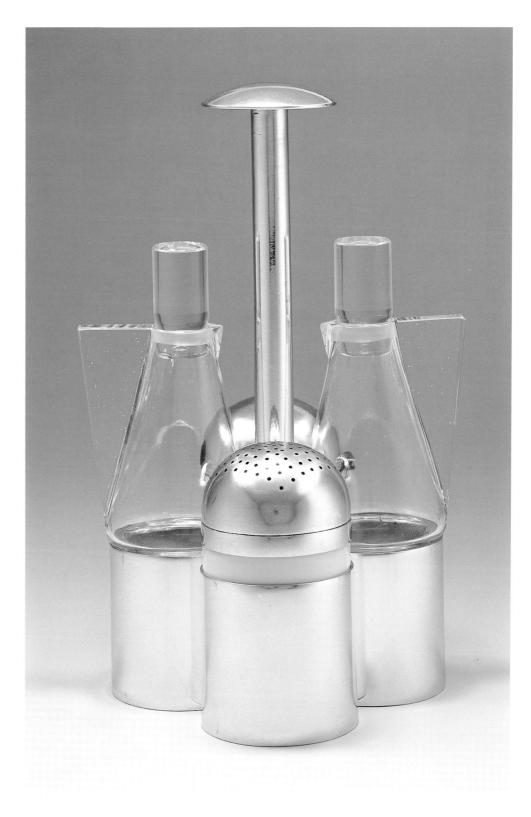

77. CRUET STAND (*KARAFFE VIERTEILIG*) FOR THE KABARETT FLEDERMAUS

Designed by Josef Hoffmann, Vienna 1909

Executed by Wenzel Bachmann & Co. for the Wiener Werkstätte, model no. M 1199

First made 1909 for fifty-two crowns

Twelve pieces produced

Silver-plated alpacca, glass, porcelain

JH, WW, rose mark

H 19.5 cm/7.8 in.

Asenbaum Collection

78. GRAVY BOAT (*SAUCIÈRE*) FOR THE KABARETT FLEDERMAUS ACQUIRED BY MAGDA MAUTNER VON MARKHOF

Designed by Josef Hoffmann, Vienna 1907

Executed by Wenzel Bachmann & Co. for the Wiener Werkstätte, model no. M 826
First made December, 1907 for fifty-five crowns
Twelve pieces produced
Silver-plated alpacca
WW
Monogram MMM
L 21.2 cm/8.5 in.
Ernst Ploil Collection

79. DESSERT PLATTER (*MEHLSPEISSCHÜSSEL RUND*) FOR THE KABARETT FLEDERMAUS

Designed by Josef Hoffmann, Vienna 1907

Executed by Wenzel Bachmann & Co. for the Wiener Werkstätte, model no. M 841
First made December, 1907 for seventy-two crowns
Ten pieces produced
Silver-plated alpacca
WW
Diameter 31.7 cm/12.7 in.
Private collection

80. PEPPER MILL FOR THE KABARETT FLEDERMAUS

Designed by Josef Hoffmann, Vienna 1907

Executed by Wenzel Bachmann & Co. for the Wiener Werkstätte, model no. M 824
First made December, 1907
Forty pieces produced
Silver-plated alpacca
WW
H 10.6 cm/4.2 in.
Ernst Ploil Collection

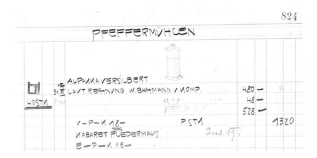

Notation for the Kabarett Fledermaus *Pfeffermühle* (Pepper mill)
(model no. M 824) designed by Josef Hoffmann
Wiener Werkstätte model book, Vienna, December 31, 1907.
MAK, Vienna

81. TWO CREAMERS FOR THE KABARETT FLEDERMAUS

Designed by Josef Hoffmann,
Vienna 1907

Executed by Wenzel Bachmann & Co. for the
Wiener Werkstätte, model nos. M 967 and M 968
First made August, 1908 for twenty-four crowns
(larger creamer)
Two pieces produced
Silver-plated alpacca
WW
H 12 cm/4.8 in. and H 5.4 cm/2.1 in.
Ernst Ploil Collection

**82. ELEVEN PIECES FROM THE "ROUND" FLATWARE SERVICE,
CONSISTING OF CAKE SERVER, BUTTER KNIFE, CORN HOLDER, KNIFE, FORK, TABLESPOON,
DESSERT KNIFE, DESSERT FORK, FRUIT KNIFE, COFFEE SPOON, MOCHA SPOON**

Designed by Josef Hoffmann, Vienna 1907

Executed by the Wiener Werkstätte, model nos. S 895, S 893, M 1278, 848, 847, 852, 849, 850, 858, 851, 853

First made December, 1907 for six crowns apiece (tablespoon)

118 tablespoons produced

Silver and silver-plated alpacca

Vienna hallmark, JH, FK, WW, rose mark (butter knife)

JH, FK, WW, rose mark (corn holder)

JH, WW, rose mark (silver-plated pieces)

Monogram EB and GHB

L 21.8 cm/8.7 in. (tablespoon)

Private collection and Ernst Ploil Collection

Creating this contact between past and present things; pointing out what is eternally human, eternally lasting; this emphasis on a continuity that would otherwise be beyond our grasp—is modern style.[42]

Felix Salten, 1903

42 Felix Salten, *Gustav Klimt: Gelegentliche Anmerkungen,* Vienna and Leipzig 1903, p. 27. English translation Michael Huey.

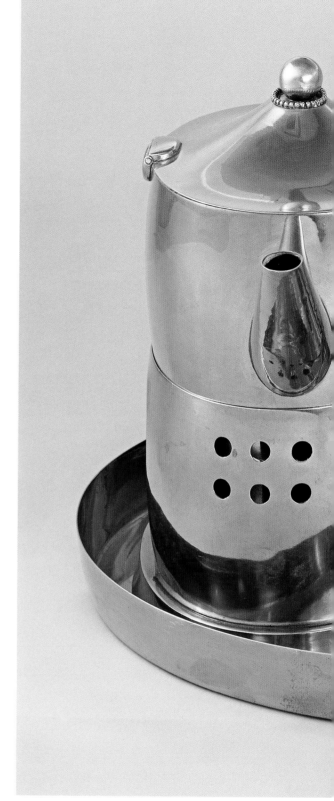

83. TEAPOT
Joseph Heinisch, Vienna 1810
Silver, fruitwood
Vienna hallmark, maker's mark IH, Austrian control marks (*Vorratspunze, Taxfreistempel*)
H 16 cm/6.4 in. Weight 415 g/16.6 oz.
Private collection

**84. TEA SERVICE CONSISTING OF TEA KETTLE AND STAND (*SAMOWAR*),
TEAPOT, CREAMER, SUGAR BOX, SUGAR TONGS, AND SERVING TRAY**

Designed by Josef Hoffmann, Vienna 1911

Executed by the Wiener Werkstätte, model nos. M 1881–M 1886

First made September/October, 1911 for 152.50 crowns (entire service)

Twenty-four to thirty-five individual pieces produced

Brass, pearwood

JH, Wiener Werkstätte, rose mark

H 21 cm/8.4 in. (tea kettle and stand)

Asenbaum Collection

4

MOBILITY AS MAXIM
OF MODERN SOCIETY

Otto Lilienthal's glider flight with the large double-decker, October 19, 1895
Vintage print by Dr. Neuhauss, Fülleborn
Photo: Deutsches Museum, Munich

Advertisement for Darmol laxative, Vienna ca. 1910
Private collection

…in many instances it is the fashion to imitate us. Not a few indeed of those who have resided for some time in England are accused of having brought back with them a pretty strong Anglomania; but it appears of a kind leading much more to the introduction of improvement, than discontent.

…The number of persons who have visited England is however very small; and, compared to the outpourings of our ever-migrating people, it almost seems as if Austrians never travelled at all. Many causes may contribute to this, but three of them are obvious. First, the government is very far from encouraging the habit among the young nobles.—Secondly, this class, the only one not retained at home by their occupations, are too much accustomed to live in luxury here, to be contented with a secondary style of expense in England; and the different rate at which not only the necessaries but the luxuries and elegancies of life are obtained in the two countries, would render frequent or long excursions to England almost ruinous to those whose incomes are proportioned to what the same style of living would require in Austria.—The third obvious reason for the rareness of Austrian travelling is founded simply upon the fact, that in this case, beyond all others, "*l'appétit vient en mangeant…*" [The appetite grows through eating].[43]

Frances Trollope, 1838

43 Frances Trollope, *Vienna and the Austrians,* London 1838, vol. 2, pp. 49–50, 51.

85. CHAMBER CANDLESTICK
Thomas Albrecht, Vienna 1816

Silver
Vienna hallmark, maker's mark TA, Austrian control mark (*Vorratspunze*)
H 7.6 cm/3 in. Weight 160 g/6.4 oz.
Private collection

In four hours I drove over here today from Vicenza on a one-seated little carriage called a *sediola,* with my entire existence in my luggage.[44]

Johann Wolfgang von Goethe, 1786

44 Johann Wolfgang von Goethe, *Italienische Reise*, Leipzig n. d., p. 62. English translation Michael Huey.

86. PAIR OF CANDLESTICKS FROM A TRAVEL SET

Johann Guttmann the Elder, Vienna 1805

Silver
Vienna hallmark, maker's mark IG
Monogram BMB
H 9.5 cm/3.8 in. Weight 534 g/21.4 oz.
MAK, inv. no. Go 2040/1978

87. CASSEROLE

Stephan Mayerhofer, Vienna 1833

Silver, fruitwood
Vienna hallmark, maker's mark STM
Diameter 19.3 cm/7.7 in. Weight 850 g/34 oz.
Asenbaum Collection

88. POCKET TELESCOPE WITH LEATHER CASE

Voigtländer and Son (?), Vienna c. 1840

Silver-plated copper, imitation tortoiseshell, glass lens
Unmarked
L 6.8 cm/2.7 in.
Michael Huey, Vienna

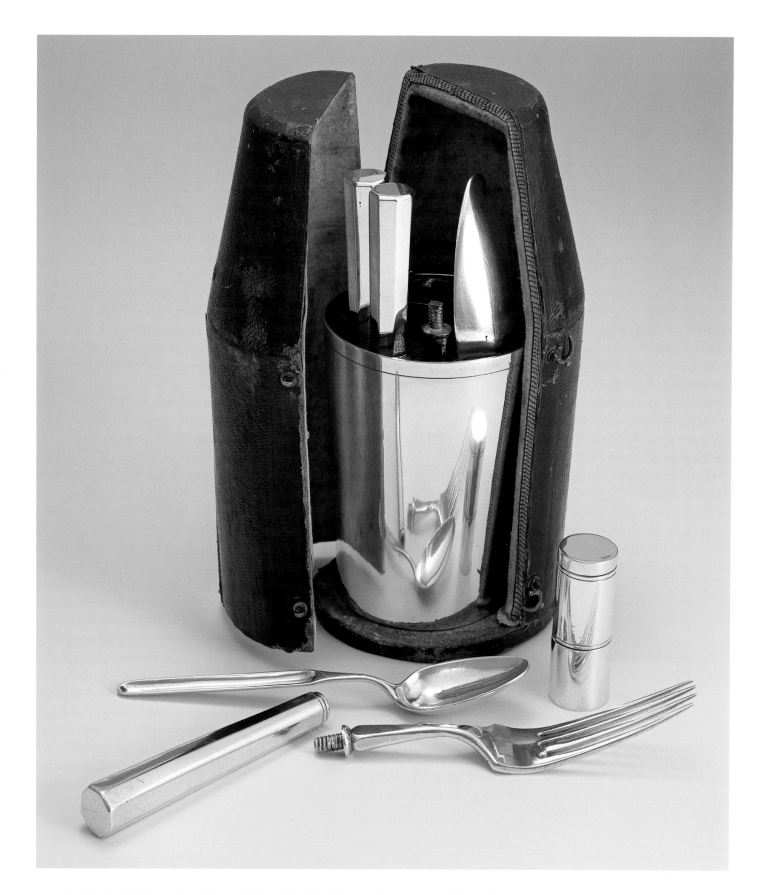

89. MILITARY TRAVEL SET CONSISTING OF BEAKER, SALT AND PEPPER SHAKER, TABLESPOON, TEASPOON, KNIFE, AND FORK

Franz Schubert, Vienna 1847

Silver, leather case

Vienna hallmark, maker's mark FS

Case embossed: "Aus/Dankbarkeit/der 7. Compagnie/Alservorstadt" (with gratitude from the 7th Alservorstadt Company)

H 18 cm/7.2 in. (with items in beaker)   Weight 333 g/13.3 oz. (silver items only)

Private collection

90. TRAVEL SET CONSISTING OF BEAKER, SALT AND PEPPER SHAKER, SPOON, KNIFE, AND FORK

Vienna 1816

Silver
Vienna hallmark, illegible maker's mark (RS or RJ?)
H 12 cm/4.8 in. (with items in beaker)
Weight 344 g/13.8 oz.
Courtney Ross-Holst Collection

The history of the mobility of household effects is made up of an abundance of curious chapters that belie what is often, in our age, perceived as the inherent stasis of dignified period surroundings. In the Hapsburg Empire in the 18th century, palace rooms were often sparsely or not at all furnished; when necessary, appropriate pieces were brought from a central *garde meuble* for use. Likewise, even the paneling, doorframes, doors, and windows of some rooms—the so-called "Dubsky" room now in the MAK, Vienna is one example—were made like clothing for the space: they could therefore also be detached and installed elsewhere later. Many became part of a dowry or inheritance and moved, with minor adaptations, from generation to generation and from palace to palace. When the imperial family stayed at the Hofburg in provincial cities such as Innsbruck and Bratislava, it brought along a variety of furnishings, including practical folding chairs with expensive coverings. Even at court in Vienna, chandeliers were dismantled and taken from other palace rooms for temporary lighting in ballrooms for festivities. Beginning in the 1820s (with wall-to-wall carpeting the current rage) castors were common in Vienna on everything from armchairs to tea tables, signaling a new kind of emancipation and mobility within the furnished space.

Though silver travel sets had existed at least since the 16th century, they became to the early 19th century what the mobile telephone was to the late 20th: a flashy accessory in acknowledgment of and concession to a new kind of personal mobility. Not unlike the cellphone, they were capable of establishing a connection—in this case psychological—to a distant place: the wayfarer's home. Travelers stopping at inns were able to surround themselves with tokens of class and status and thereby keep in touch with an idea of themselves as represented by these appurtenances: silver inkwells, candlesticks, serving platters, and cutlery. The risks faced by these early travelers were many and varied, but the travel set insured that misplacing one's identity in foreign territory was not among them.

91. FIVE-PIECE TEA SET IN TRAVEL CASE

Josef Carl Klinkosch, Vienna 1867–72

Silver, parcel-gilt (interior), ivory, wicker-work

Vienna hallmark, maker's mark ICK, court purveyor's mark

Case embossed on interior "K. und K. Hof- & Kammer Lieferant Wien"

Monogram of Prince TT

H (teapot) 12.3 cm/4.9 in. Weight (all silver pieces) 1,082 g/43.3 oz.

Private collection

92. FOLDING FORK AND SPOON

Christian Sander, Vienna 1859

Silver, steel

Vienna hallmark, maker's mark CSS

L 19.9 cm/7.9 in. and 19.7 cm/7.8 in.

Weight 97 and 81 g/3.9 and 3.2 oz.

Asenbaum Collection

93. SPICEBOX WITH THREE COMPARTMENTS FROM A TRAVEL SET

Jakob Weiss, Vienna 1840

Silver, parcel-gilt (interior)

Vienna hallmark, Jakob Weiss privilege mark

L 7.5 cm/3 in. Weight 90 g/3.6 oz.

Private collection

94. MOCHA POT FROM A TRAVEL SET
Friedrich Gindle/Wallnöfer, Vienna 1845

Silver, fruitwood
Vienna hallmark, maker's mark FG, manufacturer's privilege mark
Monogram depicting a unicorn
H 9.9 cm/4 in. Weight 147 g/5.9 oz.
Private collection

Yesterday I spoke with some peoble who had returned from Karlsbad. Jérôme Bonaparte and his entire family are there, as are the Bacciochis and a very ugly daughter of Lucien Bonaparte, who is married to a Count Possé.

On the anniversary of the Battle of Waterloo they all wore deepest black. They ride in exquisite carriages drawn by postal ponies, stroll about and eat the horrid tavern food on dishes and plates of vermeil.[45]

Marie-Henriette-Radegonde-Alexandrine
Baroness Fisson du Montet, July 20, 1819

45 Klarwill, Ernst, ed., *Die Erinnerungen der Baronin du Montet: Wien–Paris, 1795–1858*, Zurich et al. 1925. English translation Michael Huey.

95. PAIR OF CANDLESTICKS

Carl Scheiger, Vienna 1806

Silver

Vienna hallmark, maker's mark CS

H 7.6 cm/3 in. Weight 318 g/12.7 oz.

Private collection

96. INKWELL FROM A TRAVEL SET FOR FERDINAND JOHANNES WIT, GENANNT VON DÖRRING

Alois Würth, Vienna 1810
Silver
Vienna hallmark, maker's mark AW, Austrian control mark (*Taxfreistempel*)
H 6.5 cm/2.6 in. Weight 91 g/3.6 oz.
Marietta Witt-Dörring, Vienna

My companion let out a loud laugh when I informed him of my lodgings. I could not possibly stay there, he said; no one would ever socialize with me if *91, Circus Minories, Towerhill* were written on my cards. If I wished to associate with merchants, or spend time in the City, I would simply have to live on a respectable street; if I were inclined toward the West End and the aristocracy, on the other hand, it would have to be a fashionable neighborhood.

These distinctions, of course, were all Greek to me, but, if nothing else, it became clear to me that, while in England freedom might reign, equality certainly did not. I requested an explanation of his terms. There live in London two distinct races: business-people in the City; —consumers in the West End.—Solidity is the catchword in the former; glamour in the latter. Some personalities combine both natures, namely the big bankers and merchants who keep their firms in the City and their dwellings in the West End. The shibboleth of the former class is *respectable* (its meaning something like *gut* as it is used in Hamburg); that of the latter *fashionable* (up-to-date, elegant). But since in England money is the true standard of things, it is, in fact, the most expensive part of the City that is known as *respectable,* and the most expensive part of the West End that is known as *fashionable.* Oftentimes, however, one can live much better and more pleasantly—and for half the price—on another street not graced by this title, and for this reason the inns in the more expensive neighborhoods offer a messenger service. By paying the first *marqueur* (head-waiter) a yearly contribution of two guineas, one receives in return permission to appear to the eyes of the world a resident; that is to say one places the name of the hotel on his visiting cards and has all deliveries made to that address. As fate would have it, I later became associated with both races. For this reason I figured "double" on my cards. For my respectable acquaintances I lived in: *Batson's Coffeehouse;* for my fashionable ones: *Bedford Hotel, Covent Garden.* I kept the former in my right-hand pocket, the latter in the left.[46]

Ferdinand Johannes Wit, genannt von Dörring, 1819

46 H. H. Houben, *Der Lebensroman des Wit von Dörring,* Leipzig 1912, p. 28. English translation Michael Huey.

97. BASIN

Mayerhofer & Klinkosch, Vienna 1856
Silver
Vienna hallmark, maker's mark M&K
Monogram of Count HK
L 28 cm/11.2 in. Weight 915 g/36.6 oz.
Private collection

At Nussdorf, where the boat docks, one sees a Customs shed, a few scattered houses, a large number of people and coaches and a few gendarmes. Passports are handed over, and one's personal effects are courteously and casually inspected... Anyone who upon arrival does not let the steamer company take care of his personal effects—in which case he can collect them free of charge within two hours in the center of town—is acting unwisely, especially if his case contains a book, a pair of new gloves or the like. For only if he does this is the inspection carried out immediately and—as I have said—in a casual and courteous fashion. But if one absolutely insists on taking one's things with one, they are inspected at the barrier, and I witnessed how they turned everything inside out there. Out of the ladies' boxes came all the arcana of the dressing table, and out of their cases...in short, the beauties themselves, and all the things that serve as much to hide as to emphasize their charms, provided a wretched spectacle.[47]

Johan Vilhelm Snellman, 1840–41

47 Johan Vilhelm Snellman, as cited in Heinz Lunzer and Victoria Lunzer-Talos, *Abroad in Austria: Travellers' Impressions from Five Centuries,* Vienna 1997, p. 183.

98. MIRROR FROM A TOILET SERVICE

Joseph Kern, Vienna 1828
Silver, wood, leather
Vienna hallmark, maker's mark K
H 31 cm/12.4 in. Weight 1,078 g/43.1 oz.
Private collection

**99. PAIR OF CANDLESTICKS
(MADE FOR DISMANTLING)**

Eduard Schiffer, Vienna 1857

Silver

Vienna hallmark, maker's mark Schiffer, manufacturer's
privilege mark

H 13 cm/5.2 in. Weight 210 g/8.4 oz.

Private collection

**100. PAIR OF CANDLESTICKS
(MADE FOR DISMANTLING)**

Mayerhofer & Klinkosch, Vienna 1845

Silver

Vienna hallmark, maker's mark M&K

H 12.5 cm/5 in. Weight 170 g/6.8 oz.

Private collection

OBJECTS
INSPIRED BY
THE IDEA OF
MOBILITY

Robert Seymour, *Locomotion*
Hand-colored etching published by Thomas McLean, London ca. 1830
The Metropolitan Museum of Art, New York, gift of Mr. and Mrs. Paul Bird, Jr.

LOCOMOTION.)

For an explanation of the Machinery
see the next Number of the Edinburg Review.

London. Publish'd by Thos McLean. 20. Haymarket.

101. COFFEE MACHINE IN THE SHAPE OF A STEAM ENGINE
Wagenmann und Böttger, Vienna 1839
Sheet brass
Manufacturer's privilege mark
H 37 cm/14.8 in.
Technisches Museum Wien, Österreichische Mediathek, inv. no. 11526

102. COFFEE MACHINE IN THE SHAPE OF A HOT AIR BALLOON

Joachim Jaksch, Vienna 1852

Sheet brass

H 48.5 cm/19.4 in.

Technisches Museum Wien, Österreichische Mediathek, inv. no. 11525

Wenn Sie das unbekannte Flugobjekt orten, dann vernichten Sie es augenblicklich!
(If you locate the UFO destroy it instantly!) from Hansrudi Wäscher,
Nick/Wettlauf mit Maschinen (Nick/Race Against the Machines).
Hethke Comic no. 56, Schönau 1998

104. MUSTARD POT
Designed by Josef Hoffmann, Vienna 1902
Executed by Alexander Sturm & Company
Silver, glass (finial), glass inset
Vienna hallmark, cloverleaf mark
H 10 cm/4 in. Weight 207 g/8.3 oz.
Asenbaum Collection

Bergmann, custom-made Alfa Romeo automobile for Count Ricotti
Castagna body, Brescia 1913
Deutsches Museum, Munich

**105. CASTER (*PFEFFER-PAPRIKA-BÜCHSE*)
ACQUIRED BY THE WITTGENSTEIN FAMILY**
Designed by Josef Hoffmann, Vienna 1903
Executed by the Wiener Werkstätte, model no. S 53
First made 1903 for one hundred crowns
Two pieces produced
Silver, carnelian
Vienna hallmark, JH, WW, rose mark
H 7 cm/2.8 in. Weight 172 g/6.9 oz.
MAK, Vienna, inv. no. Go 2108

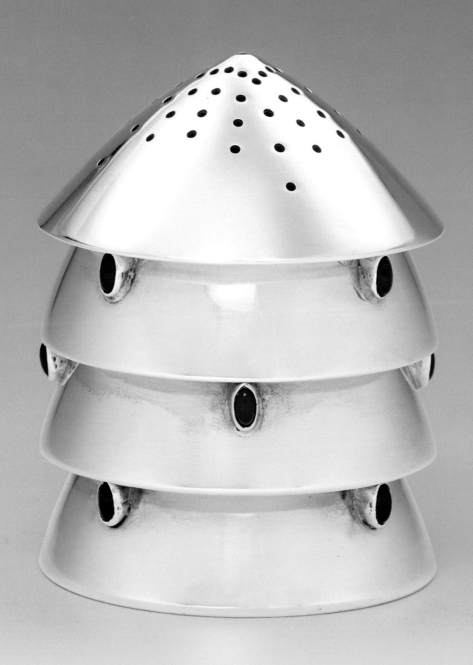

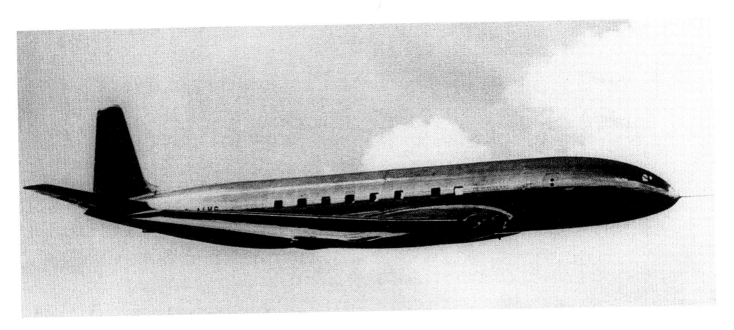

The prototype for the world's first commercial jet airliner, the—square-windowed—de Havilland *Comet* DH-106. England 1949
Illustration from Peter Dormer, *Design Since 1945*, London 2000, p. 10.

Norman F. Zapf, the locomotive *Commodore Vanderbilt*. New York Central Shops, New York 1934
Kalmbach Publishing Co., Waukesha, Wis.

In 1904 an exhibition held at the Kaiser Wilhelm Museum in Krefeld was entitled *Linie und Form* (Line and Form) and, according to W. Owen Harrod,[48] it "equated the curvilinear vocabulary of the *Jugendstil* with the ostensibly similar forms of aircraft, locomotives and naval vessels."

When Josef Hoffmann designed the egg cup model S 215 for the Wiener Werkstätte in 1904 he settled on an idiosyncratic, "streamlined" shape for an everyday form familiar all the way back to Roman times. (The shape of the "flat" cutlery he designed the same year for Fritz and Lili Waerndorfer was so novel that it led one critic to resort to not altogether flattering terms such as "anatomical tools" and "dissecting chamber" in his description of it.)[49] Hoffmann's punctuation of the skin-like surface of the egg cup with the trademark square visually interrupted the flow of the piece even as it helped to emphasize its most graceful parts and elongate its appearance. The deliberately-placed series of

hallmarks and silversmith marks on the upper side of the base referred back to this tectonic gesture and, at the same time, heightened the tension created by the interplay of "aerodynamic" and rectilinear shapes.

The tension between the two was something that continued to grow as the world began to speed up in the early 1930s. The de Havilland *Comet*, the world's first jet airliner, was originally outfitted with square windows that proved to be a serious design flaw: their disruption of the airflow caused a number of crashes in the early 1950s. ("Square holes," writes Peter Dormer, "are fatal design features in pressurized hulls because stress builds up at the corners, cracks occur and catastrophe follows."[50] This is an apt illustration of the fact that the new shapes technology provides us with must likewise evolve; eventually they begin to speak a language of their own.)

**106. EGG CUP ACQUIRED BY THE
WAERNDORFER/HELLMANN FAMILY**
Designed by Josef Hoffmann, Vienna 1904
Executed by the Wiener Werkstätte, model no. S 215
First made 1904 for forty crowns
Eight pieces produced
Silver
Vienna hallmark, JH, WW, rose mark
H 6.5 cm/2.6 in. Weight 112 g/4.5 oz.
MAK, Vienna, inv. no. Go 2057

Norman Zapf also fitted the square into his design for the *Commodore Vanderbilt,* where it has the somewhat incongruous appearance of a cottage window on a locomotive. Many Wiener Werkstätte designs share a predisposition toward the representation of speed. "It is only natural," commented Siegfried Giedion in 1948, "that an age of movement should adopt a form associated with movement as its symbol, using it in all places at all occasions."[51] Later, WW artists even made fanciful—if not to say rather outrageous—designs for automobile hood ornaments.[52]

48 W. Owen Harrod, "The Deutsche Werkstätten and the Dissemination of Mainstream Modernity," *Studies in the Decorative Arts,* New York 2003, vol. 10, no. 2, p. 24.

49 A journalist from the *Hamburg Fremdenblatt,* October 17, 1906, as cited in Christian Witt-Dörring "Checklist: Viennese Decorative Arts around 1900," in Renée Price, ed., *New Worlds: German and Austrian Art 1890–1940,* Cologne 2001, p. 463.

50 Peter Dormer, *Design Since 1945,* London 2000, p. 11.

51 Siegfried Giedion, *Mechanization Takes Command,* New York 1948, p. 610.

52 Dr. Veronika Pfolz of the MAK, Vienna kindly brought this to my attention.

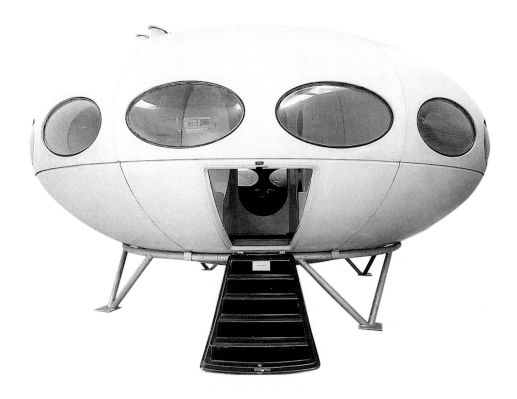

Matti Suuronen, synthetic house "Futuro"
Finland 1968
Centraal Museum, Utrecht

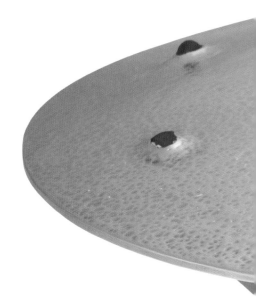

Carlo Borer, "Etienne Louis" espresso machine
Designed and executed by Carlo Borer for CB Industries.ch, Switzerland 1993–94

107. COVERED DISH (*BECHER*)
Designed by Josef Hoffmann, Vienna 1904
Executed by the Wiener Werkstätte, model no. S 99 (Josef Husnik)
First made January, 1904 for 200 crowns
Three pieces produced
Silver, carnelian
Vienna hallmarks, JH, JH, WW, rose mark
Diameter 20.2 cm/8.1 in. Weight 457 g/18.3 oz.
Asenbaum Collection

Josef Hoffmann in the studio of Koloman Moser, gelatin silver print, Vienna ca. 1898
Neue Galerie New York

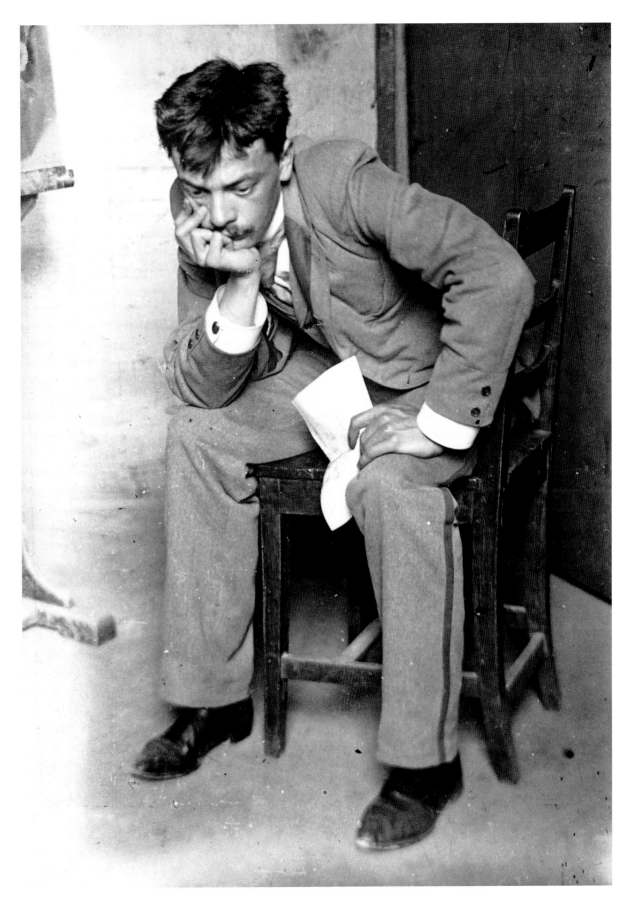

Koloman Moser in his studio, gelatin silver print, Vienna ca. 1898
Neue Galerie New York

Josef Hoffmann, rooms of the Vienna Secession at the *Kunstausstellung* in Düsseldorf, 1902; the centerpiece (cat. no. 108) was displayed in the vitrine pictured here at right.
Illustration from *Ver Sacrum,* yr. 5, vol. 21, p. 307, Vienna 1902.

Josef Hoffmann, fountain displayed at the *Kunstausstellung* in Düsseldorf, 1902; executed by Friedrich Otto Schmidt, Vienna, with bronze figures by Richard Luksch and socle reliefs by Elena Luksch-Machowska.
Illustration from *Ver Sacrum,* yr. 5, vol. 21, p. 305, Vienna 1902.

108. CENTERPIECE
Designed by Josef Hoffmann, Vienna 1902
Executed by Würbel & Czokally (Carl Würbel), Vinzenz Mayer's Söhne
Silver, blue glass inset
Vienna hallmark, JH, CW, VMS, hammer and anvil mark, 1902
Diameter 24.2 cm/9.7 in. Weight 1,050 g/42 oz. (without glass)
Ernst Ploil Collection

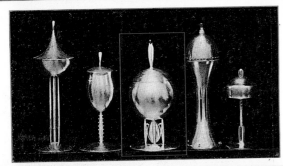

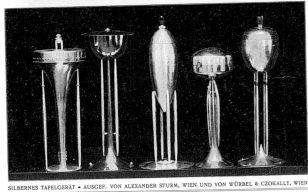

SILBERNES TAFELGERÄT ▪ AUSGEF. VON ALEXANDER STURM, WIEN UND VON WÜRBEL & CZOKALLY, WIEN

Für die Redaktion verantwortlich: H. BRUCKMANN, München.
Verlagsanstalt F. Bruckmann A.-G. München, Nymphenburgerstr. 86. — Druck von Alphons Bruckmann, München.

Josef Hoffmann, *Silbernes Tafelgerät ausgef. von Alexander Sturm, Wien und von Würbel & Czokally, Wien* (Silver tableware executed by Alexander Sturm, Vienna, and Würbel & Czokally, Vienna), 1902
Illustration from *Dekorative Kunst,* 1903, vol. 11, p. 40.

109. SPORTS TROPHY (*SPORTPREIS*)

Designed by Josef Hoffmann, Vienna 1902

Executed by Würbel & Czokally (Carl Würbel), Vinzenz Mayer's Söhne
Silver, lapis lazuli
Vienna hallmark, JH, CW, W & C, VMS, hammer and anvil mark, 1902
Monogram SW
H 21.5 cm/8.6 in. Weight 481 g/19.2 oz.
MAK, Vienna, inv. no. Go 2104

Both the architect Josef Hoffmann and the painter Koloman Moser originally worked as draftsmen in the architectural office of Otto Wagner, whose wish it was to train an army of modern architects. (Wagner later made a few, perhaps symbolic, purchases at the Wiener Werkstätte, including a frame with a relief pattern designed by Koloman Moser in 1904 and an inkwell by Josef Hoffmann from the same period.)

In the latter part of the 1890s they were members of the so-called Siebenerklub (Club of Seven), which led to the founding of the Secession in 1897. Around this time they also became professors at the Kunstgewerbeschule (Academy of Decorative Arts; today University of Applied Arts), where Hoffmann directed the architecture department; in addition, they created and oversaw the ceramics department, which had a reputation then as the most avant-garde of the academy's classes.

Under the leadership of Hoffmann and Moser, students for the first time designed and *made* ceramics at a Viennese academy. In this training the two professors promoted what they considered the ideal of an earlier age when design and production lay in one hand. Later, in practice at the Wiener Werkstätte, they abandoned this principle—in part because of their ambition to have their own designs realized—but still emphasized the contributions of individuals through a system of marks acknowledging both the designer and the craftsman. It was a tradition borrowed from England, where silver marks had been deliberately placed in a graphic, aesthetic arrangement as early as the 15th century; the idea of having separate marks for the authorship of design and production goes back to Christopher Dresser, who passed it on to Arts and Crafts designers like Archibald Knox.

By 1902 Hoffmann's reputation was firmly enough established to enable him to have his own designs made and marketed by the Viennese silversmith firms Würbel & Czokally and Alexander Sturm & Co. The founding of the Wiener Werkstätte in 1903 ended this collaboration, and Hoffmann took some of these early designs with him, so to speak, putting them into production at the WW.

These early designs are among Hoffmann's most radical. In particular, a series of silver lidded goblets—so-called *Sportpreise* (sports trophies) (cat. nos. 109 and 110)—were a kind of foreshadowing of the explosion of creativity that lay just ahead. Yet, despite their radicality—bizarre, elongated volumes perched on stilt-like legs—this group of goblets must be seen in the context of an old German silver- and goldsmith tradition: decorative goblets such as the so-called pineapple, coconut, or ostrich egg beakers made in Nuremberg and Augsburg in the 16th and 17th centuries. (Neoclassicism, too, had similar forms, especially in porcelain: spherical marmelade bowls elevated on legs in the shape of stylized lions' feet were made by Sèvres around 1810.)

Interestingly, the early post-1900 production of Würbel & Czokally, Alexander Sturm & Co., and the Wiener Werkstätte itself was marked by the ubiquitous use of polished semi-precious stones. This practice, all but unheard of in Viennese Biedermeier silver, is another medieval attribute which seems to have entered Hoffmann's vocabulary via the example of English designers such as Charles R. Ashbee and Archibald Knox.

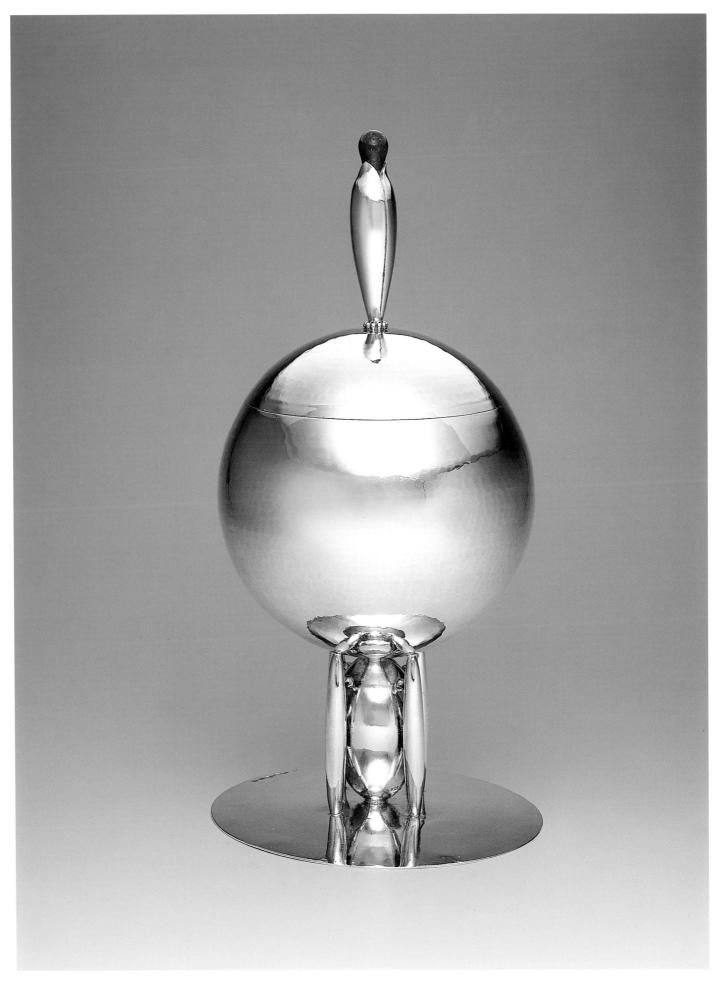

Archibald Knox, silver candlestick
London 1901
Private collection, Photo: Jean Paul Torno

**110. SPORTS TROPHY (*SPORTPREIS*)
ACQUIRED BY PAUL WITTGENSTEIN**
Designed by Josef Hoffmann, Vienna 1902
Executed by Würbel & Czokally (Carl Würbel), Vinzenz Mayer's Söhne
Silver, parcel-gilt (interior), malachite
Vienna hallmark, JH, CW, VMS, hammer and anvil mark, 1902
H 26 cm/10.4 in. Weight 305 g/12.2 oz.
Private collection

HAUS DR. SPITZER. SITZMÖBEL UND TABURETT IN DER HALLE. SCHWARZ-GEBEIZTE EICHE UND AHORN, MIT GRAUEM LEDER-BEZUG.

HAUS SPITZER. BLUMEN-GEFÄSSE AUS KUPFER UND ALPAKA.

12

Josef Hoffmann, *Haus Spitzer. Blumengefässe aus Kupfer und Alpaka* (Vases in copper and alpacca from Spitzer House), executed 1901–02

Illustration from *Das Interieur*, vol. 4, p. 169, Vienna 1903.

111. WINE COASTER

Designed by Josef Hoffmann, Vienna ca. 1902

Executed by Würbel & Czokally, Vinzenz Mayer's Söhne

Silver

Vienna hallmark, hammer and anvil mark, V. M. S, double-headed eagle

Diameter 13.3 cm/5.3 in. Weight 323 g/12.9 oz.

Clarisse Praun

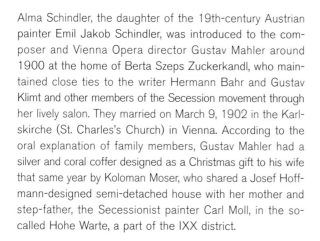

Gustav Mahler
Vintage print, E. Bieber, Berlin 1898
Private collection

Alma Schindler Mahler
Vintage print, Vienna ca. 1905
Private collection

Alma Schindler, the daughter of the 19th-century Austrian painter Emil Jakob Schindler, was introduced to the composer and Vienna Opera director Gustav Mahler around 1900 at the home of Berta Szeps Zuckerkandl, who maintained close ties to the writer Hermann Bahr and Gustav Klimt and other members of the Secession movement through her lively salon. They married on March 9, 1902 in the Karlskirche (St. Charles's Church) in Vienna. According to the oral explanation of family members, Gustav Mahler had a silver and coral coffer designed as a Christmas gift to his wife that same year by Koloman Moser, who shared a Josef Hoffmann-designed semi-detached house with her mother and step-father, the Secessionist painter Carl Moll, in the so-called Hohe Warte, a part of the IXX district.

Like Josef Hoffmann's work from 1902, this coffer was made—evidently only once—by the silversmith firm Alexander Sturm & Co. (And, like Hoffmann, Moser took his design with him to the Wiener Werkstätte: a nearly identical, though ornamentally-reduced *Schatulle* with slight variations to the keyhole and front plate where the monogram and date were placed on the Mahler version was made by the WW in 1904 as model no. S 206 and sold to the Hohenzollern Kunstgewerbehaus in Berlin for 300 crowns.)

The basic form of the box is a plain, undecorated octagon, which, by itself, could have been from 1810–20. To this, contemporary ornamentation has been affixed in a decidedly non-symbiotic manner, as though the essence of the

new style were merely a question of finding a new language for the decoration of surfaces. (A similar approach to décor was common in Vienna during another transition period—around 1800—when metal neoclassical mounts were simply added onto Josephin furniture shapes in a rather unconvincing attempt to bring them up to date.) In the later Wiener Werkstätte version this disharmony has been addressed: the leafy ornamentation, reminiscent of the English-influenced décor of Hoffmann and Moser's early work (e.g. stylized ornamentation in *Ver Sacrum*, or on the trim of the bedroom set for the daughter of Max Biach), has been removed. The personal, "private" nature of the coffer, which is emphasized by its front plate in the form of a stylized sealed envelope, remains.

The Mahlers, incidentally, also purchased at least six pieces of Wiener Werkstätte silver and metalwork, all in the year 1904: three Josef Hoffmann metal dishes (model nos. M 153 and M 154); two tall, thin Hoffmann bud vases (model no. S 356) (see cat. no. 180, same model no.); a Hoffmann tray (model no. S 164); and two Koloman Moser napkin rings (model no. S 353) (see cat. no. 123, same model no.).

After the death of Gustav Mahler, Alma Schindler Mahler had a brief affair with Oskar Kokoschka and subsequently married the architect Walter Gropius. After her divorce from Gropius, she married Austrian novelist Franz Werfel in 1929, thereby achieving in her personal attachments something akin to the concentration of events, ideas, and places embodied by her 1902 Christmas gift from Gustav Mahler.

112. COFFER GIVEN BY GUSTAV MAHLER TO ALMA MAHLER FOR CHRISTMAS 1902

Designed by Koloman Moser, Vienna 1902
Executed by Alexander Sturm & Company
Silver, coral
Vienna hallmark, cloverleaf mark
Monogram MAM (Alma Maria Mahler), 24/12/1902
W/D 13.5 cm/5.4 in. Weight 368 g/14.7 oz.
Private collection

He told me that the *Symphony no. 4* should be thought of as an old painting on gold ground. Just as he later remarked about the song *Ich bin der Welt abhanden gekommen*, he had been thinking all the while of the monuments of the cardinals in Italy—where the bodies of the clergymen lay with folded hands and closed eyes on flat stones in churches. At the time I was disturbed by this antique attitude, so foreign to our time.[53]

Alma Mahler-Werfel, 1960

53 Alma Mahler-Werfel, *Mein Leben*, Frankfurt am Main 1960, p. 27. English translation Michael Huey.

Josef Hoffmann and Koloman Moser, *Spiegel mit Dose. Silber-Arbeit* (Silver mirror and coffer) as executed by the Wiener Werkstätte
Illustration from *Deutsche Kunst und Dekoration*, vol. 15, p. 25, Darmstadt 1904–05.

Körbchen.
Silber-Arbeit.

Leuchter und
Zuckerdose.
Silber-Arbeit.

wir erst, wenn es künstlerisch gestaltet ist. — So sind Kultur und Kunst im letzten Sinne eins. Wenn wir aber auch die bisherige Auffassung von Kunst viel zu enge finden, so kann doch die Pflege dieser Gebiete gute Vorarbeiten liefern für die kommende Kultur, indem die Betrachtung der »Kunstwerke« wertvolle, für jene Kultur nötige Eigenschaften übermittelt: Wahrheit, Kraft, Rhythmus etc.

Allein dies genügt nicht; es bedarf allgemeiner und grösster Anstrengungen, wenn wir aus der vollkommenen Unkultur, der rasse- und stillosen Einrichtung unseres Lebens jenes Ideal einer Volkskunst und -kultur erreichen wollen. Vor allem ist es nötig, dass der Deutsche sich seines traurigen Kulturzustandes *bewusst* werde. Vielleicht schämt er sich, wenn er sich in seinen Bauten karakterisiert findet als eitlen Parvenü, aufgeputzt mit schäbig imitiertem Prunk, als Heuchler, der »Mietskasernen für Renaissancepaläste u. moderne Staatsgebäude für antike Tempel« auszugeben versucht; vielleicht sieht er einmal ein, wie jämmerlich es ist, von aller Welt zu borgen und sich Mode und Lebensführung von Fremden vorschreiben zu lassen. — Was wollen wir dem Fremden zeigen, der bei uns zu Gaste ist, das er nicht ebenso gut oder besser zu Hause fände? Etwa die Natur-Schönheiten unserer Berge? — Aber das deutsche Volk wird er nicht finden. Wir haben alle Rasse, alle

28

Josef Hoffmann, *Körbchen. Silber-Arbeit./Leuchter und Zuckerdose. Silber-Arbeit* (Silver Basket, Candlestick, Sugar Bowl [and Spoon]), as executed by the Wiener Werkstätte

Illustration from *Deutsche Kunst und Dekoration*, vol. 15, p. 28, Darmstadt 1904–05.

113. SUGAR SPOON (*STREUZUCKERLÖFFEL*)

Designed by Josef Hoffmann, Vienna ca. 1902

Executed prior to the founding of the Wiener Werkstätte by Alexander Sturm & Company

Subsequently executed by the Wiener Werkstätte, model no. S 195

First made by the Wiener Werkstätte December, 1904 for thirty-two crowns

Two pieces produced

Silver, turquoise

Vienna hallmark, cloverleaf mark, 800

L 14.6 cm/5.8 in. Weight 23 g/0.9 oz.

Christian Witt-Dörring, Vienna

Wohnung Dr. H. W. Wien/Salon (Salon of the apartment of Dr. H[ermann].W[ittgenstein]., Vienna),
furnished by Josef Hoffmann and the Wiener Werkstätte in 1905

Illustration from *Deutsche Kunst und Dekoration,* vol. 18, p. 457, Darmstadt 1906.

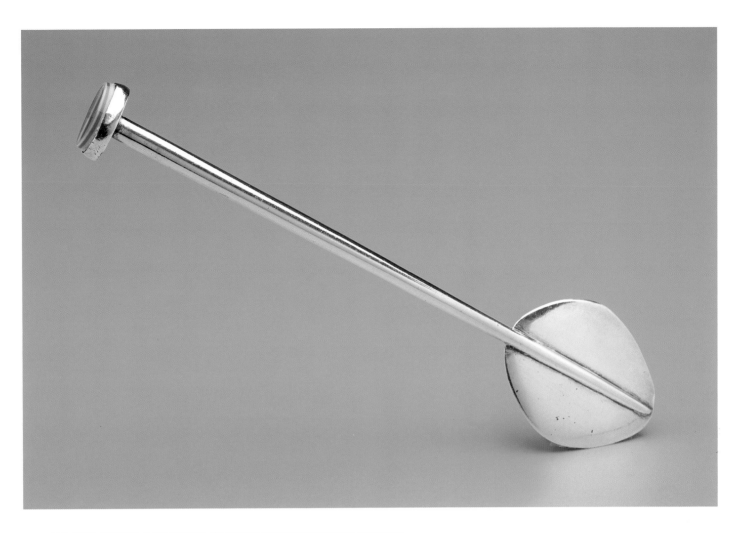

114. BUTTER KNIFE ACQUIRED BY THE WITTGENSTEIN FAMILY

Designed by Josef Hoffmann, Vienna ca. 1904

Executed by the Wiener Werkstätte, model no. S 193

First made by the Wiener Werkstätte ca. 1904 for 140 crowns

Three pieces produced

Silver, agate

Vienna hallmark, WW, rose mark

L 14.8 cm/5.9 in. Weight 33 g/1.3 oz.

Ellen and William Taubman Collection

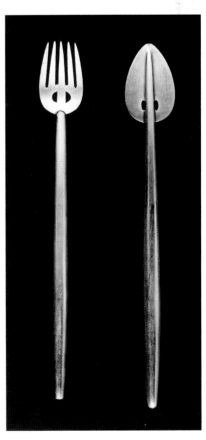

Charles Rennie Mackintosh,
silver-painted nickel fish knife
and fork
Glasgow ca. 1903
Hunterian Art Gallery, University of Glasgow,
Mackintosh Collection

The twenty-one pieces of this extensive cutlery service were made in 1902, a year prior to the establishment of the Wiener Werkstätte, for Maria Kohn, the granddaughter of Josef Kohn, a founder, together with his father Jacob, of the bentwood manufactory J. & J. Kohn. Over the course of the following years, several members of the extended Kohn family became clients of the WW and in 1904 they became directly involved with Hoffmann and Moser in the production of furnishings for the Purkersdorf Sanatorium. (Kohn was the first of the bentwood producers to make use of the most prominent architect/designers in turn-of-the-century Vienna after Adolf Loos approached the firm to produce his design for a chair for the Café Museum in 1898.) The 1906 *Studio Yearbook* reported that Hoffmann had "given much care to the solving of bentwood and wicker problems in furniture, in which he has been ably supported by Messrs. J. & J. Kohn and the Prag-Rudniker Korbwaren Fabrikation, Vienna."[54] Hoffmann's *Sitzmaschine,* arguably his most famous and radical chair design, was also produced by the firm J. & J. Kohn.

54 *The Studio Yearbook,* London 1906, p. 505.

Maria Kohn, vintage print, Eduard Josef Ehrlich,
Trebíc ca. 1905
Private collection, Vienna

115. EIGHT PIECES FROM A 152-PART CUTLERY SERVICE ACQUIRED BY FELIX KOHN FOR MARIA KOHN

Designed by Josef Hoffmann, Vienna 1902

Executed by Alexander Sturm & Company
Silver
Vienna hallmark, cloverleaf mark
Monogram MK
L 27.8 cm/11.1 in. Weight 140 g/5.6 oz. (cake server)
Private collection

115. THIRTEEN PIECES FROM A 152-PART CUTLERY SERVICE ACQUIRED BY FELIX KOHN FOR MARIA KOHN
Designed by Josef Hoffmann, Vienna 1902
Executed by Alexander Sturm & Company
Silver
Vienna hallmark, cloverleaf mark
Monogram MK
L 27.8 cm/11.1 in. Weight 140 g/5.6 oz. (cake server)
Private collection

DAS ARBEITSPROGRAMM DER WIENER WERKSTÄTTE.

Das grenzenlose Unheil, welches die schlechte Massenproduktion einerseits, die gedankenlose Nachahmung alter Stile anderseits auf kunstgewerblichem Gebiete verursacht hat, durchdringt als Riesenstrom die ganze Welt. Wir haben den Anschluß an die Kultur unserer Vorfahren verloren und werden von tausend Wünschen und Erwägungen hin und her geworfen. An Stelle der Hand ist meist die Maschine, an Stelle des Handwerkers der Geschäftsmann getreten. Diesem Strome entgegen zu schwimmen wäre Wahnsinn.

Dennoch haben wir unsere Werkstätte gegründet. Sie soll uns auf heimischem Boden, mitten im frohen Lärm des Handwerks einen Ruhepunkt schaffen und dem willkommen sein, der sich zu Ruskin und Morris bekennt. Wir appellieren an alle, denen eine Kultur in diesem Sinne wertvoll erscheint, und hoffen, daß auch unvermeidliche Fehler unsere Freunde nicht beirren werden, unsere Absichten zu fördern.

Wir wollen einen innigen Kontakt zwischen Publikum, Entwerfer und Handwerker herstellen und gutes, einfaches Hausgerät schaffen. Wir gehen vom Zweck aus, die Gebrauchsfähigkeit ist uns erste Bedingung, unsere Stärke soll in guten Verhältnissen und in guter Materialbehandlung bestehen. Wo es angeht, werden wir zu schmücken suchen, doch ohne Zwang und nicht um jeden Preis. Wir benützen viel Halbedelsteine, besonders bei unserem Geschmeide; sie ersetzen uns durch ihre Farbenschönheit und unendliche, fast nie wiederkehrende Mannigfaltigkeit den Wert der Brillanten. Wir lieben das Silber des Silber-, das Gold des Goldglanzes wegen; uns ist das Kupfer in künstlerischer Beziehung ebenso wertvoll wie die edlen Metalle. Wir müssen gestehen, daß ein Schmuck aus Silber an sich ebenso wertvoll sein kann wie ein solcher aus Gold und Edelsteinen. Der Wert der künstlerischen Arbeit und die Idee sollen wieder erkannt und geschätzt werden. Es soll die Arbeit des Kunsthandwerkers mit demselben Maß gemessen werden wie die des Malers und Bildhauers.

Wir können und wollen nicht mit der Billigkeit wetteifern; dieselbe geht vor allem auf Kosten des Arbeiters, und diesem wieder eine Freude am Schaffen und eine menschenwürdige Existenz zu erringen, halten wir für unsere vornehmste Pflicht. Alles dieses ist nur schrittweise zu erreichen.

Bei unseren Lederarbeiten und Bucheinbänden wird, ebenso wie bei allen anderen, auf ein gutes Material und technisch vollkommene Durchführung gesehen. Es ist natürlich, daß unser Dekor nur dort auftritt, wo die Struktur des Materials nicht dagegen spricht. Alle Arten der Ledereinlegekunst, des Blinddruckes und der Handvergoldung, des Lederflechtens und des Tunkverfahrens werden abwechselnd ausgeübt.

Der gute Einband ist vollkommen ausgestorben. Der hohle Rücken, das Heften mit Draht, der unschöne Schnitt, die schlecht gehefteten Blätter und das schlechte Leder sind unausrottbar. Der sogenannte Originalband, d. h. der fabriksmäßig hergestellte, mit Klischees reich bedruckte Umschlag ist alles, was wir besitzen. Die Maschine arbeitet emsig und füllt unsere Bücherkästen mit mangelhaft gedruckten Werken; ihr Rekord ist die Billigkeit. Doch sollte jeder Kulturmensch sich dieser Materialfülle schämen, denn einesteils bringt die leichte Herstellbarkeit eine geringere Verantwortlichkeit mit sich, während andernteils die Fülle zur Oberflächlichkeit führt. Wie viele Bücher sind wirklich die unseren? Und sollte man diese nicht in den besten Hüllen, auf bestem Papier, in herrlichem Leder gebunden besitzen? Sollten wir vergessen haben, daß die Liebe, mit der ein Buch gedruckt, ausgestattet und gebunden wurde, uns in ein ganz anderes Verhältnis zu demselben bringt, daß der Umgang mit schönen Dingen uns selbst verschönt? Ein Buch soll als Ganzes ein Kunstwerk sein und muß dessen Wert als solches bemessen werden.

In unseren Tischlerwerkstätten ist stets die exakteste und solideste Ausführung bedingt. Leider hat die heutige Zeit sich an solche Schleuderwaren gewöhnt, daß uns ein halbwegs sorgfältig gearbeitetes Möbel unerschwinglich erscheint. Es muß einmal daran erinnert werden, daß wir leider gezwungen sind, um den Betrag, um den zum Beispiel ein Waggon-lit gebaut wird, ein reichlich großes Haus mit allem, was darinnen ist, zu errichten. Man möge daran die Unmöglichkeit einer soliden Basis erkennen. Während noch vor hundert Jahren für manches Kabinett in Schlössern selbst damals schon Hunderttausende gezahlt wurden, ist man heute geneigt, der Moderne Uneleganz und Armlichkeit vorzuwerfen, wo sie vielleicht die ungeahnteste Wirkung erreichen würde, wenn der nötige Auftrag da wäre. Die Surrogate der stillvollen Imitationen können nur dem Parvenü genügen. Der Bürger von heute, ebenso wie der Arbeiter, müssen den Stolz besitzen, ihres Wertes voll bewußt zu sein, und dürfen nicht mit anderen Ständen wetteifern wollen, deren Kulturaufgaben erfüllt sind und die mit Recht auf eine herrliche Vergangenheit in künstlerischer Beziehung zurückblicken. Unser Bürgerstand hat seine künstlerische Aufgabe noch lange nicht erfüllt. An ihn ist jetzt die Reihe, der Entwicklung voll und ganz gerecht zu werden. Es kann unmöglich genügen, wenn wir Bilder, und wären sie auch noch so herrlich, erwerben. Solange nicht unsere Städte, unsere Häuser, unsere Räume, unsere Schränke, unsere Geräte, unsere Kleider und unser Schmuck, solange nicht unsere Sprache und unsere Gefühle in schlichter, einfacher und schöner Art den Geist unserer eigenen Zeit versinnbildlichen, sind wir unendlich weit gegen unsere Vorfahren zurück und keine Lüge kann uns über alle diese Schwächen täuschen. Es sei noch gestattet, darauf aufmerksam zu machen, daß auch wir uns bewußt sind, daß unter gewissen Umständen mit Hilfe von Maschinen ein erträglicher Massenartikel geschaffen werden kann; derselbe muß dann aber unbedingt das Gepräge der Fabrikation tragen. Wir halten es nicht für unsere Aufgabe, jetzt schon dieses Gebiet zu betreten. Was wir wollen, ist das, was der Japaner immer getan hat. Wer würde sich irgend ein Werk japanischen Kunstgewerbes maschinell hergestellt, vorstellen können? Was in unseren Kräften liegt, werden wir zu erfüllen trachten, wir können aber nur durch die Mitarbeit aller unserer Freunde einen Schritt weiterkommen. Es ist uns nicht gestattet, Phantasien nachzugehen. Wir stehen mit beiden Füßen in der Wirklichkeit und bedürfen der Aufgaben.

268

Josef Hoffmann, Koloman Moser, and Fritz Waerndorfer, *Arbeitsprogramm* (Working Program) of the Wiener Werkstätte
Published in *Hohe Warte* 1, Vienna 1904–05.

Silver workshop of the Wiener Werkstätte (with Josef Hoszfeld, *Werkmeister* [master], standing with book)
Vintage print, Vienna ca. 1905
Felicitas Kuhn Collection

WIENER WERKSTÄTTE

PRODUCTIV-GE
NOSSENSCHAFT
VON KUNSTHAND
WERKERN IN WIEN
□ R. GEN. M. U. H. □
IV. HEUMÜHLG. 6.
7. Neustiftgasse 32.

RECHNUNG . . AN . DAS . VEREHRLICHE . SEKRETARIAT . DER . . .

"SECESSION",. . . . . WIEN . . .

ZAHLBAR UND KLAGBAR IN WIEN
SANDTE AUF IHRE RECHNUNG UND GEFAHR

ZAHL	GEGENSTAND	K	H	K	H
12	Kuppeln für Opalescent-Kugeln.............à	3	–	36	–
1	Rahmen für Bild.........			30	–
			K	66	–

WIENER WERK STÄTTE 2 1898 2

WIENER WERK STÄTTE

Invoice from the Wiener Werkstätte to the Secession office

Vienna 1903

MAK, Vienna

Storefront of the Wiener Werkstätte salesroom at Graben 15
Contemporary photograph, Vienna ca. 1908
MAK, Vienna

Ausstellungsraum (Salesroom) of the Wiener Werkstätte at Neustiftgasse 32–34

Illustration from *Deutsche Kunst und Dekoration*, vol. 15, p. 4, Darmstadt 1904–05.

116. *BONBONNIÈRE*

Designed by Josef Hoffmann, Vienna 1903

Executed by the Wiener Werkstätte, model no. S 19

First made August, 1903 for 160 crowns

Three pieces produced

Silver

Vienna hallmark, JH, WW, rose mark

Diameter 16 cm/6.3 in. Weight 466 g/18.6 oz.

Ernst Ploil Collection

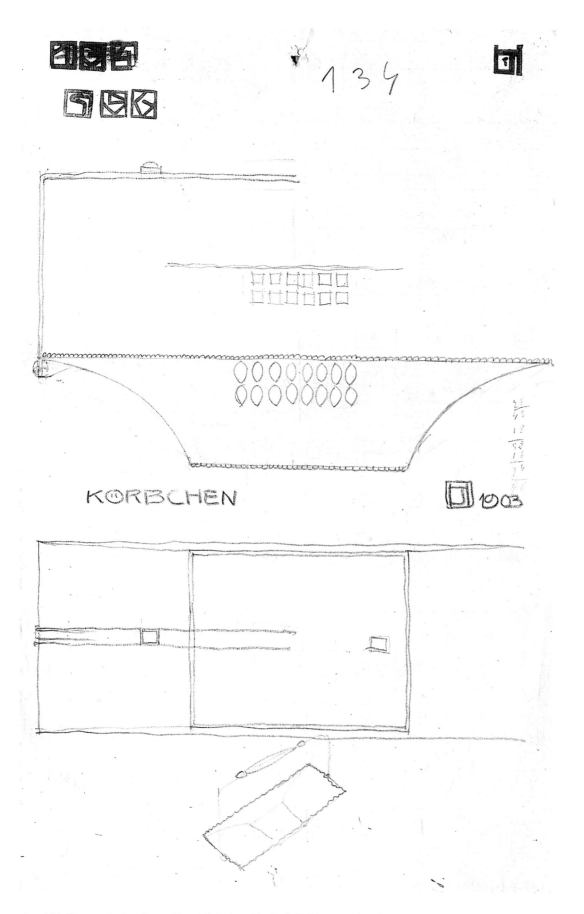

KÖRBCHEN

134

Josef Hoffmann, design for a silver *Körbchen* (Basket) (WW model S 56) with carnelian for the Wiener Werkstätte
Pencil and colored pencil, Vienna 1903
MAK, Vienna

117. BASKET (*BONBONNIÈRE*) ACQUIRED BY FRITZ WAERNDORFER

Designed by Josef Hoffmann, Vienna 1903

Executed by the Wiener Werkstätte, model no. S 56 (Josef Czech)

First made April, 1903 for one hundred crowns

Three pieces produced

Silver, carnelian

Vienna hallmark, JH, JC, WW, rose mark

W 19.2 cm/7.7 in. Weight 249 g/10 oz.

Asenbaum Collection

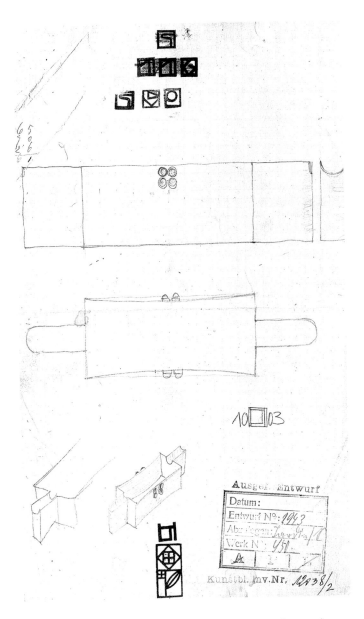

Josef Hoffmann, design for a silver *Aschen-Schale* (Ashtray)
(WW model S 50) with lapis lazuli for the Wiener Werkstätte
Pencil and colored pencil, Vienna 1903
MAK, Vienna

118. ASHTRAY (*ASCHEN-SCHALE*)

Designed by Josef Hoffmann, Vienna 1903
Executed by the Wiener Werkstätte, model no. S 50 (Josef Wagner)
First made in 1903 for eighty crowns
Two pieces produced
Silver, lapis lazuli
Vienna hallmark, JH, JW, WW, rose mark
L 16.9 cm/6.8 in. Weight 300 g/12 oz.
Ernst Ploil Collection

The decorative hammered surface of many Wiener Werkstätte pieces (*Hammerschlagdekor*), like other "innovations" often associated with the WW, actually goes back to a long-standing silversmith tradition in Austria. Adolf Loos mentions this particular tradition in his critical (and self-critical) retrospective assessment of the Chicago World's Columbian Exposition of 1893:

Years ago when I left home to acquaint myself with the architecture and decorative arts on the other side of the Atlantic, I was still fully persuaded of the superiority of German crafts. In Chicago I walked through the German and Austrian sections with a proud feeling of pleasure. I looked at the American "attempts at applied arts" with a smile of sympathy. How things have changed! My stay of many years there had as a consequence that I still turn red with shame today when I think of the embarrassment of German crafts in Chicago…

There were two divisions that saved our prestige. Austrian prestige, not German, for the Germans had nothing good to show there either. The divisions were decorative leather goods and gold- and silversmith products. At the time I harbored a

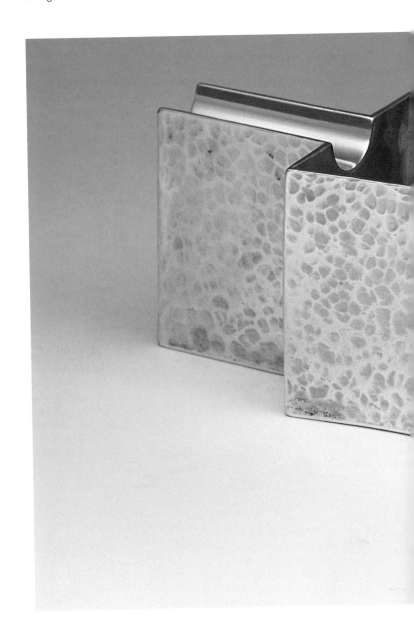

quiet fury toward these things. There were *portemonnaies,* cigar and cigarette cases, picture frames, writing sets, suitcases, bags, riding crops, canes, silver handles, field flasks—and all of it, all! was plain, without ornamental decoration, the silver goods incised or hammered at the most.

I was ashamed of this work. It wasn't applied art, I thought, it was fashion! What a horrid word! For the tried and true craftsman I still was at the time nothing could have been more pejorative.

Certainly, the Viennese liked to buy things like that… At the time I was of another mind. But now I would not hesitate to say that the silliest dandy outdid my taste back then.[55]

The one element of Loos's philosophy which he shared with Josef Hoffmann and Koloman Moser—though they were again at odds as to how it should be applied—was his imperative that the past be combed for lost qualities which, when recognized, retrieved, and re-awakened, could serve as a guide.

The hammered surface of this ashtray, designed by Josef Hoffmann in 1903 (notably just prior to the construction of the Purkersdorf Sanatorium in 1904) also contributes to its highly tectonic quality. (Purkersdorf was built for Victor Zuckerkandl, the brother-in-law of Berta Szeps Zuckerkandl, who, as an art critic, was one of the great defenders of the Wiener Werkstätte and who later had a Hoffmann-designed apartment of her own on Ringstrasse/Oppolzergasse.) Its juxtaposition of a wide central "façade" with symmetrical volumes at either end—as well as the truncation of its upper edge to form a kind of flat "roof"—are both elements Hoffmann returned to in Purkersdorf. The placement of the four semi-precious stones along the top of the ashtray's "façade" reinforce this relationship by calling to mind Hoffmann's unusual use of glazed cupboard doors in the Purkersdorf interior (entry hall), as well as the windows he placed on the upper story of the vestibule on the building's east (rough stucco) façade, where they are idiosyncratically positioned immediately below the eaves of the roof.

55 Burkhardt Rukschcio, *Adolf Loos,* Salzburg and Vienna 1982, p. 24. English translation Michael Huey.

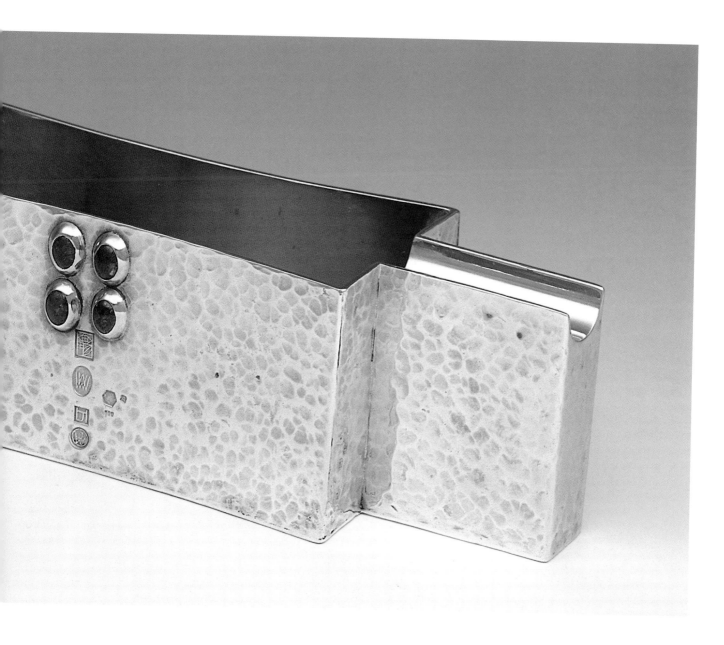

Tea caddy with pear-wood and stained pear-wood marquetry
England (?) ca. 1820
Michael Huey, Vienna

Koloman Moser (left) and Fritz Waerndorfer in the office
of the Wiener Werkstätte at Neustiftgasse 32–34

Vintage print, Vienna ca. 1905
© Imagno Brandstätter Images, Vienna

In 1903 Koloman Moser designed this rectangular coffer
with an all-over square pattern for the Wiener Werkstätte. It
was produced a second time much later, in 1908, when it
sold for 300 crowns. Its surface design relates not only to a
stunning 1802 teapot by Jacob Krautauer (cat. no. 25), but
also to a marquetry tea caddy from around 1820, both of
which may be seen as its intellectual predecessors. The coffer is a milestone piece, as it marks the first likely occasion
of the Werkstätte's all-over use of this kind of grid décor, a
practice which was abstracted beginning in the same year
(and increasingly toward 1905) in Hoffmann and Moser's
ubiquitous designs for objects made from sheet silver or
other metals with sawed-out circles or squares.

When the later cut-out pieces are compared to this earlier box,
the ironic smile that links them becomes visible. Compared and
contrasted with each other, they can be read as a play on
the negative and the positive, the open and the closed, the
solid and the ephemeral, the heavy and the light. In this they
are likewise precursors of dramatic furniture and interior
designs such as Eduard Josef Wimmer-Wisgrill's pair of
"matched" marquetry drawing cabinets from 1908 and 1912
(one is ebony and one is sycamore, both are trimmed in
mother-of-pearl)[56] and the square-motif paneling Hoffmann
devised for the living room of Karl Wittgenstein's country estate, Hochreit, which, in its intimacy, could almost be perceived
as portraying the interior of a box such as this.

56 One cabinet belongs to the Neue Galerie New York; the other is in the collection of
the MAK, Vienna.

119. COFFER (*CASSETTE*)

Designed by Koloman Moser, Vienna 1903

Executed by the Wiener Werkstätte, model no. S 21 (Adolf Erbrich)

First made in 1903

Two pieces produced

Silver, niello

Vienna hallmark, KM, AE, WW, rose mark

W 12.3 cm/4.9 in. Weight 428 g/17.1 oz.

Neue Galerie New York

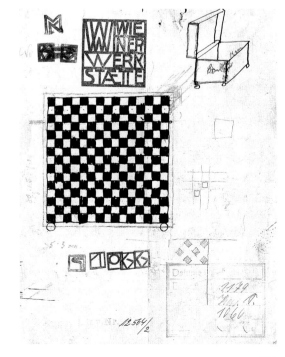

Koloman Moser, design for a
silver and niello coffer (*Cassette*)
(WW model no. S 21) for the
Wiener Werkstätte
Pencil, pen and ink, Vienna 1903
MAK, Vienna

Illustration from the 1909 (?) sales catalogue of Jacob and Josef Kohn with a *Salon-Garnitur* (Living room set) by Josef Hoffmann; the Kohn firm logo was designed by Koloman Moser.
Private collection

Felix Kohn
Albumen print, Vienna ca. 1903
Private collection

The extremely graphic quality of this candy box—versions of which were purchased by Felix Kohn and Dr. Hermann Wittgenstein—owes at least in part to the self-explanatory nature of its construction and ornamentation: the hammered sides of the box are simply pierced through with a stencil-like pattern, bent into a convex shape, welded together, and adorned with a cabochon-cut onyx stone. In 1903 Hoffmann had begun to experiment with pierced surfaces as an alternative to the application of ornamentation, and these trials—like that with the previously discussed grid-patterned coffer—inevitably led to the construction of entire objects whose thoroughly pierced surfaces are simultaneously structure and décor.

The stencil-cut pattern here has not yet reached that status, however. Interestingly, the thin walls of the box are more a play on the idea of structure than structural in and of themselves: their thinness (as well as the use of the cut-out pattern) calls to mind other materials, such as paper, which are not only easily cut, but will only stand independently if bent

into a convex shape. (This candy basket is, in effect, a kind of "permanent" version of the common—and ephemeral—paper candy box.)

The limits of the trompe l'oeil relationship of Hoffmann's silver basket to those materials is emphasized by the fact that it was not made to stand on its own body, but was placed on pill-shaped feet. This recollection of one material via another is reminiscent of a quirky element of European design favored in Vienna from at least the late 18th century onward, when porcelain and stoneware pretended to be any number of things from wood to metal to stone; in Hoffmann's early years at the Wiener Werkstätte such an imitative impulse was perhaps at most subconscious: all the talk at the time was of "honesty" toward materials. But it was subsequently (and consciously) taken to even higher heights by Dagobert Peche, who joined Hoffmann as artistic director at the Wiener Werkstätte in 1915, and who often delighted in his designs in working—in ways that now sometimes seem perverse—*against* the innate nature of his materials.

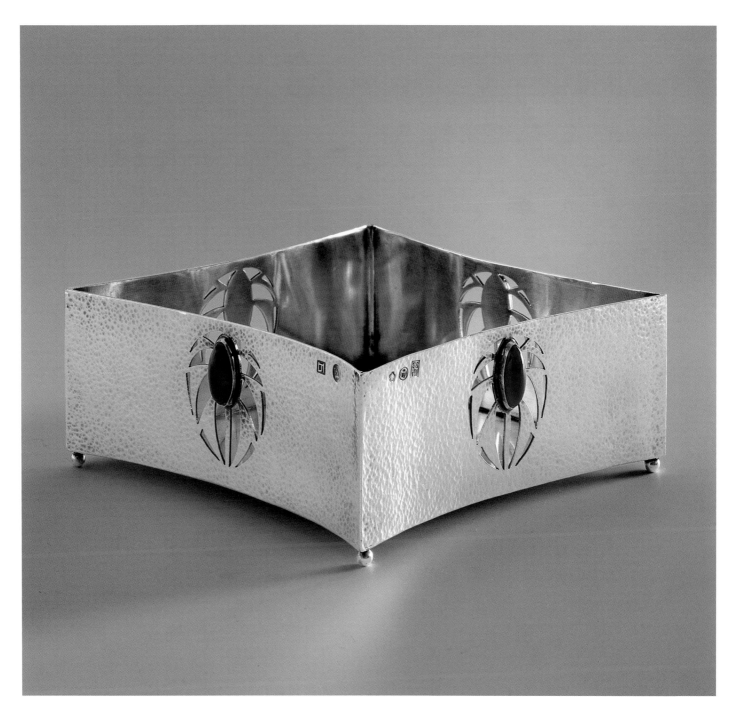

120. CANDY BASKET (*BONBONKORB*)

Designed by Josef Hoffmann, Vienna 1904

Executed by the Wiener Werkstätte, model no. S 17 (Josef Holl)

First made 1904 for 160 crowns

Four pieces produced

Silver, onyx

Vienna hallmark, JH, JH, WW, rose mark

L 18.7 cm/7.5 in. Weight 317 g/12.7 oz.

Private collection

The eleven children of Hermann Christian and Fanny Figdor Wittgenstein (l–r: Hermine "Fine"; Karl; Anna; Emilie "Milly"; Franziska "Lydia"; Ludwig "Louis" [the uncle of the philosopher]; Clothilde; Clara; Marie; Ottilie "Bertha"; Paul)
Albumen print, photograph taken for the silver wedding anniversary of Hermann and Fanny Wittgenstein, Vienna 1863
© Wittgenstein Archive, Cambridge

Like her brother Hermann, Johanna Wittgenstein was given, as part of her dowry, an apartment designed by Josef Hoffmann (Gumpendorferstrasse 8, VI. district Vienna) when she married Johannes Salzer in 1902. And, like her brother, she continued to acquire Hoffmann and Moser pieces for her home. In December, 1905 this sardine tray was purchased—presumably as a Christmas gift for the couple—by Justine Hochstetter Wittgenstein, the wife of Paul Wittgenstein. As Christian Witt-Dörring has pointed out, most of the metal pieces in the Salzer apartment made use of "rounded, futuristic-looking shapes" (in contrast to its clear, stereometric furnishings); a mustard pot (cat. no. 104; see also fig. p. 228) that stood on the dining room buffet is an example of this somewhat startling style.

Paul Wittgenstein, Johanna's father, was one of the eleven children of Hermann Christian and Fanny Figdor Wittgenstein, well-to-do members of Vienna's *haute bourgeoisie*. Though

many of the Wittgensteins eventually patronized the Wiener Werkstätte, it seems to have been the artistically-gifted and aesthetically-receptive Paul who kindled their interest.

It is instructive in this regard to examine a photograph of the eleven Wittgenstein siblings from around 1865. Viewed as an object unto itself, the photograph—when confronted with the sardine tray—illustrates not only the enormous leap in sophistication taken by Paul and other members of his family, but also, intriguingly, a certain consistency in terms of an almost puritanical clarity from the historicism of their youth to the avant-garde of their maturity. (Years later when Hermine Wittgenstein, Paul's niece, wrote of her father's collections, she claimed that the paintings were characterized by "a certain earnest placidness of composition… an emphasis on the vertical and horizontal that I should like to call 'ethical.'")[57]

57 Hermine Wittgenstein, *Familienerinnerungen*, unpubl. ms., Vienna and Hochreit June 1944, pp. 77–78. English translation Michael Huey.

**121. SARDINE TRAY ACQUIRED FOR
THE APARTMENT OF DR. JOHANNES
AND JOHANNA WITTGENSTEIN SALZER**

Designed by Josef Hoffmann, Vienna 1904

Executed by the Wiener Werkstätte, model no. M 150
First made 1904 for 120 crowns
Five pieces produced
Silver-plated alpacca, glass inset
JH, WW, rose mark
L 32.5 cm/13 in.
Private collection

Wohnung Dr. St. Berlin/Damenschreibtisch und Mappenschrank (Apartment of Dr. St.[onborough] in Berlin/Lady's writing desk and portfolio cabinet), furnished by Koloman Moser and the Wiener Werkstätte in 1905; note the silver inkwell (WW model no. S 184) (cat. no. 122) on the desk, as well as the vase (compare with cat. no. 180).
Illustration from *Deutsche Kunst und Dekoration,* vol. 17, p. 158, Darmstadt 1905–06.

One of the great early commissions of Josef Hoffmann and Koloman Moser's Wiener Werkstätte was the Berlin apartment of Jerome Stonborough and Margaret Stonborough-Wittgenstein (née Margherita, she anglicized the spelling of her name upon her marriage to the American chemist Stonborough). This apartment, too, appears to have been a kind of dowry gift to the young couple by her parents. While Moser designed the living room, which also served as a salon for Margaret Stonborough-Wittgenstein, Hoffmann did Jerome Stonborough's private study. According to the Wiener Werkstätte archive, the silver, lapis lazuli, and coral inkwell S 184 was originally purchased, somewhat surprisingly, by Hermine Wittgenstein, a sister of Margaret's who, by her own admission, was not particularly interested in design and whose taste was on the conservative side; she evidently gave the inkwell to the Stonborough-Wittgensteins as a wedding gift. In any case, it turned up together with a similarly broad-footed vase (model S 356) in contemporary photographs of the living room on Margaret's massive desk, which stood before an expansive window curtain with a large checked pattern as though it had abruptly sprung off the graph paper

Hoffmann and Moser so often used for sketching out their design ideas.

With its flared base, Moser's inkwell, which very closely resembled an Ashbee inkwell from 1900, made a perfect counterpart to the desk, which flared out at its top. The inkwell was light while the desk was dark; it was, if not exactly delicate, compact where the desk was enormous. While everyday life may have softened some of the severity of the Stonborough-Wittgenstein apartment, the general idea was clear: from the inkwell to the desk to the firescreen to the picture nails on the wall it was profoundly, unremittingly even, an expression of the Wiener Werkstätte.

As subsequent apartments show, it may or may not have been a profound expression of the Stonborough-Wittgenstein's sensibilities; Margaret, whose taste from childhood on had tended to be much more eclectic, remained attached in later life to many of the individual pieces in these rooms (including the inkwell) even as she drifted away from the corset this kind of thoroughly-designed interior represented.

122. INKWELL ACQUIRED BY HERMINE WITTGENSTEIN
FOR MARGARET STONBOROUGH-WITTGENSTEIN

Designed by Koloman Moser, Vienna 1904 (?)
Executed by the Wiener Werkstätte, model no. S 184
Made 1904 (?) for 160 crowns
One piece produced
Silver, lapis lazuli, coral
Vienna hallmark, KM, WW, rose mark
Diameter 11.5 cm/4.6 in. Weight 210 g/8.4 oz.
Ernst Ploil Collection

Charles Robert Ashbee,
silver inkpot
London 1900
Private collection

Tafel-Arrangement (Table setting) with Wiener Werkstätte items including a silver napkin ring similar to WW model no. S 354
with semi-precious stones

Illustration from *Deutsche Kunst und Dekoration,* vol. 19, p. 471, Darmstadt 1906–07.

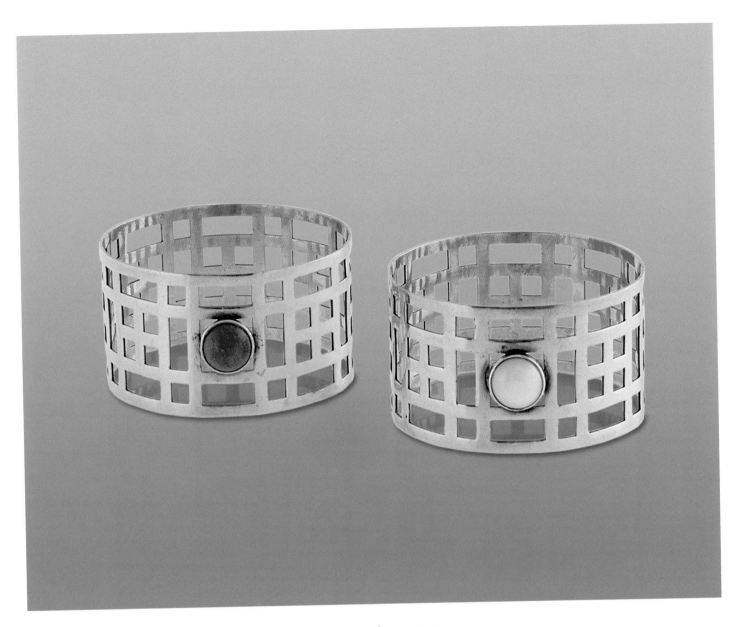

123. NAPKIN RINGS ACQUIRED BY THE WAERNDORFER/RÉMY FAMILY

Designed by Koloman Moser, Vienna 1904

Executed by the Wiener Werkstätte, model no. S 354

First made December, 1904 for fifteen crowns

Ninety-five pieces produced

Silver, amethyst, opal

Vienna hallmark, KM, WW, rose mark, Austrian control mark (*Amtsbuchstabe A*)

Diameter 5.1 cm/2 in. Weight 19 g/0.8 oz. (each)

Private collection

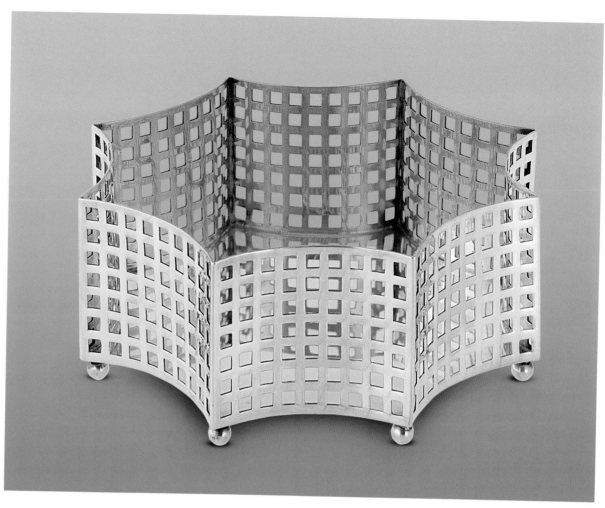

124. FRUIT BASKET
Designed by Koloman Moser, Vienna 1904
Executed by the Wiener Werkstätte, model no. S 377
First made November, 1904 for seventy crowns
Eleven pieces produced
Silver
Vienna hallmark, KM, WW, rose mark
Diameter 15.1 cm/6 in. Weight 186 g/7.4 oz.
Private collection

Marie Henneberg, possibly as a study for her
Gustav Klimt portrait
Vintage print, Dr. Hugo Henneberg (?), Vienna ca. 1901–02
Christian Witt-Dörring, Vienna

Josef Hoffmann, dining room in the residence of
Fritz and Lili Hellmann Waerndorfer
Contemporary photograph, Vienna 1902
MAK, Vienna

Fritz and Lili Hellmann Waerndorfer
Wedding photograph, Vienna ca. 1894–95
Private collection, Vienna

Fritz Waerndorfer, the industrialist financier of the Wiener Werkstätte, came from a wealthy family of cotton mill owners. In 1895 he married Lili Jeanette Hellmann. Theirs was a fast, fashionable, moneyed life: she is said to have been one of the first female drivers in Austria and to have raced automobiles. After the founding of the WW, the two commissioned alterations to their home in the so-called "cottage" district of Vienna by Josef Hoffmann, Koloman Moser, and Charles Rennie Mackintosh and his wife Margaret Macdonald, filling it with exquisite things made at the Werkstätte and by other artists associated with it. A cursory list of items acquired during the first three years of the WW's existence shows at least ninety-seven silver and silver-plated pieces—not including cutlery—that went to the Waerndorfers, from cigarette boxes and cachepots to children's toys; from toothpick holders to fruitbowls.

The "flat-model" cutlery, which rapidly achieved a certain notoriety among contemporary critics in the local and European press (one likened it to anatomical tools), was produced for a number of clients including Dr. Hermann Wittgenstein.

The Waerndorfers ordered a 106-piece set for their stark, geometrically-accented dining room.

"No other product from the Wiener Werkstätte," writes Christian Witt-Dörring, "elicited such vehement reactions as the 'flat' cutlery model." Among its enthusiastic admirers was Ludwig Hevesi, who, after dining with the Waerndorfers in 1905, claimed, "A sauce spoon could serve as the topic for a lecture on logic."[58]

Unfortunately, the Wiener Werkstätte became a money pit for Fritz Waerndorfer. In an autobiographical sketch of his father, Charley Waerndorfer (Warndof) noted bitterly that "The artists *all* abandoned him when he went bankrupt in 1913. He lost his and his wife's fortunes of 12,500,000 Kronen."[59] He emigrated from Austria, settling in the United States; he and Lili Hellmann Waerndorfer divorced in 1934. The Wiener Werkstätte itself declared bankruptcy in 1926 and, after several attempts at reorganization, closed its doors for good in 1932.

58 Christian Witt-Dörring, "Checklist: Viennese Decorative Arts around 1900," in Renée Price, ed., *New Worlds: German and Austrian Art 1890–1940*, Cologne 2001, p. 463.
59 Charley Waerndorfer (Warndof), unpubl. biographical sketch of Fritz Waerndorfer.

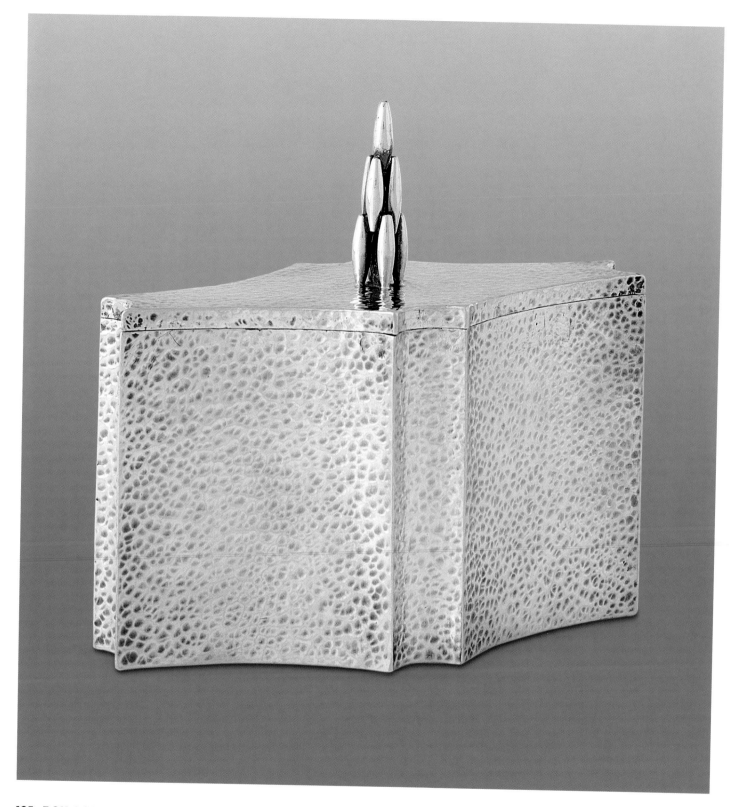

125. BOX ACQUIRED BY THE WAERNDORFER/HELLMANN FAMILY

Designed by Josef Hoffmann, Vienna 1904

Executed by the Wiener Werkstätte, model no. S 28 (Josef Holl)

First made 1904 for 180 crowns

Two pieces produced

Silver

Vienna hallmark, JH, JH, WW, rose mark, Austrian control mark *(Amtsbuchstabe A)*, Dutch import mark V

W 15.4 cm/6.1 in. Weight 518 g/20.7 oz.

Asenbaum Collection

126. FIVE PIECES FROM THE "FLAT MODEL" FLATWARE SERVICE, CONSISTING OF CRAB FORK, SARDINE SERVER, PASTRY SERVING SPOON, CHEESE KNIFE, AND BUTTER KNIFE

Designed by Josef Hoffmann, Vienna 1904–08

Executed by the Wiener Werkstätte, model nos. S 204, 231, 1009 (1907), 213, 214
First made 1904 for thirty crowns (cheese knife)
Nineteen cheese knives produced
Silver
Vienna hallmark, JH, WW, rose mark
L 17.3 cm/6.9 in. Weight 68 g/2.7 oz. (pastry serving spoon)
Private collection

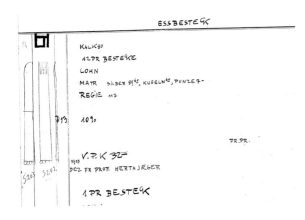

Order placed by Prof. Herta Jäger for "flat model" silver dessert knife and fork (WW model nos. S 202/203) designed by Josef Hoffmann
Wiener Werkstätte model book, Vienna, December 1903
MAK, Vienna

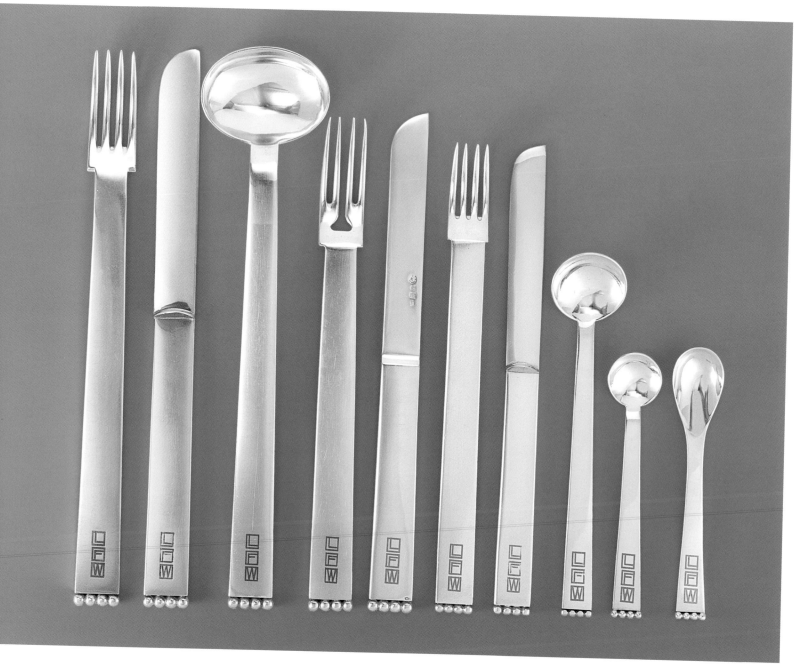

127. TEN PIECES FROM A 106-PART "FLAT MODEL" FLATWARE SERVICE ACQUIRED BY FRITZ AND LILI HELLMANN WAERNDORFER INCLUDING FORK, KNIFE, SPOON, FISH FORK, FISH KNIFE, FRUIT FORK, FRUIT KNIFE, COFFEE/TEASPOON, MOCHA SPOON AND SALT SPOON

Designed by Josef Hoffmann, Vienna 1904–08

Executed by the Wiener Werkstätte, model nos. S 24, 23, 25, 203, 202, 109, 108, 224, 266, 216
First made 1904 for twenty-seven crowns (spoon)
Silver, niello monogram LFW
Vienna hallmark, JH, WW, rose mark, Austrian control mark *(Amtsbuchstabe A)*
L 21.8 cm/8.7 in. Weight 60 g/2.4 oz. (spoon)
MAK, Vienna, inv. no. Go 2009/1967

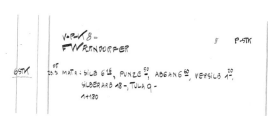

Order placed by Fritz Waerndorfer for "flat model" silver cutlery (WW model nos. S 202 and 203) designed by Josef Hoffmann

Wiener Werkstätte model book, Vienna, February/March 1905
MAK, Vienna

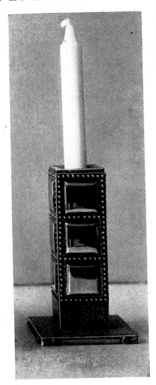

Körbchen
und Leuchter.
Silber-Arbeit.

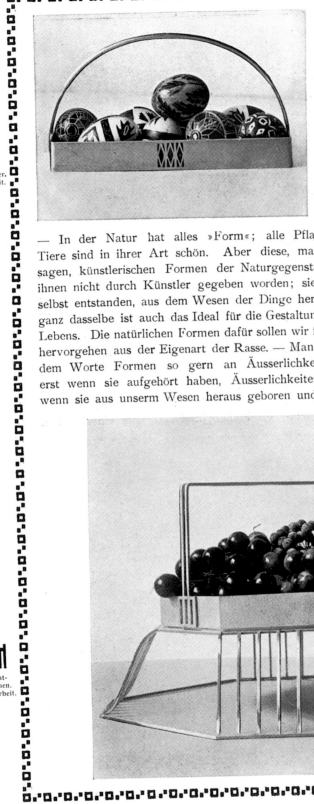

— In der Natur hat alles »Form«; alle Pflanzen und Tiere sind in ihrer Art schön. Aber diese, man möchte sagen, künstlerischen Formen der Naturgegenstände sind ihnen nicht durch Künstler gegeben worden; sie sind von selbst entstanden, aus dem Wesen der Dinge heraus. Und ganz dasselbe ist auch das Ideal für die Gestaltung unseres Lebens. Die natürlichen Formen dafür sollen wir finden, die hervorgehen aus der Eigenart der Rasse. — Man denkt bei dem Worte Formen so gern an Äusserlichkeiten; aber erst wenn sie aufgehört haben, Äusserlichkeiten zu sein, wenn sie aus unserm Wesen heraus geboren und der adae-

Frucht-
Körbchen.
Silber-Arbeit.

Josef Hoffmann, *Körbchen und Leuchter. Silber-Arbeit./Fruchtkörbchen. Silber-Arbeit.* (Silver Basket and Candlestick/Silver Fruit Basket) (WW model no. S 267), 1904

Illustration from *Deutsche Kunst und Dekoration*, vol. 15, p. 26, Darmstadt 1904–05.

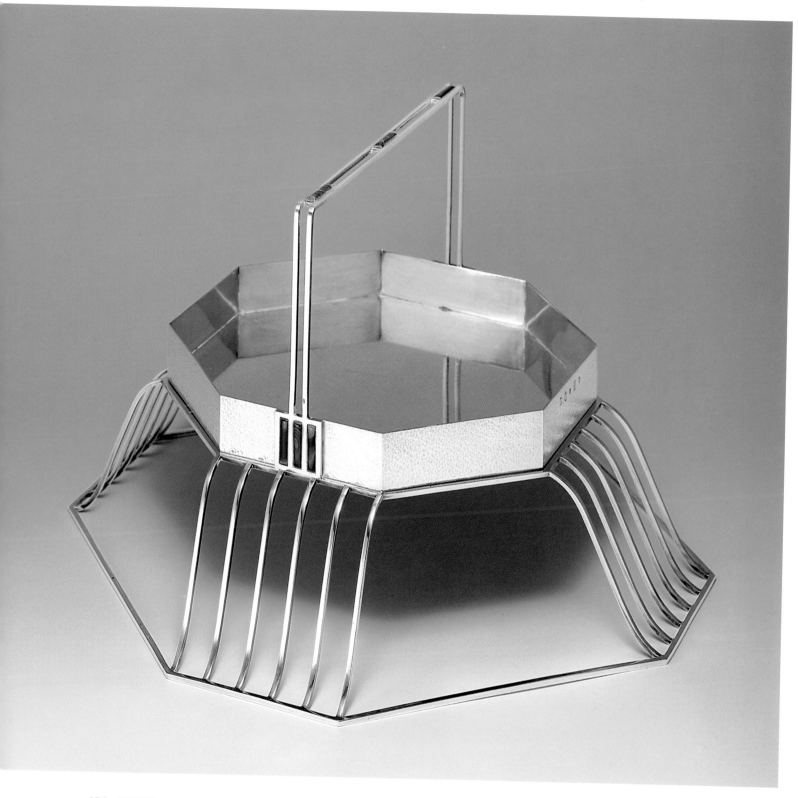

128. CENTERPIECE ACQUIRED BY H. HIRSCHWALD (HOHENZOLLERN-KUNSTGEWERBEHAUS, BERLIN)

Designed by Josef Hoffmann, Vienna 1904

Executed by the Wiener Werkstätte, model no. S 267 (Josef Hoszfeld)

Made 1904 for 450 crowns

One piece produced

Silver, malachite

Vienna hallmark, JH, JH, WW, rose mark

L/W 33.9 cm/13.6 in. Weight 850 g/34 oz.

Private collection

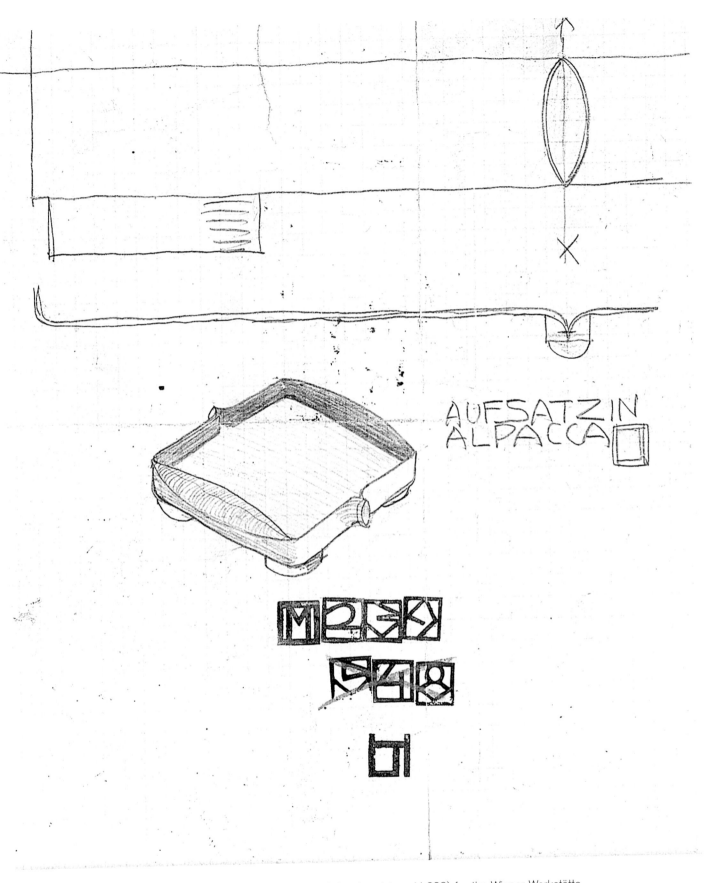

Josef Hoffmann, design for an *Aufsatz in Alpacca* (Alpacca tray) (WW model no. M 239) for the Wiener Werkstätte
Pencil and colored pencil, Vienna 1904
MAK, Vienna

129. TRAY

Designed by Josef Hoffmann, Vienna 1904

Executed by the Wiener Werkstätte, model no. M 239

First made December, 1904 for eighty crowns

Three pieces produced

Silver-plated alpacca, blue opaque glass

JH, WW, rose mark

L 33 cm/13.2 in.

Ernst Ploil Collection

Eingang zur Sonder-Ausstellung.
»Wiener Werkstätte«./Im Hohenzollern-
Kunstgewerbehaus, H. Hirschwald—Berlin,
Herbst 1904. (Entrance to the special
exhibit of the Wiener Werkstätte at the
Hohenzollern-Kunstgewerbehaus,
H. Hirschwald—Berlin, Fall 1904)
Illustration from *Deutsche Kunst und Dekoration*,
vol. 15, p. 203, Darmstadt 1904–05.

130. COFFEE POT

Designed by Josef Hoffmann, Vienna 1904

Executed by the Wiener Werkstätte, adaptation of model
no. S 292 (Adolf Erbrich)
Made November, 1904 for 220 crowns
One piece produced
Silver, ebony
Vienna hallmark, JH, AE, WW, rose mark
H 24.7 cm/9.9 in. Weight 500 g/20 oz.
Asenbaum Collection

In a letter to Josef Hoffmann regarding the Wiener Werkstätte, Charles Rennie Mackintosh wrote: "If one wants to achieve artistic success with your program (and artistic success must be your first thought) every object you pass from your hand must carry an outspoken mark of individuality, beauty, and the most exact execution."[60] This version of the Werkstätte coffee pot model no. S 292 demonstrates how Hoffmann and his colleagues took Mackintosh's admonition to heart. Far from descending to the noncommittal through its "plainness," the very terseness of its ornamental language combined with its skillful craftsmanship bears out the injunction. This stately object takes on an anthropomorphic dimension in its elegant elongation, its finial serving as the idiosyncratic dot on the "i" of individuality.

60 Eduard F. Sekler, *Josef Hofmann. The Architectural work*, Princeton 1985, p. 65.

Josef Hoffmann, *Prof. Josef Hoffmann Speisezimmer bei Herrn Dr. S.* (Dining room in the apartment of Dr. [Hans] S.[alzer]), 1902;
on the buffet in the left background stood a silver mustard pot by Josef Hoffmann (compare with cat. no. 104).
Illustration from *Das Interieur* 4, p. 2, Vienna 1903.

131. CRUET STAND (*KARAFFINE SAMT LÖFFEL*)
ACQUIRED BY IDA SALZER, NÉE FRANZ,
POSSIBLY FOR THE APARTMENT OF DR. JOHANNES ("HANS")
AND JOHANNA WITTGENSTEIN SALZER
Designed by Josef Hoffmann, Vienna 1904
Executed by the Wiener Werkstätte, model no. S 45 (Adolf Wertnik)
First made October, 1904 for 160 crowns
Two pieces produced
Silver, malachite
Vienna hallmark, JH, AW, WW, rose mark
H 17 cm/6.8 in. Weight 446 g/17.8 oz.
Asenbaum Collection

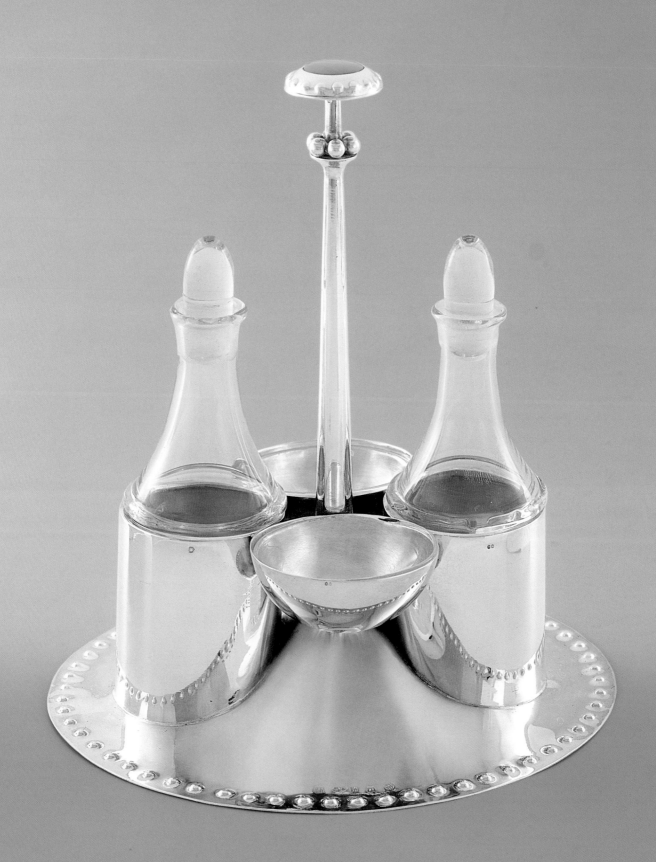

Karl Wittgenstein (with Biedermeier armchair)
Gelatin silver print, Ferdinand Schmutzer, Vienna 1908
© WestLicht, Vienna

Like the inkwell S 184, which appears to have been given to Margaret Stonborough-Wittgenstein by her sister as a wedding gift, another silver and semi-precious stone inkwell set made up of at least three pieces (inkstand S 122, blotter S 123, thermometer S 491) was evidently given by the industrialist Karl Wittgenstein and his wife to their daughter and son-in-law in 1905 for use in the Hoffmann-designed study of their Berlin apartment. Contemporary photographs show two components of this set in use on Jerome Stonborough's study desk. Hoffmann's use of neoclassical architecture as an inspiration is particularly notable in the plinth-like base of the inkstand and thermometer, as well as in their vertical features, which resemble pilasters or obelisks. "Much more up and down than sideways," as Hemingway once wrote about Switzerland,[64] these two pieces were well-suited to a room in which the vertical won out at the expense of the horizontal—even the curtains emphasized the room's height (unlike Margaret Stonborough's salon, where the desk and the curtains acted as counterweights to the verticals such as the lined wallpaper.) The blotter's elegant curve showed up again in a detail (door handle) of the sublime interior Hoffmann created for Karl Wittgenstein himself at his mountain retreat, Hochreit, in Lower Austria.

64 Ernest Hemingway "The Hotels in Switzerland," *Toronto Star Weekly*, March 4, 1922, reprinted in *Hemingway By-Line*, William White, ed., London 1989, p. 40.

134-3. THERMOMETER ACQUIRED BY LEOPOLDINE "POLDY" WITTGENSTEIN, NÉE KALLMUS, FOR THE BERLIN APARTMENT OF DR. JEROME STONBOROUGH AND MARGARET STONBOROUGH-WITTGENSTEIN

Designed by Josef Hoffmann, Vienna 1905
Executed by the Wiener Werkstätte, model no. S 491
First made August, 1905 for 180 crowns
Three square models produced
Silver
Vienna hallmark, JH, WW, rose mark
H 20 cm/8 in. Weight 325 g/13 oz.
Ellen and William Taubman Collection

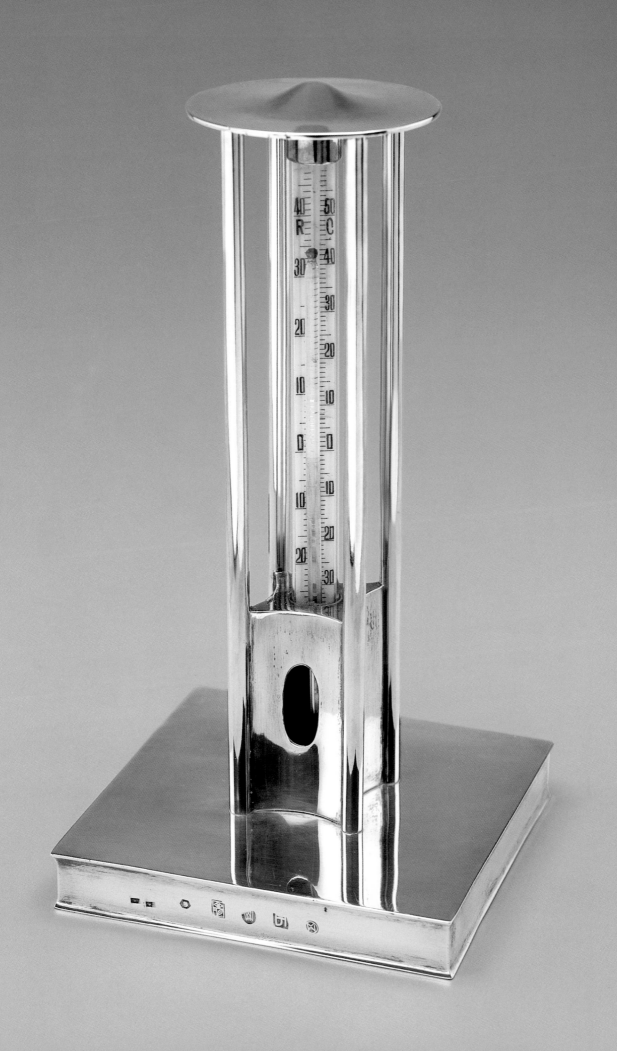

Margaret Stonborough-Wittgenstein with friends and relatives at a gathering in her residence at Kundmanngasse 19
(l–r: Marguerite Respinger; Margaret Stonborough-Wittgenstein; Primarius Foltanek; Carl "Talla" Sjögren; Ludwig Wittgenstein;
Arvid Sjögren; Count Georg Schönborn-Buchheim); note the Josef Hoffmann silver tea and coffee service, a variation of
WW model no. S 650, on the Josef Hoffmann coffee table.
Vintage print, Moritz Nähr, Vienna ca. 1930
Pierre and Françoise Stonborough, Vienna

Koloman Moser, silver *Deckelpokal* (Covered goblet)
(WW model S 501) with amber, 1905
Contemporary photograph (complete with lid) from the photo albums
of the Wiener Werkstätte
MAK, Vienna

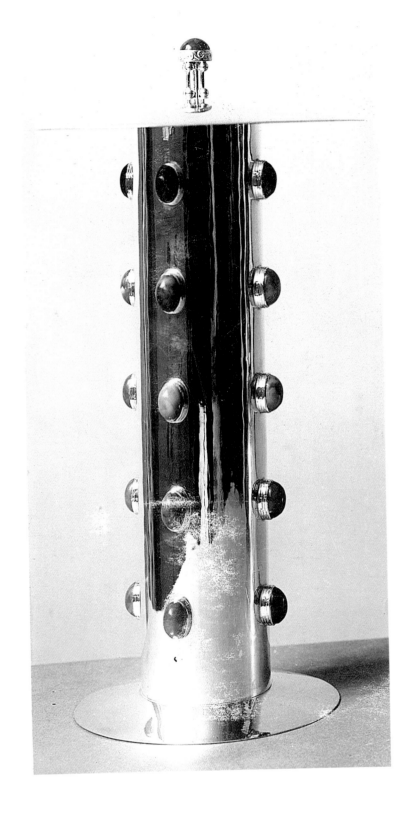

Archibald Knox, silver vase with enamel and turquoise
Executed by Liberty & Co., Birmingham 1904
Christie's, London

136. COVERED GOBLET (COVER MISSING)

Designed by Koloman Moser, Vienna 1905

Executed by the Wiener Werkstätte, model no. S 501 (Josef Hoszfeld)
Made May, 1906 for 300 crowns
One piece produced
Silver, amber
Vienna hallmark, KM, JH, WW, rose mark
H 22.2 cm/8.9 in.   Weight 317 g/12.7 oz.
MAK, Vienna, inv. no. Go 2016/1968

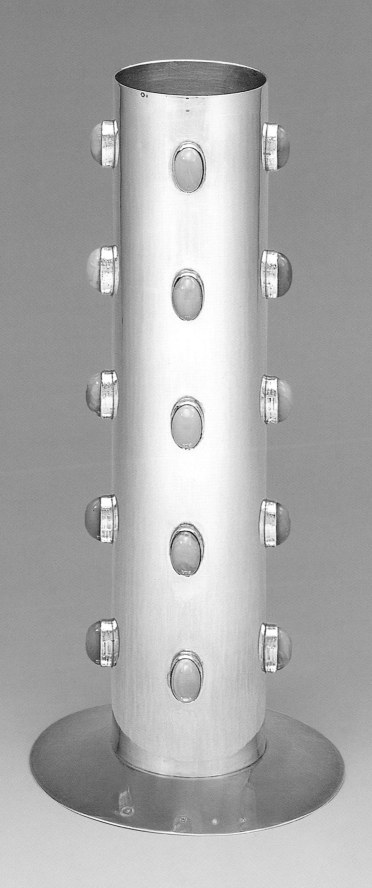

Adèle
WIEN.

I. GRABEN 19.

137. COFFER (*KASSETTE*)
ACQUIRED BY THE WAERNDORFER/HELLMANN FAMILY
Designed by Josef Hoffmann, Vienna 1905
Executed by the Wiener Werkstätte, model no. S 448 (Josef Wagner)
Made May, 1905 for 500 crowns
One piece produced
Silver, ebony, rock crystal
Vienna hallmark, JH, JW, WW, rose mark
L 25.8 cm/10.3 in. Weight 1,765 g/70.6 oz. (including wooden inset)
Asenbaum Collection

... a new golden age, new radiant and happy days seemed to return to the golf club, only perhaps names and manners, looks and clothing all betrayed something a bit too new and too brightly-colored to avoid eliciting the sometimes unjustified suspicion that all-too-new people and things are bound to evoke in an all-too-old world, a world in which neither novelty nor youth can ever replace the feeling for what is real.[65]

Curzio Malaparte, 1961

65 Curzio Malaparte, *Kaputt*, Vienna 1961, p. 375. English translation Michael Huey.

OPPOSITE PAGE: Lili Waerndorfer, née Hellmann
Vintage print, Adele Perlmutter, Vienna 1896
Private collection

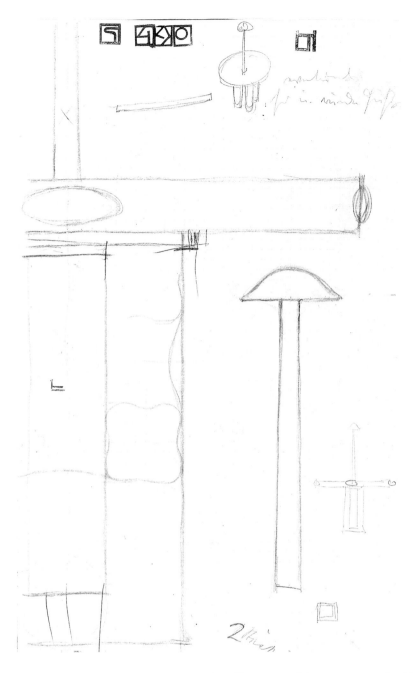

Josef Hoffmann, design for a silver *Aufsatz* (Centerpiece) (WW model no. S 490) with agates for the Wiener Werkstätte
Pencil and colored pencil, Vienna 1904–05
MAK, Vienna

138. CENTERPIECE
ACQUIRED BY DR. HERMANN WITTGENSTEIN
Designed by Josef Hoffmann, Vienna 1905
Executed by the Wiener Werkstätte, model no. S 490 (Josef Wagner)
First made February, 1905 for 650 crowns
Two pieces produced
Silver, agate
Vienna hallmark, JH, JW, WW, rose mark
H 43 cm/17.2 in. Weight 1,771 g/70.8 oz.
MAK, Vienna, inv. no. Go 2011/1967

Karl and Leopoldine Kallmus Wittgenstein
Vintage print, Adele Perlmutter, Vienna ca. 1875
Cecilia Sjögren, Vienna

Order placed by Leopoldine "Poldy" Wittgenstein, née Kallmus, for two silver *Senftiegel* (Mustard pots) (WW model no. S 458) with semi-precious stones designed by Josef Hoffmann
Wiener Werkstätte model book, Vienna 1905
MAK, Vienna

In April 1905, Leopoldine "Poldy" Kallmus Wittgenstein, the wife of industrialist Karl Wittgenstein, purchased a pair of matching mustard pots made of silver and semi-precious stones from the Wiener Werkstätte for 130 crowns apiece, possibly for use in her historicist town palace on Alleegasse, where, somewhat surprisingly, important Wiener Werkstätte and *Jugendstil* items such as a magnificent silver vitrine by Carl Otto Czeschka (see fig. p. 274) and the portrait of Margaret Stonborough-Wittgenstein by Gustav Klimt were mixed in. (Hoffmann's famous commission of the rooms at Hochreit, a Wittgenstein mountain estate, only took place in 1906; perhaps the mustard pots were purchased with the impending construction in mind, however.) The trail left by the provenance of the objects suggests that they may, alternatively, have been given to the Stonborough-Wittgensteins, who had married earlier the same year, for use in their Hoffmann/Moser apartment in Berlin. Indeed, this is one of the intriguing aspects of the two pieces: that they could have been used with equal plausibility in the plush, staid urban mansion of a sophisticated magnate and his wife; in the exquisite, jewel-box interior of an isolated hunting lodge; or in the avant-garde setting of an up-to-date apartment for a smart young newlywed couple.

The Secessionists themselves chose to emphasize the break they were making with the historicist past, but two highly influential figures in and around the movement—the financier Karl Wittgenstein and the painter and *éminence grise* Rudolf von Alt—were perhaps more representative of a connection to that past. It is instructive to compare the Alleegasse interiors and those of the Hoffmann room at Hochreit (just as it is, as Paul Wijdeveld has shown, to study the Alleegasse in the context of Ludwig Wittgenstein's "modern" house for Margaret Stonborough-Wittgenstein). From our vantage point today, they seem more obviously related than they might have earlier (see figs. 12 and 13 p. 347). The highly geometricalized and stylized spaces—particularly the part of them known in German as the *wandfeste Ausstattung* (the elements of décor actually attached to the walls, ceilings, and floors)—are both opportunities for the relentless display of lavish materials in an all-over design: gilt-edged beams, coffered ceilings, the prominent Venetian crystal chandelier, the large oval bevel-edged mirror, and the strongly-patterned carpet on the one hand are "contradicted" by gilt-edged beams, coffered walls, prominent crystal light fixtures, a large oval bevel-edged mirror above a credenza, and a strongly-patterned carpet on the other. If Hoffmann's Hochreit interior is neoclassical in certain aspects (proportion, clarity of line), it is eclectic in others (the styling of the *Gesamtkunstwerk* down to the minutest detail, its *horror vacui*). Hoffmann and Moser's mustard pots are poised with similar equivocality between the neoclassical and a Renaissance *Kunstkammer* object, a reason, perhaps, why they appealed to Leopoldine Wittgenstein.

139. MUSTARD POT
ACQUIRED BY LEOPOLDINE "POLDY" WITTGENSTEIN, NÉE KALLMUS

Designed by Koloman Moser (and Josef Hoffmann?), Vienna 1905

Executed by the Wiener Werkstätte, model no. S 458

First made April, 1905 for 130 crowns

Two pieces produced (both purchased by Leopoldine Wittgenstein)

Silver, agate, opal, moonstone, tiger's eye, tourmaline, jade, glass inset

Vienna hallmark, KM, WW, rose mark

H 10.1 cm/4 in. Weight 220 g/8.8 oz.

Asenbaum Collection

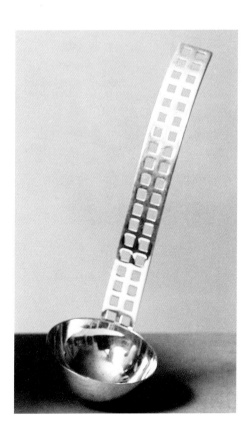

140. SUGAR BOWL (*STREUZUCKERBEHÄLTER*)

Designed by Josef Hoffmann, Vienna 1905

Executed by the Wiener Werkstätte, model no. S 609 (Adolf Wertnik)
First made November, 1905 for seventy-five crowns
Four pieces produced
Silver
Vienna hallmark, JH, AW, WW, rose mark
Diameter 20.3 cm/8.1 in. Weight 232.5 g/9.3 oz.
Private collection

Josef Hoffmann, Silver *Löffel* (Spoon)
(WW model S 610), 1905
Contemporary photograph from the photo albums
of the Wiener Werkstätte
MAK, Vienna

141. SUGAR BOWL AND SPOON

Designed by Josef Hoffmann, Vienna 1905

Executed by the Wiener Werkstätte, model no. S 582 (Josef Hoszfeld)

First made November 1905 for 120 crowns

Three pieces produced

Silver

Vienna hallmarks, JH, JH, WW, rose mark

Diameter 17.5 cm/7 in. Weight 282 g/11.3 oz.

Asenbaum Collection

Damen-Kleider Salon, Empfangsraum (Flöge sisters' fashion house reception room), furnished by Koloman Moser and the Wiener Werkstätte in 1904
Illustration from *Deutsche Kunst und Dekoration*, vol. 16, p. 524, Darmstadt 1905.

Emilie Flöge in the Flöge sisters' fashion house
Gelatin silver print, Madame d'Ora (Dora Kallmus)
Vienna, Fall 1910
© Imagno Brandstätter Images, Vienna

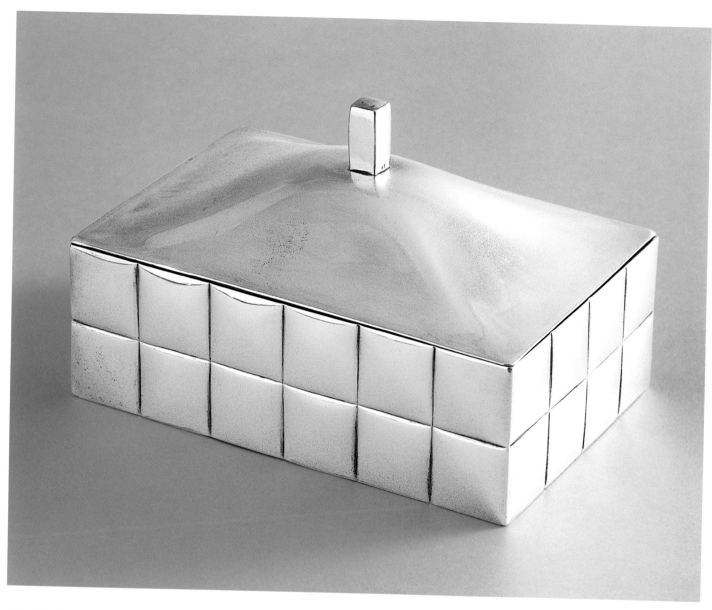

142. BOX ACQUIRED BY EMILIE FLÖGE

Designed by Josef Hoffmann, Vienna 1905

Executed by the Wiener Werkstätte, model no. S 585 (Josef Wagner)
First made October, 1905 for 250 crowns
Two pieces produced
Silver
Vienna hallmark, JH, WW, JW, rose mark
W 15.5 cm/6.2 in.   Weight 455 g/18.2 oz.
Private collection

One of two model no. S 585 silver boxes made by the Wiener Werkstätte belonged to Emilie Flöge, proprietress of the Flöge sisters' fashion boutique and intimate friend of her brother-in-law Gustav Klimt. (Emilie and Helene Flöge's salon on Mariahilferstrasse was, itself, designed by Koloman Moser and Josef Hoffmann in 1904, and it included a ravishingly-proportioned white-painted wood table by Moser now in a New York private collection.) The Flöges were proponents of wide, loose-fitting dresses for women and were considered—like their contemporary, Paul Poiret—liberators of the female form. The box here at hand is perhaps a fittingly sensual example of the Wiener Werkstätte's redefinition of the neoclassical canon and a playful take on the idea of constraint and liberation.

143. TEA AND COFFEE SERVICE ACQUIRED BY DR. HERMANN WITTGENSTEIN CONSISTING OF TRAY, TEAPOT, CREAMER, COFFEE POT, WATER JUG, SUGAR BOX, AND SUGAR TONGS

Designed by Josef Hoffmann, Vienna 1905

Executed by the Wiener Werkstätte, model nos. S 428, 493, 494, 495, 513, 514, 515 (Adolf Erbrich, Josef Holl, Josef Hoszfeld)

First made 1905 for 1,780 crowns (entire set)

One service produced (tray produced twice)

Silver, snakewood

Vienna hallmark, JH, AE, JH, JH, WW, rose mark

L (tray) 72 cm/28.8 in. H (coffee pot) 18 cm/7.2 in. Weight 5,308 g/212.3 oz.

Private collection

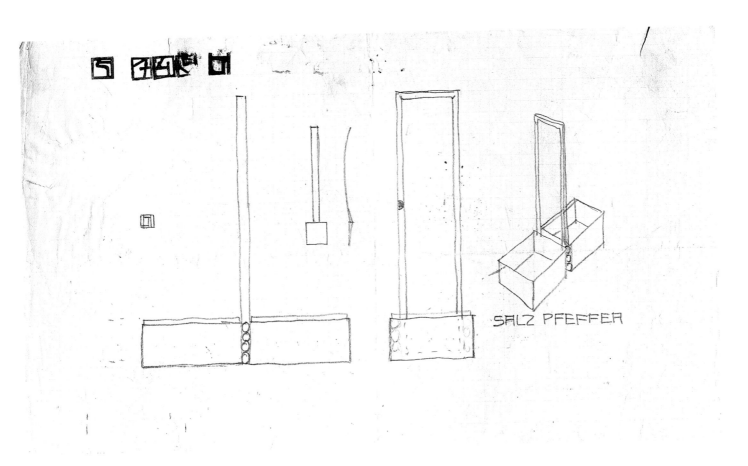

SALZ PFEFFER

Josef Hoffmann, design for silver *Salz u. Pfeffer Karaffen* (Salt and pepper cellars)
(WW model no. S 745) for the Wiener Werkstätte

Pencil, Vienna 1906
MAK, Vienna

144. SALT AND PEPPER CELLAR (*SALZ U. PFEFFER KARAFFEN*)

Designed by Josef Hoffmann, Vienna 1906

Executed by the Wiener Werkstätte, model no. S 745 (Adolf Wertnik)

First made September, 1906 for sixty crowns

Six pieces produced

Silver, original glass insets

Vienna hallmark, JH, AW, WW, rose mark

H 12.5 cm/5 in. Weight 161 g/6.4 oz.

Asenbaum Collection

Josef Hoffmann, *Kaffeegarnitur. Silber und Schlangenholz* (Silver and snakewood coffee [and tea] service),
executed by the Wiener Werkstätte in 1906
Illustration from *Deutsche Kunst und Dekoration*, vol. 22, p. 90, Darmstadt 1908.

145. COFFEE POT PURCHASED BY JENNY MAUTNER AND MORIZ SCHUR FOR KÄTHY BREUER, NÉE MAUTNER

Designed by Josef Hoffmann, Vienna 1906
Executed by the Wiener Werkstätte, model no. S 650 (Alfred Mayer)
Made January, 1906 for 180 crowns
One piece produced
Silver, snakewood
Vienna hallmark, JH, WW, AM, rose mark
H 23 cm/9.2 in. Weight 450 g/18 oz.
Private collection

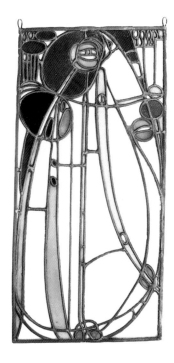

Charles Rennie Mackintosh,
glass panel
Glasgow 1902
Hunterian Art Gallery, University of Glasgow,
Mackintosh Collection

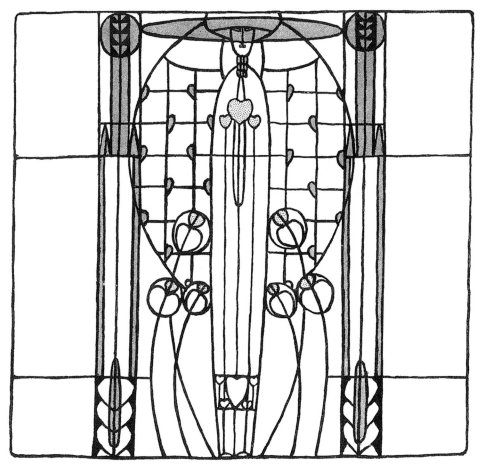

ENTWURF FÜR EIN GLASFENSTER

Josef Hoffmann, *Entwurf für ein Glasfenster* (Design for a glass window), 1901
Illustration from *Das Interieur* 2, p. 193, Vienna 1901.

146. *BONBONNIÈRE*

Designed by Josef Hoffmann, Vienna 1906

Executed by the Wiener Werkstätte, model no. S 485 (Josef Hoszfeld)

Made May, 1906 for 350 crowns

One piece produced

Silver, lapis lazuli

Vienna hallmark, JH, JH, WW, rose mark

H 18.5 cm/ 7.4 in. Weight 460 g/18.4 oz.

Asenbaum Collection

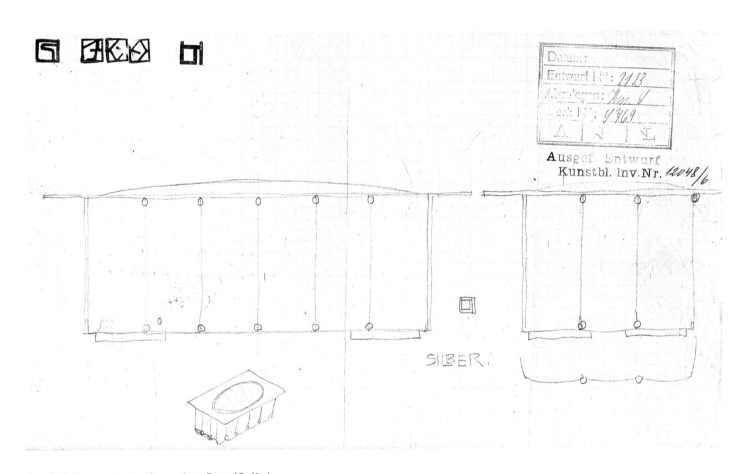

Josef Hoffmann, design for a silver *Dose* (Coffer)
(WW model no. S 769) for the Wiener Werkstätte
Pencil, Vienna 1906
MAK, Vienna

147. COFFER

Designed by Josef Hoffmann, Vienna 1906

Executed by the Wiener Werkstätte, model no. S 769 (Josef Wagner)

First made October, 1906 for 300 crowns

Two pieces produced

Silver

Vienna hallmark, JH, JW, WW, rose mark

W 19.2 cm/7.7 in. Weight 563 g/22.5 oz.

Ernst Ploil Collection

Jože Plečnik, façade of Langer apartment building at Steggasse 1, V district
Vienna 1901–03
Photo: Michael Huey, Vienna

148. JEWELRY BOX
Designed by Koloman Moser, Vienna 1907
Executed by the Wiener Werkstätte, model no. S 914 (Adolf Erbrich)
Made December, 1907 for 1,000 crowns
One piece produced
Silver, ebony, agate
Vienna hallmark, KM, AE, WW, rose mark
W 27.4 cm/11 in. Weight 2,725 g/109 oz.
Asenbaum Collection

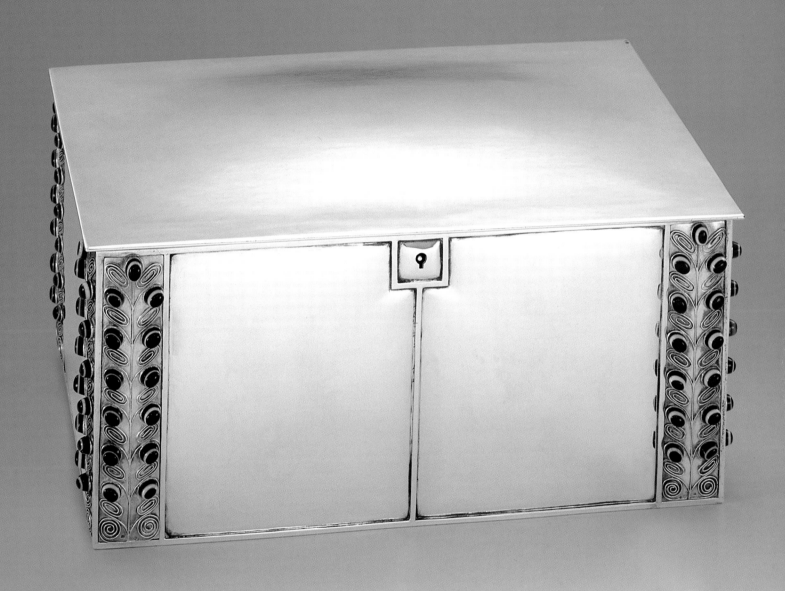

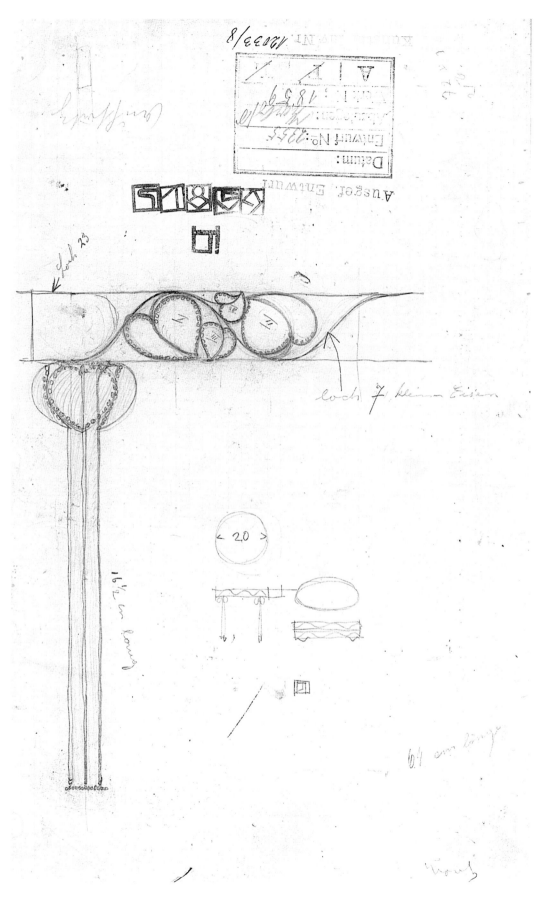

Josef Hoffmann, design for a silver *Aufsatz* (Centerpiece)
(WW model no. S 1859) for the Wiener Werkstätte

Pencil, Vienna 1910
MAK, Vienna

149. CENTERPIECE

Designed by Josef Hoffmann, Vienna 1910

Executed by the Wiener Werkstätte, model no. S 1859 (Adolf Wertnik)

First made February, 1910 for 360 crowns

Three pieces produced

Silver

Vienna hallmark, JH, AW, WW, rose mark

H 19.1 cm/7.6 in. Weight 729 g/29.2 oz.

Asenbaum Collection

Lebkuchen & Bäckerei (Gingerbread and baked goods) stand at the *Kunstschau* Vienna 1908 with society ladies in Wiener Werkstätte clothing and jewelry (center: Editha Moser, née Mautner von Markhof, the wife of Koloman Moser); a sign in the background proclaims that the gingerbread was "designed" by Koloman Moser and Carl Otto Czeschka.
Vintage print, Josef Justh, Vienna 1908
MAK, Vienna

151. TAZZA (*BONBONTASSE*)

Designed by Josef Hoffmann, Vienna 1912

Executed by the Wiener Werkstätte, model no. S 2610

First made March, 1912 for 270 crowns

Two pieces produced

Silver, lapis lazuli

Vienna hallmark, JH, WW, rose mark, Austrian control mark (*Amtsbuchstabe A*)

W/D 15.6 cm/6.2 in. Weight 281 g/11.3 oz.

Private collection

VIENNA'S EXPERIMENT
OF MODERNITY

Josef Hoffmann, overdoor relief panel for the fourteenth exhibition of the Vienna Secession
Vintage print, Vienna 1902
Photo: Österreichische Nationalbibliothek, Vienna, Bildarchiv

Adolf Loos, architectural model of the *Würfelhaus* (Cube house), address unknown
Vienna ca. 1929
Albertina, Vienna

Some of the most radical work from the Wiener Werkstätte was produced in the earliest period of the firm's existence, from 1903 to 1906. Much of this work, in which Hoffmann and Moser experimented with ideas about volume and scale, was executed—as though the pieces were prototypes, or maquettes—not in silver and other precious metals, but in silver-plated alpacca or (seldom, but occasionally) gold-plated metal. Some designs were so architectural or sculptural in nature that they seem at first glance to have been conceived either as architectural models or as objects with no purpose at all, other than that of expressing a kind of brutal beauty. (In fact, the Wiener Werkstätte took to photographing these items in use—often with odd or clumsy flower and fruit arrangements—as if to demonstrate, to *insist,* really, that they did have a purpose.) These protests notwithstanding, what this work had to say was more about structure and the interplay of volumes than about the needs of everyday life. The shapes were those of basic geometry; the attitude was that of constructivism. They are Vienna's contribution to the history of the Modern movement, ambivalent artifacts caught in a space somewhere between design and art.

Paul Engelmann and Ludwig Wittgenstein, *Gretl's Haus, Kundmanngasse* (house designed for Margaret Stonborough-Wittgenstein in 1926–28 at Kundmanngasse 19, III district, as designated by Helene Salzer, née Wittgenstein)

Vintage postcard, Moritz Nähr, Vienna, Spring 1929

© Wittgenstein Archive, Cambridge

The work of the craftsman should be measured by the same standard as that of the painter and the sculptor.[66]

66 Josef Hoffmann, Koloman Moser, and Fritz Waerndorfer, "Das Arbeitsprogramm der Wiener Werkstätte," (Working Program of the Wiener Werkstätte), in *Hohe Warte*, 15, 1, 1904–05, p. 268. English translation Michael Huey.

Josef Hoffmann, silver-plated alpacca *Jardinière* (Cachepot) (WW model no. M 459)
Executed by the Wiener Werkstätte, Vienna 1905
Musée d'Orsay, Paris

Alexander Rodchenko, *Spatial Construction No. 21*
Wooden blocks, Moscow 1921

152. COFFER

Designed by Josef Hoffmann, Vienna 1904

Executed by the Wiener Werkstätte, model no. M 238 (Franz Guggenbichler)

First made August, 1904 for 110 crowns

Six pieces produced

Silver-plated alpacca, copper

JH, FG, WW, rose mark

W/D 16.9 cm/6.8 in.

Asenbaum Collection

Josef Hoffmann, white metal *Eisform* (Ice cream mold) (WW model no. M 54)
Vienna 1903
Contemporary photograph from the photo albums of the Wiener Werkstätte
MAK, Vienna

Georges Vantongerloo, *Rapport des Volumes*
Stone, Brussels 1911
Archiv Max Bill c/o Max, Binia + Jakob Bill Stiftung, Adligenswil

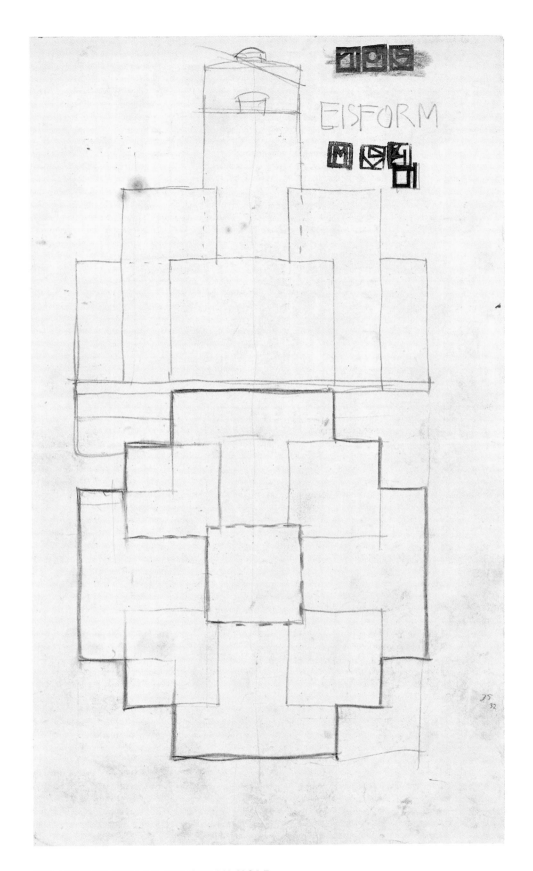

EISFORM

153. DESIGN FOR AN ICE CREAM MOLD

Josef Hoffmann, Vienna 1903

Pencil and colored pencil on graph paper

33.8 x 20.4 cm/13.5 x 8.2 in.

MAK, Vienna, inv. no. KI 12082/15

Josef Hoffmann, white metal *Eisform* (Ice cream mold) (WW model no. M 57)
Vienna 1903
Contemporary photograph from the photo albums of the Wiener Werkstätte
MAK, Vienna

Kasimir Malevich, porcelain teapot
Executed by the State Porcelain Manufactory, Petrograd 1923
The State Russian Museum, St. Petersburg

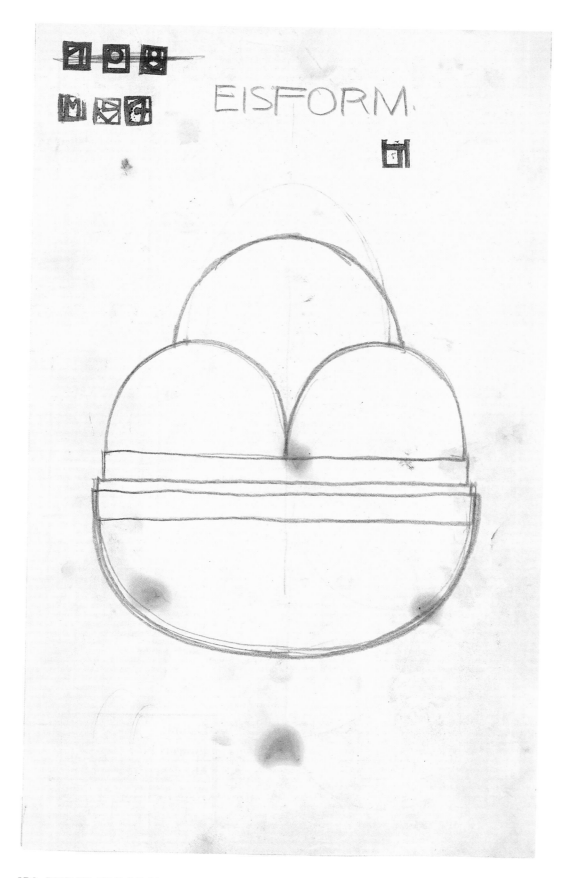

EISFORM.

154. DESIGN FOR AN ICE CREAM MOLD
Josef Hoffmann, Vienna 1903
Pencil and colored pencil on graph paper
31.5 x 20.2 cm/12.6 x 8.1 in.
MAK, Vienna, inv. no. KI 12082/13

Koloman Moser, gold-plated metal *Blumenvase*
(Flower vase) (WW model no. M 17)

Contemporary photograph from the photo albums of the Wiener
Werkstätte, Vienna 1904

MAK, Vienna

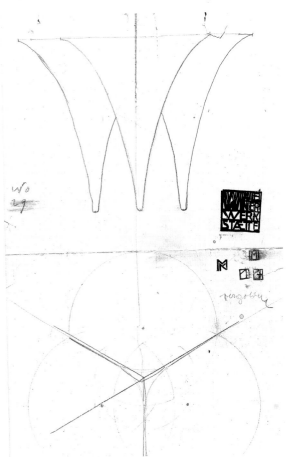

Koloman Moser, design for a gold-plated metal
Blumenvase (Flower vase) (WW model no. M 17)
for the Wiener Werkstätte

Pencil, Vienna 1904
MAK, Vienna

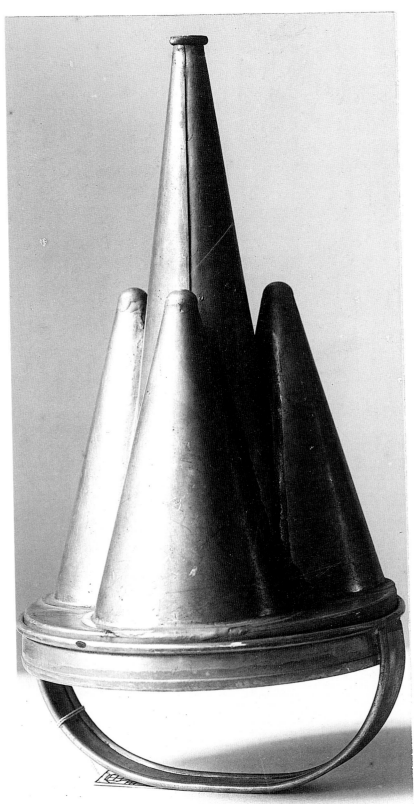

Josef Hoffmann, white metal *Eisform* (Ice cream mold)
(WW model no. M 55)

Vienna 1903
Contemporary photograph from the photo albums of the Wiener Werkstätte
MAK, Vienna

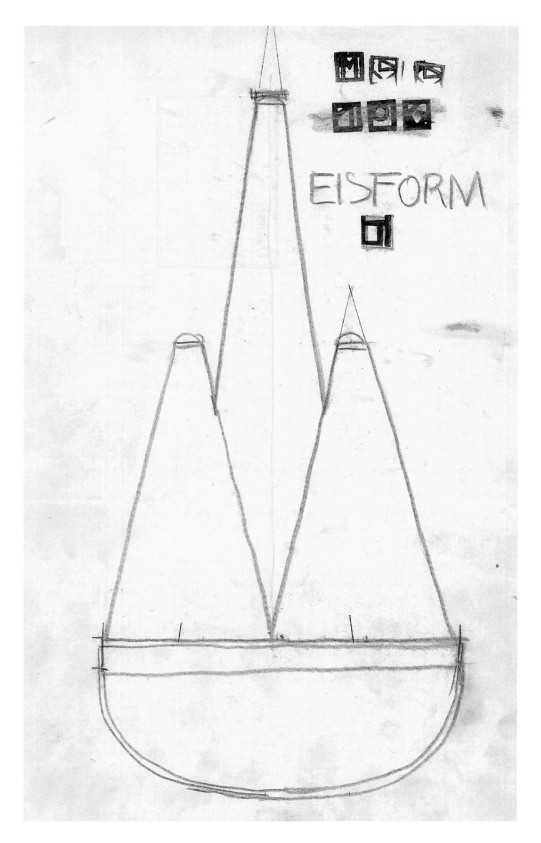

155. DESIGN FOR AN ICE CREAM MOLD

Josef Hoffmann, Vienna 1903

Pencil and colored pencil on graph paper
32.5 x 20.7 cm/13 x 8.3 in.
MAK, Vienna, inv. no. KI 12082/14

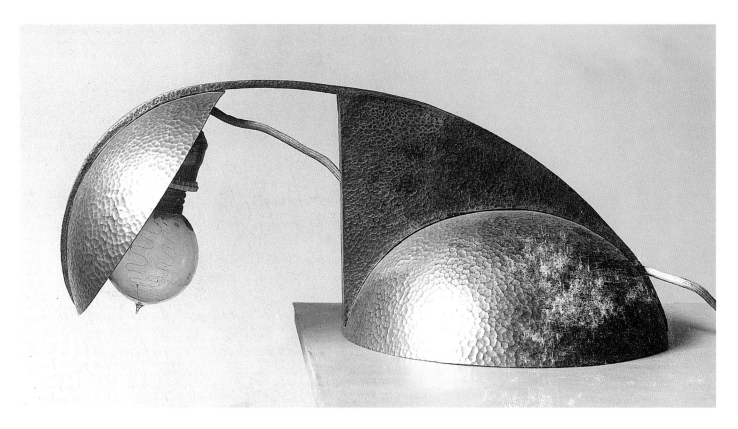

Josef Hoffmann, silver-plated alpacca *Clavierlampe* (Piano lamp) (WW model no. M 42)
Vienna ca. 1904
Contemporary photograph from the photo albums of the Wiener Werkstätte.
MAK, Vienna

Gerrit Rietveld, painted beechwood end table
for the Schröder House
Utrecht 1923
Stedelijk Museum, Amsterdam

156. LAMP
(STEHLAMPE FÜR ELEKTRISCHES LICHT)
Designed by Koloman Moser, Vienna 1903
Executed by the Wiener Werkstätte, model no. M 89
First made 1903 for 110 crowns
Eight pieces produced
Silver-plated alpacca, glass
KM, WW, rose mark
H 38 cm/15.2 in.
Ernst Ploil Collection

Josef Hoffmann or Koloman Moser, silver-plated copper
Zündholzständer klein (Small match holder)
(WW model no. M 577)
Vienna 1906
Contemporary photograph from the photo albums of the Wiener Werkstätte
MAK, Vienna

Georges Vantongerloo, *Constructie in de bol* (Construction
in the Sphere)
Painted wood, Brussels 1918
Vintage print
Frank den Oudsten, Amsterdam

Josef Hoffmann, silver-plated alpacca *Blumen-Gefäss* (Cachepot) (WW model no. M 48)
Vienna 1904
Contemporary photograph from the photo albums of the Wiener Werkstätte
MAK, Vienna

157. COFFER

Designed by Josef Hoffmann, Vienna 1904

Executed by the Wiener Werkstätte, model no. M 230

First made October, 1904 for eighty crowns

Twelve pieces produced

Silver-plated alpacca

JH, WIENER/WERK/STÄTTE, rose mark

W/D 15.7 cm/6.3 in.

Ernst Ploil Collection

Kasimir Malevich, *Architecton Gota*
Plaster, Moscow 1923 (?)
The State Russian Museum, St. Petersburg

158. VASE
(*BLUMENVASE VIERTEILIG*)
Designed by Josef Hoffmann, Vienna 1904
Executed by the Wiener Werkstätte, model no. M 73
(Josef Berger)
First made August, 1905 for ninety crowns
Six pieces produced
Silver-plated brass, brass
JH, JB, WW, rose mark
H 29 cm/11.6 in.
Ernst Ploil Collection

Josef Hoffmann, silver-plated alpacca *Weinkühler* (Wine cooler) (WW Model no. M 63) acquired by Karl Wittgenstein
Executed by the Wiener Werkstätte, Vienna 1903
Private collection

159. BOX

Designed by Koloman Moser,
Vienna 1904

Executed by the Wiener Werkstätte,
model no. M 186 (Karl Kallert)
First made 1904 for sixty crowns
Four pieces produced
Silver-plated alpacca
KM, CK, WW, rose mark
W 11.5 cm/4.6 in.
Ernst Ploil Collection

160. BOX

Designed by Josef Hoffmann,
Vienna ca. 1904

Executed by the Wiener Werkstätte
Silver-plated alpacca
JH, WW, rose mark
L 18.1 cm/7.2 in.
Ernst Ploil Collection

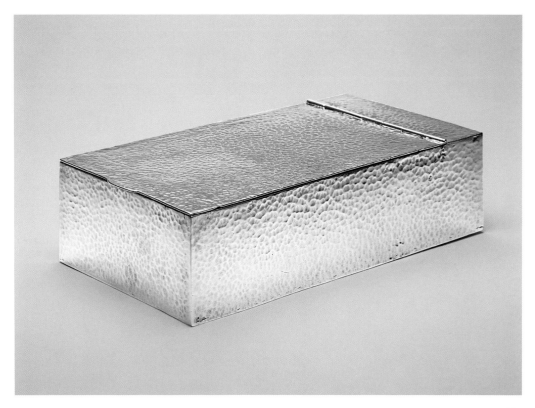

Josef Hoffmann, silver-plated alpacca
Blumen-Gefäss (Cachepot) (WW model
no. M 52)
Executed by the Wiener Werkstätte, Vienna 1903
Contemporary photograph from the photo albums
of the Wiener Werkstätte.
MAK, Vienna

Theo van Doesburg, model of
a *maison particulière*
Gouache on print, Leiden 1923
Haags Gemeentemuseum, The Hague

161. ASHTRAY (*CIGARRENSCHALE*)

Designed by Koloman Moser, Vienna 1904

Executed by the Wiener Werkstätte, model no. M 80
First made 1904 for forty crowns
Nineteen pieces produced
Silver-plated copper
KM, WW, rose mark
W/D 10.7 cm/4.3 in.
Asenbaum Collection

162. ASHTRAY (*CIGARRENSCHALE*)

Designed by Josef Hoffmann, Vienna 1904

Executed by the Wiener Werkstätte, model no. M 80
(Karl Medl)
First made 1904 for forty crowns
Nineteen pieces produced
Silver-plated alpacca
JH, MK, WW, rose mark
W/D 15 cm/6 in.
Ernst Ploil Collection

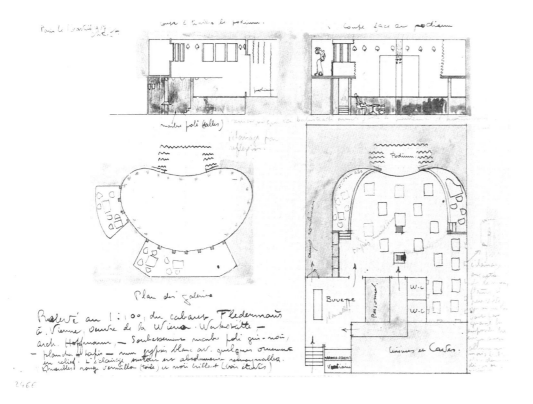

Le Corbusier, floorplan of Josef Hoffmann's Kabarett Fledermaus (1907)

Pencil and colored pencil, Vienna 1907–08

© Fondation Le Corbusier, Paris

Le Corbusier, Villa Savoye

Poissy 1928–30

Illustration from Edward Lucie-Smith, *Visual Arts in the Twentieth Century*, London 1996.

163. BOX WITH GLASS INSET

Designed by Josef Hoffmann, Vienna 1906

Executed by the Wiener Werkstätte, model no. M 563 (Josef Berger)

First made March, 1906 for fifty crowns

Two pieces produced

Silver-plated alpacca

JH, JB, WW, rose mark

Diameter 14.8 cm/5.9 in.

Asenbaum Collection

Walter Gropius, Fagus Werke
Alfeld/Leine, Germany, 1910–14
© artur/Photo: Klaus Frahm

164. ASHTRAY (*ASCHEN-SCHALE*)

Designed by Josef Hoffmann, Vienna 1904

Executed by the Wiener Werkstätte, model no. M 11

First made 1904 for thirty crowns

Four pieces produced

Copper

JH, WW, rose mark

Diameter 11.3 cm/4.5 in.

Ernst Ploil Collection

Richard Rogers & Partners, Lloyd's of London headquarters
London 1979
© Norman McGrath Photographer, Inc., New York

166. VASE (*BLUMENSTÄNDER*)

Designed by Josef Hoffmann, Vienna 1905

Executed by the Wiener Werkstätte, model no. M 457 (Johann Blaschek)
First made November, 1905 for eighty crowns
Two pieces produced
Silver-plated alpacca
JH, JB, WW, rose mark
H 29 cm/11.6 in.
Asenbaum Collection

165. VASE (*BLUMENSTÄNDER*)

Designed by Josef Hoffmann, Vienna 1905

Executed by the Wiener Werkstätte, model no. M 458 (Josef Berger)
First made October, 1905 for ninety crowns
Two pieces produced
Silver-plated alpacca
JH, JB, WW, rose mark
H 27.8 cm/11.1 in.
Asenbaum Collection

David Connor with Julian Powell-Tuck and Gunnar Orefelt, Villa Zapu, house for Thomas Lundstrom

Napa Valley, California 1984

Photo: Tim Street-Porter, Los Angeles

167. *JARDINIÈRE (BLUMENVASE)*

Designed by Koloman Moser, Vienna 1903

Executed by the Wiener Werkstätte, model no. M 18 (Adolf Wertnik)

First made July, 1903 for seventy crowns

Six pieces produced

Silver-plated alpacca

KM, AW, WW, rose mark

L 26.6 cm/10.6 in.

Asenbaum Collection

Josef Hoffmann, sheet iron, white-painted *Henkelkörbchen*
(Basket with handle) (WW model no. M 538)
Vienna 1906
Contemporary photograph from the photo albums of the Wiener Werkstätte
MAK, Vienna

Aldo Rossi, San Cataldo Cemetery
Modena 1971–73
© artur/Photo: Wolfram Jantzer

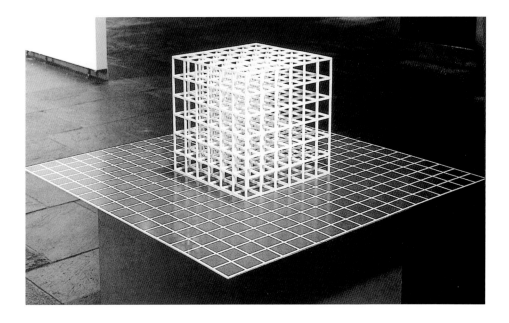

Sol LeWitt, *Untitled Cube (6)* 1968
Whitney Museum of American Art, New York

168. MANTEL CLOCK (*PENDELUHR MIT HALBSTUNDENSCHLAG*)

Designed by Josef Hoffmann, Vienna 1904
Executed by the Wiener Werkstätte, model no. M 171
Made 1904 for 300 crowns
One piece produced
Zinc-plated sheet iron, painted white; antiqued copper,
silver-plated brass, beveled glass
H 30 cm/12 in.
Ernst Ploil Collection

313

**169. FLOWER BASKET
(*BLUMENKÖRBCHEN*)**

Designed by Josef Hoffmann, Vienna 1906

Executed by the Wiener Werkstätte, model no. M 1014
First made December, 1906 for seventy crowns
Fifty-seven pieces produced
Silver-plated alpacca
WW, rose mark
H 29.1 cm/11.6 in.
Private collection

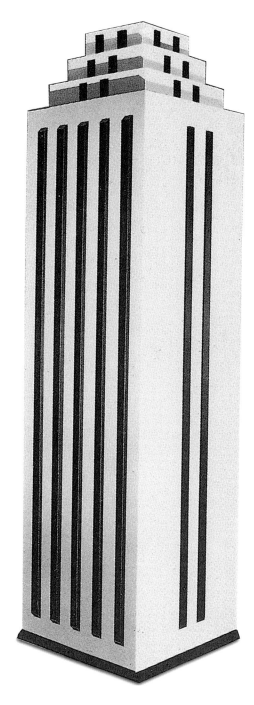

Rolf Pendias, "Skyline" cabinet, 1980s
Illustration from *Design Heute: Maßstäbe: Form-
gebung zwischen Industrie und Kunst-Stück*, exh. cat.
Deutsches Architekturmuseum, Frankfurt am Main
1988, p. 13.

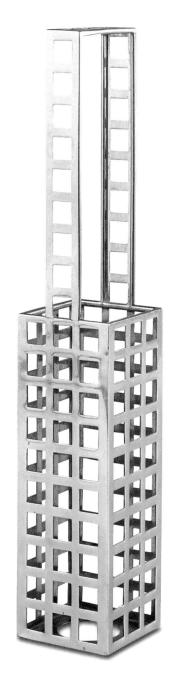

**170. FLOWER BASKET
(*BLUMENKÖRBCHEN*)**

Designed by Josef Hoffmann, Vienna 1905

Executed by the Wiener Werkstätte, model no. S 661
First made December, 1905 for twenty-five crowns
296 pieces produced
Silver, glass inset
Vienna hallmark, JH, WW, rose mark
H 24.2 cm/9.7 in. Weight 123 g/4.9 oz.
Private collection

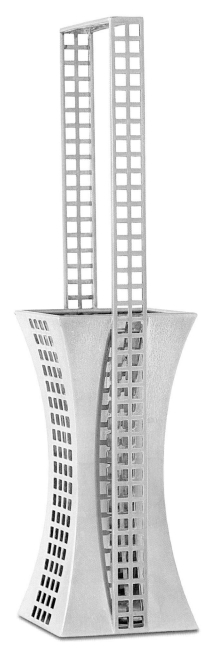

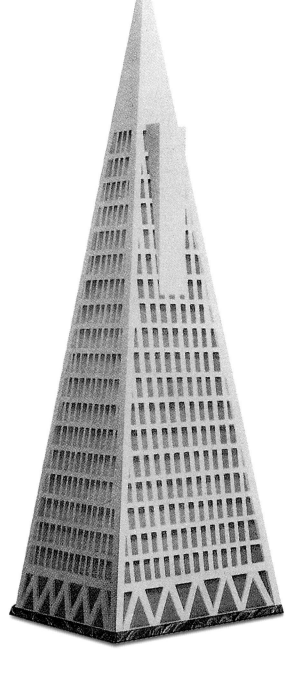

Rolf Pendias, "Skyline" cabinet, 1980s
Illustration from *Design Heute: Maßstäbe: Form-*
gebung zwischen Industrie und Kunst-Stück, exh. cat.
Deutsches Architekturmuseum, Frankfurt am Main
1988, p. 12.

171. FLOWER BASKET
(*BLUMENKÖRBCHEN*)
Designed by Josef Hoffmann, Vienna 1906
Executed by the Wiener Werkstätte, model no. S 768
First made November, 1906 for seventy crowns
Fifty-two pieces produced
Nickel-plated alpacca, glass inset
WW, rose mark
H 26.6 cm/10.6 in.
Private collection

Rolf Pendias, "Skyline" cabinet, 1980s
Illustration from *Design Heute: Maßstäbe: Form-*
gebung zwischen Industrie und Kunst-Stück, exh. cat.
Deutsches Architekturmuseum, Frankfurt am Main
1988, p. 12.

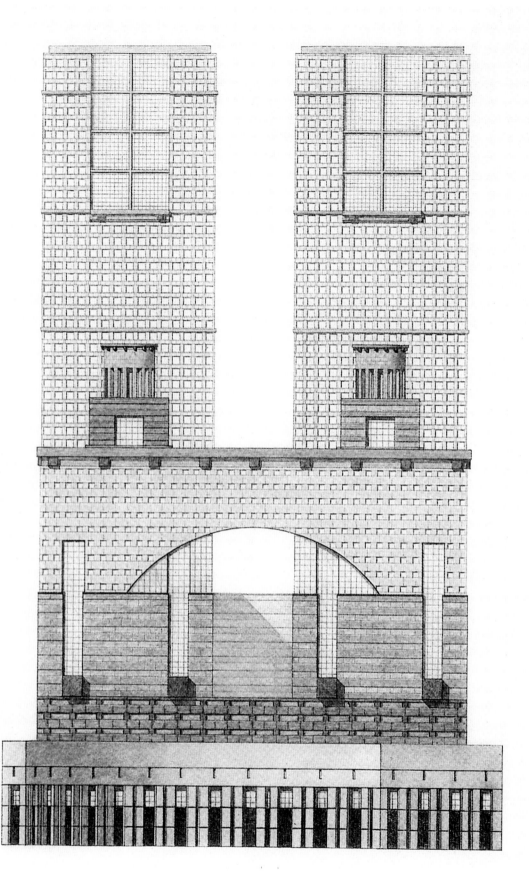

Michael Graves, plan for Columbus Circle redevelopment, view from Central Park
New York 1985
Illustration from Theodore L. Brown/Maurizio De Vita, eds., *Michael Graves: Idee e progetti 1981–1991*, Milano 1991.

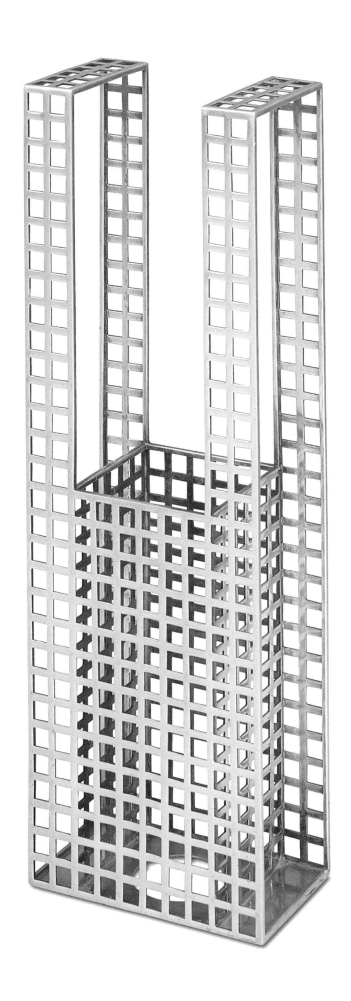

**172. FLOWER BASKET
(*BLUMENKÖRBCHEN GROSS*)**

Designed by Koloman Moser, Vienna 1906

Executed by the Wiener Werkstätte, model no. S 781

First made October, 1906 for sixty crowns

Ten pieces produced

Silver

Vienna hallmark, JH, WW, rose mark

H 21.3 cm/8.5 in. Weight 165 g/6.6 oz.

Private collection

Rafael Viñoly Architects PC, virtual design for the Samsung Cultural Education and Entertainment Center in Seoul
Planning and construction 1990–99

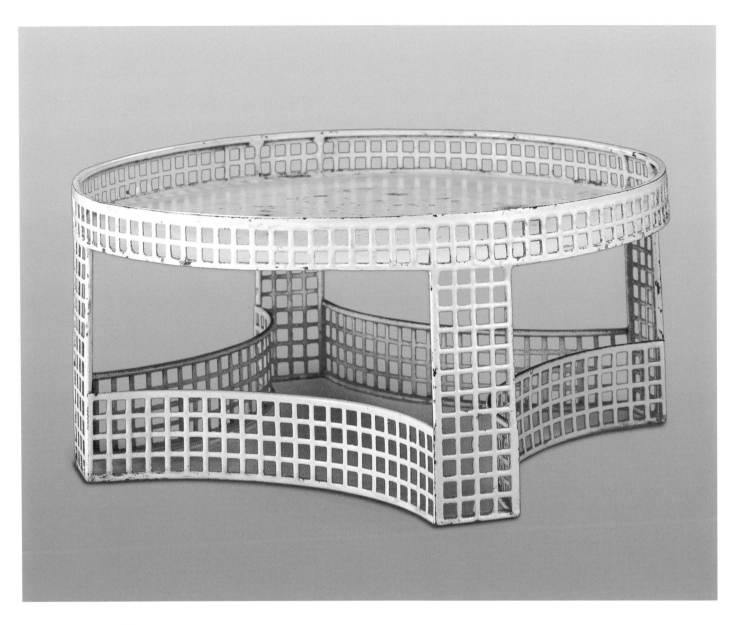

173. CENTERPIECE

Designed by Josef Hoffmann, Vienna 1904

Executed by the Wiener Werkstätte, model no. M 266
First made October, 1904 for sixty crowns
Seventy-nine pieces produced
Zinc-plated sheet iron, painted white
WIENER/WERK/STÄTTE (black rubber stamp)
Diameter 24 cm/9.6 in.
Ernst Ploil Collection

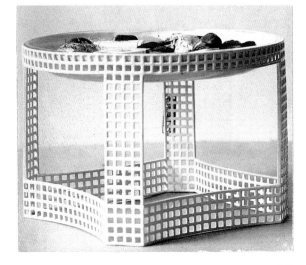

Josef Hoffmann, sheet iron, white-painted
Körbchen (Basket) (WW model no.
M 266/M 716), Vienna 1907

Contemporary photograph from the photo albums of
the Wiener Werkstätte
MAK, Vienna

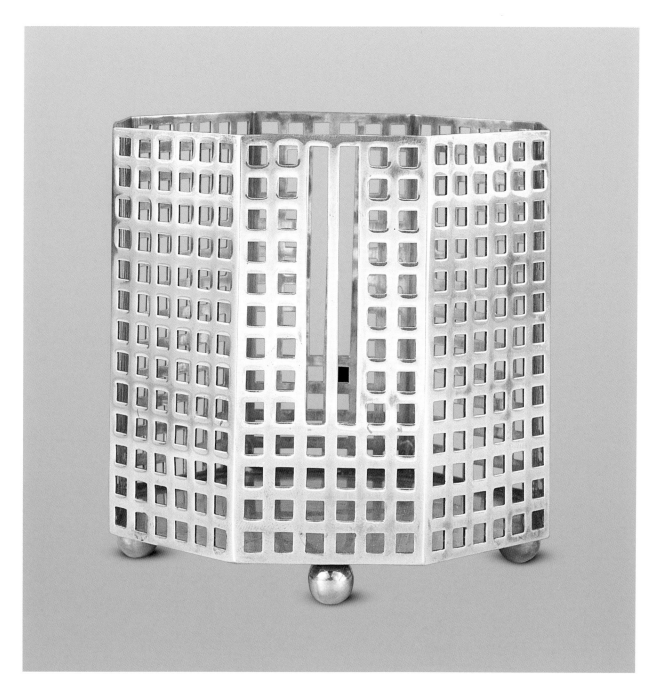

174. CACHEPOT (*BLUMENTOPFBEHÄLTER*)

Designed by Josef Hoffmann, Vienna 1905

Executed by the Wiener Werkstätte, model no. S 588

First made October, 1905 for sixty crowns

Four pieces produced

Silver

Vienna hallmark, JH, WW, rose mark

H 9.7 cm/3.9 in. Weight 189 g/7.6 oz.

Private collection

Charles Rennie Mackintosh, ebonized oak chair for the order
desk of the Willow Tea Rooms

Glasgow 1904

Glasgow School of Art Collection

175. CACHEPOT (*BLUMENTOPFBEHÄLTER*)

Designed by Josef Hoffmann, Vienna 1906

Executed by the Wiener Werkstätte, model no. S 945 (Adolf Wertnik)

First made December, 1906 for seventy crowns

Four pieces produced

Silver

Vienna hallmark, JH, AW, WW, rose mark

H 9.3 cm/3.7 in. Weight 206 g/8.2 oz.

Private collection

Josef Hoffmann, silver *Bonbonaufsatz* (Bonbon tray) (WW Model no. S 628)
Executed by the Wiener Werkstätte, Vienna 1905
Private collection

Harry Bertoia, bent chrome-bonded steel chair
Executed by Knoll, Pennsylvania 1952
Courtesy of Knoll, Inc.

Shiro Kuramata, *How High the Moon* armchair
Executed by Vitra, Birsfelden 1986

176. BASKET (*KÖRBCHEN*)

Designed by Josef Hoffmann, Vienna 1905

Executed by the Wiener Werkstätte, model no. S 509 (Adolf Wertnik)

First made September, 1905 for 200 crowns

Twenty-nine pieces produced

Silver, ivory

Vienna hallmark, JH, AW, WW, Wiener Werkstätte, rose mark

W 25.8 cm/10.3 in. Weight 470 g/18.8 oz.

Private collection

Josef Hoffmann, sheet iron, white-painted *Stehlampe 3-flammig* (Lamp for three bulbs)
(WW model no. M 456)
Vienna 1905
Contemporary photograph from the photo albums of the Wiener Werkstätte
MAK, Vienna

177. FLOWER STAND
(*BLUMENSTÄNDER*)

Designed by Koloman Moser, Vienna 1904
Executed by the Wiener Werkstätte, model no. M 182
First made 1904 for 240 crowns
Fifty-six pieces produced
Zinc-plated sheet iron, painted white
WIENER/WERK/STÄTTE (black rubber stamp)
H 160 cm/64 in.
Ernst Ploil Collection

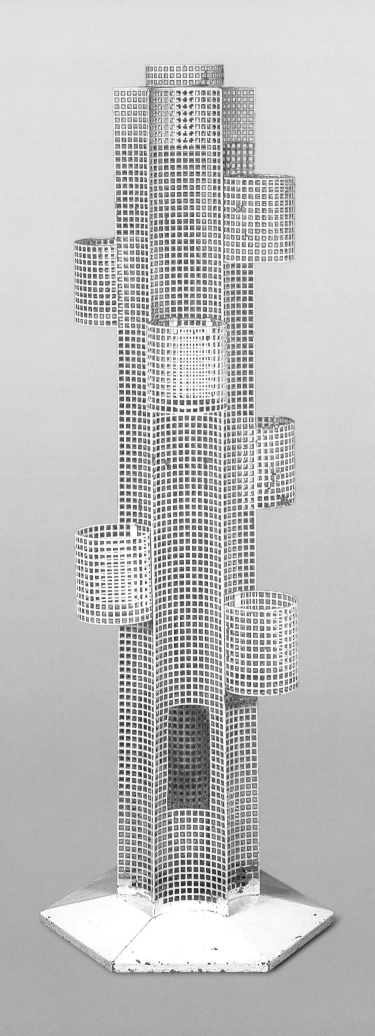

178. INKSTAND (*TINTENZEUG*)

Designed by Josef Hoffmann, Vienna 1905

Executed by the Wiener Werkstätte, model no. S 594 (Josef Wagner)
Made November, 1905 for 150 crowns
One piece produced
Silver, glass insets
Vienna hallmark, JH, JW, WW, rose mark
L 31.7 cm/12.7 in. Weight 436 g/17.4 oz.
Asenbaum Collection

Josef Hoffmann, entrance pavilion at the *Kunstschau*
Vienna 1908
Illustration from *Deutsche Kunst und Dekoration*, vol. 23, p. 33, Darmstadt 1908–09.

179. INKWELL (*TINTENFASS*)

Designed by Josef Hoffmann, Vienna 1912

Executed by the Wiener Werkstätte, model no. M 2080

First made May, 1912 for sixty-five crowns

Seven pieces produced

Silver-plated alpacca, glass inset

Vienna hallmark, JH, WIENER/WERK/STÄTTE (black rubber stamp), rose mark

H 10.7 cm/4.3 in.

Private collection

Adolf Loos, design for the *Chicago Tribune* Column
Pen and ink, 1922
Albertina, Vienna

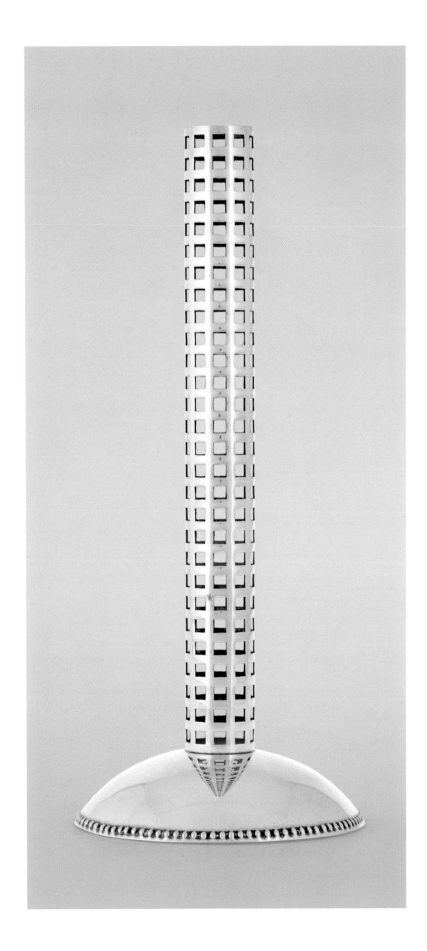

180. VASE

Designed by Koloman Moser, Vienna 1904

Executed by the Wiener Werkstätte, model no. S 356

First made November, 1904 for thirty crowns

171 pieces produced

Silver

Vienna hallmark, KM, WW, rose mark

H 21.1 cm/8.5 in. Weight 98 g/3.9 oz.

Private collection

Design for an *Oekonomisches Ziegelkabinett* (Economical brick pavilion) from Johann Gottfried Grohmann, ed., *Neues Ideen-Magazin für Liebhaber von Gärten, Englischen Anlagen und für Besitzer von Landgütern* (New Ideas Magazine for Enthusiasts of Gardens, English Parks and for Owners of Country Estates). Copperplate engraving, Leipzig 1797

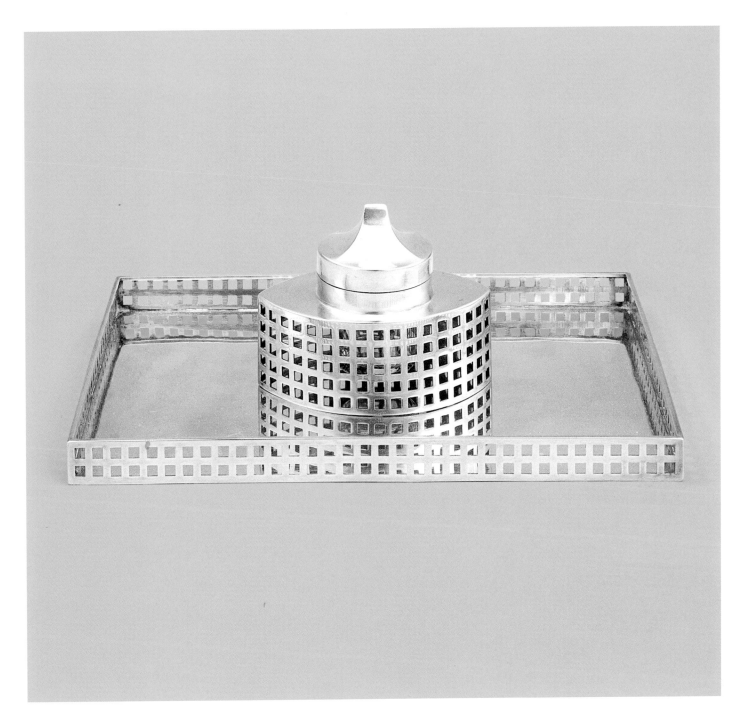

181. INKWELL AND TRAY (*TINTENFASS UND TASSE*)

Designed by Koloman Moser und Josef Hoffmann, Vienna 1905

Executed by the Wiener Werkstätte, model nos. S 545 (inkwell) and S 547 (tray)

Inkwell first made 1905 for forty crowns; tray first made October, 1905 for seventy crowns

Six inkwells produced; twelve trays produced

Silver, glass inset

Vienna hallmark, KM, WW, rose mark

L 22.1 cm (tray)/8.8 in. Weight 368 g (together)/14.7 oz.

Asenbaum Collection

Temple of Vesta in Rome (after 193 A.D.)
Stereograph ca. 1875
Michael Huey, Vienna

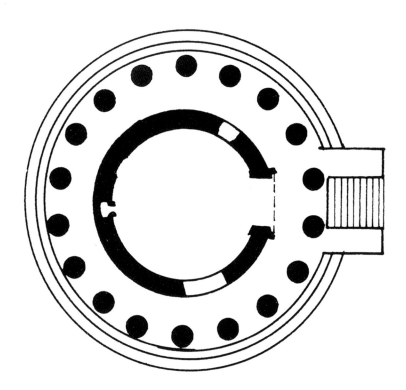

Diagram of a peristyle
from John Summerson, *The Classical Language of Architecture*, London 1996
© Thames and Hudson, London

182. COOKIE BOX (*DOSE FÜR CAKES*)

Designed by Josef Hoffmann, Vienna 1904

Executed by the Wiener Werkstätte, model no. M 123 (Adolf Wertnik)

First made November, 1904 for one hundred crowns

Eight pieces produced

Silver-plated alpacca

JH, AW, WW, rose mark

Diameter 19.8 cm/7.9 in.

Ernst Ploil Collection

1. View of the fourteenth exhibition of the Vienna Secession, 1902; plaster relief by Josef Hoffmann, Bildarchiv, Österreichische Nationalbibliothek, Vienna

ARCHITECTURAL ABSTRACTION AND THE VISION OF THE MODERN

MARKUS BRÜDERLIN

The miniature is a metaphysical exercise in balance, allowing us to create worlds with little risk.
Gaston Bachelard[1]

2. František Kupka, *Plans verticaux bleus et rouges*, 1912–13, exhibition *Ornament und Abstraktion*, Fondation Beyeler, Riehen 2001 Photo: Hasenböhler

Vienna's contribution to the history of modern abstraction is one of the yet unresolved and arguably most provocative questions in art history. After 1905, with the appearance of the *fauves* and cubism, the world's attention regarding the advent of abstract art was focused on Paris. Around 1910 a Russian émigré in Munich[2] attained "abstract terrain" in a very different way, namely via floral *Jugendstil* and a form-blurring, "impressionist" way of seeing. As early as 1902, however, an object appeared in Vienna, which, owing to its geometric/cubic, strictly horizontal/vertical composition, might be viewed as the birth of "tectonic abstraction." The astonishing thing about it was that it had not been developed in the context of the elevated, free arts—neither in sculpture nor in painting—but on a side stage, as it were, as a decorative panel in the context of a temporary exhibition space. The object in question is a roughly 1 x 1 m plaster relief installed by the architect and designer Josef Hoffmann in the fourteenth exhibition of the Vienna Secession in a niche above a connecting doorway on the wall opposite the famous Klimt frieze. In the wing on the other side of the main space, a second matching panel was installed, this time as an overdoor relief. (The whereabouts of both are unknown; they were reconstructed, though, in 1985 by the sculptor Willi Kopf.) The exhibition had been organized as an homage to the heroic Beethoven figure by Max Klinger. The Secessionists provided the decorative accessories for the show, including, among other things, Gustav Klimt's aforementioned monumental gold frieze (see above), in which the painter's style finally evolved into geometrical abstraction, despite the fact that his ornamentalism was never to achieve the radicalism of the non-representational.

3. Josef Hoffmann, Exterior façade of the Palais Stoclet Photo: *Moderne Bauformen* 23, 1914

The plaster object, in and of itself, would not have been so spectacular had not a heated debate developed surrounding

it and had its composition not been closely copied ten years later—now no longer as a decorative object, but as one of the first abstract/geometric creations in painting (fig. 2). In 1912 the Czech painter František Kupka, who had studied at the Vienna Academy from 1892 to 1895, painted the 72 x 80 cm canvas *Plans verticaux bleus et rouges* during the "cubist epidemic" in Paris; the painting demonstrated a startling formal debt to the Vienna plaster relief. (The work was shown two years ago in the exhibition *Ornament and Abstraction* at the Fondation Beyeler and was for the first time directly confronted with the replica of Hoffmann's overdoor relief—a historic moment, and one which art history had waited eighty years to witness [fig. 2].) The Hoffmann monographer Eduard F. Sekler saw it as an expression, long before its time, of the formal solutions of the neoplasticism and constructivism of the 1920s. Others, such as art historian Dieter Bogner, believe that the artifact should not be seen in isolation, but only in the decorative context of the original exhibition space in its entirety, which had likewise been designed by the architect Hoffmann (fig. 1).[3] But the semantic discussion about "autonomous art" or "ornamentation" misses the central point of Hoffmann's achievement. Hoffmann himself spoke succinctly of "crystallized stucco." "In the overdoors the essence of architecture crystallized in the truest sense of the word," Sekler concluded,[4] and Thomas Zaunschirm spoke of a "stenogram and concentrate of architectural thought."[5] Via the habitus of the relief and the manner of its integration as an overdoor panel Hoffmann seems to cry out: "Look here! I am the designer of this exhibition, and in this place I choose to demonstrate what architecture means to me: it is white, spare, cubic, and with an artistic will of expression." Bogner pointed out the compositional similarities of the relief with the spatial organization of the rooms in the "Kolo Moser" house of 1901 and the façade of Hoffmann's Palais Stoclet in Brussels, designed in 1905 (fig. 3). Hoffmann thus articulated in this artifact architecture's contribution to abstraction and truly provided, in a wider sense, a kind of early form of cubism, if we consider Juan Gris's concept *architecture plâte et colorée* or Malevich's abstract spatial constructions, the suprematist *arkhitektona* of the twenties.

Typical for the Viennese preference for the *Gesamtkunstwerk*, however, was the fact that this radical occurrence did not take place within the framework of the autonomous art avant-garde. The radicalization of form was not the result of a process of abstraction, at the outset of which a depictable "figurativity" had stood, as was the case with cubism; instead, it was much more a product of the age which could only have developed in the field of tension that existed between free experimentation with pure geometrical forms and an obsession with decorative *Sachlichkeit* (objectivity) that was the vogue in national and international architecture.

To understand this we must examine the heated debate surrounding ornamentation, a debate that made the Danube metropolis a center of the nascent modern movement and one which turned on three main points, which shall be the subject of this discussion:

First, the formal grammar of the early production of the Wiener Werkstätte (founded in 1903) was marked by a tendency toward geometricalization—its squares, spheres, cubes, and cylinders—from which Vienna's contribution to "tectonic abstraction" emanated. The taste for these forms, so typical for Viennese *Jugendstil,* must be regarded as the expression of a preoccupation with the history and theory of styles which, during the Biedermeier period and beyond, were rooted in the essence of ornamentation and the timeless forms of geometry. The prerequisite for this was the discovery, by the Viennese art historian Alois Riegl, that ornamentation had its own formal history, many thousands of years old, which was grounded in a creativity based on pure forms not primarily derived from a natural model. The purely artistic essence of ornamentation—independent of use, technique, and material—was thereby affirmed.

Second, Hoffmann and his colleagues at the Wiener Werkstätte profited from this theoretical background. Owing to this, radical formal experiments could take place within the protected space offered by everyday design. The Secessionist *Gesamtkunstwerk* ideal created a context in which these artifacts could potentially be seen as art. Paul Asenbaum has pointed out that the early products of the Wiener Werkstätte were, in fact, executed quickly and in cheap materials, as though they were intended as artistic formulae and not "real" objects that could be subjected to the stresses of daily use. Vienna introduced an ambivalent note into the history of design via this tension between autonomous art and applied production, of which I shall come to speak again later.

Third, and finally, I wish to discuss the adherence to a method of miniaturization and monumentalization, a tendency which not only connects the micro-world of handicrafts with the macro-world of architecture, but also makes up a typical element of Vienna's contribution to the vision of the modern movement itself.

THE TECTONIC AND THE CRYSTALLINE: VIENNA'S CONTRIBUTION TO MODERN ABSTRACTION

To be precise, three different aspects of Vienna's form-typological contribution to the history of abstraction must be considered. One aspect is tectonic abstraction, in which architectural thought is condensed and applied to three-dimensional objects for daily use as well as furnishings. Apart from this, the geometric surface graphics of the famous *Quadratlstil* (style with an all-over square pattern) and the checkerboard pattern should be mentioned. Marian Bisanz-Prakken has shown that—apart from Romanesque and Florentine Proto-Renaissance ornamentation, and beside Owen Jones's epoch-making publication *The Grammar of Ornament* in 1856 and other works of the British group surrounding Mackintosh—it was above all Dutch printing techniques before the turn of the (20th) century that were influential. *Das Quadrat in der Flächenkunst der Wiener Secession* (The Square in Planar Art and the Vienna Secession) evidently drew on essential impulses from the typographical decoration of text frames and decorative details as developed from the square during the 1890s by the architects Hendrik Petrus Berlage, Karel Petrus Cornelis de Bazel, and Johannes Ludovicus Mattheus Lauweriks.

4. Josef Hoffmann, ice cream mold executed by the Wiener Werkstätte, Vienna 1903 Österreichisches Museum für Angewandte Kunst MAK, Vienna

The third aspect is the interplay between the vertical cubic elements, which lends the overdoor relief more of a floating than a tectonic/constructive character, and this cements the principle of the crystalline. As noted above, Hoffmann himself spoke of "crystallized stucco;" the contemporary art critic Ludwig Hevesi added to this: "Stucco crystals in a particularly willful configuration."[6] The crystalline defines itself in relation to the fluid, with which it shares a relationship of transitory conversion, and should not here be understood in the sense of being the opposite of organic, as it was generally used during the period (Riegl). The original meaning of the Greek *krystallos* was "ice," which is to say, frozen water. Perhaps Hoffmann had this in mind when he designed a mold for ice cream in 1903—a block with an

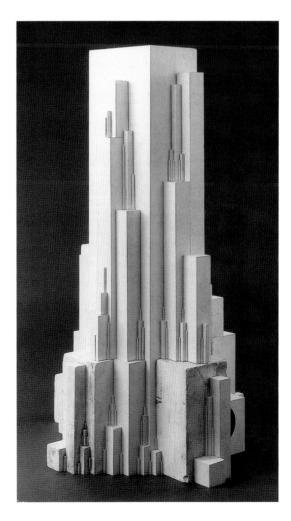

5. Kasimir Malevich, *Arkhitekton Gota*, plaster, Moscow 1923 (?) The State Russian Museum, St. Petersburg

6. Kasimir Malevich, view of exhibition *0.10*, Petrograd 1915
Photo: The State Russian Museum, St. Petersburg

arrangement of protruding shapes synthesizing the tectonic/structural and the crystalline/solid. When stood up like a miniature piece of architecture, it looked like an "ice palace" in the truest sense of the word (fig. 4). In the asymmetrically-composed overdoor relief, the "fluid" spatial idea Hoffmann developed for exhibition architecture in 1902 was solidified—in the case of this object it was "frozen." Later the crystalline grew, as did the tectonic/structural, to the size of real architecture in the Purkersdorf Sanatorium and the Palais Stoclet. Hoffmann appears to have intended to bring the three aspects into balance in accordance with the reform credo of the applied arts of the day. It is fascinating to observe how he creates objects for daily use and architecture in which the geometrical interior or surface pattern takes up and underscores the overall tectonic character, or how the cubic/crystalline also always becomes legible as tectonics and structure.

The comparison of these objects with their formal descendants—from Kupka's flat application of the overdoor relief, Juan Gris's cubist conception of *architecture plâte et colorée,* and Kasimir Malevich's visionary suprematist architectural model, *arkhitektona* (fig. 5), to the abstract, flat spatial compositions of the De Stijl movement around Mondrian and van Doesburg—makes clear, even from our present-day viewpoint, how radical the Secessionist designs were at the time, even if they were strongly influenced by the stylistic sphere of neoclassicism and Biedermeier and not directly cited by avant-garde artists like Mondrian and Malevich. It is tempting, from the postmodern perspective, to equate the sublime use of Kolo Moser and Hoffmann's *Quadratlstil* with the suprematist "black square" "nailed" to the wall of the exhibition space at the Petrograd show *0.10* by the Russian avant-gardist Malevich in 1915 as a naked, "unframed icon" (fig. 6). At second glance, however, the great differences quickly become evident—not only contextual ones, but formal ones, too.

In the first place, the square is seldom used by the Viennese as an iconic individual form; usually, it is serially-applied as a linear framing ornamentation or internalized as a checkerboard pattern in which figure and ground—black

and white squares—fill the space equally. Malevich, on the other hand, and as the title suggests, put the "black square" to use as a solitary form on "white ground," exposing it as the icon of a revolutionary, metaphysical manifesto. Suprematism is a type of mystical pantheism in which ego and cosmos, wholeness and nothingness are supposed to unite. Vis-à-vis this healing mysticism, the Secessionist square seems to accept a decorative role and to address itself to issues capable of being treated in the ornamental use of geometric forms. "We see a new value of beauty in the repetition of a single thing. Viennese Secessionism relates strongly to this idea," said the psychoanalyst and Freud disciple Otto Gross in his 1902 text *Die cerebrale Sekundärfunktion* (The Secondary Function of the Cerebrum): "It does us good to stay with one and the same formal image and to associatively develop further from it that which is essential, ideal.…Via simplicity to harmony—that is the art of high culture."[7]

Wilhelm Worringer confirmed this view six years later in his well-known 1908 book *Abstraktion und Einfühlung* (Abstraction and Empathy). In the face of the physiological/perceptive argumentation of Gross he broke with Riegl's psychology of style and perception. Worringer discusses prehistoric geometricalization together with the new abstract designs of his own day. While the former is about finding orientation in chaos and the complexity of an outside world that cannot be, a feeling for the "thing itself" is awakened in mankind "as the final resignation of knowledge" when "after thousands of years of development the human spirit has run the gamut of rational realization. What was previously instinct is now an end product of realization,"[8] and, later—taken almost verbatim from Riegl—"These abstract forms governed by laws are therefore the only ones (and the greatest ones) in which man can find rest in light of the monstrous confusion of the world."[9] Free from any sort of artistic/mystical explanation of the world, the square here, too, becomes a manifesto.

If we look more closely at the interdisciplinary nourishment available in turn-of-the-(20th)-century Vienna, from the positivism of the philosophy of language, from psychoanalysis to Riegl's formalist art theory to the invention of Gestalt theory by Christian von Ehrenfels, then we must recognize that the geometric formal experiments were more than just decorous, extravagant whims. With their interdisciplinary exchange, the Viennese quietly foreshadowed a process the representatives of the avant-garde likewise subsequently attempted to instate with revolutionary fervor. While the starting point for the Viennese was the graphic decoration of surfaces and, in particular, the experimental practice of designing objects for everyday use, in the twenties it was to be painting, and this in three different parts of Europe: in Holland with the De-Stijl movement surrounding Mondrian and van Doesburg; in Weimar in 1919 with the founding of the Bauhaus; and in Russia, where Malevich—in a parallel to Hoffmann and Moser eighteen years before with the Wiener Werkstätte—began in the 1920s to take active part in the reform and reorganization of craftsmen's workshops. All of life and society, so the theory went, was to be permeated with the suprematist design idea and thereby renewed. In the Petrograd art school GINChUK, Malevich taught the practice of design for the

7. Kasimir Malevich, porcelain teapot, executed by the State Porcelain Manufactory, Petrograd 1923
The State Russian Museum, St. Petersburg

porcelain industry (fig. 7). The artists' union UNOWIS at the art school in Witebsk was at work on a comprehensive program to turn the constructivist aesthetic into useful forms for furniture and buildings for the revolutionary worker masses. Much has been written about the failure of this transfer of art into decoration, but the Russians and the Dutch dared to do something that went against the grain of the functionalist modern movement and yet still somehow lay at the utopian/aesthetic heart of the movement: they turned the doctrine of "form follows function" around to read "function follows form." "The production of art and design was not to be based on the needs of everyday life; on the contrary, everyday life was to be altered by the productive energy of art,"[10] wrote Helga Behn, referring to the efforts of the Russians.

FUNCTION FOLLOWS FORM: VIENNESE OSCILLATION BETWEEN AUTONOMOUS AND APPLIED ART

Sparseness and the paring down of forms usually signal, in the psychology of styles, a tendency toward the functional; since the advent of the ideology of the modern movement this has been the principal standard applied to the decorative arts. This remains true despite Ernst H. Gombrich's having pointed out that a certain *Zeitgeist* and character may not necessarily be deduced from a given mentality of styles and forms.[11] Biedermeier was repeatedly cited as a model by reformers around the turn of the (20th) century, because of its reduction of things to the basics, behind which lay as much interest in comfort as in enlightenment and reason. Loos sang praises of this Austrian derivative of neoclassicism and, for his efforts, has, over the years, gained a reputation as a conservative revolutionary. In 1904–05 the essay "Biedermeier als Erzieher" (Biedermeier as Instructor) appeared in the magazine *Hohe Warte*.[12] Accordingly, and particularly in the early period of their design practice from about 1902–05, both Moser and Hoffmann made frequent references to this regional, early 19th-century style. Elsewhere the consistent application of the primacy of function before aesthetics reached its zenith in the late 19th-century doctrine of the American architect Louis Henri Sullivan: "form follows function"—an injunction that was never quite so easy to carry out as it sounded. Vienna, however, as the hometown of the *Gesamtkunstwerk,* never subordinated art to purpose, and early on developed the same unusual (aestheticizing) formula as the Russians—though for an entirely different set of reasons—in resistance toward the all-too-materialistic, purpose-oriented mantra of progress. Here, too, Sullivan's doctrine was turned on its head.

Otto Wagner's idiosyncratic terminology *Nutzstil* (functional style) is a rhetorical expression of the ambivalence with which every one-sided radicalization of the modern movement was met in Vienna. On the one hand, this necessity of the age was accepted; on the other, it was constantly subverted by a typical local ambiguity. Eventually Adolf Loos appeared on the scene to rant against the concealed aestheticism of his countrymen and against ornamentation itself. Nevertheless, he himself spoke the language of aesthetic appearance on more than one occasion, as when, for example, he included in the façade

of his Michaelerplatz building a neoclassical portico whose columns were merely non-load-bearing props. The tenet of purposefulness was also included in the platform of the Wiener Werkstätte in 1905: "We begin with purpose; usefulness is our first condition…"[13] Reduction to the elementary, however, was more closely aligned with pleasure taken in forms than symbolization of function, and the designers of attractive "useful objects" were soon confronted with the charge of creating "unfunctional" pieces. The producers saw no other option than to show their products in use in photographs: the sculptural fruit bowls were pictured full of fruit, bizarre vases were pictured with curious flower arrangements. This did not always have the desired effect: Hoffmann's "flat model" cutlery from 1903–04 may have been regarded less as something to eat with than as flat, miniature sculpture (fig. 8).

Any number of examples for the sublime Austrian zigzag course between function and aesthetics could be listed. An additional one, perhaps, will find room here: Otto Wagner fitted the marble sheets he used to face the exterior façade of the famous Postsparkasse building in 1906 with rivets whose heads, covered with aluminum caps, produced the desired decorative pattern of points. The sheets, though, were actually held in place by a special (separate) construction. Only when the mortar had dried in the brick (under)façade into which the decorative rivets had been set did the facing acquire its final fastening: "function follows form"![14]

THE FIRST VIENNA MODERN MOVEMENT: FROM SUGAR BOX TO INDUSTRIALIST VILLA

The ambivalent tension between form and function becomes quite apparent in Hoffmann's overdoor relief—in its indecisiveness between autonomous art manifesto and applied wall décor. This ambivalence is further emphasized by an additional effect: the object is simultaneously legible as a monumentalized stucco crystal and as miniaturized architecture. Is the sprawling exhibition architecture concentrated in this "crystallized stucco," or should one regard the relief as a spore, an ideal nucleus that could grow to the size of real architecture? The smaller the object shrinks, the more the pure formal thought, the idea, emerges; the larger it becomes, the more its form has to hold its own amidst the reality of the functional. The pre-modern movement in Vienna was particularly devoted to this kind of play with scale.

The catalogue section of this publication contains a group of images showing sugar boxes, as well as white-enameled, geometrically-perforated fruit and flower baskets, vases, etc. resembling reduced models of neoclassical temples or modern buildings like Corbusier's Villa Savoye. Interestingly, the converse effect also sometimes holds true: Hoffmann's realized architectural projects often bear an uncanny resemblance to enlarged jewelry boxes. In 1985, when I saw the newly-made wood model of the Palais Stoclet for the exhibition *Traum und Wirklichkeit* on a workbench at the Hochschule für Angewandte Kunst (University of Applied Arts) in Vienna, it was standing among wooden crates and furniture and was only at a second glance recognizable as a model of the villa in question. The Palais Stoclet is perhaps

8. Josef Hoffmann, five pieces from the "flat model" silver flatware set executed by the Wiener Werkstätte (cat. no. 126), Vienna 1904–08
Private collection

9. Adolf Loos, design for the *Chicago Tribune* Column, pen and ink, 1922
Albertina, Vienna

the most evident example in recent architectural history of the monumentalization of miniature form. (The tabernacle is exactly the reverse—a miniaturization of monumental forms.) In pre-modern art theory one would have spoken of a kind of mannerism, as the décor of classical architecture always had a particular dimensional relationship to the human body; in other words, the viewer had to be able to relate to the intellectual and physical dimension of architecture in what were considered "appropriate" ways. The slightly larger than man-size fillings in fluted Corinthian columns, for example, form a bridge between the anthropological scale and the dimension of the entire column or the façade itself. Nothing could simply be blown up or shrunk at will. Both historicism and the modern movement rendered this law of scale out of effect—for very different reasons. A taste for the *Gesamtkunstwerk*, for instance, encourages playfulness with dimensions: from toothpicks to skyscrapers, everything is subjected to the same formal strictures, the result being that skyscrapers were, in fact, created that looked like toothpicks. Postmodernism put a very fine point on this kind of mannerism, as Philip Johnson's so-called "Lipstick Building" in New York—in the form of a gigantic lipstick—shows. According to Peter Gorsen, the technique of size transferal serves the overall artistic unity of genres: "Hoffmann monumentalizes small craftsmen's forms and

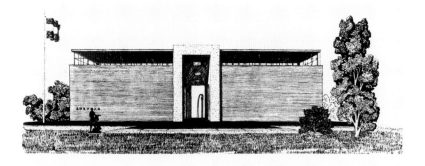

10. Josef Hoffmann, Austrian Pavilion at the Biennale in Venice in 1934
Illustration from Eduard F. Sekler, *Josef Hofmann: The Architectural Work*, Princeton 1985, p. 431.

minimalizes large architectural ones…Hoffmann polarizes architectural and applied arts forms in such a way as to enable an exchange between their differing sizes and qualities. The sterile antithesis of architecture and decorative arts was never to his taste…"[15]

The Viennese, perhaps more than others, have developed a method for size transferal, however, which far exceeds practical aspects of design and they tend to see design and architecture as a condensed version of their way of looking at the world. Josef Frank, a representative of the "second" Viennese modern movement (ca. 1920), described in his 1931 essay "Das Haus als Weg und Platz" (The Home as Passage and Resting Place) how the spatial organism of a city should serve as the model for planning the interior organization of a dwelling. From this position, the size transferal can go either way—either toward the macrocosmic or the microcosmic. The city of Vienna, as the residence of the Hapsburg Reich, became a representation of the empire's entire sovereign territory; in the row of structures strung like pearls along the Ringstrasse it also represented the canon of Western architecture's stylistic development (parliament—classical; city hall—Gothic; university—Renaissance).

11. Dagobert Peche, *Town Blocks* executed by the Wiener Werkstätte, Vienna 1918
MAK, Vienna

A. E. I. O. U., or *Austria est imperare orbi universo* (Austria's destiny is to rule the world) was the motto of Emperor Frederick III (reign as emperor 1452 to 1493). The city became a world stage or, rather, a world on a pinpoint, with the capacity of depicting the entire globe (saves on traveling). If young British aristocrats were expected to circumnavigate the sphere without dirtying their gloves and boots in the course of their "initiation," Austrians had the fiacre brought out for a drive around the Ring—a kind of historic predecessor of today's Disneyland (though certainly cheaper: nowadays a streetcar ticket is the only price of admission). After the loss of the Hapsburg territories and the end of Austrian universalism this miniaturization always had a melancholy and regressive cast. A psychoanalytical view of the populace collectively might hold that sad memories of the country's fall from imperial superpower status had mixed together with an individual penchant for dreaming and a desire to be consoled like a child. And from the child's point of view, everything is large. He who reduces the size of his environment, on the other hand, feels like Gulliver in Lilliput. This effortless slide between small and large and back again is key. "The more cleverly I make the world miniature, the better I possess it," writes Gaston Bachelard.[16] He continues: "I feel more comfortable in miniature worlds. They can be surveyed with ease…The miniature is a metaphysical exercise in balance, allowing us to create worlds with little risk."[17] Apart from the social reform aspect, the early design ideas and miniature architecture of Hoffmann and his colleagues were probably inspired by this demiurgic impetus, which—in this phase of the "first Vienna modern movement"—still had a progressive orientation: it was about enlargement, conquering the world of design, from the cookie tin to the worker's settlement, albeit refraining from the usual industrial production method. (Reduction to crafts eventually turned the Wiener Werkstätte into a purveyor of luxury goods for an exclusive clientele. The transferal from the autonomous/artistic to an application that would have benefited a larger circle of users never took place.)

Naturally, experimentation with models and playing with scale was not the exclusive specialty of the Viennese modern movement. As previously mentioned, the artists of the Russian Revolution and the Dutch both understood the finite canvas to be a kind of test-tube for a much larger order that would have a greater effect on life itself. Together with El Lissitzky and professional architects, Kasimir Malevich began in 1919 to translate his flat, suprematist, elementary forms into space: the square into the cube, the rectangle into the rectangular prism. "Consciousness has overcome the flat surface and has moved ahead to the art of spatial creation," he wrote in 1924 in his UNOWIS manifesto. As a result, those odd, white, sculptural plaster models were born which Malevich dubbed *arkhitektona* (fig. 5). As the name suggests, they were visions of a future suprematist architecture. Malevich understood them as models for the existence and movement of humans in cosmic space, thus very early on foreseeing the utopia of interplanetary flight, space stations, and future aero-cities. His visionary spirit thereby rivaled that of the French Revolutionary architects Étienne-Louis Boullée and Claude-Nicolas Ledoux nearly 150 years earlier. They designed universal programs of visual concepts whose power of expression not only had the task of rationally organizing space, but moreover rearranging communities in a political and moral sense. They were complete utopian images that nevertheless were conceived to cancel themselves out in the moment of their realization. "This ideal (of revolution) could only be clouded in the moment of its realization…for it was betrayed and deformed less from its enemies than from those who wished to guarantee its practical realization," wrote the historian Jean Starobinski.[18] In these generally "unrealizable" designs the modern contradiction between aesthetic utopia and societal practice—form of presentation and form of use—was articulated for the first time. This also becomes apparent in El Lissitzky's constructivist speaker's tribune for Lenin, famously developed between 1920 and 1924. As a sketch it seemed persuasively monumental; as a twenty-meter high realization, however, it would have been absurd. The same can be said for Adolf Loos's design for a skyscraper for the *Chicago Tribune*, which he proposed to construct in the shape of an enormous Doric column (fig. 9). No epoch has thought up quite as many architectural utopias as the modern movement; in general, it is a good thing that most of them remained in model or "cookie tin" form, including Alfred Speer's plans for Hitler's Berlin. In its narrow scope between jewelry box and industrialist villa, the Viennese cosmology seems quite tame when compared with French and Russian Revolutionary architecture. Nevertheless, Hoffmann attempted again in his 1934 project for the Austrian pavilion at the Biennale in Venice—which was inaugurated, incidentally, in his absence—to reconcile monumental and small forms (fig. 10). The propaganda of newly born Austro-fascism demanded a monumental self-depiction. Hoffmann alluded to this with the high central main portal, while at the same time working against it with the horizontal, finely fluted body of the building, which called to mind an enlarged coffer. Friedrich Achleitner judged this trick a "masterly balancing act between fascistic pathos and Viennese aesthetics."[19] But the tide had actually begun to turn again as early as 1911.

THE SECOND VIENNA MODERN MOVEMENT: FROM INDUSTRIALIST VILLA TO SUGAR BOX

Upon the completion of the collective project of the Palais Stoclet, upon which nearly the entire crew of the Wiener Werkstätte, including Gustav Klimt, worked together with Hoffmann, a new, regressive tendency toward miniaturization began to manifest itself. In 1915 Dagobert Peche, whom Hoffmann had met in 1911, joined the Wiener Werkstätte; there was a simultaneous turning away from architecture and toward the decorative arts, for which there was a very pragmatic reason: "In the Vienna of the First World War and the period between the wars there were simply not enough clients for Peche's in no way purpose-oriented building projects."[20] Over time he became the perfect foil for the tectonics of Hoffmann, who continued to dominate the

architectural side of things. Architecture becomes interior design with Peche, painterly décor, even a plaything, such as his *Town Blocks* (fig. 11), which was actually put into production by the Wiener Werkstätte in 1918. While this "introversion of the architectural" (Rainald Franz) was his own personal artistic path, he shared the fate of a dearth of clients with his contemporaries of the second Vienna modern movement, Josef Frank and Oskar Wlach.

"Outwardly restrictive circumstances hindered the development of monumental architecture; it never surpassed the everyday…but in the realm of fantasy it nevertheless confronted major challenges in meaningful ways with straightforward yet generous solutions."[21] This statement from the aforementioned essay published in 1904–05 in *Hohe Warte* on the Biedermeier epoch also applies to this second Vienna modern movement. The "realm of fantasy" referred to, however, was stage decoration during the pre-March period of the 19th century.

The so-called Third Vienna Modern movement—the architectural scene after the Second World War—was characterized by the work of Hans Hollein, Hermann Czech, Coop Himmelblau and others in the 1960s and 1970s; likewise lacking major commissions, they, too, worked in a sort of "Neo-Biedermeier" mode and, in so doing, made Vienna to one of the birthplaces of postmodernism. The "circumstances" of their day provoked their fantasies, which prospered in the brilliant, intimate atmosphere of store design and local renovations. "High r. p. m. in a small space," is how the architectural critic Dietmar Steiner summed up the obsessive inventive spirit of the so-called "little architecture" scene.

And today? Nowadays new skyscrapers loom as one approaches Vienna by air. Vienna has become a city of the world! Yet somehow one still has the feeling of flying over a "set table" (*ein gedeckter Tisch*): here a vase by Hoffmann, there a flower stand by Moser. In 1980 Hollein created a tea service in the form of an aircraft carrier (fig. 12). Previous to that he had put a photo collage together showing an "aircraft carrier city" in the middle of the landscape (fig. 13). Have Hollein and his colleagues now enlarged

their designs? Or was that just Loos's Doric column again, some 150 m high?

The contributions made by Vienna to the modern movement (as well as the postmodern movement)—tectonic abstraction; the aestheticizing backward loop "function follows form;" and the cosmological play with scale—should, in and of themselves, have encouraged the writing of a long-overdue piece entitled "Learning from Vienna." What this cultural laboratory has developed from Biedermeier to Secessionism and on to the postmodern is remarkable, particularly so when an exhibition of silver is enough to drive these points home once again.

1   Gaston Bachelard, *Poetik des Raumes* (The Poetics of Space), Munich 1975, p. 191.

2   Wassily Kandinsky lived in Munich on and off from 1896 to 1914.

3   See Dieter Bogner, "Die geometrischen Reliefs von Josef Hoffmann," *alte und moderne Kunst,* yr. 27 (1982), issue 184/185, pp. 24 ff.

4   Eduard F. Sekler, *Josef Hoffmann. Das architektonische Werk,* Salzburg 1982, pp. 60 f.

5   Thomas Zaunschirm: "Wien und die Anfänge der Abstraktion," in *Orient und Okzident im Spiegel der Kunst,* exh. cat. Stadtmuseum, Graz 1986, p. 468.

6   Ludwig Hevesi, *8 Jahre Secession,* Vienna 1906 (cited after Bogner 1982 [see note 3], p. 32).

7   Otto Gross, *Die cerebrale Sekundärfunktion,* Leipzig 1902, p. 69 (cited after Gabriele Koller, *Die Radikalisierung der Phantasie: Design in Österreich,* Salzburg and Vienna 1997, p. 42).

8   Wilhelm Worringer, *Abstraktion und Einfühlung,* Munich 1908, p. 25.

9   Ibid. See also Dieter Bogner: "Das 'constructive' Ornament—Der Beitrag Wiens zur Abstraktion," in *Ornament und Abstraktion,* ed. Markus Brüderlin, exh. cat. Fondation Beyeler, Riehen 2001, p. 38.

10 Helga Behn: "Angewandte Kunst und Architektur", in *Kasimir Malevich,* ed. Evelyn Weiss, exh. cat. Museum Ludwig, Cologne 1995, p. 157.

11 Thus the "ascetic, hardened, and rationalist Prussian Frederick the Great" resided in Schloss Sanssouci amid the most fanciful rococo decoration, while a frivolous Marie Antoinette lived in the Petit Trianon, one of the first neoclassical buildings in France. Compare Ernst H. Gombrich, *Ornament und Kunst: Schmucktrieb und Ordnungssinn in der Psychologie des dekorativen Schaffens,* Stuttgart 1982, p. 227.

12 See *Hohe Warte,* first issue, 1904–05, pp. 85–95.

13 "Arbeitsprogramm der Wiener Werkstätte" (Wiener Werkstätte Working Program), in *Josef Hoffmann zum sechzigsten Geburtstag, 15. Dezember 1930,* published by Österreichischer Werkbund, Vienna 1930, p. 21.

14 For the strange reversal of the maxim of functionalism see also Markus Brüderlin, "Genialität und Elend der Ambivalenz—Kunst der achtziger Jahre aus Österreich", in *Austria im Rosennetz,* ed. Harald Szeemann, exh. cat. MAK, Vienna, and Kunsthaus Zurich, 1996–97, pp. 190–197.

15 Peter Gorsen, "Josef Hoffmann. Zur Modernität eines konservativen Baumeisters", in Alfred Pfabigan, ed., *Ornament und Askese. Im Zeitgeist des Wiens der Jahrhundertwende,* Vienna 1985, p. 80.

16 Bachelard 1975 (see note 1), p. 180.

17 Ibid., p. 191.

18 Jean Starobinski, *1789. Embleme der Vernunft,* Munich 1981, p. 71.

19 Friedrich Achleitner, "Gibt es eine austrofaschistische Architektur?," in Franz Kadmoska, ed., *Aufbruch und Untergang: Österreichische Kultur zwischen 1918 und 1938,* Vienna et al. 1981, p. 592.

20 Rainald Franz, "'Kosmetik' der Architektur. Dagobert Peche und die Architekten der Zweiten Wiener Moderne," in Peter Noever, ed., *Die Überwindung der Utilität: Dagobert Peche und die Wiener Werkstätte,* Stuttgart 1998, p. 32.

21 "Biedermeier als Erzieher" 1904–05 (see note 12), p. 93.

THE AESTHETICIZED INDIVIDUAL: SUBJECTS AND THEIR OBJECTS IN TURN-OF-THE-CENTURY VIENNA

MICHAEL HUEY

1. Josef Hoffmann, dining room in the residence of Fritz and Lili Hellmann Waerndorfer, contemporary photograph, Vienna 1902 MAK, Vienna

"Sometimes when I look over my things I think the whole of the Secession was founded for me alone," wrote Fritz Waerndorfer to Josef Hoffmann on December 23, 1902.[1] To the Secession he owed his deeper knowledge of art; many friendships and connections (evidently including those with Charles Rennie Mackintosh, whom he had visited in Glasgow two years previously); and certain prized possessions (though not, of course, his considerable fortune, which came partly from the Wärndorfer-Benedict-Mautner Cotton Mills in Bohemia and partly from his wife's well-to-do textile-producing family)[2] and this made him feel, as he put it to Hoffmann, "like a pig fattened on your mash."

When Waerndorfer, Hoffmann, and Koloman Moser founded the Wiener Werkstätte in the spring of the following year, Waerndorfer was in a position to quite literally pay his Secessionist friends back as financier and *Kassir* (treasurer) of the organization. While this bankrupted him by 1913, it also placed him, during the interim, in a position to continue to reap the sorts of benefits he had previously been dependent upon the Secession for. It is hardly surprising, therefore, that Waerndorfer took the Wiener Werkstätte even more personally than he had taken the Secession. The Wiener Werkstätte decorated his life the way it liked to decorate the homes of its major clients: from floor to ceiling, and from wall to wall.

Waerndorfer's own home on Carl-Ludwig-Strasse[3]—the contents of which are now, sadly, haphazardly dispersed[4]—was no exception in this regard, although its initial design pre-dated the Wiener Werkstätte itself by a year. It possessed a small gallery by Moser; a snug smoking room and a rather spacious, elegant dining room by Hoffmann (fig. 1); and an adjacent music room by Mackintosh (all 1902). Besides a large collection of Aubrey Beardsley graphics kept in cases, a number of landscape paintings by Gustav Klimt were hung in the gallery, along with Klimt's *Die Hoffnung I*, which held pride of place in what must have seemed like a little shrine; in addition, there were an almost embarrassing (to Waerndorfer) quantity of Georges Minne sculptures[5] and two major friezes, one by Mackintosh and one by his wife Margaret Macdonald. As the years passed, the home's inventory of Wiener Werkstätte items—in particular from the metalsmith shop, which was the first of the Wiener Werkstätte workshops to be established[6]—grew and grew.

Clearly, Waerndorfer was a special case, and it is difficult to say precisely how many of the items he is recorded as having purchased during the lifetime of the Wiener Werkstätte were given as tribute or actually sold to him. The number, during

only the first three years of the firm's existence—for silver and silver-plated items alone (not counting many-pieced cutlery services)—unfortunately does not speak for itself, but it is around one hundred, which is to say, more than Adolphe Stoclet acquired from the beginning of the Wiener Werkstätte until its archival records end.[7] When the purchases of the extended Waerndorfer clan, including the families of Samuel and Bertha Wärndorfer,[8] August and Adrienne Waerndorfer, Bernhard and Caroline "Lina" Hellmann,[9] Isidor and Jenny Mautner,[10] and Ladislaus and Margarethe von Rémy-Berzenkovich[11] are added to the list, it exceeds 225, totaling something like 12.5 percent of the total metalwork production of the Wiener Werkstätte for the period. The only comparable familial commitment to the Wiener Werkstätte metal workshop was that made by the incomparably wealthier Wittgenstein family[12] and its von Brücke, Figdor, Grossmann, Hochstetter, Kupelwieser, Salzer, von Siebert, Sjögren, and Stonborough relatives and kin.[13] Between the years 1903 and 1905 they, too, acquired some 225 Wiener Werkstätte silver, silver-plated, and other metal items for an array of town houses, apartments, villas, and hunting lodges. (In 1908 Karl Wittgenstein bought the most expensive object ever produced by the Wiener Werkstätte, a silver vitrine decorated with enamel and moonstones designed by Carl Otto Czeschka. It sold for 25,000 crowns—the equivalent, in the year 2000, of around € 100,000.)

2. Editha "Ditha" Moser, née Mautner von Markhof, the wife of Koloman Moser. She attended the Kunstgewerbeschule in Vienna both prior to and after her marriage to Moser, a professor there. Private collection, Vienna

Together, then, the Waerndorfer and Wittgenstein families alone accounted for the sale of about a quarter of the early metal production of the Wiener Werkstätte. A handful of other regular clients, including the extended families of the bentwood furniture producer Felix Kohn; at least four of the ten children of the brewer and yeast producer Carl Ferdinand Mautner von Markhof (Magda Mautner von Markhof and her half-brother Victor, as well as her sisters Herta Jäger and Editha [fig. 2], who was married to Koloman Moser); Anton and Sonja Knips; Adolphe and Suzanne Stoclet; Max and Anna Biach; and Hugo and Marie Henneberg,[14] along with artists associated with the Wiener Werkstätte, contributed another fifteen percent or so. The family of Dr. Seewald, for instance, purchased some twenty-five Wiener Werkstätte items in 1903–05 for the furnishing of a heretofore unidentified, rambling eight-room apartment designed by Koloman Moser[15] (fig. 3). This lends a certain element of truth to the idea that the Wiener Werkstätte, if not the Secession, had, in fact, been founded for them alone—in any event, its existence owed to the loyalty of

3. Four views of the apartment of "Dr. S."—Dr. Seewald—designed by Koloman Moser in 1903–05 MAK, Vienna

individuals and families such as these, even if their dedicated patronage was never enough to place the Wiener Werkstätte on solid financial footing. (When Dagobert Peche joined the Wiener Werkstätte in 1915 this reliance on patronage was still a problem and, in fact, formed the basis of one of his primary criticisms.)[16]

The concentration of the early Wiener Werkstätte metal products in the hands of these few families had its parallel in the concentration of the designs for those products in the hands of what were at the beginning the Wiener Werkstätte's only two designers, Josef Hoffmann and Koloman Moser;[17] together they supplied the drawings for over nine hundred metal objects (not including jewelry) in the first three years of the Wiener Werkstätte. Though some were variations on a single theme, and others the result of an overall design for a house or an apartment, the number is still astonishing. It amounts, more or less, to one new design six days a week for three years straight. (At the same time, they were turning out hundreds of designs for furniture, glass, ceramics, and other items, too.)

Certain of the individuals and families for whom these interior spaces were conceived can be taken as exemplars for the social milieu of the clients of the Wiener Werkstätte in general and the nature of their relationships to the Wiener Werkstätte and its designers. The genealogical connections that sometimes existed between them, as well as the quasi-genealogical business and social relationships that often brought them into one another's circle, show how intimate (and how similar) the group of patrons of the Wiener Werkstätte itself was.

In 1908, for example, at the *Kunstschau Wien,* a group of (second) society ladies including Editha "Ditha" Moser, Lili Waerndorfer, Sonja Knips, and Berta Zuckerkandl—all of whom lived in (or would, within a decade or so, live in) Hoffmann- or Moser-designed homes—turned out partly in Wiener Werkstätte fashions to sell gingerbread and baked goods "designed" by Moser and Carl Otto Czeschka, together with Wiener Werkstätte products (fabrics, handbags, postcards) in what can only be described as a kind of "bake sale," presumably to help raise consciousness—if not money—for the Wiener Werkstätte (fig. 4 and pp. 278–280). This participation on a very personal level illustrates the kind of engagement the Wiener Werkstätte could (and did) rely on, a reliance that led, at times, to an overstepping of boundaries, as when in 1906 Waerndorfer went behind Moser's back to ask for a loan of 100,000 crowns from the affluent Editha on the argument that bolstering the Wiener Werkstätte would secure her (estranged) husband's existence.[18] Though infuriated by Waerndorfer's action, Moser himself proposed in turn that "friends" of the Wiener Werkstätte might each pay a sum of 10,000 crowns as a kind of advance on "guaranteed" future purchases. Friends? Commercial ventures do not, as a rule, place their eggs in that particular basket, though the Wiener Werkstätte seems to have benefited from doing so, at least in the short term, in accordance with Malcolm Gladwell's theory of the connectors, mavens, and salesmen who make a "tipping point" happen.[19]

It was undoubtedly no coincidence that Editha Moser, Lili Waerndorfer, Sonja Knips, and Berta Zuckerkandl (who championed the Wiener Werkstätte over decades in print)[20] also shared a liking for specific Wiener Werkstätte items: of the four, every one (or her spouse) had purchased a certain small white-painted basket (WW model no. M 270/271) from the Wiener Werkstätte in the past. (Most Wiener Werkstätte metal products were produced in more limited quantities, sometimes only a few times, or just once.) Other objects in their homes, too, connected them—in terms of taste—with many of their contemporaries. Both the Waerndorfers and the Knipses, for example, owned a number of items from a certain Koloman Moser silver, glass, and niello toilet service (WW model nos. S 324–327, S 338), parts of which had also been acquired by Paul Wittgenstein, his son Dr. Hermann Wittgenstein, and their cousin Prof. Dr. Wilhelm Figdor. The Zuckerkandls and the Koloman Mosers likewise acquired Moser-designed napkin rings that had been purchased by everyone from Gustav Mahler to Felix Kohn. *Tout Vienne* and beyond, it appears, bought perforated white-painted sheet iron flower vases/paper bins (either WW model no. M 132, M 133, or M 134): the Wittgensteins,[21] the Figdors, the Hellmanns, the Mautners, the Bloch-Bauers, the Seewalds, the Hennebergs, and the Stoclets. Like every fashion, the Wiener Werkstätte had inspired its own groupies, and it is interesting to consider what, apart from many of their possessions, these people had in common.

Karl Kraus commented—in the verbal sneer that became his fixed expression—that the big "success" achieved by Gustav Klimt and the Secession at the World's Fair in Paris in 1900 was the derision of their imported art by Parisians as *goût juif.*[22] Adolf Loos was not long in responding, as Burkhardt Rukschcio suggests, with an article entitled *Die Emanzipation des Judentums* (The Emancipation of Jewry) which was in equal parts an appeal to Jews to refrain from "building a new [aesthetic] ghetto" and an attack on Hoffmann and other Secessionists for, as it were, measuring the ghetto for curtains. ("Yes, there are Aryan Moritzes and Siegfrieds, just as there are Aryan owners of Hoffmann interiors. They are the exceptions.")[23] Loos likened the Hoffmann commissions of Jews who were looking to thereby create a new identity for themselves to "caftans"—Jews who believed to be distancing themselves from their past, he said, were merely exchanging one kind of caftan for another. Arthur Schnitzler, too, maintained that turn-of-the-century Jews in Vienna had fled into aestheticism as a diversion from other options of a social or political nature that were closed to them.

Does it matter—or what, then, does it say—that a striking number of the clients of the Wiener Werkstätte were Jews? Or, at least, Jews by the standard of the infinitely nuanced, caste-like distinctions applied by the Viennese toward many who did not see themselves as Jewish at all? There were very few high nobles on the client list, with intriguing exceptions such as the so-called "red" count, Harry Kessler,[24] the Anglo-German art patron, writer, and activist (who did not, however, buy metalwork) and the dubious Count Strasnitzki; the Princesses Lubomirska and Reuss (who bought, seemingly as a fluke, one or two items); and the King of Bulgaria (who also did not make his acquisitions from the Wiener Werkstätte metalsmith shop). Evidence such as a photograph of the historicist dining room in an unidentified Austrian palace shows how such clients, who certainly did not rearrange their lives to accommodate the Wiener Werkstätte (as many of its passionate supporters did by allowing Hoffmann or Moser to design complete environments for them) took note of the firm's existence and conceded it minimal space in their lives (fig. 5). The otherwise highly conservative table setting nevertheless included, at each place setting, a little Wiener Werkstätte-inspired,[25] grid-metal, navette-shaped basket for a flower arrangement. Similarly, the posh but otherwise primly self-restrained Hotel Bristol in Vienna ordered thirteen silver flower baskets (WW model no. S 661) for its tables; an oil painting by Hans Stalzer entitled *Ein Festabend im Speisesaal des Hotel Bristol im Jahre 1910* (Festivities in the Dining Room of the Hotel Bristol in 1910) shows what effect this had (fig. 6).[26]

The majority of Wiener Werkstätte clients were untitled; if they bore titles, they tended to be minor ones. Unsurprisingly, there are a great many little-heard-of barons and baronesses on the list. The entrenched impermeability of the upper echelons of Viennese society was not only a barrier to the socially-ambitious; it was an affront to the enterprising and those who had every reason to feel that their accomplishments had earned them the right to "represent." (And, as Berta Zuckerkandl pointed out,[27] many of them even considered themselves a "new" kind of aristocracy.) They were excluded from court; no matter what they did or earned, the second society was the highest social level available to them. Without these individuals—among them were many with Jewish roots who were to various degrees assimilated and into the second and third generation of family money—it is difficult to imagine what the market for the Wiener Werkstätte might have been. The "actual audience" *(das eigentliche Publikum)* of their age, as Stefan Zweig[28] put it, they were a class in search of a luxury market, and one not based primarily on court tradition; a subject, one might say, in search of a verb. Indeed, a grammar-based joke at the time referred to the so-called "Haben-Wittgenstein" and the "Sein-Wittgenstein" families;[29] another began with the question, "Might I ask if you are an adherent of the modern movement?" "Do you take me," went the punchline, "for an anti-Semite?"[30]

Oskar Kokoschka noted in his autobiography that "Most of my sitters were Jews. They felt less secure than the rest of the Viennese establishment, and were consequently more open to the new and more sensitive to the tensions and pressures that accompanied the decay of the old order."[31] It could be argued that the same held true—and for the same reason—with the Wiener Werkstätte. It is important to remember that for many (like Kraus, despite his own Jewish heritage) if not most of the Viennese at the turn of the century, the Wiener Werkstätte was an institution suitable chiefly for scorn or lampooning. An entire body of literature grew out of poking fun at the Secession and its adherents (fig. 7), and, as the aforementioned joke shows, the ridicule was clearly in part racially or religiously motivated. The snide term *goût juif* with its myriad connotations seems almost certain to have been a local invention—probably Kraus's own—and not a French one.

There can be little doubt that the Wiener Werkstätte was a minority, word-of-mouth movement among acquaintances, friends, and relatives who were in the know. (Adolphe and Suzanne Stoclet became devotees of the Wiener Werkstätte after wandering, one summer afternoon in 1903, into the garden of Carl Moll, the step-father of Alma Mahler, who showed them his Hoffmann-designed house and offered to introduce them to the architect.)[32] The location of its showroom at Neustiftgasse 32 in the seventh district was, as Ludwig Hevesi kindly put it, "rather peripheral,"[33] but what it sold, it sold there best. In Germany several galleries in

Berlin, including the Hohenzollern Kunstgewerbehaus[34] (see cat. no. 128), and the Dresdner Werkstätten für Handwerkskunst in Dresden[35] (fig. 8) did a fairly brisk business with Wiener Werkstätte consignment pieces. According to the Wiener Werkstätte archives, just under a quarter of the metalwork production from 1903 to 1905 went to these German retailers, who were, however, at liberty to return unsold items—and did so regularly (of twenty-three pieces sent to a show at the Berlin Secession in 1905, for instance, all twenty-three were shipped back to Vienna). In Vienna, beginning in December 1905, Wiener Werkstätte metalwork items were shown at the Galerie H. O. Miethke and, as Hevesi relates, in 1906 they were on display at a second downtown location: the Kunstsalon of Eugen Artin at Stephansplatz 4.[36] The journal *Kunst und Kunsthandwerk* called Artin (whose son was the field- and braid-theory mathematician Emil Artin) a "Modernist" and said of his "original" exhibition space that it had been "decorated in a modern manner by Adolf Böhm."[37] Judging from the amount of entries marked *retour* in the Wiener Werkstätte archives, Artin seems not to have sold much (Miethke did somewhat better);[38] the *Gesamtkunstwerk* atmosphere of the Wiener Werkstätte showroom appears to have been more important than its location in "selling" the idea of the firm. In Vienna, at least, its products performed marginally when shown isolated from the overall context of the Wiener Werkstätte.[39] As early as February, 1905 the Wiener Werkstätte evidently attempted to place work on consignment in Brno, with the Gebrüder Klein; of the twenty-four items sent, twenty-two are explicitly marked as having been returned.

Earlier even than Miethke, Artin, or the Gebrüder Klein, though, another name—Fanto—intriguingly and insistently shows up in the Wiener Werkstätte archives in a similar light. In June and July of 1904 individual silver and silver-plate items totaling seventy-nine in number went to the mysterious Fanto (with no further designation). The name calls to mind first and foremost the Jewish industrialist David Fanto,

4. *Lebkuchen & Bäckerei* (Gingerbread and baked goods) stand at the Kunstschau Vienna 1908 with society ladies in Wiener Werkstätte clothing and jewelry (center: Editha Moser, née Mautner von Markhof, the wife of Koloman Moser); a sign in the background proclaims that the gingerbread was "designed" by Koloman Moser and Carl Otto Czeschka, vintage print by Josef Justh, Vienna 1908 MAK, Vienna

5. Dining room in an unidentified Austrian palace, ca. 1905. The table is set with traditional china and glassware together with Wiener Werkstätte-inspired flower baskets. Christian Witt-Dörring, Vienna

6. Detail from an oil painting by Hans Stalzer entitled *Ein Festabend im Speisesaal des Hotel Bristol im Jahre 1910* (Festivities in the Dining Room of the Hotel Bristol in 1910). A Wiener Werkstätte silver basket for flowers in the background contrasts with a more conservative flower basket in the foreground. Hotel Bristol, Vienna

7. Book cover lampooning Josef Maria Olbrich's Secession building, Vienna 1901 Christian Witt-Dörring, Vienna

Aus den Schaufenstern der Dresdner Werkstätten für Handwerkskunst

Aus den Schaufenstern der Dresdner Werkstätten für Handwerkskunst: SPEISEZIMMER (22)

9. Ex libris of Lotti (?) Fanto, née Winterberg, Vienna ca. 1905 Michael Huey, Vienna

10. Felix Kohn, ca. 1903 Private collection

11. Karl Wittgenstein, ca. 1880 Pierre and Françoise Stonborough, Vienna

whose oil refineries allowed him to finance the construction of the "Palais Fanto," a luxurious apartment building where he made his home, on Schwarzenbergplatz in 1917.[40] There is no known Fanto residence commissioned in the year 1904 which would warrant the purchase of items in this quantity, nor, moreover, their nearly immediate return. The language of the entries in the Wiener Werkstätte archives suggests, on the contrary, that "Fanto" was the name of the owner of the earliest location where Wiener Werkstätte products were exhibited for sale on consignment—perhaps, as a later entry in the Vienna city registry implies, a jewelry shop. Of the seventy-nine pieces in question, seventy-two were returned to the Wiener Werkstätte.[41] Seven items—a metal match holder, wine cooler, and candlestick, together with a silver "samovar" (tea-urn), box, egg-cup and spoon, and saucière—are marked as having been "sold" instead of

returned. Tellingly, the cutlery pieces "acquired" and returned by Fanto in July 1904 are for one person only: presumably they were used as a pattern to put on display. David Fanto had three brothers—Adolf, Friedrich, and Edmund[42]—whose occupations are unknown, and any of whom might have been the elusive Fanto in question. The only remaining clue at present is a Secessionist-style ex libris made for an "L. Fanto" (fig. 9), which documents the modern taste of at least one branch of the Fanto family (the spouse of Friedrich Fanto was Lotti, née Winterberg).

These firms played a decided role in helping the Wiener Werkstätte gain a certain recognition, but there were nonetheless many whose attachments to the Wiener Werkstätte were of an older and more personal nature. The

bentwood furniture manufacturer Felix Kohn (fig. 10), for example, who purchased around fifty individual Wiener Werkstätte metal items prior to his death in 1905, may have known Hoffmann as early as 1902, when he bought a magnificent Hoffmann-designed silver flatware service from Alexander Sturm & Co. for the wedding of his daughter, Maria, to W. F., the industrialist. Several years prior to that, in 1898, Loos had asked J. & J. Kohn to produce his design for a chair for the Café Museum, and by 1904 Kohn was producing Hoffmann designs for the furnishing of the Sanatorium Purkersdorf (which, incidentally, belonged to Victor Zuckerkandl, the brother-in-law of Berta).

Even more intricate are the ties between the Wittgenstein family—one of the most influential families in the monarchy beginning in the second half of the 19th century[43]—and the Wiener Werkstätte. Paul Wittgenstein (see p. 210), the third eldest of the eleven children of Hermann Christian and Fanny Figdor Wittgenstein and a man so passionate about art and objects that he asked to be (and, by all accounts, was) buried not only together with sketches he had made of his favorite paintings in the academy in Venice, but also with a little Biedermeier gilt-bronze jewelry holder in the form of a temple,[44] seems the likely candidate for his family's discovery of the Secession and, later, the Wiener Werkstätte. In 1899 he gave the commission for one of the first important Hoffmann interiors, the remodeling of the so-called Bergerhöhe, a hunting lodge in Lower Austria. He ordered Hoffmann-designed apartments for two of his children, Johanna and Hermann Wittgenstein, upon their marriages in 1902 and 1905, respectively, and one for himself in 1916–17. His brother, the industrialist Karl (fig. 11), became a patron of the Secession and, in 1900, himself asked Hoffmann to build an office for the Wittgenstein Forestry Administration and a dwelling for the forester in Hohenberg; in 1906, he further engaged Hoffmann to renovate the interior of a hunting lodge on his own estate, the Hochreit, not far from the Bergerhöhe. (One of the two brothers—most likely Paul—also had Hoffmann's only sacred structure built, a Protestant church in St. Aegyd.)

In 1876 Paul Wittgenstein had married Justine Hochstetter, whose younger sister Helene commissioned an important Hoffmann house at the Hohe Warte in 1906–07; in addition, two of the nieces of Justine and Helene—Anna and Maria Hochstetter—both worked for the Wiener Werkstätte. Indeed, Anna Hochstetter had married Kurt von Schmedes, a representative of the firm.[45] Paul Wittgenstein was therefore the focal point of a far-reaching network of relatives and friends whose sympathies toward the Secession and the Wiener Werkstätte were expressed in the very real terms of cash outlay and hands-on work.

But how had this scion of a distinctly upwardly-mobile family (in terms of income, property, and society standing) originally come to learn of the existence of the Secession and become involved with the avant-garde? Like all his siblings, he had grown up in a home that counted Johannes Brahms, and, later, Pablo Casals and the members of the Rosé Quartet among its friends. His parents had taken in the *Wunderkind* violinist Joseph Joachim and paid for his education with Felix Mendelssohn-Bartholdy. Perhaps most notably, however, as Hermine Wittgenstein, Paul's niece, explains, "We knew a great many…artists personally or had formed friendships with them, such as Rudolf von Alt, from whom I own marvelous pictures from every period…"[46]

The aged watercolorist von Alt—he was eighty-five the year the Secession was founded—may have been the key figure in connecting the Wittgenstein family and Secessionists like Hoffmann. Himself a founding member and honorary president of the organization, his name was eventually emblazoned—together with that of Karl Wittgenstein and Theodor Hörmann—on the wall of the entry hall of the Secession building.[47] But long before that time he must have been a kind of *éminence grise* in a family whose cultural aspirations led them to seek out friendship with, and to purchase impressive quantities of paintings from, one of the most accomplished and prominent 19th-century Austrian artists. Von Alt's commitment to the Secession and his touching engagement for its cause at his high age must surely have struck a chord with someone as dedicated to the arts as Paul Wittgenstein.

If Paul Wittgenstein was remarkable for his steadfast interest in and support of Hoffmann and the Wiener Werkstätte, his brother Karl Wittgenstein was no less so for the extravagance of his patronage and the way in which he made room in his life for the Viennese Modern movement and its material manifestations.

In 1898 he donated funds for the construction of Joseph Maria Olbrich's Secession building. After his retirement the following year at the age of fifty-two and withdrawal from the active management of his business affairs—he had built an empire that included the largest iron and steel-producing industries in the monarchy—he traveled around the world with his wife, Leopoldine, née Kallmus, and then, increasingly, devoted himself to further philanthropic activities and patronage of the arts. Until that time, their town house on Alleegasse (later Argentinierstrasse 16, razed in the 1950s) must have been, as a photograph of the "red salon" (fig. 12) post-dating the year 1908 illustrates, a document of luxurious, but "safe," taste. The addition of the Secessionist elements seen in the photograph, such as the 1901 Max Klinger statue *Die Kauernde* (Crouching Woman); a black-stained oak fire screen by Hoffmann with Czeschka-designed embroidery in 1906; and the Czeschka vitrine in 1908 may not have changed its fundamental attitude, but at the time—and in an interior where each individual piece

12. The "red salon" in the Wittgenstein town house on Alleegasse (Argentinierstrasse 16) ca. 1905. Note the firescreen and the silver vitrine (see comparison to cat. no. 150) by Carl Otto Czeschka.
Photo: Bildarchiv, Österreichische Nationalbibliothek, Vienna

13. The Hochreit hunting lodge, interior designed by Josef Hoffmann for Karl Wittgenstein, ca. 1906
© Wittgenstein Archive, Cambridge

14. Margaret Stonborough-Wittgenstein, ca. 1905
Pierre and Françoise Stonborough, Vienna

so clearly represented something else (money, above all, but also the security it brings, expressed as sedate aesthetic conservatism)—they must nevertheless have had a certain shock value. (The famous portrait of Margaret Stonborough-Wittgenstein [see p. 175], commissioned by her parents from Gustav Klimt upon her marriage to Dr. Jerome Stonborough in 1905, was also displayed for some time in a Hoffmann frame in this room, just to the left of where the photographer in the interior view was standing.) These things were not a departure from the ideal of lavish display—not one of them was inexpensive, and the vitrine was quite possibly by far the most expensive item in the room[48]—but they did signal a leave-taking from anonymous and noncommittal good taste.

In a way (and isolated from the question of whether it can truly be called a triumph of style), the "red salon" in the Alleegasse is *more* modern in its accommodation of the new beside the old—at least from the vantage-point of our present-day eclecticism—than the thoroughly-designed Wiener Werkstätte interior Hoffmann conceived for Karl Wittgenstein's Hochreit (fig. 13) in 1906, which might merely be considered the equivalent of the Alleegasse's once-rigid, strictly historicist interior in a new set of clothes, as Loos might have put it.

15. *Wohnung Dr. St. Berlin/ Speisezimmer* (Apartment of Dr. St.[onborough] in Berlin/ dining room), furnished by Josef Hoffmann and the Wiener Werkstätte in 1905 Illustration from *Deutsche Kunst und Dekoration*, vol. 17, p. 149, Darmstadt 1905–06.

The turn-of-the-century Viennese writer Richard von Schaukal, both a critic of the avant-garde and, upon occasion, a client of the Wiener Werkstätte,[49] took disapproving note of this kind of substitution of one style for another in *Die Mietwohnung. Eine Kulturfrage* (The Rental Apartment: a Question of Culture) in 1911:

> Those who married in the year 1897 were still set up with Renaissance furniture, the happy couples of the following years received for the same dowry "English" or new German households….It is as though people believe "culture" to be raised by a degree when the "fashionable" man humbly concedes to the demands of his tailor that the vest from now on be worn at a length two buttonholes longer than previously. "They" are wearing jackets long, tailored over the hips and cut tightly across

the waist "this year." "People" have "mahogany" sitting rooms, "no longer" [neo-] rococo salons. And this is deemed "progress!"[50]

Margaret Stonborough-Wittgenstein (fig. 14), one of the three daughters of Karl and Leopoldine Wittgenstein, was a direct beneficiary—or victim, depending on how one regards it—of just such a "new" dowry. Like her cousins Hermann and Johanna Wittgenstein, she, too, received an apartment outfitted by Hoffmann (and Moser) when she and her husband moved to Berlin as newlyweds (fig. 15). Apart from its furnishings, the apartment contained at least thirty-four metal items purchased at the Wiener Werkstätte in 1905–06, from a variety of lamps and light fixtures to flower vases and a silver tea and coffee service that accompanied her from one residence to the next for the rest of her life.[51]

There is little doubt that the apartment appealed to Margaret Stonborough-Wittgenstein's taste and sophisticated sense of style. On April 18, 1905 she wrote her mother:

> Our apartment is the most beautiful thing imaginable and terribly *gemütlich*. Moser—who has once again been awfully nice—and I arranged furniture for three days, hung pictures, and painted frames. Now the apartment is, at least outwardly, in order and Jerome and I are thrilled and praise you and the Wiener Werkstätten [sic] daily.[52]

And yet it is interesting to observe, through photographs of the furnishings of successive apartments and homes, how

16. Study (?) in the apartment of Margaret Stonborough-Wittgenstein in the (now demolished) Palais Erdödy on Krugerstrasse with the Koloman Moser writing desk from her Berlin apartment, Vienna ca. 1920.
Pierre and Françoise Stonborough, Vienna

17. Salon in the apartment of Margaret Stonborough-Wittgenstein in the (now demolished) Palais Erdödy on Krugerstrasse with Josephin furnishings, a Koloman Moser bookcase (to the right of statue, with Renaissance chest), and a Josef Hoffmann table (in front of statue) from her Berlin apartment, Vienna ca. 1920.
Pierre and Françoise Stonborough, Vienna

18. Salon with mixed furnishings
including a Dagobert Peche
table in the residence of
Margaret Stonborough-Wittgenstein
at Kundmanngasse 19
Vienna, ca. 1930
Pastel drawing by
Hermine Wittgenstein.
Pierre and Françoise
Stonborough, Vienna

the presence of her own personality seems to grow and the presence of the various designers' personalities seems to recede. Over time, she visibly liberated herself from the kind of programmatic interior Berlin represented, even while continuing to hold on to and cherish individual pieces from that first apartment. Her own feeling about objects and what could be done with them began to take precedence;[53] her grandson, Pierre Stonborough, believes that the renovation of the Villa Toscana in Altmünster around 1914, during which she worked with the Otto Wagner pupil Rudolf Perco, was a turning point.[54] The juxtaposition of a Moser desk with other pieces in the apartment she rented at the (now demolished) Palais Erdödy on Krugerstrasse in Vienna during the First World War, to say nothing of the Moser cabinet she placed with Josephin seating furniture and a classical figure in its salon (figs. 16, 17), is striking to say the least. "Even in her youth," wrote her sister Hermine,

> her room was the embodiment of resistance against everything conventional and the opposite of a so-called little girl's room…Lord knows where she found all the interesting objects she used to decorate it with.…Although feminine needlework was not her strong point, she designed for herself the most unusual embroideries, for example…the anatomical image of a human heart with the veins and arteries, not naturalistic, but seen instead strictly as an ornament.[55]

Hoffmann and Moser filled her first apartment; by the time her brother Ludwig Wittgenstein designed a house for her in 1926 to 1928 (together with Paul Engelmann) it was an empty showcase, a stage, with no built-in or (new) architect-designed furniture whatsoever. What was put on display, in a manner of speaking, was space itself. (His own participation notwithstanding, the philosopher still regarded the structure as an "unhealthy, glass-house plant.")[56] Here, too, however, she made use of her—now aging—Hoffmann and Moser furniture and objects (in the breakfast room, chairs from the Berlin dining room were gathered around an Austrian rococo table), together with caned and gilt Kohn bentwood side chairs, Viennese neoclassical porcelain and silver, Chinese screens and lacquer chests, found objects and—good heavens!—comfortable, colorful, no-name chintz and satin-covered armchairs. At the same time she was freeing herself from the constraints of design, she was still actively interested in and supportive of the Wiener Werkstätte, as demonstrated by the purchase of a rococo-inspired green, yellow, and black lattice-painted dressing table by Dagobert Peche in 1918, as well two fanciful Peche cabinets[57] in 1920, some of which she mixed in with the rest (fig. 18) and some of which went to Altmünster.

Times change, and fashions change. Fortunes rise and fall. And through it all "the odds" remain, as William Maxwell once said, firmly "upon objects."[58] They outlive their immediate usefulness, perhaps, but then they outlive us, and, in so doing, gain a new usefulness as markers of where we and others have been. Their allure fades, and then it grows strong again, and the objects—be they admired or despised—are altered only in our perception. They are, after all, and at all times, nothing more or less than what they have always been. In the case of Wiener Werkstätte interiors (and, as follows, with its metalwork) the changes in perception have been cataclysmic. Almost without exception its products were damned by the generation of the children of their original purchasers and, as a consequence, sold, packed away, neglected, lost. (Apart from the Palais Stoclet, the two Wittgenstein interiors at the Bergerhöhe and Hochreit are among the only basically intact Hoffmann interiors remaining.) The aged Heinz Wittgenstein, for example, who had lived in rooms furnished by the Wiener Werkstätte as a child, acknowledged with alarm the renaissance of interest in the Wiener Werkstätte. He and his siblings had always referred to the Hoffmann dining room in their apartment as the "mausoleum."[59] Hoffmann himself, upon meeting Heinz's cousin Friedrich "Fritz" Wittgenstein, the youngest son of Hermann Wittgenstein, merely said, "So you're the poor fellow who had to grow up in the apartment I designed."[60]

For Katsi, dear friend (1945–1999)

1   Waerndorfer to Hoffmann, (former) collection of Mrs. Karla Hoffmann, Vienna; as cited in Peter Vergo, "Fritz Waerndorfer as Collector," *alte und moderne Kunst,* vol. 177, summer 1981, pp. 33–38. "Sometimes when I look over my things I think the whole of the Secession was founded for me alone. My two friends, that is, my special Viennese friends, are friends because of the Secession…I never would have had any idea about Minne had it not been for you—in short I feel like a pig fattened on your mash. Oh, well." (*Wenn ich mir so meine Sachen manchmal anschau' kommt's mir vor wie wenn die ganze Secession nur für mich gegründet worden wäre. Meine zwei Freunde, resp. Wiener Specis, habe ich durch die Sec.,…von Minne hätte ich keinen Dunst ohne Euch— kurz ich komme mir vor, wie ein an Eurem Fett gemästetes Schwein. Macht aber nix.*)

    Waerndorfer twice altered the spelling of his surname, which had begun as Wärndorfer; after emigration to the United States in 1913 he legally changed it to Warndof in the Chatham County, Georgia, Court in 1918.

2   The size of the Waerndorfer fortune, i.e. that of Fritz and Lili Hellmann Waerndorfer, was estimated at 12,500,000 crowns by Charley Waerndorfer/Warndof, Waerndorfer's son, in an unpublished essay on his family. While the Waerndorfer/Hellmanns were undoubtedly wealthy, this amount—which corresponds to about € 52,000,000 (year 2000), may have overshot the mark. (For information on the relative values of currency in Vienna, see Roman Sandgruber, "Geld und Geldwert. Vom Wiener Pfennig zum Euro," in *Vom Pfennig zum Euro: Geld aus Wien*, exh. cat. Historisches Museum der Stadt Wien, Vienna 2002, pp. 62 ff.)

3   Today Weimarer Strasse 59, at the corner of Colloredogasse, in the nineteenth district of Vienna, a part of town known then—and now— as the "cottage quarter." The name alludes to the suburban character of the district while at the same time falling short of disclosing the true nature of the homes there, on a lesser scale but not unlike the way mansions in Newport are called "cottages."

4   Vergo 1981 (see note 1), p. 36. After the Waerndorfers' bankruptcy, the house and its contents were sold to Wilhelm and Martha Freund. It is not clear whether they were the minor clients of the Wiener Werkstätte referred to in the Wiener Werkstätte (metalwork) archives merely as *"Freund"* between 1903 and 1923; whether they were related to Ella Freund, who appears twice in the same archives by name and as *"Miss Freund"*; or both. The famous Margaret Macdonald gesso panels from the music room—long believed lost—were discovered in the Österreichisches Museum für Angewandte Kunst MAK (Austrian Museum of Applied Arts) in the course of major renovations in 1990.

5   Ibid., p. 34. "I won't even tell you what all I have by Minne in marble." (*Was ich alles in Marmor von Minne habe, sag' ich Ihnen gar nicht.*) Letter from Waerndorfer to Hermann Bahr, January 5, 1903.

6   See Werner J. Schweiger, *Meisterwerke der Wiener Werkstätte*, Vienna 1990, p. 6. "With three trained craftsmen, the silversmith Karl Kallert and the metal workers Konrad Koch and Konrad Schindel, they moved into the apartment in the fourth district at Heumühlgasse 6; in the two rooms they set up the silver and metal workshop, in the smallest room the office was 'established'." (*Mit drei geschulten Handwerkern, dem Silberschmied Karl Kallert und den Metallarbeitern Konrad Koch und Konrad Schindel, bezog man die Wohnung im vierten Bezirk, Heumühlgasse 6; in den beiden Zimmern wurden die Silber- und Metallwerkstätte eingerichtet, im Kabinett "etablierte" sich die Direktion.*) Incidentally, as Schweiger explains, these rooms were furnished with Biedermeier furniture.

7   The (surviving) archives of the Wiener Werkstätte, now in the collection of the MAK, were acquired in the year 1955 as a gift from Alfred Hofmann, the lawyer who had settled the Wiener Werkstätte bankruptcy. From 1990–93 Gabriele Fabiankowitsch, working for the MAK, used them to create a computer data bank, preparing the way for the systematic processing and analysis of thousands of pages of documentary material. Though the archives list nearly every item made by the Wiener Werkstätte by model number, together with information on dates, materials, production costs, sales prices, and purchasers, the punctiliousness of the firm's record-keeping seems to vary over time and from item to item. Together with the Wiener Werkstätte model books and photo albums, they remain, nonetheless, the most important indicator of how the Wiener Werkstätte functioned, and who its clients were.

8   The parents of Fritz and August Waerndorfer. (Samuel and Bertha Wärndorfer used the traditional spelling of the family name.) Leopold Wolfgang Rochowanski's 1950 version of the founding of the Wiener Werkstätte included mention of Waerndorfer's hesitation when a second, larger sum of money was asked for. Waerndorfer is then reputed to have said, "I will speak with my mother." (…*ich werde mit meiner Mutter sprechen.*) As cited in Schweiger 1990 (see note 6), p. 6.

9   Waerndorfer married Lili Jeanette Hellmann, the daughter of Bernhard and Caroline Hellmann, in 1895.

10 Jenny Mautner, née Neumann, was the sister of Waerndorfer's mother, Bertha.

11 Margarethe von Rémy-Berzenkovich, née Hellmann, was a sister of Lili Hellmann Waerndorfer.

12 In 1885, when he was thirty-eight years old, the value of Karl Wittgenstein's stock holdings alone was already around two million crowns; the greater part of his fortune was amassed during the 1890s. During the Nazi regime two of his children, Hermine and Paul, were listed in the *Vermögenserhebung* (inquiry into property) of April 27, 1938, as the fourth wealthiest Jews in Austria, with a personal wealth of 5,010,000 Reichskronen each. Three other siblings—Helene, Margarethe, and Ludwig—also outlived their parents and would, according to law, have received a similar inheritance. Margarethe, who became Margaret Stonborough-Wittgenstein and an American citizen upon her marriage, was, presumably for the latter reason, not placed on the list. Ludwig had famously returned his inheritance to the family. Helene's absence from it is a puzzling question.

13 For a reliable and detailed genealogy of the Wittgenstein and Salzer families over the past century and a half see Georg Gaugusch, "Die Familien Wittgenstein und Salzer und ihr genealogisches Umfeld," *Adler: Zeitschrift für Genealogie und Heraldik*, vol. 21, issue 4, October/December 2001, pp. 120–145.

14 The Hennebergs lived in a house built and decorated by Hoffmann in 1904–06. Max Biach had Hoffmann remodel an apartment in 1902, the Knipses had him design a country house and boathouse in 1903, and the Stoclets commissioned their eponymous *Palais* from Hoffmann in 1905–11. Both Sonja Knips and Marie Henneberg were also the subjects of important portraits by Gustav Klimt. As Christian Witt-Dörring pointed out in a lecture at the Neue Galerie in 2002, there was a strict division between the clients of Josef Hoffmann, who often had their portraits painted by Klimt, and those of Adolf Loos, who far more frequently turned to Oskar Kokoschka for portraiture. Klimt was, himself, a client of the Wiener Werkstätte, purchasing at least seventeen pieces of Moser and Hoffmann jewelry from 1903–06, including five Hoffmann brooches. In addition, he bought a silver Hoffmann *Bonbonnière* (WW model no. S 975) in 1907.

    Several of the other names on the list of regular clients during the years 1903–06 are less well-known abroad. Other important clients such as the families Ast, Gomperz (the family of the ceramist

Lucie Rie [?]), Koller, and Primavesi made the greater share of their purchases after 1906.

15 Together with Christian Witt-Dörring, I have been able to identify the owner of this apartment, known in the pertinent literature only as "Dr. S.," as the (still enigmatic) Dr. Seewald. See *Deutsche Kunst und Dekoration,* vol. 26, Darmstadt 1905, pp. 534, 538–541.

16 Dagobert Peche, *Der brennende Dornbusch* (The Burning Bush), originally unpublished manuscript from 1922 discovered and transcribed by Philipp Häusler, posthumously published in *Dagobert Peche and the Wiener Werkstätte,* exh. cat, New Haven 2002, pp. 171–172. "Josef Hoffmann set up this undertaking on a subsidized basis and was concerned, and actually content, that the houses he built were filled with the applied arts it produced." (*Josef Hoffmann stellte dieses Unternehmen auf die Basis des Mäzenatentums und war bedacht und damit eigentlich befriedigt, wenn die Häuser, welche er baute, mit dem von ihm erzeugten Kunstgewerbe gefüllt waren.*)

17 The Wiener Werkstätte produced a design for a silver creamer by Carl Otto Czeschka for the first time in December, 1905. Beginning in the following year his designs were produced on a regular basis— some twenty-eight in 1906.

18 Werner J. Schweiger, *Meisterwerke der Wiener Werkstätte,* Vienna 1990, p. 9. Editha Moser placed half that sum at the disposal of the Wiener Werkstätte. It was over this issue, among others, that Koloman Moser left the Wiener Werkstätte in 1907.

19 See Malcolm Gladwell, *The Tipping Point: How Little Things Can Make a Big Difference,* Boston et al. 2000, pp. 34 ff. Later on, when its "friends" moved on to preoccupations with other fashions, the Wiener Werkstätte's dependency on them became a deficit.

20 Zuckerkandl's reviews appeared in the *Wiener Allgemeine Zeitung* and the *Neues Wiener Journal,* the former a newspaper published by her brother Julius Szeps. Their father was Moriz Szeps, one of the most highly admired/highly despised career newspapermen in late 19th-century Vienna. The publisher of the liberal *Neues Wiener Tagblatt* (and, later, the *Wiener Tagblatt*), he made and lost a small fortune, was a personal friend and confidant of Crown Prince Rudolf, and eventually became the father-in-law of Georges Clemenceau.

21 See photograph of the dining room of the Berlin apartment of Margaret Stonborough-Wittgenstein, where such a flower vase stands on the dining table.

22 Karl Kraus, *Die Fackel,* no. 41, 1900. As cited in Burkhardt Rukschcio, *Adolf Loos,* Salzburg and Vienna 1982, p. 70.

23 Rukschcio 1982 (see note 22), p. 70.

24 Kessler was, incidentally, an acquaintance of Berta Zuckerkandl. He betrayed their friendship by reporting her political activities—together with her sister Sophie Clemenceau she attempted to negotiate a separate peace between France and Austria in 1915—to the Foreign Office and the Chancellery of the Reich in Berlin. See Lucian O. Meysels, *In Meinem Salon ist Österreich: Berta Zuckerkandl und ihre Zeit,* Vienna and Munich 1984, pp. 148, 291.

25 These baskets, which were likely produced by the Viennese firm Argentor, clearly plagiarized the Wiener Werkstätte design vocabulary, if not a specific design. (They strongly resemble WW model nos. M 648 and M 627, both of which, however, have handles.)

26 The painting still hangs at the top of the grand staircase today.

27 "For the artists of today wish for nothing other than that for which the art of yore wished. And they can do it, as well. Out of the strong foundation of *Sachlichkeit* the highest blossom of 'Cellinesque' art has grown. That is to say, decorations for an aristocratic lifestyle." (*Denn diese Künstler von heute, sie wollen nichts anderes, als was die Kunst von einstens gewollt hat. Und sie können es auch. Aus dem starken Fundament der Sachlichkeit ist eine höchste Blüte "Cellinesker" Kunst entstanden. Das heisst adeligen Lebensschmuckes.*) Berta Zuckerkandl, "Wo halten wir? Zur Eröffnung der kunstgewerblichen Ausstellung bei Miethke" (February 1905), *Zeitkunst. Wien 1901–1907,* Vienna and Leipzig 1908, pp. 38 ff.

28 Stefan Zweig, *Die Welt von Gestern,* Frankfurt am Main 1970, p. 28.

29 A play on words involving the immensely rich and untitled Wittgenstein family and the princely—but less rich—family Sayn-Wittgenstein-Sayn. In German the verb *haben* means "to have;" the verb *sein,* which is pronounced the same way as Sayn, means "to be."

30 *Es ist Erreicht! Katalog der Kunstvereinigung Rebellion,* Vienna 1901, p. 34. (*Darf ich fragen, ob Sie der Moderne angehören? Seh' ich aus wie e Antisemit?*)

31 Oskar Kokoschka, *Mein Leben,* Munich 1971, pp. 64 ff. (*Meistens waren es Juden, die mir als Modell dienten, weil sie viel unsicherer als der übrige Teil der im gesellschaftlichen Leben fest verankerten Wiener und daher auch für alles Neue aufgeschlossener waren, viel empfindlicher auch für die Spannungen und den Druck infolge des Verfalls der alten Ordnung in Österreich.*)

32 Eduard F. Sekler, *Josef Hoffmann. The Architectural Work,* Princeton 1985, p. 98.

33 Ludwig Hevesi, *Acht Jahre Secession,* Vienna 1906, p. 484. (*…recht peripherisch gelegen…*)

34 In the Wiener Werkstätte archives these items are listed under the name of the representative of the Hohenzollern Kunstgewerbehaus, H. Hirschwald.

35 *Dresdner Hausgerät,* sales catalogue of the Dresdener Werkstätten für Handwerkskunst, Dresden 1906, pp. 81, 83.

36 Hevesi 1906 (see note 33). I am grateful to Elisabeth Schmuttermeier for bringing this to my attention.

37 *Kunst und Kunsthandwerk,* yr. 3, Vienna 1900, p. 151.

38 Twenty-one of the forty-four items listed in his name are marked as having been "sold;" three are marked *retour,* and the fate of the remaining items is unknown.

39 In 1907 the Wiener Werkstätte opened a branch at Graben 15 in the inner city, where sales appear to have been steady.

40 The architects of the building were Ernst von Gotthilf-Miskoczy and Alexander Neumann. Today part of the Palais Fanto houses the Arnold Schönberg Center.

41 In addition, twenty-three pieces of jewelry were likewise "acquired" and returned.

42 Anneliese Fanto and Georg Gaugusch kindly provided genealogical information pertaining to the Fanto family.

43 "The Vienna stock exchange fears God, Taussig, Wittgenstein and, apart from that, nothing else on the face of the earth…" (*Die Wiener Börse fürchtet Gott, Taussig, Wittgenstein und sonst nichts auf der Welt…*) was Karl Kraus's wry assessment of Karl Wittgenstein's (financial) power. *Die Fackel,* no. 17, 1899.

44 Hermine Wittgenstein, *Familienerinnerungen,* unpublished manuscript, Vienna and Hochreit June 1944, p. 191. As Hermine Wittgenstein indicates, Paul Wittgenstein's enthusiasm for—and seriousness about—the work of Hoffmann may have led to his breaking with his nephew, the philosopher Ludwig Wittgenstein, over the construction of a house for Margaret Stonborough-Wittgenstein on Kundmanngasse in 1926–28.

45 Information from Monika Krünes Sarnitz, the niece of Anna Hochstetter, as told to Stefan Asenbaum and Michael Huey in June, 2002.

46 Wittgenstein 1944 (see note 44), p. 77.

47 During the Nazi regime, the Secession chose to remove all three names rather than just Wittgenstein's, as the authorities had demanded. The names have since been returned. (According to Hermine Wittgenstein, the idea to remove all the names in protest had been that of the painter Josef Engelhart, who was married to Doris Mautner von Markhof, the sister of the aforementioned Victor and the half-sister of Magda.) See Wittgenstein 1944 (see note 44), p. 76.

48 The vitrine cost, as previously mentioned, some 20,000 crowns. According to Tobias G. Natter, Klimt quoted a price of around 5,000 crowns for the portrait of Margaret Stonborough-Wittgenstein. See *Klimt und die Frauen,* exh. cat. Österreichische Galerie Belvedere, Vienna 2000, p. 111.

49 Von Schaukal purchased a Hoffmann coal bin (WW model no. M 469) in about 1904–06.

50 Richard von Schaukal, *Die Mietwohnung. Eine Kulturfrage,* Munich 1911, p. 34. *(Wer im Jahre 1897 geheiratet hatte, war noch mit Renaissancemöbeln versorgt worden, die glücklichern Verlobten der nächstfolgenden Jahre erhielten bereits für dasselbe Ausstattungspauschale "englische" oder neudeutsche… Es ist das so, als ob man die "Kultur" um eine Schichte gehoben meinte, wenn der "fashionable" Mann dem Schneider darin ehrfürchtig Folge leistet, daß die Weste nunmehr um zwei Knopfspannen tiefer ausgeschnitten getragen werde. "Man" trägt das Sacco "heuer" lang über die Hüfte hinabgeschmiegt und streng in die Taille geschnitten. "Man" hat ein "Mahagoni" Sitzzimmer, "nicht mehr" einen Rokokosalon. Und das sind "Errungenschaften"!)*

51 Photographs of the tea- and coffee-service in use by or in an interior belonging to Margaret Stonborough-Wittgenstein exist from 1905 until the 1950s.

52 Margaret Stonborough-Wittgenstein, correspondence with Leopoldine Kallmus Wittgenstein, cited in Ursula Prokop, *Margaret Stonborough-Wittgenstein: Bauherrin. Intellektuelle. Mäzenin,* Vienna 2003, p. 56. *(Unsere Wohnung ist das Schönste, was man sich vorstellen kann, und riesig gemüthlich. Moser, der wieder riesig nett war, und ich haben drei Tage lang Möbel aufgestellt, Bilder gehangen und Rahmen angestrichen. Jetzt ist die Wohnung wenigstens äusserlich in Ordnung und Jerome und ich sind begeistert und loben Euch und die Wiener Werkstätten [sic] täglich.)*

53 According to Ursula Prokop, she even made designs of her own for cups and glasses, and, with Eduard Wimmer-Wisgrill, designed a table centerpiece she intended to have produced by the Wiener Werkstätte in the fall of 1910. See Ursula Prokop (see note 52), p. 71.

54 As told to Michael Huey in November, 2002. Pierre Stonborough surmises that, since Perco's reputation was slighter than Hoffmann's, Margaret Stonborough-Wittgenstein was able to prevail with her own ideas.

55 Wittgenstein 1944 (see note 44), p. 123. *(Schon in ihrer Jugend war ihr Zimmer die verkörperte Auflehnung gegen alles Hergebrachte und das Gegenteil eines sogenannten Jungmädchenzimmers.…Gott weiss woher sie alle die interessanten Gegenstände nahm, mit denen sie es schmückte.…Und obwohl weibliche Handarbeiten nicht ihre Force waren, entwarf sie für sich selbst die merkwürdigsten Stickereien, z. B. um nur eine zu nennen, die anatomische Darstellung des menschlichen Herzens mit den Kranzgefässen und Arterien, aber nicht naturalistisch, sondern rein als Ornament empfunden.)*

56 "…es fehlt ihm die Gesundheit…(Treibhauspflanze)." Ludwig Wittgenstein, *Vermischte Bemerkungen,* Frankfurt am Main 1994, p. 80.

57 New Haven 2002 (see note 16), cat. nos. 1 (showcase for the *Kunstschau* 1920), 5 (cabinet for the *Kunstschau* 1920), and 24 (dressing table).

58 As cited in Brendan Gill, *Here at The New Yorker,* New York 1975, p. 116.

59 *Die Gruft.* As told by Christina Wesemann-Wittgenstein to Michael Huey, September 2002.

60 As told by Friedrich Wittgenstein to Paul Asenbaum, December 2002. *(Du bist also der arme Bua, der in meiner Einrichtung hat aufwachsen müssen.)*

IN ALL DIRECTIONS: TRAVEL AND ITS MEANINGS IN A MODERNIZING EUROPE

J. S. MARCUS

A European traveler at the beginning of the 18th century—like a traveler at the beginning of the 8th—depended on horses, and on the condition of the roads, which, unless they were built along surviving stretches of Roman road, were often impassable. Horses sank up to their bellies in mud; wheels rotted in mid-journey.

People traveled for the same reasons they do today—for business, for safety, for salvation. The word "refugee" was first used at the end of the 17th century, to describe the Protestants who fled France after the Edict of Nantes was revoked. (Our age's "economic" refugees are like pilgrims, trying to cure their poverty at the shrines of capitalism.)

Traveling for pleasure was not unknown, just impractical. As late as the 1770s, a trip by stagecoach from London to Glasgow could take up to three weeks if the weather was bad; on foot, in good weather, the trip took four weeks. There were hardly schedules. A gun was let off to let people know that a coach had come in.

Inns were egalitarian, and utilitarian; lively and meager. Travelers were expected to bring their own cutlery. The City Museum in Sheffield has in its collection a silver fork, from around 1725, that still suggests the Middle Ages, except for the neat screw attached to the head and the handle's narrow joint. The fork and its matching, unscrewable knife are almost flat, and fit exactly into a small leather pouch. Compactness in design has nautical origins, as a set of tricks to save space during long journeys at sea. On stagecoach journeys, compactness was a source of luxury and a mere necessity, like arriving at one's destination.

■

Ideas are like travelers, who take their time and then return home changed. John Locke was inspired by Descartes, whose works he happened upon while a student at Oxford. Tens of thousands of Huguenots fled to England, read English books, and wrote back to France about the new ideas of Locke and Isaac Newton. In turn, Voltaire and Montesquieu were inspired to move beyond the *finesse* (as Diderot would later put it) of Nicolas de Malebranche, Descartes's disciple, and reimport French logic as "sensible" English truth.

Voltaire made the journey to England in 1726, and, like many travelers, starting with Marco Polo, wrote a book about what he saw. In *Letters Concerning the English Nation,* Voltaire made a general, well-reasoned appeal for reason itself, and along the way managed to popularize the anecdote about Newton and the apple. What Voltaire especially admired about England was its government, as he understood it; the English, he thought, had "drowned the Idol of arbitrary Power." The book, which appeared in France in 1733, with the title *Lettres philosophiques*, would later be called "the first bomb thrown at the ancien regime."

Thanks to Voltaire, the English style was all the rage in mid-18th-century France. Work on the *Encyclopédie* began in the 1740s, as a translation of the two-volume *Cyclopedia,* by the Englishman Ephraim Chambers. The editor, Denis Diderot, had made a name for himself as an English translator.

The *Encyclopédie* was the intellectual event of a century noted for intellectual events. It had universalist aspirations ("It is the aim of an encyclopedia," we learn, from its eponymous entry, "to collect the knowledge that is scattered across the earth") and a compact form. The world, it was discovered, could be wondrously contained in seventeen volumes of text and eleven volumes of plates.

The *Encyclopédie* is like a travel book, which also collects impressions, and facts, and contains illustrations; and like an atheist's bible. It is an illustrated guide to everything, meant to free its readers from blind belief in something.

■

The French Revolution was immediately preceded by great advances in road construction. Beginning in 1764, a man named Pierre Trésaguet began to build roads with stone foundations, and then covered them with gravel. The roads were arched, or cambered, which encouraged natural drainage; and there were curbstones.

Because of Trésaguet, France's aristocrats could flee more quickly when the revolution came, and Napoleon's armies could begin their brief age of victory in what might be called reasonable haste.

The Grand Tour straddles the revolution in roads and the revolution in ideas. Starting in the 17th century, English aristocrats made the invariably difficult journey down to Italy, and later, in Lord Byron's footsteps, on to Greece, as a way, really, of fitting in back home. Of course there were pleasures to be had, and knowledge to be gained, and, usually, a book to be written. But the pleasure and the knowledge were incidental, and the books were anecdotal, fanciful. *Gulliver's Travels* satirized English society, not English travel writing.

The England that 18th-century grand tourists returned to was in no way free from class prejudice or prerogatives. Those prejudices and prerogatives, however, were free of religious pretension. In the 1710s, the middle reaches of England's upper classes began to dabble in Freemasonry, more or less a Whiggish fad. Freemasonry quickly spread to Europe, popularizing the ideas of the Enlightenment in exclusive, even secretive lodges. Freemasons, like the *philosophes* (many of whom were Freemasons themselves), never doubted that they were trying to improve on, or even to replace, Christianity by providing a secular religion of morality. In his Masonic dialogues, Gotthold Ephraim Lessing went a step further, and suggested that Freemasonry was a kind of pre-condition for citizenship in a world ruled by reason rather than by God's anointed sovereigns.

1. Leopold Kupelwieser, *Land-partie der Schubertianer von Atzenbrugg nach Aumühl* (Excursion of the Schubert Society from Atzenbrugg to Aumühl), watercolor, 1820 Historisches Museum der Stadt Wien

Freemasonry came to Austria with Francis Stephen of Lorraine, the husband of Maria Theresa, who had been initiated in England, in 1731. His coronation as Holy Roman Emperor—who ruled absolutely, with Divine Right—included unlikely, Masonic formulas.

■

Eighteenth-century Germans were vaguely unified, or just held in suspension, by the fancifulness of the Holy Roman Empire, an illusion (neither holy, nor Roman, nor an empire) that towards its close had become like an illusion of an illusion. In Goethe's *Faust,* the empire is a cause for wonderment, anti-Newtonian in all but words, in that it falls apart and still hangs together. The empire's decline inspired the tiny, expansive, and infinitely complicated—the par- ticular—worlds of Jean Paul, whose foolish, lonely, provincial geniuses move from one south German town to another with extravagant effort and muted pomp, as mock explorers; his stories can seem to be about the futility of travel, about stasis. A traveler, he explains, is like an invalid caught between worlds. Jean Paul—who might be thought of as the Holy Roman Empire's greatest satirist—first used to great effect the word *Doppelgänger.*

■

For Germans, the Enlightenment has as much to do with Reason as with the reaction against it. The imitation of Englishness, of Frenchness, and of French imitations of Englishness, quickly led to an authentic, artistic corrective, a Sturm and Drang, the aesthetic temper tantrum that made an idol out of personal expression. The German *Denker* are a mood away from the French *philosophes*. "I am not here to think," wrote Kant's student, and Goethe's tutor, Johann Gottfried Herder, "but to be, feel, live!"[1]

Goethe's Werther shot himself in 1774, and it was like the first bomb thrown back at the Enlightenment.

Germans had their own tradition of traveling over the Alps, for business, and for knowledge, and, by the 18th century, for position at home; *Kavalierreise* was the German expression for the Grand Tour. Yet a German in Italy does not suggest a fop or an amateur in the English manner, but a shift in understanding—a Dürer, a Winckelmann.

Goethe went to Italy in 1786. His two-year journey was highly documented, and subsequently mythical, recalling, in its origins, the traveler's pause in the dark forest at the beginning of *The Divine Comedy*. At thirty-seven, Goethe was like Dante; he "had lost the path that does not stray." *Die Leiden des jungen Werther* (The Sorrows of Young Werther) had made Goethe, after Voltaire, the most famous writer in Europe. But that early success and his official duties in Weimar had become like the walls of a crypt. Life in all its variety began for him in Italy, where he traveled anonymously. The account of his trip, rewritten in the form of a diary, appeared decades after the fact, in installments. *Italienische Reise* (Italian Journey) is filled with serene contradictions, like Tischbein's famous portrait, *Goethe in der Campagna* (Goethe in Campagna), with its subject in alert repose, dressed in a contemporary suit with antique trappings, suggesting, somehow, the temporal and the eternal. "Auch ich in Arkadien!" is the book's epigraph, but could also be its postscript.

Italian journey could be in the plural. There was an outer journey—indeed almost a field expedition (the descriptions of nature are more impassioned, and more frequent, than descriptions of art)—and an inner journey; a *Kavalier-* and *Geistesreise.* Goethe returned to Weimar ready to write the masterpieces that would catapult him above literary movements, and then beyond history itself. His life, as transformed in Italy, stands for the totality of experience, and the triumph of genius; for an idea of inner progress that would be summoned up in the new, secular, and transcendent meaning of a previously theological term, *Bildung.*

In 1812, Rahel Varnhagen published her correspondence about Goethe, a guide of sorts to the master's genius. During the French Revolution, a cult of Reason had been declared:

2. Carl Spitzweg, *Engländer in der Campagna* (Englishmen in Campagna), oil on paper, 1835–1836 Preussischer Kulturbesitz, Nationalgalerie Berlin, inv. no. 1591

there were Republican celebrations on the altar at Notre Dame, renamed a Temple of Reason. Varnhagen, a converted Jew, is credited with starting a "Goethe cult." "Goethe" and *Bildung* would become the magic words for Central Europe's Jewish middle classes. Travel metaphors come to mind. Goethe was a guide to German *Kultur; Bildung* was a passport out of the ghetto.

After Italy, Goethe settled for good in Weimar, and became a kind of tourist attraction, a living version of an antique monument.

■

The 19th century began, arguably, in 1815, and was, for a generation, characterized by a political restoration and a technological revolution. In 1829, the year Goethe published the final installment of *Italienische Reise,* the first passenger train service, driven by a locomotive called the *Rocket,* began service between Liverpool and Manchester. The first passenger steamboat, called the *Comet,* began running in northern England, on the River Clyde, in 1812.

Karl Baedeker, who revolutionized the travel habits, and desires, of Europeans, started that revolution in 1832, the year of Goethe's death, when his family's Coblenz printing house bought the rights to *Rheinreise von Main bis Cöln* (A Journey on the Rhine), a *Reisebild* by Johann August Klein. *Reisebilder*—previously a subgenre of Romantic literature— did not need to be correct, just atmospheric. Baedeker had the idea of checking facts, and ranking attractions, and, after his fame grew, of traveling anonymously, disguised as one of his readers. The Baedeker guides were practical and efficient: compact. They soon appeared in translation— in France, in 1848, and, to an even greater effect, in Britain in 1861.

Not surprisingly, the word "tourist" is of English origin, first coming into use around 1800. ("A traveler nowadays is called a tour-*ist*," we learn from one Samuel Pegge, in a book published that year, called *Anecdotes of the English Language,* one of many imitations of Dr. Johnson's *Dictionary.*) A few years after the appearance of the first English Baedeker, Thomas Cook conducted his first organized trip to Switzerland, once a stopping-off point on the Grand Tour; he announced the trip in advance, in *Cook's Excursionist and Advertiser.*

The turn toward Switzerland was significant. Cook's early tours had been to England's Lake District (made popular by the Romantic poets) and to Scotland (made popular by the novels of Sir Walter Scott). After the rapid expansion of the railroad, these destinations became available even to working-class tourists. Cook diverted middle class imaginations toward more sublime, and expensive, settings. Thomas Cook was responsible for popularizing the need to get away, and the need to get away from those who were getting away; for the restoration in the travel revolution.

■

Once abroad, the English tourist epitomized a kind of unenlightened traveler. Heine, in his satire of Goethe,

among others, *Reise von München nach Genua* (A Journey from Munich to Genoa), runs into English tourists in Innsbruck's Hofkirche; they misread their guidebook, wonder why Rudolf Hapsburg posed for a sculptor while wearing a dress. Heine's Italy is almost invisible, blotted out with tourists: "One can no longer imagine an Italian lemon tree without imagining an English lady sniffing at it."[2] And in a growing concern for travel writers it is blighted by political oppression, in this case, Hapsburg oppression. The theme of Carl Spitzweg's 1835 painting, *Engländer in der Campagna,* is contemporary anxiety. The Englishman of the title has his face in a guidebook, and his wife is clutching her purse.

■

The Industrial Revolution was the application of reason to the physical world; or, in a metaphor popular at the time, the marriage of science and practicality. For us, the early symbol of that revolution is James Watt's steam engine, patented in 1776. For Watt's European contemporaries, there was more inspiration to be had from the new, Parisian air balloon released by the Montgolfier brothers, over the Champs de Mars, in 1783.

The concerted application of reason to human affairs began not with the republican passions of the French Revolution, but with the passionate reforms of the Hapsburg Empire, under Maria Theresa and her son, coregent, and successor, Joseph II. They were advised—like Joseph's successor, Francis—by Josef von Sonnenfels, editor of the influential journal *Der Mann ohne Vorurtheil* (The Man without Prejudice) and the grandson of the Grand Rabbi of Berlin, turned Catholic and Freemason.

Joseph—directly inspired by the ideas of the *philosophes* and the Freemasons, and the model for Sarastro, the wise ruler in *The Magic Flute*—was the most enlightened, and most despotic, of Europe's enlightened despots. He abolished the feudal privileges of the Church, brought about religious toleration, suspended censorship, and gave Austria the most modern administration in Europe; until his frustration got the better of him and he reinstalled censorship, cracked down on the Freemasons, and planted the seeds of nationalist resentment. By the end of his reign, his bureaucrats had ceased to be agents of reason, and were on their way to becoming agents of a police state; the freedom from religious dogma had been replaced by a dogmatic idea of the state itself.

In 1790, the year of Joseph's death, Johann Pezzl wrote a travel guide to Vienna "for the unbiased German public," called *Skizze von Wien* (Sketch of Vienna). Pezzl compares "Old Vienna" of 1770 with "New Vienna" of 1790; the "old" spies ("in wartime and against the enemy") with the "new" spies ("in peacetime and against the state's own employees and subjects"); the "old" state ("sick from constipation") with the "new" state ("sick from too many purges"). It says something about Pezzl, or about Vienna, that his barbs were meant to be amusing, as much as true.

The reign of Joseph inspired 19th-century liberal-minded Austrians to go on hoping for reform. And it inspired 20th-century critics of liberalism to find a place where everything started to go wrong; critics who realized that when power is concentrated, reform and reaction are like *Doppelgänger,* variations on a single, anti-democratic theme. Hannah Arendt, in *The Origins of Totalitarianism,* titles her first chapter, "The Equivocalities of Emancipation and the Jewish State Banker," in which the Josephin privilege of toleration is seen not as a hopeful advance towards full citizenship, but as an ominous substitute for it.

In the shrunken "Austrian" empire of Francis I, Vienna became a refuge from the Enlightenment. North German Romantics, turned archconservative Catholics, arrived and became part of the circle around the strict, appealing priest Klemens Maria Hofbauer; Jesuits reappeared. The caretaker of Enlightenment ideas was, arguably, none other than Prince Metternich, whose repressive domestic policies and system of national alliances were inspired by Reason and utility. For Metternich, feudalism and clericalism, like republicanism, didn't make sense.

■

Fanny Arnstein—wife of the Hapsburg court banker Nathan Arnstein (ennobled in 1797), and childhood friend of Rahel Varnhagen—oversaw the most glittering salon of her time. The temporary mingling of the second society, which had begun to include people like the Arnsteins, with members of the nobility had ended by the 1830s. But a kind of mingling between Jews—who could be ennobled, but could not become citizens until 1848— and the highest reaches of the nobility persisted, on the boards of the new railroads.

■

The horse-driven railroad between Linz and Budweis started running in 1825; the first stretch of the Nordbahn, connecting Vienna with Silesia, was functioning in 1836. The Austrian Danube Steamship Company, connecting Germany to the Black Sea, was established in 1829; and the Austrian Lloyd, headquartered in Trieste, in 1836. But Austria's industrialization was paradoxical: it led the way on the continent in the development of railroads and shipping, and—because of bureaucratic indifference and state censorship—lagged behind in economic output; rushed forward, and fell back.

The empire acquired a habit of ignoring or harassing its inventors. Josef Ressel, a Bohemian working in Trieste, developed the first modern propeller in 1826, but he was forbidden to experiment with it. In 1815, a Viennese tailor named Josef Madersperger had invented the first sewing machine, but he couldn't get anyone to market it. Ressel and Madersperger are somehow ridiculous—small, indeed forgotten, giants; Biedermeier characters.

■

The Napoleonic Wars had been a time of uncertainty and deprivation, and of shifting political loyalties. The Biedermeier virtues of discretion, thrift, domesticity, and political indifference were like jovial versions of wartime exigencies. Unlike the rest of Western Europe, Austria never experienced an economic boom in the years after Waterloo;

the drawn-out fact of shortages turned into the charm of modesty. There was a fad for smallness, for quaint interiors, and calming exteriors. There was a kind of monumental smallness; quaint mountains served nicely as placid backdrops.

There were small concerts at private houses, discreet journeys to the countryside around Vienna. Freemasonry had been outlawed by Francis; open-minded Viennese replaced it with an exclusive, egalitarian, vaguely subversive, nonsense club, the Ludlumshöhle. The trappings of Freemasonry lingered on in journeymen's use of geometric shapes and simple patterns; in the dignity—the idyll—of the craftsman at work.

Biedermeier literature abounds in images of travel, of discreet, pleasant journeys turned inward. *Am Strome* (On the River) is a poem by Johann Mayrhofer, set to music by his great friend, Franz Schubert. "It seems to me that my life is/Together with the river bound./Have not I on its banks/Both pleasures and sorrows found?"[3]

Pleasing images of travel were also images of entrapment; Anastasius Grün—the pen name of Count Anton Alexander Auersperg—titles his virulent indictment of repressive, Franciscan Vienna *Spaziergänge eines Wiener Poeten* (The Strolls of a Viennese Poet). And discreet pleasures can reveal inner horrors. *Am Strome* concludes with the speaker addressing the river: "Flow onward to the distant ocean/Mustn't tarry too long here./I, too, long for milder climates—/Bliss is foreign to earth's sphere."[4]

An excursion leads to contemplation, and contemplation leads back to the self, and to the fact of mortality. In his guide, *Wien und die Wiener* (Vienna and the Viennese), Adalbert Stifter includes a long section on the catacombs, with a preface that describes civilization as transient, and *Bildung* as futile in the face of death. In Schubert's *Winterreise,* life itself is nothing but a doomed journey: "A stranger I arrived," begins the first song, "a stranger I depart."[5]

■

The second invention of the screw propeller, patented in 1836 by the Swedish captain John Ericsson, changed the history of ship building, and led to the transatlantic steamer. The Englishman Robert McAdam improved on Trésauget's techniques, and invented the first paved road. By the 1850s, the "macadamized" Cumberland Road stretched for nearly 1,000 miles, from Virginia to Illinois, opening up the American West. In 1875, the inventor Siegfried Marcus drove the world's first automobile, powered by a single-cylinder internal combustion engine, through the streets of Vienna. It was considered too noisy, immediately banned by the police, and quickly forgotten.

The new Dual Monarchy—which both disguised and determined, slowed down and then sped up, Austria's decline—invented numerous, contradictory expressions to describe its authority, was at once imperial, royal, and constitutional; codified every possibility but that of disintegration.

3. *In the Model Railroad Club,*
Alfred Eisenstadt, Berlin 1931
From Susan Buck-Morss,
Dialektik des Sehens,
Frankfurt am Main 1993.

Austria-Hungary finished off its rail network in the 1880s, with attending motives that Sigmund Freud would later call regressive—with vengeance and greed. Hungary built its rail lines as far as possible from Austrian territory, forbade rail links that did not connect through Budapest, virtually impoverished Austrian Dalmatia and Hungarian Croatia. The railroad meant to connect Austria's distant crown colonies, Galicia and the Bukowina, was the financial scam of its time, condemning its Jewish, noble, and ennobled Jewish directors to ruin and embarrassing the country by causing the stock market to crash during Vienna's 1873 World's Fair.

■

Europe's expositions—starting with the Great Exhibition in London, in 1851—were both practical and fantastical, trade shows tuned into tourist attractions; international and nationalist; temporary utopias. In 1867, fifteen million people visited the second Paris exposition. Hundreds of thousands of workers were given free tickets, strolled through the grounds to look at goods they could never afford, were encouraged to inspect machines that would replace them. Vienna's World's Fair celebrated the new Ringstrasse prematurely. The new theater and opera and parliament and museums—the temples of *Bildung,* monuments to a liberal ascendancy—were either unfinished or hadn't been started. The crash of 1873 was like a premonition. Political anti-Semitism takes on a recognizable form after the crash. Liberalism—newly arrived in Austria, as a kind of Western European import—begins to seem old-fashioned. The Ringstrasse is obsolete before it can be completed, becomes like a permanent World Exposition, a previous utopia.

■

Europe's first passenger trains, like European society, were divided up into classes. The wooden benches of third class remained unchanged for nearly a century, fourth class meant standing up in a cattle car. European visitors to America were often surprised that up until after the Civil War America had only one class of travel.

The first generation of train travel coincided in America with the development of so-called patent furniture. A piece with many functions was reduced to its constituent, patentable parts, which could be combined in diverse, space-saving ways; form did not only follow function, but was indistinguishable from it. Comfort, mobility, and utility were combined in such wonders as the piano-bed of the 1860s (which also boasted a bureau, two closets, a washbasin, a pitcher, and a towel), the wildly popular Wilson Adjustable Chair of the 1870s (advertised in six different positions, including parlor chair, child's swing, and full-size bed), and the hammock-tricycle of the 1880s. Patent furniture's one lasting creation was the Pullman sleeping car, which promised to bring luxury travel to the masses. The *Pioneer*, Pullman's first, appeared in the 1860s, just as the first luxury hotels were being built in Switzerland and on the Riviera.

Patent furniture lost its appeal by the 1890s. The Chicago World Exposition of 1893 introduced Americans to a European idea of luxury. The once urgent, but simple pleasure of saving space gave way to the more urgent pleasure of cluttering up space.

■

John Ruskin hated trains, he hated their look, their smell, and their practicality, their sameness. In his autobiography, he recalls the "complex joys and ingenious hopes, connected with the choice of the traveling carriage." What attracted him was a carriage's "cunning design"—the "distribution of store cellars under the seats, secret drawers under front windows, invisible pockets under padded lining, safe from dust, and accessible only by insidious slits or necromantic valves like Aladdin's trap door." Ruskin is a prophet of sorts, a bridge between the Europe of the *Encyclopédie* and the Grand Tour, and the Europe of Thomas Cook and Friedrich Nietzsche. His celebrations are also lamentations; the world, as he imagined it, became a trap. He stands not for the totality of experience, but for the burden of it; for things that don't fit together, for incompleteness and failure; for genius as a kind of self-defeating spectacle. He died with his century, in 1900, by which time the word "Waterloo" had taken on another meaning as the name of a train station.

■

Trains were an obvious improvement over carriages. Steamships improved on clippers; telephones on telegraphs. Progress was not just a technological feat; it was a creed, both the cause of change and its result.

19th-century French thought has an expansive, but practical streak. Its placid confections, positivism and socialism, suggest what one might call a worldly utopia, a mechanized paradise. For Henri de Saint-Simon, and for Pierre Joseph Proudhon after him, the benefits of industry were manifest; for Proudhon, progress meant nothing short of "the march of society into history." In 1855, the year of the first Paris exposition, Victor Hugo ("the man of the 19th century," claimed one obituary writer, upon Hugo's death in 1905, "as Voltaire had been the man of the 18th"), called progress "the footstep of God himself."

History, as such, takes on another, no less manifest meaning for Karl Marx ("an alienated Jew pretending to be a Hegelienated Jew," in the words of a late 20th-century New Yorker), who insisted, as a matter of scientific fact, that mankind, led by the new working classes, will progress toward perfection. There are early, ominous signs in these modern wonders. Europe's completed train network, perfected in the first years of the 20th century, allowed, by design, for both mass travel and mass mobilization. The *Pioneer* made its maiden journey, and its name, in 1865, by carrying the body of the assassinated President, Abraham Lincoln, from Washington, D.C. home to Illinois. The trains crossing Europe's borders—carrying Thomas Cook travelers, with their new hotel vouchers and their patented, Baedeker fold-out maps—made Europe all the more aware of borders. The continent, indeed the world, is suddenly smaller. The race, for colonies, for navies, is on. The new assembly lines of Detroit have their origins in the slaughterhouses of Cincinnati and Chicago. The world had its first glimpse of an American assembly line in Vienna, at the 1873 exposition, with a panoramic view of a Cincinnati packing plant.

■

The Hapsburg Monarchy is an exception. It has no overseas colonies. (It has colonies inside its own borders.) The world around it is shrinking; but the world it makes up is getting bigger, its constituent parts are breaking away from the whole. The competing nationalisms of the late monarchy recall the petty states of the Holy Roman Empire. In the early years of the new century, the new Austrian Parliament has stopped functioning. Members yell at themselves in their various languages; Czech nationalists filibuster with toy instruments; tourists crowd the gallery, amused by the chaos. The atmosphere, really, is one of armed particularism; and the most rational form of government seems to be the most old-fashioned. The aged Francis Joseph—preferring to see out the end of his reign without electricity, without water closets—shuts down Parliament several times and must rule directly, at least in name, as a kind of mechanized despot.

■

By 1900, the Hapsburg nationalities have favored resorts, usually found at the end of secondary train lines. German nationalists prefer the Salzkammergut and the Tyrol. Poles prefer Zakopane. (The *Zakopanski* style would later become the Polish national style.) Slovak intellectuals assemble at Luhatschowitz, where half-timbered "Slovak" cabins are embellished with Czech modernist decorations. On Adriatic beaches, Croats avoid Hungarians. In Borszek, in Transylvania, the Rumanians time their arrival with the departure of the Germans.

Europe's privileged classes convene one last time in the years before the war, in the monarchy's most exclusive spas. English gentry, trying to avoid the middle-class bastions in Switzerland and the Riviera, headed for Meran in the Tyrol. Russian aristocrats met each other in Abazzia. ("I can still identify its crenellated, cream-colored tower in old pictures,"[6] writes Vladimir Nabokov, half a century later, of a villa his family rented in Abazzia in 1904.) Karlsbad, the most illustrious of all, had associations with Goethe, who visited thirteen times—began, in fact, his Italian journey from there. Like other luxury firms, the Wiener Werkstätte opened up a store in Karlsbad, and its artists rendered the town on postcards.

Many of the monarch's finest resorts had a Jewish, or vaguely Jewish, reputation. Karlsbad supported a number of Jewish marriage brokers (though Jewish guests were encouraged by their hotels to take their promenade at early, unfashionable hours). Bad Ischl, where Franz Joseph spent his summers, attracted Vienna's cultivated upper-middle classes. Invoking the liturgical phrase, "People of Israel," Karl Kraus mocked their denied Jewishness by referring to them as the "people of Ischl." Kraus, who had his own brand of denied Jewishness, was in turn dubbed the "Ischl Heine."

Tourism was an early target of Kraus's. Tourists were for Kraus what refugees would be for Bertolt Brecht—bearers

of ill tidings; or, even worse, of inauthenticity. The prosperity that tourism was supposed to bring was a kind of false, decorative prosperity, a sign of spiritual impoverishment.

Kraus, along with his friends Adolf Loos and Arnold Schoenberg, were their era's enlightened cranks, promoting a kind of impatient rationalism as a weapon against the aestheticizing pageants of their adversaries. They presided over their followers, perhaps, like despots, but were on the whole repudiated or ignored. The fact of their genius had to be sent abroad and then re-imported, often from Germany, like the automobile.

■

The hero of Jules Verne's novel, *Around the World in Eighty Days,* is an English dandy. He wears Savile Row suits and has his drinks at the Reform Club with "ice brought at great expense from the American lakes." His trip, which requires every mode of transportation, recalls the improvisations of the Grand Tour. The novel is reportage as fantasy, and inspires a world-wide contest.

Verne's double is H. G. Wells, whose fantasies are more practical, and more sinister. In 1895, Wells publishes *The Time Machine,* which imagines the world progressing to the point of near extinction. His hero glimpses the end of life on earth in a view of giant crabs covered in algae. But Wells, really, is an optimist: that final vision of advanced primitiveness is meant to instruct us, to help up to change ourselves. Our age's great historian of ideas, Isaiah Berlin, calls Wells "the last preacher of the morality of the Enlightenment."

■

In his 1902 film, *A Trip to the Moon,* Georges Melies invents the "dissolve" as a way of connecting one scene with another. The effect is at once rapid and dreamy; succinctly magical.

■

Does history move in cycles?

No, answers Isaiah Berlin, in *spirals,* in apparent recurrences. Not at all, says Gertrude Stein, time is a cubist painting, a composition with neither beginning nor end; Stein will look back on World War One as a cubist war, as topographically scattered, and temporally defiant. Perhaps, suggests Marcel Duchamp, whose painting, *Nude Descending a Staircase,* is cinematic. A figure in motion can be anywhere—everywhere—but in truth is at the very end.

■

War mimics peace, up to a point. Fritz Haber, imperial Germany's preeminent chemist, conducts experiments that lead to the isolation of nitrates—to artificial fertilizers and then to poison gas. German airships, once something out of Jules Verne, bomb wartime London, in a scene from H. G. Wells. Central Europe's spa towns—which profited from the medicalization of tourism, and made mild illness fashionable—are converted into sprawling hospital wards.

4. Leopold Drexler, postcard view of Karlsbad, printed by the Wiener Werkstätte Österreichisches Museum für Angewandte Kunst MAK, Vienna

5. Sticker with Minnie Mouse on a German warhead From Susan Buck-Morss, *Dialektik des Sehens,* Frankfurt am Main 1993.

6. *Présentation de quelques nouveautés* (Presentation of Some Novelties) From Susan Buck-Morss *Dialektik des Sehens,* Frankfurt am Main 1993.

Goethe's journey to Italy, and what might be called his cult of life, has an odd echo in Ernst Jünger's books about his trip to the front, in a cult of death. "The shame of the age" for Karl Kraus is to be found in the wartime Swiss plan to take tourists to see the front once peace has been declared, in the militarization of tourism.

Literary postmortems of the Hapsburg Empire began even before the war started, but reach an elegiac *finesse* in Joseph Roth's *Radetzkymarsch,* published in 1932, in time for the demise of the first Austrian Republic. Francis Joseph's double in the novel is an orthodox rabbi. Roth understood that the lowest Jew, like the highest noble, had nowhere to go in an empire-less world.

Hapsburg literature ends, arguably, with the Israeli novelist, Aharon Appelfeld, born in the 1930s in the former Bukowina, in German-speaking, Rumanian Czernowitz. In *Badenheim 1939,* Jews assemble in an Austrian-sounding resort that gradually turns into a ghetto; finally they are loaded onto cattle cars, to be deported to death camps as fourth-class passengers from the previous century. They move into the cars like grains of sand move through an hourglass.

A rocket is a primitive train, a comet is an antiquated boat. Robert Musil writes in *The Man without Qualities* that "it is the fulfillment of man's primordial dreams to be able to fly."[7] *The Man without Qualities*—recalling Sonnenfels's journal— is an unfinished, unfinishable postmortem both of the Hapsburg Empire and of the mechanized world that replaced it.

Aerodynamics is a branch of physics that studies the motion of air and other gaseous fluids. It has its origins in antiquity, in the Greeks' observations of birds in flight. The word first appears in German in 1835, and then in English a few years later. Principles of aerodynamics are first applied to industry in the 1880s, as a way of making trains run more efficiently. The topic takes on a new importance in Germany at the beginning of the 20th century, with wind tunnel experiments at Friedrichshafen, where Graf Zeppelin was building his airships.

The first man to apply the results of these experiments to the design of airships is Paul Jaray, from Vienna. Jaray is a man with qualities, as, I believe, Robert Musil might have it. He wanted to be an artist (he had studied painting and music), but ended up at the Maschinenbauschule. He was *gebildet,* in the late-Hapsburg sense; but his cultivation allowed him to take an active role in life. (Musil's hero, Ulrich, is paralyzed by what he knows; all his qualities are for naught.) Though by the terms of Musil's novel, even Jaray is doomed: he lives in a world in which "mathematics" is "the new method of thought itself;" a world in which man has thought his way past the possibility of thought, in which action becomes meaningless, mere motion.

Jaray was responsible for the airship *Bodensee,* built in 1919— the model for all subsequent airships, until the Hindenburg disaster, and the beginning of what was called "streamlining."

Streamlining came to imply its opposite, as was quickly seen in the bloated, vaguely rounded surfaces of art deco. The Arts and Crafts movement, as inaugurated by Ruskin's friend William Morris, was a school of design derived from a theory of social interaction. Streamlining progressed from being a design theory to a theory of social utility; one talked— indeed, one still does—of streamlining a company.

In Jaray's Zeppelin, we notice our jet engines and our rockets, our bombs and our cellphones: our shiny round present-tense, as ourselves.

∎

The age of jet travel has rendered travel absurd; we leave one city from an airport that is a double for the airport that we land in; the city we left behind reappears as the city where we have just arrived.

The airplane itself reminds us, perhaps, of Ruskin's coach, in the cunning of its design. Tables fall out of seats; cushions are said to be life preservers.

But the wonder of flight does not belong to our era; the routine of flight does. Can routine ever inspire wonder?

The September 11 attack, with its demonic utility, had a scattering effect, was at once mythical and science-fiction like. It was Promethean, and it was anti-Promethean, like two pieces of flint creating fire.

∎

Heinrich von Kleist's "On the Marionette Theater" reminds me of patent furniture. It expands in unexpected directions, then folds up neatly into a Promethean allegory. We have defeated our creator, it tells us, and our creations will defeat us. But, it could be argued, there is hope, in that the reverse is also true.

> "Well my good friend," said Herr C, "you now have everything you need if you are to understand me. We see that in the same measure as reflection in the organic world becomes darker and feebler, grace there emerges in ever greater radiance and supremacy.—But just as two lines intersecting at a point after they have passed through infinity, will suddenly come together again on the other side, or the image in a concave mirror, after traveling away into infinity, suddenly comes close up to us again, so when consciousness has, as we might say, passed through an infinity, grace will return; so that grace will be most purely present in the human frame that has either no consciousness or an infinite amount of it, which is to say either in a marionette or in a god."
>
> "But," I said rather distractedly, "should we have to eat again of the Tree of Knowledge to fall back into the state of innocence?"
>
> "Indeed," he replied; "that is the final chapter in the history of the world."
>
> From "On the Marionette Theater"[8]
> Heinrich von Kleist, 1810

∎

The plane has landed where we didn't expect, away from the terminal. There is only one way out, down the steps, right on to the runway.

We walk, single file, out and down. And do we feel it? Do we all feel it? It is the air itself, our vessel, and now our solace, running along our faces, down our bodies, to our stiff legs, as they touch ground.

1   See Isaiah Berlin, *The Crooked Timber of Humanity,* New York 1991, p. 40.

2   See Gretchen Hachmeister, *Italy in the German literary Imagination: Goethe's "Italian Journey" and its reception by Eichendorff, Platen, and Heine,* Rochester N.Y. 2002 *(Man kann sich keinen italienischen Zitronenbaum mehr denken, ohne eine Engländerin, die daran riecht…).*

3   *Ist mir's doch, als sei mein Leben / An den schönen Strom gebunden. / Hab' ich Frohes nicht am Ufer, / Und Betrübtes hier empfunden.*

4   *Fliesst fort zum fernen Meere / darfst allda nicht heimisch werden. / Mich drängt's auch in mildre Lande – / Finde nicht das Glück auf Erden.*

5   *Fremd bin ich eingezogen / Fremd zieh' ich wieder aus.*

6   Vladimir Nabokov, *Speak, Memory,* London 1967, p. 61.

7   Robert Musil, *The Man without Qualities,* New York 1996, p. 35.

8   Kleist. "On the Puppet Theater," included in *Selected Writings,* edited by David Constantine, London 1997, p. 167.

See p. 394 for Selected Bibliography

LOOKING AT
THE PAST THROUGH
MODERNIST EYES

CHRISTOPHER WILK

Viennese silver of the early 19th and early 20th centuries presents an impressive record of craftsmanship and design in the history of silver. Those pieces shown in the chapter entitled "From an Ideal of Simplicity to the Modern Commodity" demonstrate an extraordinary interest in what we might term today simplified, geometric, and largely unornamented form. Austrian neoclassical silver of the early 19th century (which has often been lumped under the catch-all Biedermeier label) is little known beyond specialists; those who see it for the first time are apt to remark on its "modern" appearance. Similarly, anyone unfamiliar with the work of Josef Hoffmann from the early 20th century is liable to comment on how "advanced for their date" or how "of today" such objects look. Although it would be misleading to suggest that most silver manufactured in Vienna between 1780 and 1918 was plain in form and lacking in applied ornament, there is a sufficient quantity of such objects to suggest that it constitutes a tradition of design in Viennese silver.[1]

When we look at the objects in this exhibition and see in them qualities of simplicity and modernity of form, we do so largely through the filter of 20th-century modernism, specifically the style and polemical ideals of architecture and design in the 1920s exemplified by the work of Le Corbusier and Mies van der Rohe, as well as, after 1925, that of Walter Gropius and the Bauhaus School.[2] Hard as we try to consider and evaluate the form and decoration of these objects in terms of the period of their making, the way we look at things which have geometric shapes and unornamented surfaces is entirely framed by a point of view and aesthetic sensibility that became increasingly known at the end of the 1920s, was widely imitated during the 1930s, and in the 1950s and 1960s became common currency in Europe and North America. Although the modernist viewpoint was modified over time—especially as a result of a gradual acceptance of the broader range of 19th-century design during the 1960s and 1970s, and owing to the rise of post- and even anti-modernism in the 1970s and 1980s—it continues to be a dominant point of reference today. Early 20th-century modernism remains not only the prevailing model for looking at objects which are described today as "modern" but, in many circles, the term focuses attention on their appearance and formal characteristics.[3] In order to understand this, it is necessary to consider what form this modernist interpretation took. This is largely a question of historiography. Before turning to that, however, it is worth briefly considering how these forms arose within the context of their period of making.

18th-century neoclassicism provided both the formal and ideological basis for the simplified, geometric forms of the early 19th century. Neoclassicism held powerful sway across Europe well into the 19th century and all of the pieces in

this exhibition from that period can be accurately described as neoclassical. Viennese silversmiths would have had a plethora of models from across Europe to consider including those of France and, crucially, the simpler examples of English neoclassical silver. That influence can be seen particularly clearly in pieces that are identifiably English in character (figs. 1–3), as well as in pieces where the borrowings are less obvious.

Neoclassicism hence provided an ideology of simplicity which derived both from the ancient world and from its 18th- and 19th-century interpretations. J. J. Winckelmann wrote in his widely read *History of Ancient Art* that "All beauty is heightened by unity and simplicity."[4] One of the most famous descriptions of ideal form and simplicity in an object of the early 19th century is the story of the poet Goethe's admiration of a rush basket he traveled with. It was strong and large but folded down to a small size when not in use. "It comes close to the classical [model] for it is not only as rational and functional as possible, but has, moreover, at the same time the most simple, pleasant form, so that one can safely say: It is the pinnacle of perfection."[5] Although it would be tempting to link Goethe's equation of rationality and functionality with perfection of form, and to use it to describe silver contemporary with his account of the basket, there are insufficient contemporary descriptions of specific objects to allow a clear understanding of the meaning of these words in the early 19th century. Certainly it would be unwise to assume that simplicity of form inevitably allowed for cheaper production, thereby creating an economic argument for the development of these manifestations of neoclassicism. While there is some evidence that unornamented forms were cheaper to make and henceforth might have an appeal on that basis (the accounts cited in cat. nos. 13 and 14 indicate this was at least sometimes the case), simple forms could be exceptionally demanding of their skilled makers. Indeed, the high degree of perfection in the shaping and surface-finishing of a relatively unornamented piece means it is possible that these types of objects were not always cheaper to make and, indeed, may have been more expensive. As in the case of ceramics, where firing faults could be disguised by the strategic placing of painted motifs, three-dimensional forms in silver were difficult to produce to outstandingly high standards of unadorned surface quality.

Equally important to the style of the silver shown here was the 19th century development of a specific central European neoclassicism into what came to be called the Biedermeier style, which was so prevalent and well-developed in Vienna from around 1815. Like many such terms, it is an imprecise one and covers a range of types of design up to 1848. Most Biedermeier furniture, however, and much silver placed emphasis on the plain surface and largely eschewed applied ornament. Within its ideology, it equated simplicity with the domestic and with domestic privacy, and made neoclassicism meaningful within a specific local framework. If 18th-century neoclassicism in its most general terms resonated for Viennese designers, importers, and consumers in the late 18th and early 19th centuries, by 1900 Viennese architects and designers were profoundly and specifically influenced by Biedermeier neoclassicism. Indeed, it is not inappropriate to speak of a Biedermeier revival beginning

1. Franz Würth, silver teapot
(cat. no. 52),
Vienna 1803

2. Alois Würth, silver wine coaster
(cat. no. 49),
Vienna 1828.

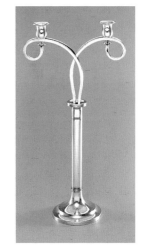

3. Stephan Mayerhofer,
one of a pair of silver-plated
candelabra
(cat. no. 19),
Vienna ca. 1820

4. Henry Cole, *Drawings of Simple Objects for Child Education,* England ca. 1850

5. Jakob Krautauer, silver and niello teapot (cat. no. 25), Vienna 1802

6. Koloman Moser, silver and niello coffer (cat. no. 119), Vienna 1903

in the 1890s, which became widespread in the first decade of the 20th century.[6] Around 1900 the Biedermeier era was seen as a period of national inventiveness and success, the last moment before the rise of 19th-century historicism, when a profound sense of home *(Heimat)* translated into a style of design appropriate for everyday life.[7] While there is little contemporary writing that refers directly to metalwork, there are many examples of Biedermeier being put forth as a "teacher" or "model" for designers of the day, not to be copied but as an exemplar both in terms of attitude and in terms of an approach to form.[8]

Retrospective descriptions of Biedermeier written around 1900, not unsurprisingly, employed a language that could equally well describe new work, including Viennese silver. Joseph August Lux, who was closely associated with Josef Hoffmann, referred to the "matter-of-fact simplicity" of Biedermeier as well as its "practical usefulness."[9] Reflecting the writings of both Winckelmann and of the arts and crafts designer William Morris, he wrote that "only on this basis do we come to beauty". In the context of a discussion of architecture in the city he remarked, "How beautiful a cityscape would be if the façades of houses had unmade-up faces…smooth walls without ornament, light and clean."[10] There was, accordingly, a clear consciousness of the value of reducing ornament and emphasizing geometric volume. Lux wrote, "How advantageous is this simplicity and how ornamental this lack of ornament is."

At the same time it is worth noting that this revival represented an increase in popularity rather than a rediscovery of something forgotten. The Viennese had never completely given up Biedermeier and around 1900 it was not uncommon to see modern, architect-designed interiors furnished with Biedermeier, including those by Hoffmann or Adolf Loos.[11] There were even instances of designers of 1900 creating new objects by modifying or altering Biedermeier pieces.[12] The tradition of mixing contemporary and Biedermeier objects in interiors continues in Vienna today.

While the interest in Biedermeier was strong in Vienna around 1900, it is important to remember that designers of the day were deeply concerned with creating a distinctly modern visual culture without recourse to what Hoffmann, Moser, and Waerndorfer called "the mindless imitation of old styles."[13] However, in ways that would have seemed unthinkable by the 1920s, they saw no contradiction in consciously drawing inspiration from the past in order to create their modern style. Indeed, despite the different and sometimes antagonistic approaches of Hoffmann and Loos, both sought to link their work with the vital traditions of Austrian design and, in both cases, Biedermeier was seen as the last flourishing of national creativity.[14] And while Hoffmann also looked to others for inspiration, including the Scottish architect Charles Rennie Mackintosh, his aesthetic of geometric simplicity is inconceivable without the example of Biedermeier neoclassicism which surrounded him. Simplicity, in this case, came at a price, however. Wiener Werkstätte silver—the cost of which is well documented—was extremely expensive. This appears to have been largely a matter of the number of hours required to re-make pieces (sometimes five or six times) which had not met the extraordinary levels of perfection demanded by Hoffmann.[15]

When we turn to the question of the retrospective view of the objects in the exhibition, it is necessary to consider how the modernist view came to be so well established that, despite continuous reinvention, it has continued to affect the way we view objects of the past. In his seminal book, *Pioneers of the Modern Movement from William Morris to Walter Gropius,* published in 1936, Nikolaus Pevsner offered an original history of the antecedents and beginnings of 1920s modernism that was to shape fundamentally subsequent writing on the subject.[16] He described his modern movement as beginning with the ideas and designs of William Morris and arising in opposition to the "profound artistic dishonesty" represented by the Victorian battle of the styles, by the ravages of the industrial revolution, and by debased artistic theory of the period.[17] Pevsner traced a lineage for modernism which included what he described as unself-conscious developments in 19th-century-engineering (mainly in iron and steel); advanced painting of the 1880s and 1890s; art nouveau architecture and design; and the work of early 20th-century architects including Auguste Perret, Tony Garnier, Loos, Frank Lloyd Wright, and Gropius. The latter represented, significantly, both the culmination of Pevsner's story of the pioneers and, implicitly, through the buildings and the products of the Bauhaus after 1925, the personification of the mature phase of the modern movement.

However much Pevsner admired Morris—especially his "decorative honesty"—he acknowledged the backward-looking nature of his teaching, especially his exclusion of the aesthetic dimension from design in favor of craft and his hatred of the machine.[18] When it came to illustrating designs he admired, Pevsner lauded the extraordinary "simplicity," "directness," reductiveness, and lack of ornament in Christopher Dresser's work. In the work of C. F. A. Voysey and others, Pevsner focused on the "simplicity" and "cleanness… of their shapes."[19] Plain surfaces, lack of applied ornament, and constructural honesty were his ideals. Although Pevsner cited other English designers who moved towards accommodation of the machine, his real heroes came from the turn of the century and included Henri van de Velde, Otto Wagner, Loos, and Wright. He quoted Loos approvingly: "To find beauty in form instead of making it depend on ornament is the goal towards which humanity is aspiring." While Pevsner allowed for the ornament of art nouveau—as part of a turning to nature and away from the past—he attached greatest importance to simpler, geometric form, exemplified by Peter Behrens's street lamps that demonstrated "purity of form [and] the simplest geometrical forms."[20] Similarly, he waxes lyrical about a Loos interior in which "nothing… can strictly speaking be called ornament."[21]

With the exception of the designs of a very select few and, of course, the work of engineers, 19th-century design, as Pevsner characterized Morris's view, "bristled with atrocious vulgarity."[22] Pevsner, as an art historian, was more moderate in his views than most contemporary modernist architects and designers who—except as regards engineering and perhaps the ancient world—turned their backs, at least publicly or in print, on the past. So, despite the interest of Mies van der Rohe, for example, in neoclassicism, it would have been inconceivable in modernist circles for Biedermeier to be cited during the 1920s as a model for contemporary design. But Pevsner's story, though it represented the views of modernist architects and designers, was more nuanced. To those views he added an art historian's analysis of the dynamics of style, an interest in decorative arts objects, and an appreciation of, in particular, the contributions of Morris and of late 19th-century painting.

Although first published in 1936, Pevsner's book must have gained a much wider audience when it was published in a second edition in 1949 by the Museum of Modern Art, New York, under the new title *Pioneers of Modern Design*.[23] This followed the publication in the previous year of another book by a polemicist for modernism, a book which helped begin the rehabilitation of the 19th century, especially mid and late 19th-century design: Siegfried Giedion's *Mechanization Takes Command*.

Giedion's book was a brave and wide-ranging attempt to explain the history and role of mechanization in Western culture. Unlike his earlier *Space, Time and Architecture* (1941), which identified a new tradition of modern architecture and argued on its behalf, *Mechanization Takes Command* did not concern itself with architecture, although, in one chapter, Giedion considers the seminal contribution of modernist architects as the form-givers of 20th-century furniture. While covering topics including agriculture and manufacturing, much of the book concentrates on mechanization and the home. Ultimately, Giedion was interested in how technology and industrialization affected aspects of daily life, whether baking bread or sitting. It also emphasized, as might be expected, the 19th century, though Giedion's 19th century extended much wider than Pevsner's and helped change the image of that period. He focused attention on the merits of neglected 19th-century design, particularly domestic appliances and furnishings.
Though the subject of Giedion's book was mechanization, there was also an underlying interest in aesthetics and the development of a modern style. Like Pevsner, Giedion looked to 19th-century British design reformers as pioneers of a new attitude which embraced plainness and simplicity. He drew parallels between Cole's *Drawings of Simple Objects for Child Education* and Ozenfant's purist drawings of daily objects (1925) and, through his modernist eyes, glimpsed "the abstract forms inherent in industrial production" (fig. 4).[24] Giedion viewed the 19th century as inventive and exuberant though stylistically confused, but searched for exceptions. One was 19th-century bentwood furniture which, echoing Le Corbusier, he described as "form purified by serial production."[25]

It was, however, during the 1960s that, within the context of a Victorian revival, some writers and exhibition organizers, including architects and designers, sought in the 19th century the beginnings of modern design.[26] The reasons for turning to the 19th century were several. The general attitude toward the period had softened and this led many to seek quality and value in 19th-century design. There was a desire to revise the Pevsnerian view of the 19th century as a period characterized solely by over-ornamented, historicizing design redeemed only in the work of certain British design reformers, above all, William Morris. Publications, most notably Herwin Schaefer's *19th Century Modern, the Functional Tradition in Victorian Design,* sought out the modern in other areas of 19th-century design and it gradually became common to describe the "rational" or "functional" tradition in the 19th century.[27]

Schaefer and his contemporaries took their framework from Pevsner but, encouraged by Giedion, turned their attention to different categories of objects, including both elite and mass-market items with an emphasis on the sometimes anonymous vernacular as well as on the industrial. Schaefer specifically rejected Pevsner's emphasis on "artistic creativity" and the work of "artist-craftsmen" in the 19th century.[28] He defined "functional design" as "abstract, often geometric and devoid of decoration, but emphasizing utility," and set out to show its origins in the 19th century.[29] The categories of objects he considered were a mixed bag. Despite describing the importance of industrial and vernacular objects in particular, he included many high-design types as exemplars of functional, rational design. British and American machinery, French and German scientific instruments, English ceramics, Austrian bentwood, and American Shaker furniture became touchstones of early or proto-modernism as did the simpler forms of 18th- and 19th-century silver, including Austrian. Schaefer specifically illustrated a coffee pot by Lorenz Wieninger and a silver pitcher by Benedikt Ranninger in what must have been the only appearance of Viennese silver in a book covering so broad and international a range of objects. In doing this he invented a new history of modern design with a wider cast of characters than ever before and elevated the status of many object types he discussed.

The style of the 1920s, albeit reinterpreted and often shorn of its aesthetic subtleties, can be said to have triumphed in the 1960s and 1970s as a true international style, gaining an acceptance it never achieved in the 1920s and 1930s. Yet it was at the same time, perhaps owing to its ubiquity in poor-quality, commercial interpretations, that reaction against it gained momentum. The Victorian revival might be described as a sign of a rapidly-developing disenchantment with modernism. Beginning tentatively in the 1960s and then more emphatically in the 1970s and 1980s, designers and writers explicitly looked for alternatives. Modernism's most central tenets, notably the eschewing of ornament and decoration and the striving for simplified geometric forms, were rejected. "Less is more" became "less is a bore."[30] Debates about the nature of "post-modernism" began to emerge, signaling a perceived end of modernism. Such debate encouraged the investigation of neglected or hitherto spurned areas in the history of design, and modernism came to be seen as a historical style. There was, in parallel, a strident anti-modernism which saw modernism as a destructive force and objected to its equating morality and rationality with a particular type of architecture.[31]

The renewed interest in ornament and decoration, and in neglected areas of the history of architecture and design, led many to Vienna. Despite its simplified appearance, Viennese silver of 1900 offered a model for the use of decoration without recourse to historicism. It was hugely admired and imitated in the 1980s (though the results seemed, even then, distinctly historicist). The interest in Vienna 1900 led many to Vienna 1800 as the audience for Biedermeier spread beyond specialists, designers, or those who had grown up with it. The art and antique market's appetite for new and less fashionable (and cheaper) areas of collecting also raised the profile of Viennese wares and brought them to new audiences. The fact that among these objects were highly simplified designs—rare though they were outside of the realm of furniture—resonated with a public used to the vocabulary of modernism.

Despite the disenchantment with modernism in recent decades, and its proper categorization as but one of many styles of the 20th century, it remains fundamental to our view of the past and of the present. With its utopian agenda which rejected the past, it claimed a ground different from the neoclassical or from the anti-classical (e.g., Gothic or chinoiserie). Even those who are unsympathetic to the appearance and/or the ideology of modernism have had to acknowledge its centrality as a point of reference over the last seventy-five years. It has profoundly shaped our attitudes to the objects shown in this exhibition. Modernism sticks in the collective unconscious in ways that have barely been analyzed. This selection and interpretation of the present collection of historic Viennese silver is part of that process.

1   First suggested in *Moderne Vergangenheit: Wien 1800–1900,* exh. cat. Künstlerhaus Vienna 1981.

2   Modernism is a word that covers a very broad range of work and ideologies. At the time, it was identified by a variety of terms, many of which referred not only to architecture but to the wider design environment, including the domestic interior. Many of these terms were used as or derived from book titles; all identified self-consciously modern, forward-looking design: e. g., *Internationale Architektur, Neues Bauen, Die neue Baukunst, Modern Architecture, International Style.* For a useful summary see the bibliography in Kenneth Frampton, *Modern Architecture,* London 1985. Modernism, as used here, encompasses what in architectural circles has long been called the International Style, following the Museum of Modern Art's eponymous exhibition and publication of 1932, although the latter term has never found an agreed application to objects designed for the interior.

3   Early modernists denied any interest in form or style (e.g., Ludwig Mies van der Rohe, *G,* no. 2 [1923], quoted in P. Johnson, *Mies van der Rohe,* New York 1953, p. 189). However, it is indisputable that in its dissemination, especially through architecture and design magazines in the western world, modernism was portrayed as a new design style. Although today historians also generally disparage any concentration on the aesthetics of modernism at the expense of its cultural context and political agenda, to ignore its aesthetic dimension is to fail to engage with its full meaning.

4   J. Winckelmann, *History of Ancient Art,* 2nd ed. 1776, translated and published London 1850, p. 43, cited by Adrian Forty, *Words and Buildings,* London 2000, p. 252.

5   Johann Peter Eckermann, *Gespräche mit Goethe in den letzten Jahren seines Lebens,* Leipzig 1910, pp. 276–277 (*Er kommt der Antike nahe, denn er ist nicht allein so vernünftig und zweckmässig als möglich, sondern er hat auch dabei die einfachste, gefälligste Form, so dass man also sagen kann: er steht auf dem höchsten Punkt der Vollendung.*).

6   *Moderne Vergangenheit Wien 1800–1900,* exh. cat. Künstlerhaus, Vienna 1981; G. Himmelheber, "Biedermeier als Vorbild" (Biedermeier as Model) in G. Himmelheber, *Kunst des Biedermeier 1815–1835,* Munich 1988; and, covering a slightly wider period in terms of architecture, Stanford Anderson, "The Legacy of German Neoclassicism and Biedermeier: Behrens, Tessenow, Loos and Mies," *Assemblage,* 15, August 1991, pp. 63–87.

7   Joseph August Lux, "Biedermeier als Erzieher" (Biedermeier as Instructor), *Hohe Warte,* yr. I, vol. 8, pp. 146–147, reprinted in *Moderne Vergangenheit* (see note 5), pp. 86–87.

8   Ibid., and Hartwig Fischel, "Biedermeier als Vorbild" (Biedermeier as Model), *Das Interieur,* 2, 1901, pp. 65–73.

9   Lux, p.149 ("*diese sachliche Einfachheit,*" "*praktische Brauchbarkeit*").

10 Ibid., pp. 153–154 (…*wie lieblich ein Stadtbild aussehen müsste, wenn die Fassaden der Wohnhäuser ein ungeschminktes Gesicht zur Schau trügen, glatte, schmucklose Wände.…*).

11 For a summary of Hoffmann's Biedermeier interests see Eduard F. Sekler, *Josef Hoffmann: The Architectural Work*, Princeton 1985, chapter V, esp. p. 110. See also Hoffmann's use of Biedermeier furniture *Deutsche Kunst und Dekoration*, vol. 12, no. 10, July 1909, p. 209 (H. H. house) and *Internationale Kunstausstellung Rom 1911, Oesterreichischer Pavillon,* Vienna 1911, p. 109.

12 An unpublished corner cabinet made for the Mautner von Markhof family has a Biedermeier base and a top designed by Koloman Moser.

13 Josef Hoffmann, Koloman Moser and Fritz Waerndorfer, *Working Program* (of the Wiener Werkstätte), Vienna 1905, p. 1, translated in Werner J. Schweiger, *Wiener Werkstätte,* London 1984, p. 42.

14 Hoffmann wrote of the search to "find tradition" to avoid imitation, in "Einfache Möbel" (Simple Furniture), *Das Interieur,* vol. 2, 1901, p. 196. Loos in "Architektur" (1910) in *Sämtliche Schriften,* Vienna 1962, p. 312, wrote of the connections between 1800 and 1900 and of his need, "to begin again at that point [ca. 1800] where the chain of development had been broken."

15 Wiener Werkstätte Archive, MAK, Vienna. On the re-making of pieces, information from Mr. Grohmann, son of the last financial director of the Wiener Werkstätte, as told to Stefan Asenbaum in October 1969.

16 Although Pevsner's book followed Henry-Russell Hitchcock's *Modern Architecture: Romanticism and Reintegration,* New York 1929, Pevnser was the first to give the decorative arts a prominent place in the story of modernism.

17 Nikolaus Pevsner, *Pioneers of the Modern Movement from William Morris to Walter Gropius,* London 1936, p. 20.

18 Ibid., pp. 61, 25–26.

19 Ibid., pp. 62 and 146.

20 Ibid., pp. 32 and 197.

21 Ibid., p. 190.

22 Ibid., p. 20, changed in later editions to read, "practically all industrial art was crude, vulgar, and overloaded with ornament", 1975 edition, p. 20.

23 It was subsequently revised and/or reprinted a remarkable eighteen times between 1960 and 1991. The book's new title must have contributed to the use of the term "modern design," which became more widespread in the post-war period.

24 Siegfried Giedion, *Mechanization Takes Command,* New York 1948, p. 359.

25 Ibid., p. 492.

26 There were, of course, earlier instances of the interest in the 19th century, starting with the publication of Kenneth Clark's *The Gothic Revival,* London 1927. This widened in the 1950s to embrace the Victorian period as a whole. Highlights around the 1950s included the installation of Victorian period rooms at the Brooklyn Museum and the Victoria & Albert Museum's exhibition *Victorian and Edwardian Decorative Arts* (1952). It was not until the second half of the 1960s, however, that a full-blown Victorian revival can be said to have begun, and the interest in finding the beginnings of modernism in the 19th century was of less interest than finding new areas of collecting.

27 Herwin Schaefer, *19th Century Modern; The Functional Tradition in Victorian Design,* New York 1970, and *Die verborgene Vernunft: Funktionale Gestaltung im 19. Jahrhundert,* ex. cat., Munich 1971.

28 Schaefer 1971 (see note 26), p. 198.

29 Ibid., p. 18.

30 Robert Venturi, Denise Scott Brown and Steven Izenour, *Learning from Las Vegas,* Cambridge MA 1972.

31 David Watkin, *Morality and Architecture,* London 1977, rev. 2001.

MOIST AND DRY

JOSEPH RYKWERT

Until the end of the 17th century, there was really only one way of designing: both rational and pious, it was overlaid by notions of a primarily Roman, august antique past, as well as Scripture. The attribution of the design of the Temple in Jerusalem and its furnishings to God Himself found broad acceptance. It followed, therefore, that the Temple architecture and its contents expressed universal, cosmic harmony. The inner secrets of that harmony had been studied by the oldest philosophers, notably by Pythagoras, and its confirmation and warrant was man's body, which—so Scripture declared—was made in the Image of God. (Vitruvius, the only Roman writer on architecture, subsequently made the body fit both the square and the circle, and read all the measurements a builder might need out of it.) This view was held firmly by most artists from Alberti to Poussin and Bernini, quite independently of whatever stylistic label was pinned to them, and it was inherited by one of Bernini's most brilliant disciples, Johann Bernhard Fischer von Erlach. Fischer von Erlach's junior and rival, Lukas von Hildebrandt, was already affected by its eclipse.

Three developments overshadowed that enduring doctrine. The first was associationist psychology; the second, the so-called "higher criticism" of biblical texts; the third and final was the powerful impact of the growing new science of archaeology.

An associationist view of art decreed that there was no fixed, permanent rule for beauty: René Descartes, in his treatise on music, already declared the voice of a friend more agreeable than that of an enemy, and certain sounds beautiful because we associate them with pleasant circumstances. Beauty needs to be "tuned" to hearing: *ad…delectationem requiritur proportio quaedam obiecti cum ipso sensu.* His follower, the Parisian architect Claude Perrault, extended this view to the visual arts by dividing beauty into two distinct kinds: the first is positive beauty, which can be appreciated by anyone with common sense (which, as Descartes observed, opening his *Discourse on Method* with a smile, is the most equably distributed of human faculties since no one thinks himself deficient in it). Bilateral symmetry, fine materials, and good workmanship are its features. The second kind of beauty is more subtle and arbitrary. It results primarily from proportions, which cannot be estimated accurately by the sense of sight—nor can they be considered invariant. Perrault, who was a comparative anatomist of great distinction as well as an architect, maintained that the eye, which is a very complex instrument, transmitted data indirectly to the brain and was, for this reason, fallible. (He held that the ear, by contrast, was so simple mechanically that it enjoyed direct contact with the brain and therefore greater fidelity). Great and sometimes apparently irrational differences in the proportions of columns, which Perrault noted, seemed to confirm his skepticism and linked his discoveries to a new, critical archaeology. Roland Fréart, Lord of Chambray, already published a book comparing the prescriptions for the orders

by "modern" authors, such as Alberti and Palladio, with surviving antique examples. First printed in 1650, it became a standard handbook for architects and was often republished—the English version was made by the great diarist John Evelyn. King Louis XIV and his chief minister, Jean-Baptiste Colbert, commissioned a young architect, Antoine Desgodetz, to measure all the main ancient buildings remaining in Rome and had his results published in a splendid folio in 1682. It also became a standard textbook for a century and more and was often reissued. But then columns were being almost obsessively measured and compared at this time, since they were regarded in their different orders as the main carriers of proportional wisdom.

The Temple in Jerusalem, described in various Old Testament texts, was given an *interpretatio christiana* by virtue of a number of references which spoke of the Body of Christ as its representation. A very seductive though fanciful restoration of it was provided by two Spanish Jesuits, Juan Bautista Villalpando and Jeronimo Prado, in an opulent three folio-volume commentary on the Book of Ezekiel published between 1595 and 1603; among other ideas, it suggested that the classical orders, i.e. Doric, Ionic, and so on, took their origin from the one God-given order of the many columns of the Temple. Fischer von Erlach knew that commentary well, as he knew the exalted ideas of another Jesuit, the Romano-German polymath Father Athanasius Kircher, a mathematician, musician, and orientalist whom he had met during his long Italian apprenticeship. Kircher had written much about magnetism, optics, and acoustics before he devoted himself to oriental matters and linguistics. He was the first serious student of Egyptian hieroglyphics and the first to compare them to other picture-writings, particularly Chinese ideograms. When Fischer von Erlach published the very first general history of architecture toward the end of his life in 1721, the *Entwurf einer historischen Architektur,* he opened it with an account of the Seven Wonders of the world, to which he added, as the very first of the world's wonders, the Jerusalem Temple reconstructed after Prado and Villalpando. It is a sign of the times that his text is in French and German—Italian was no longer the lingua franca of the arts.

Fischer's most important executed church project, the Karlskirche, was built in fulfillment of a vow by the Emperor Charles VI to his namesake, St. Charles Borromeo, when Vienna was threatened by the plague in 1713. It faced the great brick-and-earth walls which had protected the city during the last major siege (by the Turks in 1683) and stood in more or less open country. The Turks remained close, both as a familiar presence and as a threat—they had retaken Belgrade in 1739—but they were not altogether alien; it was from them that the Viennese learned their quintessential habit of coffee-drinking. In his *Entwurf* Fischer had given Turkish and Arab architecture, as well as Chinese and Thai buildings, almost the same weight as those of Rome.

The design of the Karlskirche was radical. Its "modern" elliptical dome was entered through an "antique" hexastyle portico—and it was flanked by two giant columns in deliberate emulation of those of the Jerusalem Temple (Jachin and Boaz); those in Rome (of Trajan and of Marcus Aurelius); as well as, by metonymy, those of Constantinople, the second Rome—the minarets of the church of Hagia Sophia. They could further be recognized as referring to the two columns on the arms of Charles V, whose imperial crown over the shield also suggested the shape of the dome. All these citations reiterated the implication that Vienna, the imperial capital, could be considered the third Rome.

Fischer's enthusiasm for Prado and Villalpando was, in a way, out of his time. The conflicting texts that described the Temple—the older authorities tried to harmonize them—were being reconstructed as historical documents by new scholars. One of them engaged Claude Perrault to produce a completely new column-less reconstruction of the Temple. Throughout the 17th century battle raged about this and related issues; various exalted authorities, Isaac Newton and Sir Christopher Wren included, became involved in these discussions. Models, sometimes huge, were made of the reconstructions and toured around Europe as exhibition pieces.

Although the conflict was fierce and prolonged, even in Paris itself, the conclusion was a foregone one. The authority of the scriptural examples would be considered as problematic as that of antique precedent, while religious backing for the grand theory had also been fatally weakened. Pleasure derived from the proportions of buildings was increasingly considered arbitrary—and associative. This implied that while positive beauty was easily procured, the architect's or designer's art and skill depended on taste, and taste was best formed on the example of the ancients, since those proportions and ornaments we have seen in great and important antique buildings will be the ones our eyes and minds will prefer.

If the mechanism of sight is much less precise than that of hearing, then there is no mathematically ascertainable harmony to proportion. Which is why—although there is no absolute rightness about antique examples, and their ornaments are the product of convention—architects and painters need to study them nevertheless in order to discipline their wayward fancies. Perrault, whose teaching this was, was a child of the *grand siècle,* and his most famous design was the eastern façade of the Louvre, conceived for the *grand monarque.* His ideas circulated throughout Europe, and his projects were known through popular engravings.

After Louis XIV's death in 1715, the arts took a turn which Perrault did not—could not—foresee. While all Europe was still emulating Versailles and its park, the Parisian circles formed in the *grand siècle* as a refuge from the court—the salons—quickly became the dominant social force and alternative centers of influence. Sovereignty passed to the dissolute but astute Duke of Orléans as Regent (for the infant Louis XV), and he ruled in effect from his quarters in the Palais-Royal, while the more brilliant ladies—Mme du Deffand was perhaps the most famous—dominated society through their social assemblies. In that atmosphere, the Grand Style of the Great King simply lapsed. The ornamental and allegorical *machines* dependent on ancient example were inappropriate to the intimate scale of such gatherings. The dethroned antique examples could be treated with some license: they could be infracted and inflected in various ways.

Such is the origin of the manner which dominated Europe from the Paris of the Regency. It turned away from a demoted antiquity to favor motifs derived from nature: shells and bats' wings, driftwood, knobby Chinese-style rocks and coral, wispy plants. All provided a repertory which could be woven through and even grafted onto the older, persisting structures. This new kind of ornament was familiar from garden buildings and fountains, from grottoes—hence its name, *rocaille,* later corrupted to *rococo,* to rhyme with *barocco.* From garden and grotto, it was promoted into the salons, the new reception-rooms of palaces. In painting it was given a sublime if evanescent incarnation in the work of Watteau. With time, it proliferated over churches in Austria and Bavaria where, in an orgy of gold and silver that framed delicious pastel colors, it offered the promise of a fluffy, weightless paradise. And yet—with the notable exception of the Zwinger in Dresden, there are virtually no rococo exteriors. Even if projects for them (such as Gilles-Marie Oppenordt's for St. Sulpice in Paris) have survived, none were built. The most obviously *rocaille* interiors, such as the Wies church, or *Vierzehnheiligen,* shelter in the most sober, barely inflected, exteriors.

Rocaille interiors abound in France, Italy, Prussia, and Bavaria—and, of course, in Austria. So do *rocaille* furniture, silver and other decorative arts. Yet for all its charm, its very virtues meant that it lacked structure and thrust. So willful a fashion could not last, and—by reaction—had to make room for a new sobriety. That move started in France and Italy even before 1750. A motive for this recoil was a distrust of the artificialities of courtliness, and a confidence in the natural virtue of direct, unmediated sentiment. A new anthropology was growing in France around the primitivism of Rousseau, and in Britain around the skepticism of his friend David Hume. It fed on the discovery by travelers, particularly in the South Seas—Bougainville, Cook—of "primitive" peoples "uncorrupted" by civilization. These savages seemed in some way like some of the ancient Greeks.

Pictorial information about the ways of remote antiquity had come from images on painted vases which had been collected episodically since the 16th century but had become increasingly fashionable in the 18th. These vases were thought to be Etruscan (and therefore even more "primitive" than Greek ones). Their different shapes now provided an early model for a new kind of earthenware; the famous English manufacturer Wedgwood even re-named his pottery works "Etruria." It was a common enough mistake at the time.

In building, the most radical revolution was prompted by a small—and at first unillustrated—book called *An Essay on Architecture,* published anonymously by an obscure Jesuit, Marc-Antoine Laugier, in 1751. He proposed to purify architecture by offering the primitive hut as a model for all building. This hut was limited, according of him, to four posts supporting a double-pitched roof. These were its two elemental features, while the admittedly necessary walls, windows and all the rest were mere "licenses." The wide use of pedimented centerpieces in palace façades was condemned as capriciousness—along with a great many other contemporary commonplaces. Laugier's little book became an overnight success, acquired its famous frontispiece in a later edition, and was widely translated. It chimed in with that increasing demand for simplicity which dominated the second half of the 18th century when *rocaille* was stripped from essential structures like so much clinging water-weed; the Cartesian teaching of Perrault was then extended into a belief that the simpler the form, the more it would appeal—certainly to common sense. It took another half-century before Étienne-Louis Boullée and his disciple Jean-Nicolas-Louis Durand could finally assert that the sphere and the cube were the best of all forms.

But while the *Abbé* Laugier was purifying architecture in Paris, another *Abbé*, Johann Joachim Winckelmann, a German settled in Rome, undertook the radical examination of ancient art which became the model not only for the future history of art, but a structural model for historians generally. "He must be considered"— so Hegel thought—"to have developed a new organ for the spirit, a completely new approach to the field of art."[1] For all that he also set up Roman Hellenistic art as a model of beauty for learned Europe—in the belief that the works he admired were of the great classical Greek period.

Between rococo and the new sobriety of which Winckelmann was the prophet and legislator, there was an intermediate stage when "a mixture of grotesque stucco and painted ornaments, together with the flowing *rinceau* with its fanciful figures and winding foliage" would be considered as adding "a greater beauty to the whole," as the Adam Brothers wrote, introducing the survey of their work in 1773. Although the recipe reads like a description of *rocaille,* it no longer looked like it. The ornament was stiffened, ironed out, and the prototypes were no longer natural forms but supposed Etruscan and Greek (in fact Roman) decoration, even if this very fashionable manner still had a rococo relationship to structure.

In 1777, at the time of *Wilhelm Meister,* the young Goethe combined cube and sphere, the eternally stable and the ever-changing, into a memorable altar to Good Fortune in his garden at Weimar. Of course, the older Goethe was to despise romanticism and consider himself plainly "classic;" "A new expression has occurred to me," he said to Eckermann in April 1829 (they were discussing the latest Parisian writing), "I call classic what is healthy, and romantic what is ill…Most of what is new is not romantic because it is new, but because it is weak, sickly and ill and what is old is not classic because it is old, but because it is strong, fresh, jolly and healthy…"[2]

As in Goethe's garden altar, the forms of pure geometry and those which were shaped by human use—since need manifests the inner working of nature—became the forms of elegance. The quality of materials could be nakedly displayed. And for quite different reasons, in a quite different context, an analogous change came over design about a century later. Even at the time when Goethe asserted the sanity of classicism, there was an uneasy sense among younger artists (architects especially) that their age, whether classic or romantic, relied too much on the past for style. The unease became articulated after 1850 in a belief that a new art, wholly dependent on nature and owing little to the past, to history, would be needed

for the coming age. The great prestige of biology inevitably directed artists' attention to plant forms.

Any number of designers, William Morris most conspicuously and prolifically, invented patterns for textiles, for wallpapers, for glass—even for furniture—which owed less and less to the past, but more and more to meticulous, explicitly morphological representations of plants and flowers. Morris and his mentor, John Ruskin, had a crowd of disciples, all of whom were concerned with the shifting relation between art and industry; they believed that their work would transform that relationship and act as social leaven. The movement now goes by the name Arts and Crafts and it persisted well into the 20th century. It was in the last decade of the 19th, however, that fin-de-siècle and the expectation of a new age prompted a lavish outgrowth of the new ornament into a style which involved not only furniture and interiors, but also buildings and urban planning. Even someone as quintessentially "classical" and modern as Otto Wagner was affected by the wild, flowery fashion—while its tendrilly character sometimes deserved the nickname *Schnörkelstil,* which the Viennese used for the rococo.

Foreseeably, it did not last long with him. The so-called *Majolika-Haus* (Wienzeile 40) and its neighboring building (both 1898–99) are the closest he came to adopting it; in 1900 he commissioned Adolf Böhm, an explicitly "art nouveau" Viennese artist, to fill the windows of the studio he added to his villa with swirly, floral stained-glass. These forms likewise affected some of the stations he designed for the *Stadtbahn* (subway and elevated train), particularly the opulent imperial pavilion at Hietzing, near Schönbrunn, of 1896–98 and the metal-and-marble station near the *Karlskirche;* but these were exceptions to the rule; simpler stations—those along the *Gürtel* (beltway), for instance— had freed themselves of vegetal elaboration. It was a transition Wagner and others of his generation and the next needed to go through as part of a maturing process.

But, of course, the manner had infected his pupils Josef Maria Olbrich, Josef Hoffmann (these two received the Viennese Academy's Rome Prize), Jože Plečnik, and Emil Hoppe, as it affected German and Austrian designers we no longer associate with it at all—Bruno Paul or Peter Behrens. It was Olbrich who designed the headquarters of the Secession, the grouping of the "advanced" Viennese artists: Gustav Klimt, Koloman Moser, Alfred Roller, and others. Its building, crowned by what the Viennese called the "golden cabbage" (*goldenes Krauthappl*), shows the passage from a vegetative tendril-and-whiplash profusion to a geometricized discipline imposed—paradoxically—on the very plant-forms which were the repertory of art nouveau. Olbrich left Vienna in 1900, however, to become—with Behrens—the crucial member and principal architect of the artists' colony on the Mathildenhöhe in Darmstadt. Their two houses became its first showpieces, though they were soon overshadowed by Olbrich's masterpiece: the Ernst-Ludwig Haus, a group of artists' studios whose opening was the occasion of a great festival. The main event was the very ceremonial handing over of a symbolic gift to Duke Ernst-Ludwig of Hesse-Darmstadt: the gift was a crystal.

Crystals, not plants, became the paradigmatic natural phenomenon for artists from then on. This coincided with a transformation of scientific culture. The new era of physics began with Konrad Roentgen's discovery of X-rays in 1895. In the decade that followed, the researches of Lord Rutherford on gamma rays and of Pierre and Marie Curie on uranium, the speculations about the relation between mass and energy (which would culminate in Einstein's first communication about general relativity in 1905) all instantly attracted public attention. From that time, through all the many variations of cubism, speculation about physics captured the imagination of artists (though not always their understanding). Foliage, tendrils, and *Schnörkel* were of no further interest to them.

When the young textile manufacturer Fritz Waerndorfer lightheartedly suggested to the architects Josef Hoffmann and Koloman Moser that a workshop on the Arts and Crafts model might be initiated in Vienna, they were enthusiastic. In 1903 the *Wiener Werkstätte* experiment began. Waerndorfer had—perhaps on Hoffmann's urging—befriended Charles Rennie Mackintosh in Glasgow; it was Mackintosh who designed a very simple "WW" Werkstätte mark and letterhead, though Hoffmann and Moser preferred to use a more elaborate design of their own in the end.

Hoffmann and Moser often and insistently declared themselves disciples of the English Arts and Crafts movement, and although their methods and their forms acknowledged this debt, their designs and those of their colleagues were dominated from the beginning by primary geometries, rather than natural forms: the cube, the sphere, the cylinder. Their first major collaborative project, the sanatorium at Purkersdorf, was also one of the earliest buildings outside France to use the new in-situ reinforced construction techniques of François Hennebique.

The two movements of ideas and of taste, a century and a half apart, seem almost exactly parallel: the first begins with a transition from the damp, moist, and wanton *régence rocaille* to the hard and crystalline neo-antique sobriety of the *goût grec* of Louis XV's time, as enthusiastically patronized by the demure Mme de Pompadour; the second is a mutation of the organic-vegetative-tubercular-Liberty style of the fin-de-siècle into the crystalline geometry of 20th-century proto-modernity.

The forbidding sanity of that first neoclassicism in the 18th and early 19th century was gradually eased and slurred by the allure of other styles and periods quite different from that of the idealized Greeks—until styles became so intermixed, so hybrid, so mongrel even, that an unhistorical, biology-based, ornamental discipline emerged in the latter part of the 19th century as the appropriate, radical remedy for the confusions of eclecticism. The biological ebullience of art nouveau/*Jugendstil* was a prelude, in turn, to that powerful movement which has not, as yet, been given any sure, undisputed label—perhaps because it claims to be no style at all. Its forms are said to arise, unmediated and bare, from the dictates of structural necessity, inner function, and elementary geometry. That claim is often disputed; yet for all the various evasions it has prompted and even invited, we have never quite freed ourselves from its trammels.

The texts about the Temple are I Kings 5–6; Ezra 5 or Ezekiel 40–48; and II Chronicles 1–5. There are other texts in the Mishna and in the Talmud. A description of Herod's temple was also given by Josephus. For the principal New Testament references see Matthew 26:61 and 27:40; Mark 14:58; and John 2:19–21.

1   Georg Friedrich Hegel, *Ästhetik*, vol. 1, Friedrich Bassenge, ed., Berlin and Weimar 1965, p. 71. (*Denn Winckelmann ist als einer der Menschen anzusehen, welche im Felde der Kunst für den Geist ein neues Organ und ganz neue Betrachtungsweisen zu erschliessen wussten.*)

2   Johann Peter Eckermann, *Gespräche mit Goethe*, Ernst Beutler, ed., vol. 24, Zurich 1948, p. 332. (*Mir ist ein neuer Ausdruck eingefallen. Das Klassische nenne ich das Gesunde und das Romantische das Kranke… Das meiste Neuere ist nicht romantisch weil es neu, sondern weil es schwach, kränklich und krank ist, und das Alte ist nicht Klassisch weil es alt, sondern weil es stark, frisch, froh und gesund ist…*)

VIENNESE SILVER: A STYLISTIC OVERVIEW

ELISABETH SCHMUTTERMEIER

1. Ulrich Link (?), vermeil goblet,
Vienna 1610
Private collection

2. Joseph Ignaz Würth,
silver tureen and stand for
Duke Albert of Saxe-Teschen,
Vienna 1779–81
Sterling and Francine Clark
Art Institute, Williamstown,
Massachusetts

3. Johann Pfeiffer, silver coffee pot,
Vienna 1740
Private collection

4. Franz Hartmann, silver teapot
and creamer
Vienna 1816
Private collection

Is it merely a coincidence that the first documented craftsman in Vienna, "Bruno de Wien, aurifex," who was identified in a Salzburg document on January 13, 1177,[1] was a goldsmith? In 1156 Vienna—situated toward the eastern edge of the Holy Roman Empire—became the residence of the Dukes of Babenberg and, thereby, an important administrative and trade center offering a variety of craftsmen work and the incentive to settle. The Hapsburgs,[2] too, who followed the Babenbergs as rulers, encouraged Vienna's tradesmen and craftsmen, since a wealthy capital in their sovereignty had a positive effect on their position of power within the empire. The oldest known craftsmen regulation for Viennese goldsmiths was therefore not decreed by the mayor or city council, but by the ducal brothers Albrecht III (1349/50–95) and Leopold III (1351–86) von Hapsburg on October 13, 1366. The fact that the craftsmen required valuable precious metals—which were also used in large amounts for the minting of coins—as the raw material for their products explains the special interest of the court in goldsmiths. The Viennese goldsmiths' guild, whose members numbered between twenty and thirty in a given year, was similar in stature to those in other cities of the empire.

Vienna's location on the eastern border of the imperial realm and the wars that came about as a result of this exposure, together with the religious wars of the 16th and 17th centuries,[3] which forced even the court to retreat from Vienna on several occasions, brought a constant series of economic ups and downs for the city. Astonishing quantities of precious metal objects were destroyed either as a direct or indirect result of the wars. In addition, changes in taste as well as in eating and drinking habits rendered many luxury goods out of date and no longer suitable for everyday use. Experts estimate that just two to four percent of the total production of earlier goldsmith work has survived until our day. Viennese silver prior to the end of the 18th century belongs to this group of absolute rarities, with only sacred objects surviving in greater numbers, since their worth lay primarily in an intellectual/spiritual dimension and not in a fashionable/aesthetic one.

If one considers the few precious metal objects from the 16th through the mid-18th century that have come down to us, their obvious proximity—both stylistic and typological—to the work of the most important goldsmith centers in the German-speaking realm (Nuremberg, Augsburg) is immediately apparent (fig. 1). Shapes and ornamentation were copied by Viennese goldsmiths and executed in exceedingly high craftsmanship quality, as is documented by numerous commissions from the court known from archival records, as well as by surviving work.[4] From the mid-18th to the early 19th century a formal rapprochement with French goldsmith work took place. The table service made by the Viennese goldsmith family Würth for Duke Albert of Saxe-Teschen (1742–1822) is an example (fig. 2), as are

diverse opulent (French style) neoclassical tureens by Georg Hann,[5] still very much in the spirit of the ancien régime, or a number of surviving coffee pots (fig. 3). Borrowings from English neoclassical "Adam silver"[6] can be discerned in some teapots, baskets, trays, or candlesticks, although their particular spare shapes and delicate ornamentations also mirrored the taste of the age in general (fig. 4).

The Viennese court seems to have endorsed the neoclassical style: the head silver chamberlain, Count von Dietrichstein, mentions in an internal document from 1778 "the authorization to complete the plain table silver for sixty persons."[7] Spareness in keeping with the ideals of the Enlightenment also went along with the personal style of the Hapsburg ruler Joseph II (1741–90). Whether the court table silver, which was almost completely re-made during the period of his solitary governance in the years 1783–84 by the Viennese silversmiths Ignaz Joseph Würth (1743–92) and Ignaz Sebastian Würth (1747–1834), consisted of sober shapes is something that can no longer be verified, as it was melted down again by his nephew, Emperor Francis II (1768–1835).[8] Joseph's personal hot chocolate pot (cat. no. 2),[9] in any case, which survives to this day, fulfilled the strict, functional criteria.

Toward the end of the 18th century financial means—the bourgeoisie, which had been strengthened both socially and economically, was flush with money—personal taste, and social environment began to be instrumental in the individual's formal/aesthetic perception and to play a part in his selective process. Plain, usually "cheaper" wares (because of the reduction in time required to make them) were offered for sale together with highly decorated pieces that were complicated to make.[10]

The true age of some plain, spare Viennese silver is often cause for bewilderment on the part of specialists who might be tempted to date these "modern" 19th century forms to the 20th century. Their stamped hallmarks, however, attest to the year of their making. This is particularly the case with certain simple, unornamented pieces that were usually part of toilet or traveling services. Because of what they were used for, they had to be functionally designed to fit into traveling cases while both saving space and being easy to stack. In addition, they had to have the capability of being easily and quickly cleaned while on the road. This is where formal simplicity is most often found, as rich ornamentation would have contradicted the purpose.

In the first half of the 19th century, gold- and silversmiths throughout the Hapsburg monarchy followed the lead of Vienna, which set the standard of taste throughout the realm.[11] An elongated candlestick type with a trumpet-shaped base, corseted shaft, graduated nozzle, and engraved, frieze-like décor taken from antiquity —known primarily in England—was thus popular from Prague and Brno to Budapest, Graz, and Ljubljana, to name only a few locations. When Viennese products are compared with contemporary products from elsewhere in the domestic and foreign markets during this era, the well-considered proportions and subtle decoration of the Viennese objects immediately stand out.

The comparison amongst themselves of Viennese objects made before and after 1800 makes it evident that the proportions of items for everyday use improved markedly after the turn of the century. Likewise, the relationship between shape and ornamentation also became more harmonious. These improvements may have had their roots in a crafts reform ushered in by Reichskanzler Prince Wenzel Kaunitz. After April 10, 1785 those who wished to become Meister, or master craftsmen, were required to pass a drawing examination,[12] which, in turn, made it necessary to attend drawing instruction and gain familiarity with the classical orders and their proportions.[13] The master drawings of gold and silver artisans from the first half of the 19th century correspond quite precisely to the stylistic development of executed models.[14]

After the 1780s shapes from classical antiquity began to be varied, though the ornamentation tended to play a subordinate role. It was not usually applied over the entire surface of the pieces, but used instead discriminately to emphasize individual zones. Where the formal vocabulary of antiquity lacked tried and true exemplary types, as was the case, for instance, with coffee and tea services, the elements were independently designed according to practical and functional criteria and most obviously adapted to contemporary taste in their extremities (the shapes of handles, spouts, or feet) and also through the selection of antique decorative motifs such as palmetto leaves, laurel friezes, egg and dart patterns, etc. Antique vessels for liquids were the model for neoclassical oval or cylindrical wine and water jugs (fig. 5). The long, drawn out metal and wood handles, turned and bent in various directions, emphasized the antique effect further. Viennese silversmiths often reduced the forms of their silver objects to the essentials and added to them simple, classical ornaments, all the while adhering to proportions familiar from antiquity. From this they developed, over time, the autonomous local style manifested in their plain, elegant, and fanciful silver objects.

Around 1825–30 a change began to take place in the formal appearance of silver objects such as pots, "samovars" (hot-water kettles and stands), boxes, candlesticks, beakers, baskets, and centerpieces for fruit, confections, or chocolate. Types that had once been characterized by their height were now made low and squat and preference was given to convex and partly curved shapes. Three-dimensional garlands of roses came into use as a favored decorative motif that was placed above the base and below the nozzle of candlesticks or on the shoulder and neck regions of pots.

After around 1840 the shapes of tablewares and other goods for everyday use filled out even more and became ever-more opulent; the lines of their silhouettes were oriented toward the forms of the baroque and rococo. Bulges and humps were raised up from or pressed into sheet silver on the ever-squatter shapes of objects (fig. 6). Indented or sharp-cornered ribs that can even take the form of ridges or tines often distinguished the surface of "samovars," coffeepots, teapots, or sugar boxes (fig. 7). Many objects were decorated with such abandon that their function was difficult to guess upon quick glance. Individual blossoms,

bouquets, or leaves were used as ornamentation, in addition to the aforementioned rose motifs. The ornamentation was usually sculpturally chased from the metal, which increased the dynamic of the lively contours of the object. Chased or pressed acanthus leaves also competed with the rose pattern, and upon occasion they covered the entire surface of the container (fig. 8) or were used to form feet, handles, or spouts. In this way ornamentation began to take on a partially structural role.

Until the end of the 19th century a variety of differing styles dominated the shapes of objects. Inspiration was taken not only from European styles (Romanesque to rococo), but also from the types and ornamentation of the Orient and Far East. Simple, undecorated shapes were in the minority after historicism began to hold sway.

Historically, the quality and value of objects was reflected in the complicated, handicraft method of their production. This did not mean, however, that the use of machines in production beginning in the 1820s was originally seen as a negative development. On the contrary, this cost-effective means was regarded as progressive and, therefore, initially admired by consumers. Only toward the middle of the century did cheap mass production lead to its taking on negative connotations.

After 1895 a massive artistic change took place in Vienna, as it did in the rest of Europe, which perceived the seventy-year reign of historicism as no longer befitting the age. Four designers followed the international trend and accepted the edicts of floral *Jugendstil*, but in a more measured manner than was the case in Belgium and France. The exuberant, curvilinear forms were thus also put to use on Viennese pieces. In this context, stylized plant motifs made of curved, sometimes spiral lines, were beloved as decoration; enamel was used as a color accent.

5. Johann Guttmann, silver wine jugs
Vienna 1806
Private collection

6. Emerich Scheinast, silver sugar box
Vienna 1850
Private collection

7. Franz Teltscher, silver tea kettle and stand
Vienna 1840
Private collection

8. Maker IK., silver trophy
Vienna 1838
MAK, Vienna

A group of artists and architects, including the architect Josef Hoffmann (1870–1956) and the painter and graphic artist Koloman Moser (1868–1918), opposed this trend, taking their inspiration instead from England and Scotland. They espoused geometric contours and stereometric shapes, as well as the spare use of decoration. Free from the constraints of outside firms, they were able to realize their aesthetic visions, supported by the metal workers and gold- and silversmiths who executed applied arts objects according to their specifications in the Wiener Werkstätte, which they founded together in 1903 based on the ideas of the London Guild of Handicrafts. Until 1907 objects with plain surfaces and *Hammerschlagdekor* (hammered décor) were made in precious and non-precious metals; like the grid baskets these, too, were derived from basic geometric forms. Occasionally semi-precious cabochon-cut stones were set into the sheet silver as color accents; sometimes stylized motifs were cut out from it. Simultaneously with the departure of Koloman Moser from the Wiener Werkstätte[15] its style of metalwork underwent a fundamental change. The formerly straight walls of silver decorative arts objects began to soften and curve, and stylized flower and leaf motifs started to cover surfaces. Wiener Werkstätte products achieved a highpoint in fluidity and the use of ornamentation in the late 1910s and early 1920s in the exceptionally creative designs of Dagobert Peche (1887–1923), whose work placed the artistic idea in the foreground. Apart from the Wiener Werkstätte a series of Viennese firms (Oskar Dietrich, Alexander Sturm, Brüder Frank, and Eduard Friedmann) executed silver and metalwork designs by students of Hoffmann and Moser at the Kunstgewerbeschule (Applied Arts Academy) in very high quality. The work of this next generation, which was striving to attain the standards of its masters, belies these artistic roots, even if it does not live up to the more radical experiments of its predecessors.

The collapse of the Hapsburg monarchy in 1918 and the grave economic and social disruptions that followed meant, with very few exceptions, the professional and artistic downfall of the silversmith's craft in Vienna. Altered living conditions with less call for display, as well as the appeal of "easy care" materials in objects for everyday living have until now precluded a "renaissance" in Viennese silver. Although objects executed in silver have been on the retreat from usage in everyday life since that time, they have nevertheless established a secure place in public and private collections as highly sought-after collectibles.

1 Gustav Otruba, "Alter, Verbreitung und Zunftorganisation des Goldschmiedehandwerks in Österreich," *Uhren/Juwelen*, vol. 5, Vienna 1967, p. 55. The document mentions the fact that the goldsmith Bruno, who died prior to 1170, sold his vineyard in Währing (near Vienna) to the Michaelbeuern monastery near Salzburg.

2 After the male line of the Babenbergs died out in 1246 and the short intermediary reign of King Ottokar of Bohemia (about 1233 to 1278), the Hapsburgs were awarded Austria as a fiefdom in 1282. Their reign ended in 1918.

3 In 1529 the first siege of Vienna by the Turks took place; in 1683 the second siege occurred. Vienna suffered major damage in the course of the wars between Protestants and Catholics, as the religious schism cut through all levels of society and, therefore, also through the reigning family.

4 Camillo List, "Wiener Goldschmiede und ihre Beziehungen zum kaiserlichen Hofe," *Jahrbuch der kunsthistorischen Sammlungen des Kaiserhauses*, vol. 17, Vienna 1896, p. 292.

5 A silver covered tureen with stand, made by Georg Hann in 1788, is today in the metal collection of the MAK (inv. no. Go 1817/1908).

6 Robert Adam (1728–1792) was active as an architect and decorator in England; he designed furniture, metalwork, fireplace surrounds, wall treatments, etc. whose classical shapes and delicate ornamentation were thought to "re-awaken the spirit of antiquity." His work became increasingly popular in England after 1760, and his reputation quickly grew in France and the United States as well.

7 The internal letter from February 25, 1778 from head silver chamberlain Count Karl Dietrichstein (1702–1784) regarding the authorization for the completion of the plain table silver also discusses the melting down of two table surtouts, out of which seventeen dishes could be made. Haus-, Hof- und Staatsarchiv, OmeA Prot. 39, 1778, fol. 210–211.

8 The two coinages of the imperial table silver in 1793 and 1810–11 raised the status of both table porcelain and, somewhat later, table bronze, making it *hoffähig* (acceptable for use at court), since without them court festivities could not have been held for lack of tableware.

9 The silver chocolate pot with ebony handle and engraved monogram J II and crown was made around 1780 by Ignaz Sebastian Würth. Museen des Mobiliendepots, Silberkammer, Vienna, inv. no. 180368/ 003–006.

10 The art dealer and founder of the Salzburg Baroque Museum, Kurt Rossacher, shows in his article "Moderne Form in altem Wiener Silber" (*alte und moderne Kunst*, year 18, issue 127, 1973, p. 58) how it became a virtue to "seek beauty through the effect of well-balanced silver surfaces, through the proper relationship of form and material thickness, and by making function visible.…This type of design also demanded a client who combined purchasing power with good taste. The taste that eschews ornamentation can only rise from the refinements of a mature culture. The naïveté of the nouveaux riches or the recently ennobled usually seeks out garish ornaments and loves artificial splendor."

11 A certain type of silver wine and water jug, which was derived from Greek jugs for liquids, appears to have been first fashioned by Viennese silversmiths. Compare a silver wine jug by Paul Mayerhofer, Vienna 1807 (inv. no. Go 1836/1941) and a pair of silver wine and water jugs, Prague 1815 (inv. no. Go 1247/1904) from the collections of the MAK, Vienna.

12 Gabriele Fabiankowitsch, *Funktion und Wesen des Zeichenunterrichts für Handwerker und seine Auswirkung auf die Möbelentwürfe des Empire und Biedermeier in Wien,* dissertation, Salzburg 1989, pp. 23 ff.

13 After 1767 "Journeymen and apprentices of the commercial professions, gold and silver workers, 'composition' workers [bronze workers], leather workers, sword makers, and knifesmiths…" were admitted to the Graveurschule (Engravers' Academy), which was founded by the painter and copper engraver Jakob Schmutzer (1733–1811). The drawing of models formed the basis of instruction. In: Walter Wagner, *Die Geschichte der Akademie der bildenden Künste in Wien*, Vienna 1967, p. 33.

14 The master drawings of the *Rechtswerber* (applicants) from the first half of the 19th century can be found in the library of the MAK, Vienna. They depict both sacred and profane objects, as well as jewelry.

15 Differing opinions between Koloman Moser and the financier of the Wiener Werkstätte, Fritz Waerndorfer, over the economic course of the firm together with Waerndorfer's planned financial involvement of Moser's wife caused the artist to leave the Wiener Werkstätte.

Inventory of the estate of Baroness Anna Maria von Mayrhofen in Klebing, including a page of silver items, 1827. Christian Witt-Dörring, Vienna

A "BOURGEOIS CENTURY?": SOCIETY AND HIGH CULTURE IN VIENNA 1780–1920

WILLIAM D. GODSEY, JR.

The period roughly separating the reign of Joseph II from the collapse of the monarchy has become known, not without good reason, as the "bourgeois century" in both Hapsburg and in European history generally. We all know the traditional story. Joseph II's "enlightened" assault on entrenched privilege and the old regime, however clumsy, ill-starred, or frustrated it may have been, unpleasantly jolted an already tottering and conveniently doomed "feudal" order. The emperor may have gone to his grave a disappointed, thwarted, and broken man, but his initiative at modernization was very soon followed by powerful economic, social, and political forces of change that he would nevertheless have found difficult to accept. A preliminary phase of industrial activity in Austria around 1800 early presaged the industrial revolution; a conspicuous bourgeoisie soon appeared on the scene; and events in France and Germany in the years after 1789 bode ill for the august, the blue-blooded, the courtly, and the titled. The arbiters of tone and style became the Geymüllers, the Arnsteins, and the Frieses, instead of the Dietrichsteins, the Esterházys, or the Auerspergs. Culturally, the "Biedermeier" is associated almost exclusively with the middle class and indeed "Biedermeier" and "burgher" have come to seem practically interchangeable. Given Vienna's later cultural fluorescence in the fin-de-siècle, which incontestably owed its brilliance to the capital's wealthy haute-bourgeoisie—known as the "second society"[1]—, the preoccupation with its social precursor in the first half of the 19th century has been both understandable and warranted.

And yet, nagging if mostly unexpressed doubts have remained, sometimes even among the chief exponents of the thesis of an early *embourgeoisement* of the Hapsburg Empire, about the social and cultural power of the middle classes in the decades after 1780. Their rise has been accompanied—so the usually implicit assumption—by the corresponding slip of the old aristocracy, whose continuing pomp and exclusiveness after its essential disappearance from history's stage has been written off as desperation in a hopeless situation. In a world dominated by bourgeois values, bourgeois money, and bourgeois taste, the magnates could no longer compete. Merit rather than birth and classical simplicity rather than baroque show became the bywords. The old élite shut itself up in its country houses, turned its back on modern culture, cultivated its piety, and sank into an ever more irrelevant and puerile obscurity. This picture owes much to the lively interest in the history of the middle classes in recent decades, to occasional declarations by grandees themselves, such as Prince Felix Schwarzenberg (1800–52), who claimed that few of his equals were fit for public service, and to the very real "fall" of the aristocracy in the 20th century.

But its allegedly quick disappearance and the dawn of "bourgeois society," which has been dated to the end of the 18th century, are very difficult to reconcile with what we know about the Hapsburg nobility in the early modern period or with more recent findings for the 1800s about its European counterparts. In his pioneering *The Making of the Hapsburg Monarchy,* the English historian Robert J. W. Evans has depicted the incomparable social, cultural, and economic power of the magnates, who entered an effective alliance with dynasty and Church during the Counter-Reformation and thereby maintained an unparalleled and unthreatened position deep into the 18th century. With latifundia scattered across Bohemia, Moravia, Inner and Lower Austria, and Hungary, they were collectively surpassed in their wealth only by the British territorial establishment. Unlike their French and German opposite numbers, they endured no devastating structural blows before 1848. Titles neither were abolished as in France nor did they become subject to intrusive bureaucratic regulation as in Bavaria;

the traditional estates constitutions (landständische Verfassungen) such as were extirpated in much of Germany around 1800 remained intact in the Hapsburg territories until 1848; and much evidence suggests that the old compact between the House of Austria and the aristocracy, supported and sanctioned by bureaucracy and Church, went through its last, great revival precisely in the decades—the Restoration and the Pre-March—that we have come to think of as the beginning of the "bourgeois century."

Furthermore, given the obdurate staying power of other early modern European élites that had encountered greater challenges in the upheavals between 1789 and 1815, there is good reason for rethinking the temporal categories of late modern Hapsburg history. Bourgeois ascendency arguably set in later—in the second half of the 19th century—was more halting, and was never as self-evident before the First World War as previously believed or as was the case elsewhere. After all, the Hapsburg state retained, down to its demise, meaningful political and constitutional elements, such as the monarchy, the court, a parliamentary upper house, and an electoral system slanted in favor of wealth, that lent themselves to the exercise of a disproportionate, if increasingly behind-the-scenes influence by traditional nobles. Cultural trends in Vienna, the seat of the court and the aristocracy, are hardly to be understood outside of this context. The applied arts, including the design, manufacture, and purchase of products such as porcelain, glass, and silver, must have depended far into the 19th century principally on the patronage of representatives of the old order.

A modern bourgeoisie as the chief carrier of any likewise modern culture in the decades around 1800 in Vienna is difficult to imagine given, above all, the lack of industrialization that would have created such a class. The consensus among historians is that the Hapsburg Monarchy did not begin to industrialize until the late 1820s and that even then a slow and gradual, if respectable, take-off rather than the proverbial "spurt" occurred. The later 18th century first witnessed "some of the structural changes that normally accompany modern economic growth," but neither they nor the reforms of Joseph II ultimately produced industrialization or a meaningful modern bourgeoisie. Except for a few years of strong performance around the turn of the century, industrial growth actually stagnated for much of the period from the 1780s to the 1820s. This is not to argue that some new enterprises, such as the textile mills of Johann Joseph Leitenberger (1730–1802), who was the first entrepreneur in Austria to use English spinning machines, did not portend later developments. Even after its beginning, though, modern industrialization spread very unevenly across the Hapsburg lands, with no "spurt" ever occurring even in the more "advanced" western regions and an initial noticeable increase in such activity coming as late as the 1870s in Hungary. The fevered expansion of the 1850s and 1860s in Cisleithania was followed by the long depression that set in after the famous financial "crash" of 1873 and that lasted into the 1890s. Other indicators, such as the high proportion of the population still living in the countryside, which had not sunk below the fifty percent mark even by 1910, would appear to justify the label of "industrializing agrarian state" applied to the Hapsburg Monarchy down to the First World War.[2] Large numbers of people continued to subsist in areas still dominated by their former feudal lords, the sheer size of whose estates helped them—through economies of scale and probably through strategic agrarian capitalism—to ride out the agricultural depression at the end of the 19th century better than smaller farmers. The Hapsburg economy remained less industrialized than in neighboring Germany, to say nothing of England, heavily dependent on such traditional sectors as agriculture, and thus more conducive to the relative preservation of a privileged social position of the old stratum of magnates.

Although the origins of the Viennese Biedermeier are invariably attributed to "bourgeois" inspiration, the class that might have incorporated such values was very small indeed in the initial decades after 1800. Of the 500 entrepreneurs identified by the historian Ingrid Mittenzwei as making up Vienna's "early bourgeoisie," some one-third came from the traditional branches of banking and wholesale trade, neither of which was especially "modern" in terms of the industrial age and whose representatives rather recalled the agents (Hoffaktoren) that had been a familiar sight at the Hapsburg court in earlier times. This sector tended to dominate the "bourgeoisie;" their names—Arnsteiner (later Arnstein), Henikstein, Fries, Geymüller, Wertheimer—often figured among the more prominent of the group as a whole; and they sometimes exhibited a taste for aping or outdoing aristocratic style that is difficult to reconcile with notions of Biedermeier intimacy and simplicity. Riches that would have challenged those of the magnates were at any rate the exception and few businessmen may be reckoned to the haute bourgeoisie in terms of their way of life. Where bankers such as Berend Gabriel Eskeles piled up thousands of guilders worth of table silver, most entrepreneurs held far less spectacular reserves. That left behind by the early 19th-century silk manufacturer Lorenz Verständig was more typical of his peers: "…two watches, four silver tablespoons, a serving spoon, and three teaspoons."[3] Recent scholarship furthermore suggests that contemporary reports of elaborate consumption by the early Viennese bourgeoisie were very exaggerated.

Other, more substantial strata of the early 19th-century Viennese population, such as the ever-increasing flock of non-noble bureaucrats and officers, were even less likely, if they lacked independent wealth, to have been in a position to set up an elaborate household with the appropriate trappings. They were miserably paid—the salaries of governmental servants declined continuously in real terms from the time of Joseph II to the third quarter of the 19th century and a high proportion could not afford to get married until they were middle-aged. The coveted rank of court councilor (Hofrat) brought in only between 4,000 and 6,000 guilders annually as opposed to the 50,000–70,000 guilders that the head of a middling house of the court nobility had at his disposal. At his death in 1815, one bourgeois official characterized as well-situated, Johann Peter Weckbecker, laid claim to silver that amounted to some six spoons. Similar relative poverty, in comparison at least to the aristocracy and the leading bankers, was also the lot of those who held military commissions.[4]

The increasingly lively trade beginning in the last decades of the 18th century in luxury articles such as silver may be traced above all to the market generated by courtiers and aristocrats whose disposable revenues were on the rise. It bears repeating that their immense landholdings, which in many cases amounted to tens of thousands of acres, and the corresponding incomes, which not infrequently reached into the hundreds of thousands of guilders, had no rival in continental Europe—either in Prussia or in France—and that these by no means went lost in the transition to late modernity. To the contrary: they profited by the agricultural revolution, by the high prices for harvests around 1800, by a flexible willingness to shift their production to meet new demand, and by their own industrial activity. The late 1790s several times witnessed bumper crops; the cost of wheat tripled between 1790 and 1806 on the exchange in Pest; and Napoleon's famous "Continental System" (1806), which diminished competition from British exports, further helped prop up the value of their estate yields. During the 18th century, many grandees had been pioneers in industrial production, a tradition that had by no means died by 1800. The Harrachs and Buquoys led in Bohemian glass; the Wrbnas, Fürstenbergs, and Salm-Reifferscheidts in iron; and the Waldsteins, Lažanskys, and Auerspergs in textiles. Thanks to their intimate ties to court and government, many aristocrats had advance warning of the notorious demonetization of 1811 and were able in time to transfer their capital to safer investments.

The sharp, but temporary, fall in agricultural prices following the conclusion of peace (1815) accelerated already emerging patterns of diversification, such as the breeding of merino sheep, which became a profitable mainstay of magnate farming during the Restoration. In the 1820s, a Moravian magnifico, Baron Carl Dalberg (1792–1859), launched the cultivation of beetroot on his estate in Datschitz for the manufacture of domestic sugar. The 1830s then saw the beginning of its widespread production, which owed much of its initial success to aristocratic entrepreneurship, which became a substantial agro-industry in the following decades, and which, given its landed base, long remained closely associated with the nobility. Although the abolition in 1848 of patrimonial administration and manorial rights dealt an irremediable blow to the age-old position of the landed aristocracy, depriving it of its domination of the countryside, handsome compensatory payments for these losses flowed into its coffers and provided new opportunities for agricultural modernization, the building and renovation of castles, and investments in banking, railroads, and insurance.[5]

If the Hapsburg aristocracy remained ipso facto the pre-eminent economic élite in an agrarian state down to 1848 and beyond, this was no less matched by its continuing social predominance. The usual treatments of Biedermeier Vienna, which are all too often emphasize such elements as the new bourgeoisie and Metternichian repression, tend to disregard the significance that accrued to the capital as the residence of Europe's premier monarchy, the continent's most blue-blooded, hidebound, and exclusive court, and a grand nobility possessed of material resources unmatched outside London. The "Restoration," a misnomer for so much of the post-1815 settlement, here hints accurately at the aristocratic renaissance that had set in by the 1820s in Hapsburg Central Europe. Where nobles in Germany gradually redefined themselves as a *national* élite in a

Herderian sense and accentuated their extraction from an original, almost mythical Teutonic caste—hence the artificial, Late-Enlightenment term *Uradel*—Hapsburg aristocrats took their cue from the *ancien régime*.

Metternich became the last great proponent of the old alliance between crown and magnates, while powerful courtiers such as Grand Chamberlain Count Rudolph Czernin (1757–1845) resolutely made sure that Viennese aristocratic society remained closed to those who were considered parvenus, upstarts, and the merely rich. In keeping with the earlier practice, which had all but died out in France and other parts of Germany, purity of noble blood—meaning possession of twelve to sixteen noble quarterings on both the maternal and paternal sides—prevailed as the standard. In this spirit, the 18th-century regulations regarding admission to court and the bestowal of its most coveted honors—the chamberlain's key *(Kämmererwürde)*, the Order of the Star-Cross *(Sternkreuzorden)*, and the post of page *(Edelknabenstelle)*—were re-confirmed in 1824. Collegiate foundations for men that required similarly elaborate ancestry for admission and that had nearly been destroyed in the revolutionary era, such as the Order of St. John of Jerusalem and the Teutonic Order, were revived. The emperor agreed that noble descent should continue to be a prerequisite for membership in the cathedral chapter in Olmütz nearly a generation after such institutions had been abolished in Germany. The relentless Czernin successfully fought off challenges for access to court, and thus to the charmed circle of the aristocracy, not by wealthy newcomers such as Baron Johann Heinrich Geymüller (1781–1848), whose famously sumptuous parties brought him no closer to consideration, but by otherwise well-connected and wellborn nobles such as Count Carl Haugwitz (1797–1874) and Count Alexander Nákó (1785–1848), both of whom he nonetheless regarded as tainted by the counting house.[6] Viennese blue-bloods had ample opportunity during the 1830s to titter at the caricatures passed around of the socially ambitious Nákó. One such depicted him as a cat balancing himself on a support beside a bowl of milk, reaching for a chamberlain's key dangling above his head, and saying: "*Si je tombe, au moins je tombe dans la crème.*"[7] (If I fall, at least I'll fall into the cream.)

The unbroken, if perhaps no longer unchallenged power of the Hapsburg aristocracy and the analogous and relative weakness of the bourgeoisie within the essentially early modern social, political, and economic structures of the Hapsburg state between 1780 and the 1840s raise as well the issue of culture. To put it another way, how "bourgeois" were the Enlightenment and the Biedermeier? The tired and tiresome cliché that the aristocracy and the imperial family somehow adapted the views and outlook of the middle classes—rather than the other way around—does not stand up in view of what has been said above, of the rigidly hierarchical nature of Hapsburg society, or of what we now understand about the nobility's own cultural past. As the American historian Jonathan Dewald has put it: "But the [early modern] period brought something more, a readiness among nobles to appreciate artistic innovation, a surprising degree of support for what was new and even challenging in contemporary culture….During the 17th and 18th centuries…nobles supported (and in some instances defined) the cutting edge of contemporary culture." Dewald and others have convincingly argued that many of the ideals that we associate most strongly with the bourgeoisie, such as individualism, the quest for privacy, and familial intimacy—all further associated with the Biedermeier —first established themselves among the early modern nobility. Along the same line, other scholarship, such as T. C. W. Blanning's look at the Catholic Enlightenment, indicates that the "bourgeois" contribution to 18th-century culture has long been overstressed. The carriers of the Enlightenment, as the membership lists of the Freemasons indicate, came in many cases from the second estate, which provided both cultural benefactors and producers. Given the Hapsburg aristocracy's resources and prestige, which had made possible its earlier endeavors and which remained undiminished in the decades after 1800, its sudden disappearance from an area so traditional and so ideal for the preservation of status would have been surprising.

Indeed, if we take a look at one established field of aristocratic patronage relevant to our topic—architecture and interior design—the first half of the 19th century marked another, if perhaps last apex. Dozens of magnates who formed the core of Viennese aristocratic society re-fashioned, refurbished, and rebuilt their seats during this period and thereby left behind artistic monuments of the first rank. In the lands of the Bohemian crown alone, neoclassicism found elegant expression in castles such as Katschina near Neuhof (Chotek), Königswart (Metternich), Datschitz (Dalberg), and Boskowitz (Dietrichstein), while the Neo-Gothic attained a new splendor in Hradek (Harrach), Frauenberg (Schwarzenberg), Eisgrub (Liechtenstein), and Žleb (Auersperg). In most cases, the gentlemen-builders themselves were closely involved in the conception and completion of the plans. Their creations were paralleled by many others elsewhere in the Hapsburg territories, as Grafenegg in Lower Austria (Breunner), Fót in Hungary (Károlyi), or Csákvár in the same kingdom (Esterházy) conspicuously suggest. Such building boomed once again after mid-century, this time in the historicist style, and an astonishing number of country houses were constructed or redone. Why aristocrats would have given such compelling and original embodiment to their own, so obviously unimpaired sense of identity, only then to have allegedly copied from the middle classes in their interiors, is an incongruity that does not hold up. The old equation of "bourgeois" and Biedermeier has in fact been powerfully, if perhaps unwittingly discredited by the catalogue of a recent exhibition of watercolor-views of aristocratic indoor living spaces revealingly called *Zeugen der Intimität* (Witnesses to Intimacy) held at Schallaburg Castle in Lower Austria (1997). These pictures more than evidence the weight placed on intimacy, privacy, family, simplicity, even marital devotion, by great noble houses such as Czernin, Waldstein, and Buquoy. There is no evidence that bourgeois style provided the inspiration, which was made even more unlikely by the lack of social contact between aristocratic women, who had a say in the appointments and furnishings of their apartments, and those from other strata. Original creative impulses—in part for silver as well—came rather from abroad, particularly from the British upper crust, which many Hapsburg aristocrats regarded as their ideal and to which they developed intimate ties. His obsession with the life of the English upper class earned Count Breunner the good-natured mockery of his peers and the nickname "milord."[8] The influx during the revolutionary era into Vienna of highborn émigrés from France, the Austrian Netherlands, and western Germany—Metternich, Crenneville, Dalberg, Bombelles, Stadion, and Rohan are just a few of the many well-known names—may have played another, heretofore neglected part in cultural transfer.

Only in the third quarter of the 19th century can we begin to speak of the eclipse of the Hapsburg aristocracy, a process that by 1918, however, was still far from complete. Though no longer lords of the countryside, the magnates continued to dominate the court, were favored politically by the curial electoral system in the diets, managed to hold onto their broad acres, and were over-represented in certain branches of officialdom. Culturally, the retreat was more clear-cut. Castles were occasionally still erected, though not on the same scale as earlier, and little evidence indicates they had much to do with new trends in the visual and applied arts.[9] In the later 19th century, their feelings of insecurity became too great in the face of the demographic shift to the cities, especially Vienna, the rise of the bourgeoisie, and the threat posed by mass politics. To the extent that grandees still collected, the past became the measure. Count Hans Wilczek (1837–1922) stuffed the eyrie he reconstructed at Kreuzenstein outside of Vienna with medieval armor and Gothic implements, while Count Karl Lanckoroński preferred the Renaissance. Modern art was left to their new rivals in what has been termed "Ringstrasse society" or the "second society"—that section of the bourgeoisie whose wealth, palaces, and patronage rivaled the aristocratic past.

A so-called "second society," even if not so named, had been characteristic of the early modern social order, where noble ideal and practice had required descent from noble stock on all sides. Those without it—the freshly ennobled, the nouveaux riches, and the increasingly numerous bureaucratic élite—all of whom laid claim to superior status, occupied a distinctly subordinate social position and took their cue from the court and those of pure blood. With the essential destruction around 1800 of the system of pedigree everywhere in Central Europe but the Hapsburg Empire, a fusion of the two upper social echelons tended to occur. Only in Vienna did the barrier remain to the end nearly impermeable, even if the number of intermarriages between the two groups rose steadily.[10] And only later in the 19th century did this "second society" truly come into its own following the consolidation and expansion of the modern banking, industrial, and trade sectors. High-ranking bureaucrats and officers, as well as the small number of entrepreneurial dynasties that had established themselves in the Pre-March, were now joined by railroad tycoons, financiers, and factory owners. The heights of this world, which was probably smaller than the haut monde in London or Berlin, were heavily, though not exclusively Jewish and their names, rather than those of the old aristocracy or even of the bourgeoisie at large, are associated with the flower of Viennese culture in the fin-de-siècle. Their contributions to our civilization have been the repeated subject of exhibitions and scholarly inquiry, and need no repetition here. Suffice it to say that the "second society" to some extent took up the legacy of the old court nobility through its supranational orientation, which was reinforced by an increasingly rabid nationalism and anti-Semitism, and through its patronage of the arts, including the applied arts as represented by the Wiener Werkstätte. It is worth speculating whether the elegance, simplicity, and "modernity" specific to Viennese silver might not be attributable to certain similarities of mindset, despite the marked differences in history and tradition, of two remarkable, truly imperial élites at home in the Hapsburg capital from the reign of Joseph II to the First World War.

1   The term "second society" refers to that stratum of upper Hapsburg society, recruited primarily from newly ennobled officers, civil servants, and the economic élite, as well as the non-noble haute bourgeoisie, that may be distinguished from the high nobility or aristocracy, also known as "first society." Given the latter's abiding attachment to the traditional concept of nobility, those without a pedigree of noble descent in both the paternal and maternal lines were inevitably excluded from its ranks. A product of the time-honored corporate order, the "second society" had emerged by the late 18th century and existed down to 1918.

2   This was down from the more than eighty percent that were living in villages and towns of less than 2,000 inhabitants in 1850.

3   Inventories of estates probably tended to minimize, for tax reasons, the amount of silver a person had owned. On the other hand, we should not forget how small the prosperous classes of the population were at the time and correspondingly how well-known the circumstances of its members were. It would have been difficult to hide large troves of silver from the authorities.

4   Apart from the aristocracy, only the top ranks of officialdom and the small wealthiest sector of the bourgeoisie could have afforded silver in larger quantities. In 1780, the market price of one kilogram of *uncrafted* fine silver was eighty-five guilders, which had gone up by 1809 to 253 guilders. The salaries of non-manual employees at the Viennese *Bürgerspital* in 1779 suggest how difficult it would have been for even the best earning to have had much in the way of silver tableware. The head of the hospital *(Spitelmeister)* brought in 1,000 guilders per year, while a doctor *(Wundarzt)* had only 400 guilders and a clerk (*Grundschreiber*) 500 guilders per annum. Even a court councillor *(Hofrat)*, whose salary was falling in real terms from the reign of Joseph II, would have found it difficult to collect large quantities of crafted silver.

5   Given the dearth of secondary literature on the 19th-century Hapsburg aristocracy, it is not surprising that not a single study has been devoted to the question of how such compensatory payments were used.

6   Haugwitz's mother was a Fries, while Nákó's paternal ancestors in earlier generations had been merchants.

7   The term "cat" was a contemporary play on Nákó's Greek Macedonian ancestry. "Crème" referred to the Viennese aristocracy's own characterization of itself.

8   Revealingly, Breunner and his family later (1834) became the subject of a major Biedermeier portrait by Friedrich Amerling.

9   The purchase of uniforms in *Jugendstil* for the court-pages, an honor that required sixteen noble quarterings, is an interesting exception.

10 The children of such unions, even if they bore the names of historic families, were excluded from the aristocracy. The case of Bertha von Suttner, née Countess Kinsky, whose mother belonged to a family of the recent nobility, is a typical case.

See p. 394 for Selected Bibliography

CREATIVE DENSITY

SYLVIA MATTL-WURM

Can "creative milieus" be produced? Certain political scientists answer the question with a definitive yes, even as they qualify that answer with prerequisites such as freedom and point out that their duration is limited. Other authors actually connect the achievement of creativity directly with the constitution of states, cities, and educational systems whose internal logic—a willingness to change as recipe for success—allows them to become "creative milieus par excellence."[1] Historically, this applies in particular to cities when they are confronted with a process of renewal. For openness and public life, new ideas must be presented, discussed, and exchanged. Mobility and flexibility, plurality and tolerance (on the part of carriers of the political system), but also acceptance of conflict and competition are preliminaries for the invention of the new.[2] In the following essay it is not my intent to subscribe to this view part and parcel, but merely to examine the lone aspect of real productivity in cities and urban areas, and even this discussion shall be restricted to two especially outstanding periods in the biography of Vienna. I shall not necessarily be guided by the image of a "constructive" or positive creativity, for, as David Harvey notes, renewal and transformation are just as dependent upon "creative destruction."[3]

Looking back over most recent history, we see that the significance of distinct phases of intense developmental spurts and the seizure-like release of creative potential is not to be doubted. The fin-de-siècle serves as the model in this case for the parallelization and connection of artistic, scientific, and political innovations, as well as innovation in the realm of everyday culture. Vienna, as the capital and residence of the Hapsburg realm, takes a crucial position in the scientific discourse surrounding the success of the Modern movement, and, in the course of the past two decades, innumerable publications have reflected upon Vienna's true contribution.[4] If we go back slightly further in the history of the city of Vienna and attempt to locate similarly intense culmination points in processes of change and creativity, it is above all the period of the Enlightenment that deserves our attention.

The Enlightenment, which in the Hapsburg state can be defined as the period of the (co)-regency of Joseph II (1765–90)—roughly twenty-five years— is one of the most fascinating periods of transformation in European history and in the history of its major cities. The Enlightenment was introduced from the top down in Austria, and it led the region from a religiously-integrated baroque world into a secular, rational environment, as well as from the court/feudal system to an early-bourgeois, proto-modern society. Vienna evolved during these explosive years of the late 18th century from a relatively provincial imperial residence with a bigoted character to a large city with a population that held worldly, urbane views.

Looking back from our vantage point, these processes of change had their most distinct effect in the architecture that transformed the cityscape during those years. By this I mean the dissolution of class representation in the body of the city itself and the conquering of new social spaces by its citizens. In contrast to the ostentatious buildings of the court/feudal system during the first half of the 18th century (such as the Church of St. Charles, the imperial stables, Schloss Schönbrunn, or numerous aristocratic palaces, many of which still exist today, such as Daun-Kinsky, Harrach, and Lobkowitz) the 1770s and 1780s were marked by monumental public buildings for the purpose of serving the regulation of population in accordance with contemporary scientific standards (the general hospital, psychiatric ward [the so-called *Narrenturm,* or fool's tower], the Josephinum [educational facility for training military physicians], and barracks). The opening to the general public of two parks and hunting grounds near the city, even though these measures had first and foremost to do with an absolutist population policy, encouraged—apart from political reforms of which I shall come to speak later—the growth of a public sphere.

MOBILITY

The conversion of the Prater (1766) and the Augarten (1775) to recreational areas, together with the alteration of the glacis surrounding the city walls (today's Ringstrasse) into a kind of *corso,* as well as the opening of the gardens of aristocratic palaces to the public (e.g. Palais Liechtenstein) created for the first time a terrain for genuine bourgeois self-depiction. The Viennese very quickly took possession of these new city areas and they developed into large-scale spaces for popular entertainments and urban attractions. Thus there were in the year 1782 some forty-three taverns (*Praterhütten,* or Prater huts), two ring-toss arenas and two visual attractions (camera obscura). Contemporary publications also reported in detail about the thousands of Viennese who filled the only bridge connecting the city and other nearby towns on their Sunday evening return from the Prater—and the traffic snarls that were the result. Commercial theater, concerts, and entertainment events (and the mass transport systems they required), together with the regulation of opening hours for visits to gardens and collections allowed for the rise of new forms of communication and a new, profane sense of time.

PUBLIC LIFE AND OPENNESS

In the years of the Enlightenment new-fangled institutions such as "casinos" were likewise established; as a rule the so-called educated-classes gathered there, where they could eat, gamble, make music, read newspapers, and discuss events. The first great dance halls also date from this period, and in 1792 there were already six of them. A number of suburban theaters were founded, such as the Leopoldstadt Theater, the Freihaustheater in Wieden (the site of the premiere of Mozart's *Die Zauberflöte),* or the Theater in der Josefstadt. The number of *Trakteure* (comparable to today's snack bars), the beer halls, and above all the coffee houses increased significantly during the 1780s.[5] They all constituted new, bourgeois-coded spaces for urban pleasure, mixed in with forms of discourse in public life. A significant meeting of the various classes took place here and new forms of communication unrelated to courtly distinctions were developed: according to contemporary reports, in the thirty-some *Trakteure* in the center of Vienna civil servants, officers, priests, musicians, craft apprentices, servants in aristocratic households, etc. all gathered together. In the beer halls it was usually lackeys, students, artists, clerks, and the middle bourgeois who spent their evenings here discussing the news of the day. The coffee houses appear to have developed into the refuge—even at this early stage—of the (still rare) intellectuals: one came here to "study, play, chat, sleep, negotiate, rant, and to haggle; to hatch intrigues and plots, build castles in the air, and to read newspapers and journals," in the words of the Josephin city chronicler Johann Pezzl.[6] In some of them, smoking tobacco was allowed, in almost all of them billiards were played, and yet it seems that it was the exchange of opinions that stood at the forefront of interest. Here, too, we thus encounter the sudden spurt of change that led to the formation of a genuine bourgeois public distinct from the closed hierarchical milieus of aristocratic salons and the social theatrics of court festivities.

In the introduction to his 1992 book on urban intellectuals Walter Prigge[7] wrote: "The French Revolution freed knowledge from feudalism. Secrets and privileges were done away with, the democratic institutions of knowledge opened out onto the city and the world, which was explored geographically in the development of global markets. The city, [i.e. Paris] becomes a universe of knowledge, and this urban universe contains in the classical architecture of the city the collected knowledge of the world—in particular, the academy and the museum were the places where this knowledge was made public and available for everyone. Cities as spaces for the circulation of revolutionary ideas are the prerequisite for the cultural and political revolutionizing of society. Salons, cafés, and literary circles formed communicative zones within the city, and in these places the population became enlightened. In this manner the city public became the true medium of the bourgeois intellectuals: urbanity and public exchange versus aristocratic regimentation and absolute power."

All of this is true (to a certain extent) for Vienna as well: while the intended foundation of an academy of sciences (in opposition to the Catholic university) failed, scholarly lectures were nevertheless held for the public (the "mechanical courses" of Joseph Walcher, for instance), and, after the removal of the imperial paintings collection to the Belvedere and its restructuring, it was opened to the general public. For the first time the court library kept regular opening hours, and "reading corners" (*Lesekabinette*) were increasingly established in the city as central clearing houses for literature, where members who paid monthly or yearly membership dues could read books—and above all, newspapers—for a very minimal fee and even have them delivered to their homes. Apart from the cafés it was chiefly the literary circles, the first Viennese bourgeois "salons," and the lodges of the Freemasons that were carriers of the (self-) Enlightenment. (The first Viennese salons, incidentally, were led by women as a rule. The most famous of them was probably that of Fanny von Arnstein.) In them could be found local scholars and artists, as well as foreign ones on their way through Vienna ("a little music, friendly conversation in

1. Bird's eye view of Vienna with outlying towns, 1769–74 Copperplate engraving by Joseph Daniel Huber, Vienna 1774–76 Historisches Museum der Stadt Wien

confidence, literary news, discussion of books, travel, works of art, theater, the events of the day, and interesting novelties related with spice, judged, and illuminated, make up the entertainment and shorten the long winter evenings for the cosy circle."[8]). Many of these institutions were closely connected to the playing of music, such as the salon of the Leopold Auenbruggers (Auenbrugger, a physician, was the inventor of the so-called *Auskultationsmethode* [auscultation method] for the diagnosis of lung illnesses), or that of Gottfried van Swieten, the son of the famous university reformer and physician Gerard van Swieten. Here was created—with one fell swoop, as it were—a public whose opinions rested on reason, information, and criticism.

NETWORKS

At this time I would like to take up a theory of Karl H. Müller,[9] who in his study of social-scientific creativity in the 20th century laid the parameters for creativity itself. One of his important operationalization theses is that of network description and network design. Müller speaks of networks of communities that communicate via their individual components, such as manners of thought, people, research units, clusters, specialty media, marketplaces, systems, and the like, all the way to topics, methods, basic perspectives, theories, and models, thereby guaranteeing a highly creative, interdisciplinary transfer of knowledge. In fin-de-siècle Vienna private research bodies (like Freud's psychoanalytic discussion group), late-Enlightenment popular scientific societies (such as the Urania), and institutions (university

2. Otto Wagner, *Ideal design for the XXII district*, pen and ink and pencil, Vienna 1910–11 Historisches Museum der Stadt Wien

3. Monument for Emperor
Joseph II with his decrees
Copperplate engraving,
Vienna ca. 1792.

MONUMENT IOSEPHS II.

institutes or museums) in strict or loose coupling with political parties and associations (the Social-Democratic cultural and educational organizations, for instance), the quality press, and free social gatherings (e.g. the salons of Marie Lang or Berta Zuckerkandl) constituted an extraordinarily stimulating process of exchange, creating the basis for numerous innovative crossings between the arts and the sciences.

In addition to the salons and literary societies we can, with all due caution, identify a further institution around 1790 that prefigured such network structures: the Freemasons. The climate under Joseph II was favorable toward Freemasonry and, after his Freemason Decree (1785), which allowed the founding of one to three lodges per town with a maximum of 180 brothers, the lodges experienced another strong upswing. Humanitarian and scientific discussions on the highest intellectual level of the day took place in them, and their effect on the broader public should not be underestimated. The discussions in the True Harmony Lodge (*Zur wahren Eintracht*) were, for example, printed up in an edition of 1,000 in the Freemason journal. The lodge published *Physikalische Arbeiten der einträchtigen Freunde in Wien* (Work in Physics by the Harmonious Friends in Vienna) and the *Wiener Realzeitung* (Viennese Real Newspaper)—the chief organ of the Enlighteners—as scientific periodicals. Today the membership rosters of the Viennese Freemason lodges during the 1780s read like a fictitious early *Who's Who*: the internationally recognized mineralogist Ignaz von Born (1742–1791), who presided over the Viennese lodge according to the model of the Paris lodge Aux neufs soeurs, making it a lodge of scholars; the political scientist Joseph von Sonnenfels (1732–1817); or Franz von Zeiller (1751–1828), author of the general code of civil law. Johann Peter Frank, founder and first director of the general hospital, and the anatomist and art collector Joseph Barth were lodge brothers, as were the writer Aloys Blumauer, Johann Ratschky, Johann Baptist Alxinger, and the composers Joseph Haydn and Wolfgang Amadeus

Mozart. Count Georg Festetics, one of the most important Hungarian reformers, was a member; so was the poet and world-traveler Georg Forster. There were adherents of revolutionary movements among them, like Baron Siegfried Taufferer and Martin Prandstetter. But there were also conservatives such as Count Leopold Kollowrat-Krakowsky, the court chancellor, and Count Franz Saurau, who uncovered the Jacobin plot. The sculptor Franz Anton Zauner; the famed "Moor" Angelo Soliman, page of Prince Liechtenstein; the publisher Pasquale Artaria; the engraver Jakob Matthias Schmutzer; and the actor, theater director, and librettist Emanuel Schikaneder (who wrote the libretto for Mozart's *Die Zauberflöte)* likewise all belonged to Viennese lodges.[10] Helmut Reinalter, the preeminent scholar of the history of Austrian Freemasonry, saw the lodges first and foremost as meeting places for discussions, as centers of communication, places for personal contact and the exchange of writing, and as sites where the ideas of the Enlightenment were transferred.[11] These ideas were undoubtedly the unifying element. Thus it was that Joseph II culled his censors (Gottfried van Swieten, Joseph von Sonnenfels, Aloys Blumauer, or Joseph von Retzer) from the circle of the Freemasons when it came to an attempt to more or less successfully steer and control the flood of printed material in circulation, a flood brought about by recent expansions of press freedom.

PLURALITY AND TOLERANCE

Exhaustive research has shown, using the example of Wolfgang Amadeus Mozart, just how much the democratic principles of Freemasonry entered into his artistic work and how nearly identical his social environment and circle of friends were with the network of the "Masons." The Berlin historian Ingrid Mittenzwei identified an additional cluster in the Enlightenment as the new class of bourgeois entrepreneurs. Even though this class encompassed but a very small segment of society, the high number of ennoblements among its members shows the weight this early economic bourgeoisie carried. We find among its ranks Nathan Adam Arnsteiner, Thomas Ligthowler, Franz Wilhelm Natorp, Johann Michael Puchberg, Johann Baptist Puthon, Johann Thomas Trattner, Joseph Paul Weinbrenner, Karl Abraham, and Raimund Wetzlar von Plankenstein.[12] Most of these names can also be found in the lists of the Freemason lodges or in the group of patrons of Mozart. For the educated bourgeoisie, just as for the economic bourgeoisie, a very high immigration rate and multi-confessionality is characteristic. Ignaz von Born came from Siebenbürgen (Transylvania, today part of Rumania), had studied in Prague, and was, among other things, a member of the English Royal Society before coming to Vienna; Joseph von Sonnenfels had a Jewish background and studied in Leipzig and Vienna; the Artaria family emigrated from northern Italy. By far the greatest share of immigrants came from the Hapsburg or German territories. Smaller groups came from non-Hapsburg Italy, the Netherlands, from France, England, Greece, or Switzerland, whence came technological transfers of particular note.

The Swiss influenced ribbon production, the metalwork industry received decisive new impulses from England (Ligthowler), and the silk industry from France. Many among the new elite were Jews or Protestants, like the Evangelical textile industrialist Johann Fries (1719–1785), who became a count after the Edict of Tolerance was decreed. For the first time he was able to acquire land, and he had a town palace erected (today Palais Pallavicini) facing the Hofburg. Joseph II's Patent for Jews remained far behind the position of the Enlightenment, however. On the one hand it made the universities accessible and allowed Jews to carry out a profession or create industries, but at the same time it continued to forbid them to buy property or build synagogues. It encouraged the integration of the "tolerated" Jews belonging to the upper classes, but kept close watch over the new immigration of Jews. Residency papers for Jews in Vienna were tied to a certain amount of capital. Extremely high, tightly controlled residency fees were indicative of the reigning anti-Semitism.

It is well-known that the Austrian "Enlightenment" was shaped from above. Joseph II was not only interested in promoting a concentration of intellectuals and scientific experts in Vienna, he actively encouraged it. Paradoxically, he hoped to use it to anchor new, even "revolutionary" thinking in all levels of society and, at the same time, to secure the absolutist state with their political loyalty. Public opinion was therefore to be both shaped and manipulated according to his views. As Michel Foucault has said: the "Enlightenment" was to serve the founding of (self-) disciplinary groups. The changes brought about by the two decades of "Enlightenment" in the capital city and imperial residence—I call them the city's fast-paced years—were lasting. The most so was, in my opinion, the destruction of the regime of time and space ordered by the court calendar, the church, and governing bodies of the classes, all of which began to take a back seat to the conventional opening and closing hours of the theaters, collections and museums, and parks and restaurants. The restructuring of the city into zones of work, culture, and recreation—which in the case of the Prater, with its freely-accessible attractions for the city crowd, brought about a new urban culture leading to the perception of the city as a place of diversity—proved to be just as long-lived. In these few years "spaces" were established such as the salons, the "reading corners," and the scientific faculties at universities, all of which produced a social milieu in which the modern city could see its reflection. Nor was the political system of "Restoration" that followed able to eradicate it in its entirety. (Under Francis II, who followed his father Leopold II on the throne in 1792, many of the Josephin reforms were taken back again. The perfection of the secret police force, in particular, had as its effect the far-reaching retreat of the civilian public from public affairs.)

"There can be no doubt that a certain measure of openness, tolerance, and prosperity encourages innovation…"[13] wrote Joachim Jung regarding the psychological basis of creativity. Creativity means bringing forth something new, and it has as its prerequisite the courage to question the past or to destroy it. Perhaps we can draw parallels in light of this to fin-de-siècle Vienna: both in the period of the Enlightenment and again around 1900 the state, the city, and thus society as well all seem to be in a phase of complete restructuring. During both these times the question of democratization, or anchoring politics within the populace, was debated—in

both cases as a method of stabilizing the monarchy and popularizing it. In both periods this decision was connected to a counter-movement to the baroque/Catholic milieu, based on science, and in both radical modernization movements (national or social revolutionary scenarios) formed the (international) context. In one case, just as in the other, the transformations went hand in hand with far-reaching cultural changes: in the first period an urban, bourgeois elite culture, and in the other an urban mass-cultural industry.

The cultural phenomena of the fin-de-siècle in Vienna have been dealt with in detail in other parts of this catalogue. For that reason, I would like to confine my discussion to the mere mention of certain revolutionary "inventions" of the Viennese Modern movement, which were the subject of highly-regarded exhibitions in the wake of *Traum und Wirklichkeit*.[14] The phrase relates in particular to the discovery of the "unconscious" as the virtual opposite of civilization by Sigmund Freud, the radical formalization of aesthetics by Arnold Schönberg, the tension between serial municipal planning and individualistic microarchitecture with Otto Wagner, and the theory of an unbridgeable gap between ethics and a scientific/rational view of the world with Ludwig Wittgenstein. Put differently, the Viennese Modern movement, inasmuch as this designation is a fitting one, may be characterized by the destruction of concepts of bourgeois identity and subjecthood, providing an anchor for the gradual rationalization of modern life.[15] But to what extent is the urban constellation of Vienna around 1900 reflected in these discoveries? In *Culture and Political Crisis in Vienna*[16] John W. Boyer pointed out the hybrid forms of modernization of the city under Christian Socialist governance (after 1897): new technologies such as poured concrete were not put to use for housing, but for church building; communal public relief was bolstered financially, but the underprivileged had to put up with being personally controlled by Christian Socialist party functionaries; the city underwent a democratization, but only for those persons and groups known to be adherents of the Christian city government. With the communalization of traffic and energy policies, the first social housing in the city, the founding of communal insurance companies and savings-banks, etc. Vienna experienced a "municipal revolution"; but the ideology carrying the revolution was neither universal nor humanist, but populist, xenophobic, and anti-Semitic. Vienna found itself in a kind of latent civil war: from the school system to the funerary ritual, Viennese society was divided into political, confessional, and ethnic "camps" whose conflicts forced the taking of sides and made dubious the possibility for the existence of an autonomous sphere for scientific and artistic projects divorced from issues of class and milieu.[17] With this as its background, the Viennese Modern movement could also be characterized by its anti-empirical, even anti-urban attitude,[18] by its face-to-face communities, expressed most radically in Schönberg's demand for the abolition of the anonymous public and the organization of artistic life along the lines of new kinds of Illuminated Societies.[19] The "flight" of Viennese intellectuals into aestheticism in light of the dilemma of populist politics, as diagnosed by Carl Schorske—the Wiener Werkstätte and its hybrid strategy between Renaissance-oriented *Gesamtkunstwerk* and highly capitalist marketing concept is one example—need not necessarily be seen as a contradiction to the previously presented thesis of a "skeptical Modern movement"; it might just as readily be understood as the reverse of this reaction to ambivalent urban processes in Vienna.

But let us return to the comparison of the "material" prerequisites for the release of creative potential in the Vienna of the Enlightenment and that of the fin-de-siècle. Both phases are marked by higher than average, rapid growth of the city. The first census took place in 1754 and counted 175,609 inhabitants. The suburbs, in particular, grew with great speed and appear to have been bursting at the end of the 18th century. At the century's close Vienna counted some 220,000 inhabitants, an addition of nearly one quarter to the total population.

The explosive decades prior to 1900 brought to Vienna growth of a kind that today seems comparable only to non-European major cities. Within two decades the population tripled, swelling from 720,000 inhabitants in 1880 to two million in 1900. The financial and administrative center of the Austro-Hungarian monarchy, Vienna was thus one of the largest cities in Europe. Both timeframes saw a wave of absolute acceleration: in the 1770s the first steps toward general time/space mobility were taken, and the movement away from strict traditional municipal structures controlled by court, guilds, and church began. At the turn of the (20th) century there was explosive growth in urban traffic systems (elevated trains and subways, streetcars), communal infrastructure (electrification), and new technical networks of communication such as the underground pneumatic post, combined rail and postal deliveries, and the telephone. (The latter served 24,000 customers in 1900, and in 1911 Vienna counted—here in a leading role—some 189 *kiosks* or pay telephones in public places and on the street.) Finally, in 1896 the pictures themselves began to move: the first (documented) "permanent" cinemas were established in Vienna between 1903 and 1905. By 1909 there were already sixty-two.[20]

Networking as a prerequisite for intellectual/artistic creativity stood on a completely different footing around 1900 with a whole new universe of communication media at hand. Countless newspapers, technical periodicals, and trade journals were in circulation, offering intellectuals new forums for publicity. In this context of impersonal communication the formation of small, comprehensible clusters became necessary. Thus certain non-party-affiliated forums began to crop up, such as the so-called Fabier-Gesellschaft (Fabier Society) with the banker Otto Wittelshöfer and the Social Democratic parliamentarian Engelbert Pernerstorfer among its members; the Ethical Club, founded by the philosopher Friedrich Jodl; the free-thinking society Free School; or Rosa Mayreder's General Austrian Women's Society.[21] If we look at the arts scene around 1900, this cluster formation was highly differentiated. In 1895 Josef Hoffmann (who had been studying in Vienna since 1892), the architect Joseph Maria Olbrich, the painter Koloman Moser, and others joined together in a loose association of artists against the establishment, the Siebenerklub (Club of Seven). In 1897 nineteen artists founded the "progressive" Vienna Secession from the "old" Künstlerhaus. It had its own building (the Secession) and its own magazine (*Ver Sacrum*). The

Secessionist Felician Myrbach was placed at the head of the newly-founded Kunstgewerbeschule (Academy of Decorative Arts, today University of Decorative Arts) in 1899. He, in turn, brought the generation of thirty-year-olds to the school, among them Josef Hoffmann and Koloman Moser. Later on they were joined by Alfred Roller, Carl Otto Czeschka, Bertold Löffler, and Franz Metzner.

Creative individuals and intellectuals during both periods of change were recruited from the monarchy's pool of immigrants. In 1910 fifty percent of the Viennese population had been born elsewhere. Most of Vienna's inhabitants came from Bohemia, Moravia, Slovakia, Hungary, Galicia, etc.; in addition, there were small minorities such as Italians, Bulgarians, Greeks, or Turks. The same era saw the high point of urbanization of Eastern/Central European Jews. At the turn of the century Vienna was not only the second-largest Czech city in Europe (around 410,000), but also the third-largest Jewish city in Europe (after Warsaw and Budapest; 1900: 146,926; 1910: 175,318). Between 1880 and 1920 it was still the fourth-largest city in Europe and because of the way it drew international immigrants—in contrast to cities like London, Paris, and Berlin, which grew through domestic immigration—it held a special place among the cities of the world.[22] As the "melting-pot" of the Austro-Hungarian monarchy Vienna was thus comparable in diversity to cities like New York or Chicago.[23]

In recent years research has concerned itself to a great extent with those protagonists of the Viennese Modern movement (Freud, Wittgenstein, Karl Kraus, Schönberg, Mahler, Viktor Adler…) with Jewish roots.[24] We can still profit from applying Mario Erdheim's ethno-historic transferral of the concept of "marginal man" here: neither foreigners—if only because of the overwhelmingly "German" cultural self-perception of the Jewish citizens of the Hapsburg monarchy—nor truly integrated (owing to the efficacy of a "second" society fed by the aristocratic/class tradition and its highly differentiated and anti-Semitic nuanced codes of inclusion and exclusion), the sons and daughters of Jewish *Gründerzeit* (founding period) families were extremely well-equipped and qualified to reflect critically on the dominant culture and to develop it further in creative ways.[25] Often there were family networks that helped to financially support the Modern movement through entrepreneurs with Jewish ethnic roots. They helped to realize projects which went on to become icons of the "creative milieus" around 1900. An example would be the industrialist Fritz Waerndorfer, who made possible the founding of the Wiener Werkstätte and used his personal means to keep it, as best he could, on solid financial ground. Furthermore, he had established good connections to the English workshop movement and British designers. As the case may be, the "creative milieus" around 1900 are almost unimaginable without such informal networks. Other conclusions along the lines of an ethnification of the Viennese Modern movement seem to me, however, highly problematic.

If we review again "Vienna 1770–1790" and "Vienna 1890–1910", these two phases of intensified creativity prove to be the result of conservative modernizing strategies dictated from above and the intellectual movements that attended and opposed them. Things become somewhat unfocused thereby (in comparison to the sites of "classic" transformations to the Modern movement, such as London, Paris, Chicago, Berlin, or New York), and strict couplings of artistic, social, and political tendencies are difficult to document with facts. Instead, perhaps, we can in closing venture to expand the theory of prefiguration of variants of the Modern movement in the context of Vienna: once—1770–1790—as the production of a bourgeois lifestyle "ahead of its time," the second time—1890–1910—as an anticipation of postmodernism.

1   Wolfgang Mantl, "Lassen sich kreative Milieus schaffen?," in: *Kreatives Milieu: Wien um 1900,* Emil Brix and Allan Janik, eds., Vienna 1993, p. 242.

2   Mantl 1993 (see note 1).

3   See David Harvey, *The Condition of Postmodernity,* Cambridge, Mass. and Oxford 1991, p. 16.

4   Diverse exhibitions such as *Traum und Wirklichkeit: Wien 1870–1930* in Vienna in 1985, *Die fröhliche Apokalypse: Wien 1870–1938* at the Centre Georges Pompidou in Paris in 1986, or *Vienna 1900: Art, Architecture and Design* at the Museum of Modern Art in New York in 1986.

5   For example, from forty-eight coffee houses in 1779 to seventy in the year 1790.

6   Johann Pezzl, *Skizze von Wien: Ein Kultur- und Sittenbild aus der josefinischen Zeit,* Gustav Gugitz and Anton Schlosser, eds., Graz 1923, pp. 365 ff.

7   Walter Prigge, *Städtische Intellektuelle: Urbane Milieus im 20. Jahrhundert,* Frankfurt am Main 1992.

8   Pezzl 1923 (see note 6), p. 145.

9   Karl H. Müller, "Sozialwissenschaftliche Kreativität in der Ersten und Zweiten Republik," in *ÖZG,* yr. 7, issue 1, 1996.

10 Helmut Reinalter, "Die Freimaurerei in Österreich von der Aufklärung bis zur Revolution 1948/1949," in *Zirkel und Winkelmass: 200 Jahre Grosse Landesloge der Freimaurer,* exh. cat. Historisches Museum, Vienna 1984, p. 7 ff.

11 Helmut Reinalter, "Die französische Revolution," in *Freimaurer: Solange die Welt besteht,* Vienna 1993.

12 Ingrid Mittenzwei, "Zwischen Vergangenheit und Zukunft. Wiener Wirtschaftsbürger am Ende des 18. Jahrhunderts," in *Genie und Alltag: Bürgerliche Stadtkultur zur Mozartzeit,* Salzburg and Vienna 1992.

13 Joachim Jung, "Die psychologischen Grundlagen der Kreativität," in Brix and Janik, eds., 1993 (see note 1).

14 *Traum und Wirklichkeit: Wien 1870–1930,* exh. cat. Historisches Museum, Vienna 1985, covered the entire spectrum of the Viennese Modern movement from the operetta *Die Fledermaus* to Otto Wagner's Postal Savings Bank Building, communalization during the Lueger period, the early workers' movement, Theodor Herzl's *Judenstaat* (Jewish state), Arnold Schönberg's chamber symphony, the Adolf Loos's building on St. Michael's Square, Ludwig Wittgenstein's *Tractatus,* and the international exhibition of new theater techniques in 1924.

15 See in particular Jacques LeRider, *Das Ende der Illusion: Zur Kritik der Moderne,* Vienna 1990; Allan Janik and Stephen Toulmin, *Wittgensteins Wien,* Munich and Vienna 1984.

16 John W. Boyer, *Culture and Political Crisis in Vienna: Christian Socialism in Power, 1897–1918,* Chicago and London 1995.

17 See Alfred Pfoser, "Schnitzler gegen Lueger. Schnitzlers Stadtansichten—Von den Vorzügen und Grenzen seines Werks beim Studium des Wien um 1900," in *Metropole Wien: Texturen der Moderne,* Roman Horak et al., eds., Vienna 2000.

18 See the example of Karl Kraus and his satirical depiction of Vienna as an ensemble of barriers and confused spaces (outside of the lecture halls) in António Ribeiro, "Metamorphoses of the Flâneur: From 'Ringstrasse' to 'Rua dos Douradores'," in *New Comparison: A Journal of Comparative and General Literary Studies,* no. 21, Spring 1996.

19 By this I mean the call for the "co-structuring" of musical events by a competent concert public.

20 Siegfried Mattl, "Wiener Paradoxien. Fordistische Stadt," in Horak et al. 2000 (see note 17), vol. 1, pp. 35 ff.; Werner Michael Schwarz, *Kino und Kinos in Wien: Eine Entwicklungsgeschichte bis 1934,* Vienna 1992.

21 Friedrich Stadler, "Spätaufklärung und Sozialdemokratie in Wien 1918–1938," in *Aufbruch und Untergang: Österreichische Kultur zwischen 1918 und 1938,* Franz Kadrnosky, ed., Vienna et al. 1981, pp. 441 ff.

22 Peter Eppel, "Foreword" and Michael John, "Mosaik, Schmelztiegel, Weltstadt Wien? Migration und multikulturelle Gesellschaft im 19. und 20. Jahrhundert," in *Wir. Zur Geschichte und Gegenwart der Zuwanderung nach Wien,* exh. cat. Historisches Museum Vienna, Vienna 1996; Moritz Csaky, "Sozio-kulturelle Wechselwirkung im Wiener Fin de siecle," in *Wien um 1900: Aufbruch in die Moderne,* Peter Berner et al., eds., Vienna 1986.

23 Klaus Zapotosky, "Soziologische Analysen der Kreativität," in Brix and Janik 1993 (see note 1), pp. 33 ff.

24 Steven Beller, *Vienna and the Jews 1867–1938: A Cultural History,* Cambridge 1989; Robert S. Wistrich, *The Jews of Vienna in the Age of Franz Joseph,* Oxford 1989.

25 See Mario Erdheim, *Die gesellschaftliche Produktion von Unbewusstheit: Eine Einführung in den ethnopsychoanalytischen Prozess,* Frankfurt am Main 1984.

BIOGRAPHIES OF VIENNESE GOLD- AND SILVERSMITHS

DIETHER HALAMA

INTRODUCTION

The biographies of the gold-, silver-, and metalworkers whose work appears in this catalogue were compiled during the years 1996 to 2003 in the framework of a research project whose goal it was to make a survey of the biographies and marks of all gold- and silversmiths and jewelers active in Vienna during the period from 1780 to 1922. The project stood under the guidance of Dr. Elisabeth Schmuttermeier (MAK, Vienna) and was financed through grants from the Jubiläumsfonds der Österreichischen Nationalbank (Jubilee Fund of the Austrian National Bank), the Verein Archiv der Wiener Silberschmiedekunst (Association of the Viennese Silversmith Archives), the Neue Galerie New York, the Kunsthistorisches Museum Vienna, and the MAK. The MAK will publish the entirety of the almost 5,000 biographies put together in the course of this project for the first time concurrent with the appearance of this catalogue in the form of a CD-ROM.

THE BIOGRAPHIES

The strongly divergent length of the following biographies reflects the differing amounts of information offered by the available source materials pertaining to the individuals at hand. While the members of the Viennese silversmith family Würth—one of the best-known such families around 1800—are fairly well documented, far less is known about other important craftsmen such as Benedikt Ranninger or Lorenz Wieninger.

The biographies were divided into two main groups, according to the overall concept of the exhibition: Viennese gold-, silver-, and metalworkers active prior to 1900, and those represented by later work. In the framework of this second category, the silver- and metalworkers of the Wiener Werkstätte are listed separately.

The individual biographies were conceived in a standard format. For ease of use, they were organized in three parts: 1. personal data and family information, 2. the actual biography with significant professional and private data, 3. special functions in the guild.

Regarding the organization in further detail:

1. Personal data and family information: after the family and given names, with the most common variants in spelling, follow biographical dates (date and place of birth and death). The family environment—parents, spouse, children, and other relatives—is only mentioned if these people also have a direct connection to the professional activity of the craftsman in question. For this reason only gold- and silversmiths or other metal craftsmen appear.

2. The actual biography: this section begins with education and professional career. The basis for a skillful craftsman was an apprenticeship—usually lasting four to six years—with a gold- or silversmith. If this information is missing from a biography it means only that that individual did not absolve his apprentice years in Vienna and is therefore not entered into the apprenticeship books of the Viennese gold- and silversmiths' guild.

Only in exceptional cases are the journeyman (assistant) years that followed documented, since no systematic records were kept in the guild of the journeymen employed in the various workshops. For this reason this type of information can often only be acquired through common addresses—the journeymen and apprentices customarily lived in the same household as the master—in registries or schedules.

After a certain number of journeymen years (usually six to ten, but sometimes more) the journeyman could apply to the magistrate of the city of Vienna for consent to ply an independent trade, the so-called *Gewerbeverleihung* (trade license). In order to be allowed to work as a "civil master" (*bürgerlicher Silberarbeiter*) or "with authorization" (*befugter Silberarbeiter*) the journeyman had to fulfill a number of conditions.

In the case of civil gold- and silverworkers or jewelers this meant passing the master examination, which consisted of drawing instruction at the Kaiserliche Akademie der Bildenden Künste (Imperial Academy of Fine Arts) together with the completion of a masterpiece. The new master was then accepted into the guild, and shortly afterward he was awarded the rights of a burgher of the city of Vienna. Since it was guild policy for many years to keep the number of masters as low as possible for reasons of (non-)competition, only very few journeymen could become masters, unless they were the sons of gold- or silversmiths and could take over the business of their fathers. Another often-practiced method was that a journeyman married—after the death of the master for whom he was working—the master's widow and continued the business.

In the case of the merely "authorized" craftsmen, on the other hand, who originally stood outside the guild and were therefore not bound by such restrictions, an independent professional career began with the acquisition of the "authorization."

With trade license in hand, the civil or authorized gold- or silversmith was allowed to use his own maker's mark—usually with his initials. It was required that every newly-made mark be stamped into the "mark boards" of the marks authority for controlling purposes.

After the trade license follow the most important events in the professional career of the individual craftsman. Among these are the granting of further trade rights such as the *Landesfabriks-Befugnis* (National Factory Permit) (the right to open branches in the capital cities of other Austrian crown lands, as well as to use the imperial crest, the double-headed eagle, in business dealings); the title of *kaiserlich-königlicher österreichischer Handwerker* (Imperial and Royal Austrian Craftsman); the granting of patents for new inventions; or the participation in important exhibitions. Collaboration with other craftsmen (often family members) is also mentioned—as far as it is known—as well as the relocation of the place of business from one suburb or (later) city district to another and the opening of salesrooms in what is today the inner-city, or downtown Vienna.

This section also includes a list of the special accomplishments of the individual in public life. Since certain Viennese gold- and silversmiths achieved great standing and wealth, they were often entrusted with high offices in the service of the city administration: in the *Stadtrat* (the city council, divided into "outer" and "inner" council), in social services (administrator of funds for the poor, district director for the poor, burgher hospital economic commission member), or in the burgher guard. This exceptional status among the burghers of the city is also shown in the awards of honorary burgher rights and distinctions; in a few instances there were even ennoblements.

At the conclusion of this section the date of the completion of independent trade activity is given. If the return of the trade license was concurrent with the death of the person in question it is not listed separately, since the date of death is listed at the beginning of each individual biography. It was not uncommon, however, that businesses continued to be run by a widow, a son, or another employee.

3. Special functions in the guild: many silverworkers held particular offices on the board of the guild. In the late 18th century the "old and young chairmen," the "old and young drawing masters," and the "old and young assessors" stood at the head of the guild. In the early 19th century the "chairman and sub-chairman" were supported by a "commission" with twenty-four members; after 1851 there was a "newer and an older commission," and after 1862 "spokesmen" along with the "commission."

A number of civil masters were also active in positions in the *Witwenkasse der bürgerlichen Gold-, Silber- und Galanteriearbeiter* (Widows' Fund of the Civil Gold-, Silver- and Notions Workers), which had been founded in 1793, a voluntary organization for the support of the widows of gold- and silversmiths—and occasionally destitute masters themselves. At its head stood the "director" and "vice-director" together with four "administrators" and six "assessors."

BIOGRAPHIES OF THE VIENNESE GOLD- AND SILVERSMITHS AND METALWORKERS PRIOR TO 1900 WHOSE WORK APPEARS IN THIS CATALOGUE

Albrecht, Thomas (cat. no. 85)
(Dates and trade investiture unknown)
Listed during the years 1815 to 1817 as an authorized silverworker in Vienna-Strozzigrund.

Binder (Bindner), Ignaz (cat. no. 16)
Born ca. 1772 in Vienna, died May 29, 1835 in Vienna-Wieden.
On February 11, 1813 he was awarded the right to set up trade as an authorized silverworker; his workshop was in Vienna-Leopoldstadt. On February 27, 1818 he became a civil silverworker and, on October 16, 1818 became a burgher of the city of Vienna. In 1824 he moved his workshop to Vienna-Wieden. After his death in 1835 the shop was run by his widow Magdalena until 1836.

Blasius, Carl (cat. no. 20)
Born ca. 1771 in Bratislava, Hungary (today Slovakia), died October 22, 1834 in Vienna-Windmühle.
In 1804 he married Josepha Huber, widow of the civil silverworker Joseph Huber (born ca. 1761 in Vienna, died April 24, 1802 in Vienna-Windmühle), and took over the workshop she had previously run as the widow of the latter in Vienna-Windmühle.
On October 5, 1804 Carl Blasius was awarded the right to set up trade as a civil silverworker; on November 2, 1804 he became a burgher of the city of Vienna. After his death in 1834 the workshop was run by his widow Josepha until April 6, 1842. She received a pension until 1848 from the Widows' Fund, of which her husband had been a member since 1804.
Beginning in the year 1830 and until his death Carl Blasius was a member of the guild commission.

Bock (Beck), Ludwig (cat. no. 63)
(Dates unknown)
On June 14, 1811 he was awarded the right to set up trade as an authorized silverworker; his workshop was in Vienna-Mariahilf. On October 30, 1817 he became a civil silverworker and on November 7, 1817 he became a burgher of the city of Vienna. He retired January 8, 1848.

Domanek (Domanöck), Antonius Mathias (cat. no. 1)
Born April 21, 1713 in Vienna, died March 8, 1779 in Vienna.
Apprenticed with the civil goldworker Joachim Michael Salecker in Vienna and was released from service in 1732. Later he studied at the Vienna Graveurschule (Engravers' School) under Raphael and Mathias Donner. In 1736 he was awarded the right to set up trade as a civil goldworker; his workshop was in Vienna. On March 13, 1738 he became a burgher of the city of Vienna. After a journey through France, Germany, Spain, and England he became a member of the Vienna Academy in 1747. After 1767 he was the first director of the so-called k. u. k. Posier- und Graveur-Academie (Royal and Imperial Embossers' and Engravers' Academy), which he had founded. In 1773 he retired from office and returned his goldsmith trade license. His son Franz Anton Domaneck (born May 23, 1746 in Vienna, died August 1, 1821 in Vienna-Leopoldstadt) also worked as his father's assistant at the academy.
Among his most important surviving work is the gold breakfast service for Maria Theresa, Queen of Hungary and Bohemia and Archduchess of Austria, and her husband, Emperor Francis I Stephen (Kunsthistorisches Museum Vienna), as well as numerous medallions.

Dub (Dubb), Thomas (cat. no. 44)
Born December 22, 1811 in Volenice, Bohemia (today Czech Republic), died March 19, 1889 in Vienna-Rudolfsheim.
Apprenticed with the civil silverworker Franz Friseck in Vienna-Josefstadt. On January 23, 1839 he was awarded the right to set up trade as an authorized silverworker; his workshop was in Vienna-Neubau. In 1848 he moved to Vienna-Schottenfeld. On March 10, 1851 he became a civil silverworker and on April 24, 1851 he became a burgher of the city of Vienna. On September 15, 1859 he was allowed to establish an authorized factory as a "gold- and silverware manufacturer." Within a few years the enterprise had gained a good reputation for the production of cutlery. In 1873 the firm took part in the Vienna World's Fair with various silver goods and was distinguished with a certificate of recognition. After Thomas Dub's death in 1889 his son and collaborator of many years, Vincenz Karl Dub (born ca. 1852, died March 15, 1922), took over his father's business and turned it into one of the leading cutlery manufactories of the day in Austria.
During the years 1862 to 1874 Thomas Dub was a member of the guild commission, was on its board of directors, and served as its spokesman.

Forgatsch (Fergatsch), Georg (cat. nos. 21 and 42)
Born April 18, 1772 in Kosice, Hungary (today Slovakia), died January 29, 1832 in Vienna-Wieden.
On August 4, 1807 he was awarded the right to set up trade as a civil silverworker, and on August 29, 1807 he became a burgher of the city of Vienna. His workshop was in Vienna, but in 1822 he moved it to Vienna-Wieden and, later, to Vienna-Laimgrube. Finally, in 1831, he returned it to Vienna-Wieden.
He retired March 22, 1832.

Gindle (Gendle), Friedrich (cat. no. 94)
Date of birth unknown, died ca. 1859 (not in Vienna). He was a descendant of perhaps the best-known goldsmith family of the same name from Schwäbisch-Gmünd.
On December 11, 1829 he was awarded the right to set up trade as an authorized goldworker; his workshop was in Vienna-Neubau. After his death the business was run by his widow Elisabeth until 1876.

Guttmann (Gutmann), Johann, Sr. (cat. no. 86)
Born 1754 or 1755 in Prague, Bohemia (Czech Republic), died June 20, 1823 in Vienna-St. Marx.
On July 16, 1782 he was awarded the right to set up trade as a civil silverworker after having completed his masterpiece, a "plain goblet chased from a single piece." On February 22, 1783 he became a burgher of the city of Vienna. His workshop was in Vienna. In 1818 he closed his business. From 1793 to 1795 he was sub-chairman, and from 1786 to 1798 chairman of the guild.

Guttmann (Gutmann), Johann, Jr. (cat. no. 33)
Born between 1780 and 1785 in Vienna, died ca. 1816 (likely not in Vienna).
Son of the civil silverworker Johann Guttmann, Sr. (see above).
Apprenticed 1795 to 1801 with his father.
On May 5, 1812 he was awarded the right to set up trade as a civil jeweler (*bürgerlicher Juwelenarbeiter*), and on July 9, 1812 he became a burgher of the city of Vienna. His workshop was in Vienna until 1814 and subsequently in Vienna-Wieden.

Haas, Caspar (cat. no. 13)
Born ca. 1764, died February 11, 1840 in Vienna-Wieden.
On December 11, 1801 he was awarded the right to set up trade as a civil silverworker, and on February 12, 1802 he became a burgher of the city of Vienna. His workshop was located in Vienna.
In 1821 he was selected for the "outer council" of the city. In 1825 he moved his workshop to Vienna-Wieden. He retired November 14, 1836. In the guild he had been sub-chairman from 1819 to 1820, chairman from 1821 to 1825, and a member of the commission from 1830 to 1836. In the Widows' Fund, to which he had belonged since 1802, he served as assessor and administrator between 1824 and 1839. During

the last years of his life he received—he was likely destitute—a pension from the fund.

Hann (Han), Johann Georg (cat. no. 31)
Born ca. 1756 in Vienna, died April 17, 1812 in Vienna.

Apprenticed with the civil silverworker Lorenz Reinhart in Vienna and was released from service in 1774.

On May 18, 1780 he was awarded the right to set up trade as a civil silverworker after having completed his masterpiece, a "plain goblet chased from a single piece." On June 16, 1781 he became a burgher of the city of Vienna, where his workshop was located.

For his outstanding accomplishments in the Wiener Bürgergarde (Vienna Burgher Militia)—which had proven its usefulness during the Napoleonic wars from 1797 to 1809—he was promoted to 1st lieutenant of the 1st Burgher Regiment.

He served in the Widows' Fund as assessor from 1793 until his death.

Heinisch (Heintsch), Joseph (cat. nos. 10, 14, 83)
Born between 1765 and 1770 in Vienna, died May 26, 1834 (likely not in Vienna).

Son of the civil silverworker Johann Michael Heinisch (born ca. 1731, died December 20, 1780 in Vienna-Mariahilf).

Apprenticed 1780 to 1786 with his father; after the death of the latter with the civil silverworkers Andreas Hesser and Anton Karl Wipf in Vienna.

On November 16, 1802 he was awarded the right to set up trade as a civil silverworker, and he became a burgher of the city of Vienna on January 14, 1803. His workshop was located in Vienna-Mariahilf; in 1807 he relocated to Vienna. Although he had shut down his business in 1828, his license was only returned by his widow after his death November 2, 1835. She received support from the Widows' Fund, of which her husband had been a member since 1803, until her death in 1837.

Huber, Bartholomäus (cat. no. 34)
Born between 1777 and 1779 in Alt-Frauenhofen, Bavaria, Germany, died May 24, 1865 in Vienna-Josefstadt.

In 1807 he worked as an apprentice with the civil silverworker Jakob Krautauer in Vienna. On May 24, 1811 he was awarded the right to set up trade as an authorized silverworker; his workshop was located in Vienna-Leopoldstadt. In 1844 he moved to Vienna-St. Ulrich, and in 1851 to Vienna-Josefstadt. He retired in 1857.

Jaksch, Joachim (cat. 102)
(Dates and trade investiture unknown)

From 1849 to 1861 listed as a civil sheet-metalworker in Vienna-Laimgrube and Vienna-Mariahilf.

Kain (Kainn), Johann (also Ignaz) (cat. no. 26)
Born ca. 1763, died April 30, 1840 in Vienna-Leopoldstadt.

On September 6, 1813 he was awarded the right to set up trade as a civil jeweler, and on September 16, 1813 he became a burgher of the city of Vienna. His workshop was located in Vienna, but he moved it to Vienna-Leopoldstadt in 1823. After his death in 1840 his son (?) Stanislaus Kainn (active until 1872) took over the business.

Kern, Joseph Anton (cat. nos. 35, 67, 68, 69, 98)
Born 1790 in Vienna, died August 12, 1832 in Vienna.

Son of the civil silverworker and sub-chairman (later chairman) of the guild Martin Kern (born 1758 in Szemet/Misérd [?], today Nove Kosariská, Slovakia died November 3, 1818 in Vienna), the brother-in-law of the civil gold notions worker (bürgerlicher Goldgalanteriearbeiter) Johann Hollauer von Hohenfelsen (born ca. 1761 in Prague, died March 1, 1831 in Vienna) whose second marriage was to Joseph Kern's sister Anna (born 1790/92 in Vienna, died February 2, 1868 in Vienna).

Apprenticed with his father from 1801 to 1806 in Vienna.

On April 3, 1812 he was awarded the right to set up trade as a civil silverworker; he likely became a burgher of the city of Vienna in the same year. His workshop was located in Vienna, and in 1821 he opened his own salesroom on Kohlmarkt. In 1824 he was selected for the "outer council" of the city and he later also served as Armenvater (administrator of funds for the poor). Likewise in 1824 he was first listed as königlich-ungarischer adeliger Goldarbeiter (gold- and silverworker of the royal Hungarian guard) and in 1826 also as k. k. Hof-Kammer-Silberarbeiter (imperial and royal court-chamber-silversmith). After his death in 1832 the business was run by his widow Anna (born ca. 1788 in Vienna, died April 8, 1846 in Vienna), alone at first and, after 1841, together with her son Heinrich Kern (born ca. 1815). On November 6, 1850 the latter turned in his license.

Joseph Anton Kern counted among the most renowned Viennese silversmiths of his era. Aside from tableware and sacred instruments he also made gold and silver medallions. His products reached a wide public through numerous advertisements and articles in newspapers and journals.

He was sub-chairman of the guild in 1829 and chairman from 1830 to 1832. In the Widows' Fund, of which he was a member from 1813 on, he was assessor from 1820 until after 1830.

Klama, Michael (cat. no. 56)
Born ca. 1783 in Vienna, died after 1828.

Apprenticed from 1795 to 1801 to the civil silverworker Wilhelm Schwegerl in Vienna-Laimgrube. On June 27, 1815 he was awarded the right to set up trade as a civil silverworker, and on June 30, 1815 he became a burgher of the city of Vienna. His workshop was located in Vienna-Wieden; after 1819 it was in Vienna-Josefstadt, and later still in Vienna proper. He is last mentioned in 1828 in Vienna-Mariahilf.

Klima, Johann (cat. no. 6)
Date of birth unknown, died after 1848.

On July 2, 1812 he was awarded the right to set up trade as an authorized silverworker; his workshop was located in Vienna-Spittelberg. On June 21, 1816 he became a civil silverworker, receiving also on July 27, 1816 the rights of burgher of the city of Vienna. He is last mentioned in 1848.

In the guild he was a member of the commission from 1830 to 1845.

Klinkosch (after 1880: Ritter von), Josef Carl (cat. no. 91)
Born February 28, 1822 in Vienna, died June 8, 1888 in Vienna-Leopoldstadt.

Son of the civil and, later, imperial and royal court silverworker (k. k. Hof-Silberarbeiter) Carl Klinkosch (born 1797 in Vienna, died October 14, 1860 in Vienna-Leopoldstadt). In 1848 he married Elisabeth Swoboda (born October 27, 1830 in Vienna, died November 6, 1910 in Meran, Tyrol, today South Tyrol, Italy), daughter of the civil/imperial and royal court jeweler Wenzel Johann Swoboda (born between 1797 and 1798 in Vienna, died October 26, 1860 in Vienna).

Apprenticed from 1834 to 1839 with his father in the gold-, silver-, and metalware factory Mayerhofer & Klinkosch in Vienna-Leopoldstadt, which was under the direction of the latter.

On November 10, 1843 he was awarded the right to set up trade as a civil silverworker, and became a burgher of the city of Vienna on January 25, 1844. After study trips through Italy and, likely, other European countries he took over partial control of the factory from his father in 1847, becoming its director in 1853. In 1860 and 1861 he was a member of the Vienna city council. After the departure of his business partner Stephan Mayerhofer, Jr. he became the sole owner of the business in 1869, which was known after that date under the name J. C. Klinkosch. In the same year he was awarded the title k. k. Hof- und Kammerlieferant (Purveyor to the Imperial and Royal Court and Chamber). By producing work after designs by renowned artists such as Theophil Hansen or Gustave Deloye, as well as through his participation in the World's Fair in Vienna in 1873 and in Paris in 1878, Josef Carl Klinkosch was able to garner an international reputation for the firm. He was distinguished with the Ritterorden der französischen Ehrenlegion (Knight's Order of the French Legion of Honor) and the Eiserner Kronen-Orden III. Klasse (Iron Crown Order, III. Class)—which carried with it the honor of hereditary knighthood—for an ornate shield commissioned by Emperor Francis Joseph I and shown at the Paris World's Fair of 1878. In 1884 he retired from business life for health reasons and turned the factory over to his two sons, Isidor (born June 16, 1852 in Vienna, died January 13, 1914 in Vienna) and Arthur *Ritter* von Klinkosch (born May 10, 1854 in Vienna, died October 4, 1899 in Vienna). After the end of the First World War the firm was sold to the Berndorfer Metallwaren-Fabrik Arthur Krupp A.G. and only closed in 1953.

Koch, Joseph Franz (also Johann) (cat. no. 43)

Born ca. 1806 in Vienna, died March 5, 1859 in Vienna-Neubau.
Apprenticed 1817 to 1822 with the civil gold notions worker (*bürgerlicher Goldgalanteriearbeiter*) Stephan Eduard Starkloff in Vienna-Neubau and the authorized goldworker Franz Heber.
On August 12, 1833 he was awarded the right to set up trade as an authorized silverworker. His workshop was located in Vienna-Neubau.

Kohlmayer (Kollmeier), Georg (cat. no. 22)

Born ca. 1780 in Vienna, died September 5, 1844 in Vienna.
Apprenticed 1795 to 1800 with the civil silverworkers Andreas Kirstorffer and Joseph Stelzer in Vienna.
In 1811 he married Anna Fautz (born ca. 1782, died 1853), widow of the civil silverworker Franz Xaver Fautz, who died in 1811. Kohlmayer took over the workshop she had run in the interim in Vienna.
On June 25, 1812 he was awarded the right to set up trade as a civil silverworker, and on July 8, 1812 he became a burgher of the city of Vienna. He retired December 12, 1838.
He was a member of the guild commission from 1835 to 1839.

Köll, Anton, Sr. (cat. nos. 32 and 54)

Born ca. 1767 in Vienna, died October 16, 1854 in Vienna-Mariahilf.
Apprenticed from 1780 to 1786 with the civil silverworker Johann Georg Brandmayr in Vienna. In 1797 he was awarded the right to set up trade as a civil silverworker, and on July 7, 1797 he became a burgher of the city of Vienna. His workshop was located in Vienna, but in 1812 he relocated it to Vienna-Leopoldstadt. In 1822 he was selected for the "outer council" of the city. In 1833 he moved again to Vienna-Mariahilf, returning in 1836 to Vienna proper. On October 15, 1841 he retired and turned the business over to his son Anton Köll, Jr. (born ca. 1800 in Vienna, died May 10, 1857 in Vienna-Mariahilf), who had worked there since 1827. In 1846 Anton Köll, Sr. received the Gold Salvator Medal of the city of Vienna.
He served as sub-chairman of the guild from 1815 to 1818, and as a member of the commission from 1830 to 1854. He was an assessor in the Widows' Fund from 1798 on; after 1830 he was its vice-director and from 1846 until his death in 1854 he was its director.

Köll (Kell), Franz (cat. no. 39)

Born ca. 1769 in Vienna, died January 25, 1830 in Vienna-Mariahilf.
Apprenticed from 1784 to 1789 with the civil gold- and silverworker Octavian Cogsel III in Vienna. On May 17, 1810 he was awarded the right to set up trade as a civil silverworker and on August 16, 1810 he became a burgher of the city of Vienna. His workshop was located in Vienna-Mariahilf.
In 1830 he was a member of the guild commission.

Krautauer (Krauttauer), Jakob (cat. nos. 5, 11, 15, 18, 24, 25)

Born ca. 1772 in Vienna, died April 3, 1845 in Vienna.
Son of the silverworker Ignaz Krautauer (born ca. 1738, died October 9, 1787 in Vienna).
Apprenticed from 1785 to 1789 with his father and, after the death of the latter, remained apprentice in the business run by his mother, the widow Maria Anna, in Vienna. In 1795 he was awarded the right to set up trade as a civil silverworker after completing his masterpiece, a silver coffee pot. He then took over the business from his mother. On March 11, 1796 he became a burgher of the city of Vienna, where his workshop was located. He retired in 1824. He nevertheless took part in the *Allgemeine österreichische Gewerbsprodukten-Ausstellungen* (General Austrian Decorative Arts Products Exhibitions) in 1835 and 1839, exhibiting silver goods.

He was a member of the Widows' Fund from 1801 on; beginning in 1813 he worked as one of its assessors and, after 1820, as an administrator. After 1833 (?) until his death in 1845 he was its director.

Laubenbacher, Joseph (cat. no. 17)

Born ca. 1768 in Vienna, died October 20, 1823 in Vienna.
Son of the civil silverworker Johann Georg Laubenbacher (born ca. 1717, died November 9, 1786 in Vienna), brother of the authorized goldworker Andreas Laubenbacher (born October 12, 1779 in Vienna, died after 1827).
Apprenticed from 1783 to 1788 with his father and, after the death of the latter, remained apprentice in the business run by his mother, the widow Magdalena. Later he was apprenticed with the civil silverworker Lorenz Reinhart in Vienna.
On April 10, 1804 he was awarded the right to set up trade as a civil silverworker, and on April 27, 1804 he became a burgher of the city of Vienna. His workshop was located in Vienna-St. Ulrich. In 1812 he became *Mittelansagersadjunkt* (assistant secretary) in the guild; in the same year he seems to have ended his career as a silverworker. In 1815 he became *Mittelansager* (secretary). He moved to Vienna proper. On October 9, 1823, just prior to his death, he turned in his license.
His widow Theresia (born ca. 1853, died November 5, 1832 in Vienna-Wieden) received support until her life's end from the Widows' Fund, to which her husband had belonged as a member from 1812 on.

Mayerhofer, Stefan, Sr. (cat. nos. 19, 41, 57, 70, 87)

Born in 1772 in Székesfehérvár, Hungary, died January 14, 1852 in Vienna-Leopoldstadt.
In 1797 he founded a factory in Vienna-Leopoldstadt for the production of plated iron goods. On May 31, 1805 he was awarded the national factory permit. In 1816 he was distinguished with the title of *k. k. Hof-Plattierer* (Imperial and Royal Court Plater); at the time he was making harness and carriage mounts for the imperial court. In 1822 he opened a salesroom in Vienna proper. During 1822 and 1823 he received several patents, including one for an invention to produce "silver goods of every kind and shape more easily, more quickly, and more uniformly by machine." On October 10, 1825 he was awarded the right to set up trade as an authorized silverworker. He began to work together with the civil silverworker Carl Klinkosch (the father of Josef Carl Klinkosch, see entry) in 1830; in 1836 the factory was renamed Mayerhofer & Comp. and, in 1837, Mayerhofer & Klinkosch (see entry). Stephan Mayerhofer, Sr. became an honorary burgher of his hometown Székesfehérvár in 1839. In 1844 he turned over the management of his business to his adopted son, Stephan Mayerhofer, Jr. (born 1819, died ca. 1889).

Mayerhofer & Klinkosch (cat. nos. 72, 97, 100)

In 1830 the civil silverworker Carl Klinkosch (father of Josef Carl Klinkosch, see entry) was employed at the *k. k. Privilegierte Silber- und Englisch-Plattierwaren-Fabrik* (Imperial and Royal Silver and English-plated Goods Factory) of Stephan Mayerhofer, Sr. (see above). Beginning in 1836—Klinkosch had since become foreman—the factory was called Mayerhofer & Comp. In 1837 it was renamed Mayerhofer & Klinkosch. A number of important commission for Emperors Francis I and Ferdinand were rewarded with the title of Imperial and Royal Court Silverworker in 1837. At this time the factory employed 200 workers and made various goods from pure gold and silver as well as in gold and silver plate. The firm exhibited at the *Allgemeine österreichische Gewerbsprodukten-Ausstellungen* (General Austrian Decorative Arts Products Exhibitions) in 1835 and 1839 in Vienna and was awarded a gold and a silver medal for its silver and silver-plated wares. In 1844 Stephan Mayerhofer, Sr. left the management of the business to his adopted son of the same name; in 1847 Carl Klinkosch also turned the management of the factory over to his son Josef Carl. In 1869 Stephan Mayerhofer, Jr. sold his shares of the business to Josef Carl Klinkosch. The factory, of which he was now the sole owner, was renamed Gold, Silver, and Metal Goods Factory J. C. Klinkosch. (Further details under Klinkosch, Josef Carl).

Ranninger (Ranniger), Benedikt Nicolaus (cat. nos. 7, 8, 23, 29)

Born June 14, 1782 in Eutin, Schleswig-Holstein, Germany, died February 26, 1845 in Vienna.

In 1814 he was awarded the right to set up trade as an authorized gold- and silverworker; his workshop was located in Vienna-Josefstadt. After 1825 his nephew, Wulf Heinrich Ranninger (born July 22, 1804 in Eutin, died August 12/13, 1855 in Bucharest, Romania), who eventually became an authorized silverworker, joined the workshop as apprentice, later becoming its foreman. In 1828 the two received together a patent for the invention of "a new press and turning machine with a standing spindle." In the following year Benedikt Ranninger opened a salesroom in Vienna proper. Wulf Heinrich Ranninger left the business in 1837.

Sander, Christian, Jr. (cat. nos. 61 and 92)

Born April 14, 1819 in Vienna, died July 16, 1900 in Vienna-Favoriten. Son of the authorized silverworker Christian Sander, Sr. (born ca. 1788 in Redwitz, Bavaria, Germany, died March 20, 1874 in Vienna), brother of the civil silverworker Eduard Sander (born 1822 in Vienna, died May 30, 1862).

Apprenticed 1831 to 1836 with his father in Vienna-St. Ulrich.

On December 5, 1843 he was awarded the right to set up trade as a civil silverworker, and on March 14, 1844 he also became a burgher of the city of Vienna. He worked in the business founded by his father in 1819 in Vienna-Josefstadt and took over the business with his brother Eduard (born 1822 in Vienna-Alservorstadt, died May 30, 1862) in 1849. After the death of his brother he continued to run the business on his own. From 1872 to 1875 Christian Sander worked together with the goldsmith Alfred Bryner under the firm name Sander & Bryner. In 1892 Sander & Bryner was shut down.

Christian Sander was a member of the new commission of the guild from 1858 to 1860; from 1862 to 1868 he was deputy chairman, and from 1869 to 1871 spokesman. In the Widows' Fund, of which he had become a member in 1853, he served beginning in 1868 as vice-director. After 1894 he received a pension—he was likely destitute—from the fund.

Scheiger (Schleicher), Carl (cat. no. 95)

Born ca. 1794 in Vienna, died January 14, 1820 in Vienna-Neubau. Apprenticed 1778 to 1783 with the civil silverworker Joseph Moser in Vienna.

On September 3, 1802 he was awarded the right to set up trade as a civil silverworker, and on January 1, 1802 he became a burgher of the city of Vienna. His workshop was located in Vienna-Mariahilf; after 1813 it was moved to Vienna-Neubau.

Schiffer, Eduard (cat. no. 99)

Born between 1825–30, died after 1863.

Son of the civil/imperial and royal court gold- and silverworker (*bürgerlicher und k. k. Hof-Gold- und Silberarbeiter*) Franz Schiffer (born December 24, 1800 in Essen, Germany, died September 18, 1854 in Vienna-Grinzing).

Apprenticed from 1840 to 1846 with his father in Vienna and under the civil goldworker Georg Haunold in Vienna-Schottenfeld. Subsequently he became a shareholder in his father's business, and, after the death of the latter, in the business of his stepmother Franziska (born November 4, 1814 in Sierndorf, Lower Austria, died after 1860), known as Franziska Schiffer & Sohn. On March 6, 1856 he was awarded the right to set up trade as a civil gold- and silverworker, and in the same year he likely became a burgher of the city of Vienna. In 1858 the business received the national factory permit. Franziska Schiffer left the firm in 1860 and in 1863 Ignaz Theuer (died May 4, 1865) became the new shareholder. The new name of the company was Eduard Schiffer and Theuer, Gold- Silber- und Metallwaren-Fabrik (gold-, silver-, and metal-goods factory). At the time it employed twenty workers, possessed a ten horsepower steam engine, and chiefly produced cutlery—also in base metals. Eduard Schiffer retired from business life in 1867. In the guild he had been a member of the commission from 1860 to 1863 and in 1865.

Schleicher, Jakob (cat. no. 58)

(Dates unknown)

On October 13, 1817 he was awarded the right to set up trade as an authorized silverworker. He was active until 1836 at the latest.

Schubert, Franz (cat. nos. 65 and 89)

Born November 22, 1813 in Vienna, died April 1, 1906 in Vienna-Wieden. Foster son of the civil silverworker Dominikus Würth (born August 22, 1784 in Vienna-Wieden, died August 17, 1854 in Vienna-Wieden). Apprenticed 1827 to 1832 with his foster father in Vienna-Wieden. In 1840 he worked as a journeyman in the silverware factory of Mayerhofer & Klinkosch. On October 20, 1840 he was awarded the right to set up trade as a civil silverworker, and on October 20, 1840 he became a burgher of the city of Vienna. His workshop was located in Vienna-Wieden. He closed his business in 1856 but only turned in his license in 1862.

In the Widows' Fund, a member of which he had been since 1840, he served from 1874 to 1885 as assessor. After 1885 he received from it—he was likely destitute—a pension.

Sedelmayer (Sedlmeyer), Karl (cat. nos. 30, 62, 71)

Born ca. 1766 in Vienna, died June 22, 1840 in Vienna-Mariahilf. Apprenticed 1778 to 1785 with the civil goldworker Paul Schedi, and then with the civil silverworkers Mathias Ehrentrauth and Nikolaus Wiener in Vienna.

In 1797 he was awarded the right to set up trade as a civil silverworker, and on December 29, 1797 he became a burgher of the city of Vienna. His workshop was located in Vienna-Mariahilf. He was selected for the "outer council" of the city in 1797 and retired in 1828. Until his death he was also imperial and royal district director for the poor (*k. k. Armenbezirks-Direktor*).

He was a member of the Widows' Fund from 1798 on, serving from 1837 to 1840 as assessor. His widow Theresia (born ca. 1781, died April 13, 1843 in Vienna-Mariahilf) received support from the fund until her death.

Stelzer (also Stölzer), Joseph (cat. nos. 12 and 48)

Born ca. 1758, died February 16, 1830 in Vienna-Alservorstadt. Son of the civil goldworker Leopold Stelzer (born ca. 1717, died February 2, 1780 in Vienna).

Apprenticed 1770 to 1775 with his father in Vienna. On March 20, 1783 he was awarded the right to set up trade as a civil silverworker after completing his masterpiece, a "gilt silver goblet." He took over the business of his widowed mother Catharina (born ca. 1726, died February 21, 1798 in Vienna). On August 9, 1783 he also became a burgher of the city of Vienna. He retired in 1823.

In the guild he had been sub-chairman from 1807 to 1808 and chairman from 1809 to 1814. He served as assessor from 1813 until after 1827 in the Widows' Fund, of which he had been a member since prior to 1803.

Wagenmann & Böttger (cat. no. 101)

Lacquer, tin, and composite goods factory. Partners Dr. Carl Wagenmann and Gottfried Böttger.

Founded in 1836. The factory in Vienna-Wieden with a salesroom in Vienna proper was specialized in the production of chandeliers, lamps, and candelabra, but also tin and cast goods such as tea and coffee machines, sugar boxes, writing sets, etc. in painted and lacquered finishes. The firm took part in the *Allgemeine österreichische Gewerbsprodukten-Ausstellung* (General Austrian Decorative Arts Products Exhibition) in 1839 and won a silver medal. At the time it employed twenty workers. In the years 1839 and 1840 it received a number of patents on the "invention of improved coffee machines." In 1840 or 1841 the factory was taken over by Karl Rudolf Ditmar and expanded over the course of the following decades under the name Ditmar Brothers to one of the leading lamp manufacturers in central Europe.

Wallnöfer (Walnefer, Wallnöffer), Franz, Sr. (cat. nos. 52, 53, 63, 64, 94)

Born ca. 1767–68 in Vienna, died January 26, 1858 in Vienna-Landstrasse.

Father of the civil gold notions workers (*bürgerlicher Goldgalanteriearbeiter*) Franz, Jr. (born ca. 1798, died after 1872), Carl (born ca. 1799 in Vienna, died February 13, 1872 in Vienna), and Josef (born 1802 in Vienna, died September 18, 1872 in Vienna).

Apprenticed 1781 to 1786 with the civil notions worker David Kreissl. In 1800 he was awarded the right to set up trade as a civil gold and silver notions worker, and on September 26, 1800 he became a burgher of the city of Vienna, where his workshop was located. In 1812 his business received the national factory permit. After 1820 his two sons Carl (master as of December 22, 1820) and Franz, Jr. (master as of December 8, 1822) joined the firm. The factory was relocated to Wallnöfer's own house in Vienna-Landstrasse; the salesroom remained in Vienna proper. In 1825 Franz, Jr. was named as head clerk of the business, and in 1828 both sons were entered into the public corporation, which became known as Franz Wallnöfer & Sons. The third son, Josef (master as of April 26, 1828), worked part-time (1828, 1841–44) in his father's business. In 1838 the corporation was re-named Wallnöfer Brothers by Franz, Jr. and Carl. Franz Wallnöfer, Sr. retired in 1851, followed by his sons Franz, Jr. and Carl in 1857. The third son, Josef, who had been adjunct appraiser in the k. k. Versatzamt (Imperial and Royal Loan-Bank) since 1855 and appraiser since 1865, turned in his license in 1866. Franz Wallnöfer, Sr. served from 1813 until after 1827 as assessor in the Widows' Fund, of which he had been a member since 1798. He had also been awarded the Gold Salvator Medal of the city of Vienna.

The two sons Josef and Carl were members of the guild commission for many years: Josef from 1830 to 1846, Carl from 1845 to 1851.

Wastel (Wastl), Johann Michael (cat. no. 103)

Born between 1790–95, died after 1815.

Father of the civil silverworker Johann Evangelist Wastel (born March 25, 1811 in Vienna-Mariahilf, died January 1, 1869 in Vienna).

Apprenticed 1799 to 1805 with the civil gold- and silverworker Paul Mayerhofer in Vienna-Mariahilf. On August 12, 1814 he was awarded the right to set up trade as an authorized silverworker. His workshop was located in Vienna-Mariahilf.

Weirich (Weyrich), Joseph (cat. no. 50)

Born ca. 1803 in Vienna, died August 29, 1869 in Vienna.

Apprenticed 1817 to 1823 with the civil silverworker Karl Sedelmayer in Vienna-Mariahilf. On October 6, 1834 he was awarded the right to set up trade as an authorized silverworker. In 1843 he closed down his business.

Weiss (Weihs), Jakob (cat. no. 93)

Born in 1794 in Lüneburg, Germany, died November 1, 1847 in Vienna-Alservorstadt.

In 1822 he was awarded the right to set up trade as an authorized bronze notions worker (befugter Bronzegalanteriearbeiter); his workshop was located in Vienna-Fünfhaus. Between 1824 and 1827 he received patents for an invention to "enamel notions in metal as on gold" and one for a "new enamel for notions in gold, silver, bronze, and other metals." In 1832, after having relocated to his own home in Vienna-Alservorstadt, he was awarded—now an "imperially and royally privileged gold-, silver-, and bronze-goods producer" (k. k. privilegierter Gold-, Silber- und Bronzewaren-Fabrikant)—a further patent for "producing cutlery and notions in thirteen-lot silver, and then in gold more quickly and more beautifully." In the following year he was awarded the right to set up trade as a civil silverworker. He took part in the Allgemeine österreichische Gewerbsprodukten-Ausstellungen (General Austrian Decorative Arts Products Exhibitions) held in Vienna in 1835, 1839, and 1845 with bronze jewelry and pressed silver goods and won two silver medals for his work. At the time his firm employed thirty to sixty workers and was specialized almost exclusively in the production of inexpensive silver goods; in 1844 it received the "national factory permit." After Weiss's death in 1847 the factory was run by his widow Amalie until 1850.

Weissenböck (Weisenböck), Franz de Paula Anton (cat. no. 27)

Born June 13, 1766 in Vienna, died January 23, 1836 in Vienna-Wieden.

Apprenticed from 1779 to 1785 with the civil goldworkers Johann Kössler in Vienna and Franz Willibald Weitzmann in Vienna-Neubau. On December 10, 1811 he was awarded the right to set up trade as a civil jeweler, and on January 30, 1812 he became a burgher of the city of Vienna. His workshop was located in Vienna-Neubau. After 1825 he moved it to Vienna-Mariahilf and after 1829 to Vienna-Wieden.

After his death in 1836 the business was taken over by his widow Theresia (born ca. 1776 in Linsberg bei St. Margarethen an der Sierning, Lower Austria, died February 27, 1871 in Vienna) and run until 1837; the trade license was only returned in 1844.

Wieninger (Winninger), Joseph (cat. nos. 45 and 46)

Born ca. 1793–98 in Prinzendorf, Lower Austria, died February 20, 1869 (not in Vienna).

Apprenticed from 1808 to 1814 with the civil silverworker Lorenz Wieninger. On July 2, 1821 he was awarded the right to set up trade as an authorized silverworker; his workshop was located in Vienna-Laimgrube. Until 1836 he most likely worked together with the civil silverworker Ferdinand Wieninger (see below). He returned his trade license in 1867.

Wieninger (Wienninger), Lorenz (cat. no. 9)

Born in 1768 in Prinzendorf, Lower Austria, died March 6, 1828 in Vienna-Laimgrube.

Father of the civil jeweler and silverworker (bürgerlicher Juwelen- und Silberarbeiter) Franz Wieninger (born ca. 1799 in Vienna-Mariahilf, died 1854?), as well as the civil silverworker Ferdinand Wieninger (born between 1795 and 1800 in Vienna, died after 1850).

In 1795 he worked as a silverworker journeyman with the civil silverworker Johann Renner in Vienna-Mariahilf. In 1798 he was awarded the right to set up trade as a civil silverworker, and on September 28, 1798 he became a burgher of the city of Vienna. His workshop was located in Vienna-Mariahilf; after 1806 it was located in Vienna proper. From 1827 to 1828 his son Franz worked alongside him in the workshop. After his death in 1828 his son (?) Ferdinand Wieninger (see above) took over the business and ran it until 1850.

Lorenz Wieninger had been guild sub-chairman during the years 1826 to 1828. He was a member of the Widows' Fund from 1803 on, serving from 1825 until his death as an assessor. His widow Josepha received support from the fund until her death on February 7, 1836.

Würth (Wirth, after 1827 Edler von), Alois Johann Nepomuk (cat. nos. 4, 49, 55, 66, 96)

Born September 18, 1778 in Vienna, died July 5, 1833 in Graz, Styria.

Son of the imperial and royal court silverworker (k. k. Hof-Silberarbeiter) Ignaz Sebastian Joseph (after 1827 Edler von) Würth (1746–1834, for precise biographical data and family see entry).

Apprenticed from 1792 to 1796 with his father in Vienna.

On May 8, 1804 he was awarded the right to set up trade as a civil silverworker, and on May 11, 1804 he also became a burgher of the city of Vienna. His workshop was located in Vienna proper. In 1824 he received a patent for an invention enabling the faster production of items from thirteen-lot silver, such as coffee-, punch-, and tea machines. On January 12, 1832 he retired and left Vienna.

Alois Würth was a member of the guild commission from 1830 to 1831. His widow Anna (born January 14, 1785, died October 27, 1858 in Vienna) received support from the Widows' Fund, of which her husband had been a member since 1804, until her death.

Würth (Wirth, after 1827 Edler von), Franz Joseph Seraphin (cat. no. 52)

Born May 6, 1773 in Vienna, died February 1, 1831 in Graz, Styria.

Son of the imperial and royal court silverworker (k. k. Hof-Silberarbeiter) Ignaz Sebastian Joseph (after 1827 Edler von) Würth (1746–1834, for precise biographical data and family see entry). Father of the imperial and royal court silverworker Eduard Edler von Würth (born ca. 1798 in Vienna, died June 13, 1887 in Vienna-Fünfhaus).

Apprenticed from 1783 to 1788 with his father in Vienna, and then studied in Rome for three years.

On December 13, 1796 he was awarded the right to set up trade as a civil gold- and silverworker (bürgerlicher Gold- und Silberarbeiter), and on November 3, 1797 he also became a burgher of the city of Vienna, where his workshop was located. In 1809 he took over his father's business and was named imperial and royal court silverworker. His son Eduard worked with him after the year 1824, eventually taking over the workshop with his uncle Alois Johann Nepomuk Würth and running it until 1836.

Würth (Wirth,), Ignatz Franz Joseph (cat. no. 59)

Born February 3, 1743 in Vienna, died August 17, 1792 in Vienna.

Son of the civil gold- and silverworker (*bürgerlicher Gold- und Silberarbeiter*) Johann Joseph Würth (born April 2, 1706 in Vienna, died September 30, 1767 in Vienna). Father of the civil silverworkers Aloys Andreas Matthias Würth (born February 25, 1771 in Vienna, died August 7, 1831 in Vienna), Johann Nepomuk Würth (born November 17, 1778 in Vienna, died November 7, 1828 in Vienna), and of Maria Anna Würth (born December 30, 1772 in Vienna, died December 29, 1819 in Vienna), the first wife of the civil silverworker Johann Pretsch (born ca. 1769, died January 28, 1828 in Vienna-Leopoldstadt).

On October 24, 1769 he was awarded the right to set up trade as a civil silverworker after completion of his masterpiece, a "clock case." On March 17, 1770 he also became a burgher of the city of Vienna, where his workshop was located. In 1789 he was forced to file for bankruptcy, but likely continued to work. After his death in 1792 the workshop was managed by his widow Theresia (born ca. 1743, died June 15, 1805 in Vienna) and turned over to their son Aloys Andreas Matthias Würth in 1804.

Würth (Wirth, 1827: Edler von), Ignaz Sebastian Joseph (Sebastian Ignaz) (cat. no. 2)

Born January 20, 1746 in Vienna, died January 18, 1834 in Vienna.

Son of the civil gold- and silverworker (*bürgerlicher Gold- und Silberarbeiter*) Franz Xaver Caspar Würth (born January 7, 1715 in Vienna, died February 4, 1769 in Vienna); father of the imperial and royal court silverworker (*k. k. Hof-Silberarbeiter*) Franz Joseph Seraphin Würth (1773–1831, see entry) and the civil gold- and silverworker Alois Johann Nepomuk Würth (1778–1833, see entry); brother-in-law of the civil goldworker Johann Matthias Kiermayer (born ca. 1737, died May 15, 1807 in Vienna), who was married to his sister Maria Anna (born January 30, 1744, died after 1812).

Apprenticed from 1758 to 1763 with his father in Vienna.

On May 30, 1769 he was awarded the right to set up trade as a civil silverworker after completion of his masterpiece, a "cherub chased in silver." On June 10, 1769 he also became a burgher of Vienna, where his workshop was located. Having become an imperial and royal court silverworker, in 1809 he passed the business on to his son Franz Joseph Seraphin and turned in his license in 1815.

He served as administrator of the Widows' Fund from 1793 to 1805 and subsequently as vice-director until his death.

In addition to his activity as a silverworker, Ignaz Sebastian Joseph Würth made numerous contributions in the public sphere. From 1769 to 1833, he belonged to the *ritterlich-bürgerliches Scharfschützenkorps* (Noble and Civil Sharpshooters' Corps) of the civil guards, finally becoming chief constable and commander. In 1785 he was one of the founders of the Armeninstitut bei St. Stephan (Institution for the Poor of St. Stephen's) and also, for more than forty-nine years until his death, its first director. He played a major role in establishing the Graf Wurmser'sches österreichisch-steiermärkisches Freikorps (Austrian-Styrian Volunteer Corps of Graf Wurmser)—which was successful in the French Wars—and for this was awarded the Goldene Zivil-Verdienstmedaille mit der Kette (Gold Civil Service Medal and chain) by Emperor Francis II. As a long-term member of the "outer council" (and later of the "inner council" as well) of the city of Vienna, from 1800 to 1833 he was one of the commission members of the Bürgerspitalsfonds (burgher hospital fund) which supported the Viennese poor. For all his merits, the "patriot" Ignaz Sebastian Joseph Würth was elevated to the hereditary nobility by the emperor on May 19, 1827.

BIOGRAPHIES OF THE VIENNESE GOLD- AND SILVERSMITHS AND METALWORKERS AFTER 1900 WHOSE WORK APPEARS IN THIS CATALOGUE

Wenzel Bachmann & Co. (cat. nos. 73–81)

The k. k. privilegierte Alpacca- und Chinasilberwaren-Fabrik (Imperial and Royal Alpacca- and China Silverware Factory) was founded in 1842 by the bronze worker Wenzel Bachmann (born 1817 in Krakovany, Bohemia, today Czech Republic, died January 30, 1877 in Vienna-Mariahilf). After 1853 the factory in Vienna-Gumpendorf chiefly produced Alpacca silver goods for churches, restaurants, and coffee houses, along with various luxury items. Between 1906 and 1907 it also put certain designs for the Wiener Werkstätte into production. At this time it employed over 200 workers and had machines with sixty horsepower engines. In 1918 the business, which had become a shareholder concern, was taken over by the Berndorfer Metallwaren-Fabrik Arthur Krupp A.G.

Sturm, Alexander (cat. nos. 104, 112, 113, 115)

Born May 6, 1851 in Vienna, died September 28, 1915 in Vienna-Neubau.

In 1882 he was awarded the right to set up trade as a silver goods manufacturer. The factory was located in Vienna-Neubau. In 1908 Alexander (born December 23, 1875 in Vienna, died 1949) and Adalbert Sturm (born April 24, 1877 in Vienna, died September 3, 1931) joined the firm. After Alexander Sturm's death in 1915 the two took over management of the factory.

The firm Alexander Sturm & Co. worked with designs by Koloman Moser and Josef Hoffmann until 1903 and after 1932 (1925?).

Wiener Werkstätte

In 1903 the Wiener Werkstätte was licensed in the trade for gold- and silversmiths and jewelers. The official business manager was Karl Kallert. The Werkstätte was located in Vienna-Neubau; as of July 1909 a salesroom was opened in the first district.

In July 1925 the license was returned, but work continued in the silver and metal workshops. The Wiener Werkstätte was dissolved in 1932.

Würbel & Czokally (cat. nos. 108, 109, 110, 111)

Founded in 1864 (1862?) by the silverworker Vinzenz Czokally. The silver goods factory, located in Vienna-Neubau, was taken over in 1890 by the silversmith Anton Czokally (trade license 1890, active until 1900) and managed together with the chaser and engraver Carl Würbel (born November 25, 1853 in Vienna, died May 29, 1913 in Vienna, trade license as silversmith 1899) under the name Würbel & Czokally. After Anton Czokally's departure in 1900 Carl Würbel became the sole owner. He had been awarded the gold cross with crown for service and was a member of the Decorative Arts Society and the Chamber of Commerce. After his death in 1913 the factory was again registered for business in December 1914 under the name Josef Würbel (born 1876 in Vienna, died after 1927). In April 1927 he returned the license.

The factory produced decorative arts objects in gold and silver such as sports prizes, table services, and liturgical objects. Designs by Josef Hoffmann were also produced prior to the establishment of the Wiener Werkstätte.

SILVER- AND METALWORKERS IN THE WIENER WERKSTÄTTE

Berger, Josef (cat. nos. 158, 163, 165)

Born 1874 (or November 11, 1875?) in Vienna, date of death unknown.

Apprenticed from 1889 to 1893 with the civil jeweler Josef Huber or 1890 to 1894 with the gold- and silversmith and jeweler Rudolf Balog in Vienna-Neubau.

In 1905 he was active as a goldsmith in the Wiener Werkstätte. From 1907 to 1922 he is listed as a jeweler's assistant in the guild. In March, 1923 he was awarded the right to set up trade as a jeweler in Vienna-Favoriten.

Blaschek, Johann (cat. no. 166)

(Dates unknown)

Active in 1905 in the Wiener Werkstätte as a metalworker.

Czech, Josef (cat. nos. 117 and 134/1)

Born January 1, 1874 in Staré Sedliste, Bohemia (today Czech Republic), died September 30, 1958.

Apprenticed from 1887 to 1891 with the silver goods producer Thomas Dub (see entry) in Vienna-Neubau.

He was active in 1905 as a silversmith in the Wiener Werkstätte.

Erbrich, Adolf (cat. nos. 119, 130, 143, 148)

Born 1874 in "Speichendorf" (? Speisendorf, Lower Austria), date of death unknown.

Apprenticed 1888 to 1892 with the civil silverworker Josef Szombathy in Vienna-Neubau.

He was active in 1905 as a silversmith in the Wiener Werkstätte.

In the guild he was an assistant witness for assistants' examinations from 1911 to 1922; after 1934 he was on the advisory board of the assistants' assembly.

Frank, Karl (cat. nos. 82/2, 82/4)

Born January 27, 1878 in Vienna, date of death unknown.

Apprenticed from 1892 to 1896 with the gold- and silverworker Karl Michalik in Vienna-Fünfhaus.

He was active from 1908 to 1926 as a silversmith in the Wiener Werkstätte. During the same period he was awarded the right to set up trade as a gold- and silversmith in October 1918 in Vienna-Margareten. He appears to have plied this trade until after 1938.

Guggenbichler, Franz (cat. no. 152)

(Dates unknown)

He was active in 1905 as a metalworker in the Wiener Werkstätte.

Holi, Josef (cat. nos. 120, 125, 143)

(Dates unknown)

He was active in 1905 as a metalworker in the Wiener Werkstätte.

Hoszfeld, Josef (cat. nos. 128, 136, 141, 143, 146)

Born April 18, 1869 in Vienna, died February 20, 1918 in Vienna.
Son of the civil knifesmith Ferdinand Hoszsfeld.

In 1900 he was awarded the right to set up trade as a silversmith in Vienna-Josefstadt. He ended his independent career in 1905 and worked as master silversmith in the Wiener Werkstätte. During the First World War he served as *Oberjäger* in the *Deutschmeister-Schützenkorps* (Master of the Teutonic Order Sharpshooter Corps).

Husnik, Josef (cat. no. 107)

Born August 8, 1876 in Vienna-Fünfhaus, died April 5, 1957.

Apprenticed from 1890 to 1894 with the civil silverworker Franz Rumwolf in Vienna-Josefstadt.

He was active in 1905 as a silversmith in the Wiener Werkstätte.

In 1910 he was awarded the right to set up trade as a silversmith in Vienna-Neubau. In February 1933 he closed the business, but in 1935 he began to work again.

In the guild he was a member of the commission beginning in 1921 and, after 1922, delegated master at the assistants' assemblies.

Kallert, Karl (cat. no. 159)

Born October 29, 1879 in Vienna, date of death unknown.

Apprenticed from 1893 to 1897 with the gold- and silver-goods producer Rudolf Frank in Vienna-Mariahilf.

After the year 1903 he was, as gold- and silversmith and jeweler, the official business manager of the Wiener Werkstätte. In 1905 he was listed there as master silversmith.

Mayer, Alfred (cat. nos. 133, 134/3, 135, 145)

Born 1873, date of death unknown.

Apprenticed from 1889 to 1892 with the jeweler and goldsmith Josef Wlach in Vienna proper.

In the years 1905 and 1920 (and presumably in-between) he was active as a silversmith in the Wiener Werkstätte. In March 1929 he was awarded the right to set up trade as a jeweler, gold- and silversmith in Vienna-Mariahilf.

Medl, Karl (cat. no. 162)

(Dates unknown)

He was active in 1905 as a metalworker in the Wiener Werkstätte.

Wagner, Josef (cat. nos. 118, 132, 137, 138, 142, 147, 178)

(Dates unknown)

He was active in 1905 as a metalworker in the Wiener Werkstätte.

Wertnik, Adolf (cat. nos. 51, 131, 140, 144, 149, 150, 167, 175, 176, 182)

Born June 12, 1880 in Vienna, date of death unknown.

Apprenticed beginning in 1895 with the silversmith Eduard Friedmann in Vienna proper but never ended his apprenticeship.

He was active in 1905 as a metalworker in the Wiener Werkstätte.

Selected sources:

Wiener Stadt- und Landesarchiv
Burgher books; cemetery records; guild of gold- and silversmiths: records, books, master lists; death register.

Heraldisch-genealogische Gesellschaft Adler, Vienna: ancestry lists, death announcement collection, genealogies.
Records of various Viennese parishes.
Punzierungsamt, Vienna (I district): mark boards.
MAK-Austrian Museum of Applied Arts, Vienna: Archive of the Wiener Werkstätte, drawings for master examinations (*Kunstblätterinventar*).

See p. 394 for Selected Bibliography

SELECTED BIBLIOGRAPHY

William D. Godsey, Jr.

Steven Beller, *Wien und die Juden 1867–1938,* transl. by Marie Therese Pitner, Vienna et al. 1993.

Ernst Bruckmüller et al., eds., *Bürgertum in der Habsburgermonarchie,* Vienna and Cologne 1990.

Ernst Bruckmüller, *Sozialgeschichte Österreichs,* 2nd ed., Vienna and Munich 2001.

Günther Chaloupek et al., *Wien: Wirtschaftsgeschichte,* 2 vols., Vienna 1991.

István Déak, *Beyond Nationalism: A Social and Political History of the Habsburg Officer Corps, 1848–1918,* New York and Oxford 1990.

Jonathan Dewald, *The European Nobility, 1400–1800,* Cambridge 1996.

R. J. W. Evans, *The Making of the Habsburg Monarchy 1550–1700,* Oxford 1979.

William D. Godsey Jr., *Aristocratic Redoubt: The Austro-Hungarian Foreign Office on the Eve of the First World War,* West Lafayette, Indiana 1999.

David F. Good, *The Economic Rise of the Habsburg Empire, 1750–1914,* Berkeley et al. 1984.

Waltraud Heindl, *Gehorsame Rebellen: Bürokratie und Beamte in Österreich 1780 bis 1848,* Vienna et al. 1991.

Horn 1997, *Zeugen der Intimität: Privaträume der kaiserlichen Familie und des böhmischen Adels. Aquarelle und Interieurs des 19. Jahrhunderts,* exh. cat. Niederösterreichisches Landesmuseum.

Christina Kokkinakis, *Die Familien Köchert, Wild und Zacherl: Heiratsverhalten des Wiener Bürgertums im 19. und frühen 20. Jahrhundert,* thesis University of Vienna 1993.

Ralph Melville, *Adel und Revolution in Böhmen: Strukturwandel von Herrschaft und Gesellschaft in Österreich um die Mitte des 19. Jahrhunderts,* Mainz 1998.

Ingrid Mittenzwei, *Zwischen Gestern und Morgen: Wiens frühe Bourgeoisie an der Wende vom 18. zum 19. Jahrhundert,* Vienna et al. 1998.

Helmut Rumpler, *Eine Chance für Mitteleuropa: Bürgerliche Emanzipation und Staatsverfall in der Habsburgermonarchie,* Vienna 1997.

Roman Sandgruber, *Ökonomie und Politik. Österreichische Wirtschaftsgeschichte vom Mittelalter bis zur Gegenwart,* Vienna 1995.

Ferdinand Seibt, ed., *Böhmen im 19. Jahrhundert: Vom Klassizismus zur Moderne,* Berlin and Frankfurt am Main 1995.

Hannes Stekl et al., eds., *Durch Arbeit, Besitz, Wissen und Gerechtigkeit,* Vienna et al. 1992.

Karl Vocelka, *Glanz und Untergang der höfischen Welt: Repräsentation, Reform und Reaktion im Habsburgischen Vielvölkerstaat,* Vienna 2001.

Diether Halama

Diether Halama, *Die Gold-, Silber- und Metallwaren- fabrik J. C. Klinkosch in Wien (1797–1972),* M.A. thesis, Vienna 1995.

Fachzeitung der Wiener Juweliere, Gold- und Silberschmiede, Vienna 1909–1938.

Kaiserlich-Königliche Allgemeine Hofkammer, *Beschreibung der Erfindungen und Verbesserungen, für welche in den kaiserlich-königlichen österreichischen Staaten Patente ertheilt wurden, und deren Privilegiums-Dauer nun erloschen ist,* Vienna 1841 ff.

Bernhard Koch, "Biographische Beiträge zur Geschichte Wiener Münzstempelschneider und Medailleure," *Numismatische Zeitschrift,* 82, Vienna 1967, p. 74f.

Lehmanns Allgemeiner Wohnungs-Anzeiger nebst Handels- und Gewerbe-Adressbuch für die k. k. Reichshaupt- und Residenzstadt Wien, Vienna 1859 ff.

Johann Joseph Prechtl, *Jahrbuch des k. k. polytechnischen Institutes in Wien,* Vienna 1819 ff.

Anton Redl, ed., *Handlungs Gremien und Fabricken Adressen Buch der österreichischen Statistik der Volkswirthschaft in Nieder-Österreich 1855–1866,* published by the Handels- und Gewerbekammer, Vienna n.d.

Welt-Ausstellung 1873 in Wien: Amtlicher Catalog der im Reichsrathe vertretenen Koenigreiche und Laender Oesterreichs, Vienna 1873.

Wiener Zeitung, Vienna 1703ff.

Michael Huey

Hermann Bahr, *Secession,* Vienna 1900.

Lazarus Bendavid, *Versuch einer Geschmackslehre: Mit doppeltem Register,* Berlin 1799.

Kurt Blaukopf, *Mahler: Sein Leben, sein Werk und seine Welt in zeitgenössischen Bildern und Texten,* Vienna 1976.

Max von Boehn, *Das Empire: Die Zeit, das Leben, der Stil,* Berlin 1925.

Hubertus Czernin, *Die Fälschung: Der Fall Bloch-Bauer,* 2 vols., Vienna 1999.

Peter Dormer, *Design Since 1945,* London 2000.

Johann Bernhard Fischer von Erlach, *Entwurf einer historischen Architektur,* Dortmund 1978.

Isabelle Frank, ed., *The Theory of Decorative Art: An Anthology of European & American Writings 1750–1940,* New Haven and London 2000.

Georg Gaugusch, "Die Familien Wittgenstein und Salzer und ihr genealogisches Umfeld," *Adler: Zeitschrift für Genealogie und Heraldik,* 21, 4, 2001, pp. 120–145.

Siegfried Giedion, *Mechanization Takes Command: a Contribution to Anonymous History,* New York 1969.

Ernst H. Gombrich, *Ornament und Kunst. Schmucktrieb und Ordnungssinn in der Psychologie des dekorativen Schaffens,* Stuttgart 1982.

Johann Gottfried Grohmann, *Ideenmagazin für Liebhaber von Gärten, Englischen Anlagen und für Besitzer von Landgütern,* nos.1–4, Leipzig 1796.

Eileen Harris, *The Genius of Robert Adam: His Interiors,* New Haven and London 2001.

Ludwig Hevesi, *Die fünfte Dimension,* Vienna 1905.

Horn 1997, *Zeugen der Intimität: Privaträume der kaiserlichen Familie und des böhmischen Adels: Aquarelle und Interieurs des 19. Jahrhunderts,* exh. cat. Niederösterreichisches Landesmuseum.

Rosalind E. Krauss, *The Originality of the Avant-Garde and Other Modernist Myths,* Cambridge and London 1997.

Alfons Lhotsky, *Festschrift des Kunsthistorischen Museums in Wien: Die Geschichte der Sammlungen von Maria Theresia bis zum Ende der Monarchie,* Horn 1941–1945.

London 1996, *Grand Tour: The Lure of Italy in the Eighteenth Century,* exh. cat. Tate Gallery, Andrew Wilton and Ilaria Bignamini, eds.

Adolf Loos, *Das Andere: Ein Blatt zur Einfuehrung abendlaendischer Kultur in Oesterreich,* yr. 1, no. 2, Vienna 1903.

Heinz Lunzer and Victoria Lunzer-Talos, eds., *Abroad in Austria: Travellers' Impressions from Five Centuries,* exh. cat., Österreichisches Bundes-ministerium für Auswärtiges, Vienna 1997.

Joseph August Lux, *Die moderne Wohnung & Ihre Ausstattung,* Vienna and Leipzig 1905.

Alma Mahler-Werfel, *Mein Leben,* Frankfurt am Main 1960.

Philip Mansel, *Charles-Joseph de Ligne 1735–1814: Charmeur de l'Europe,* Paris 1992.

Lucian O. Meysels, *In Meinem Salon ist Österreich: Berta Zuckerkandl und ihre Zeit,* Vienna and Munich 1984.

Andrea Mihm, *Packend ... Eine Kulturgeschichte des Reisekoffers,* Marburg 2001.

Munich 1971, *Die verborgene Vernunft: Funktionale Gestaltung im 19. Jahrhundert,* exh. cat. Die Neue Sammlung.

Munich 1992, *Josef Hoffmann Designs,* exh. cat. MAK Österreichisches Museum für Angewandte Kunst.

Waltraud Neuwirth, *Wiener Gold- und Silberschmiede und ihre Punzen 1867–1922,* Vienna 1976.

Waltraud Neuwirth, *Bestecke für die Wiener Werkstätte,* Vienna 1982.

Waltraud Neuwirth, *Wiener Werkstätte Avantgarde Déco Industrial Design,* Vienna 1984.

Waltraud Neuwirth, *Wiener Silber 1781–1866 Namens- und Firmenpunzen,* Vienna 2002.

Adolf Opel, ed., *Adolf Loos: Die Potemkin'sche Stadt: Verschollene Schriften 1897–1933,* Vienna 1983.

Derek Ostergard, ed., *Bent Wood and Metal Furniture: 1850–1946,* New York 1987.

Eduard Poetzl, *Moderner Gschnas,* Vienna 1901.

Eduard Poetzl, *Zeitgenossen,* Vienna 1905.

Renée Price, *New Worlds: German and Austrian Art 1890–1940,* Cologne 2001.

Ursula Prokop, *Margaret Stonborough-Wittgenstein: Bauherrin, Intellektuelle, Mäzenin,* Vienna 2003.

Marcel Raval, *Claude-Nicolas Ledoux 1756–1806,* Paris 1945.

Viktor Reitzner, *Alt Wien Lexikon für Österreichische und Süddeutsche Kunst und Kunstgewerbe,* Vienna 1957.

Maria Rennhofer, *Koloman Moser: Leben und Werk 1868–1918,* Vienna 2002.

Alfred Rohrwasser, *Österreichische Punzen: Edelmetall-Punzierung in Österreich von 1524 bis 1984,* Perchtoldsdorf 1984.

Burkhardt Rukschcio and Roland Schachel, *Adolf Loos,* Salzburg and Vienna 1982.

Richard von Schaukal, *Die Mietwohnung: Eine Kulturfrage: Glossen,* Munich 1911.

Elisabeth Schmuttermeier, "Wiener Silber und Schmuck des Biedermeier," in Vienna 1988, pp. 228–234.

Carl Schorske, *Fin-de-siecle Vienna: Politics and Culture,* New York 1990.

Werner J. Schweiger, *Meisterwerke der Wiener Werkstätte,* Vienna 1990.

Werner J. Schweiger, *Kunst und Handwerk 1903–1932,* Vienna 1982.

Charles Sealsfield and Karl Postl, *Austria as It Is: or Sketches of continental courts, by an eye-witness: London 1828,* Vienna 1994.

Eduard F. Sekler, *Josef Hoffmann: The Architectural Work,* Princeton 1985.

Cecilia Sjögren, "Die Familie," in *Wittgenstein,* exh. cat.Wiener Secession, Vienna 1989, pp. 99–117.

Michael Snodin and John Styles, *Design & the Decorative Arts. Britain 1500–1900,* London 2001.

Stockholm 1988, *The Triumph of Simplicity,* exh. cat. Nationalmuseum Stockholm, Uddevalla 1988.

Frances Trollope, *Vienna and the Austrians,* London 1838.

Jenny Uglow, *The Lunar Men: the Friends Who Made the Future,* London 2002.

E. C. J. Van de Vivere, *Mausoleum oder Grabmahl Ihrer Königlichen Hoheit Mariae Christinae, Erzherzogin zu Oesterreich, etc. etc.,* Vienna 1805.

Peter Vergo, "Fritz Waerndorfer als Sammler," in *alte und moderne kunst,* no. 177, Vienna 1981, pp. 33–38.

Vienna 1967, *Die Wiener Werkstätte: Modernes Kunsthandwerk von 1903–1932,* exh. cat. MAK Österreichisches Museum für Angewandte Kunst, Vienna 1967.

Vienna 1981, *Moderne Vergangenheit: Wien 1800–1900,* exh. cat. Künstlerhaus, Vienna 1981.

Vienna 1988, *Bürgersinn und Aufbegehren: Biedermeier und Vormärz in Wien 1815–1848,* exh. cat. Historisches Museum der Stadt Wien, Vienna 1988.

Vienna 1994, *Ägyptomanie: Ägypten in der europäischen Kunst 1730–1930,* exh. cat., Kunsthistorisches Museum Wien.

Vienna and Salzburg 1987, *Josef Hoffmann: Ornament zwischen Hoffnung und Verbrechen,* collection cat. MAK Österreichisches Museum für Angewandte Kunst.

Christina Wesemann-Wittgenstein, "Stefan Grossmann: Publizist, Theatermacher und Schriftsteller zwischen Wien und Berlin," *Profile, Magazin des Österreichischen Literaturarchivs,* vol. 7, Vienna 2001.

Paul Wijdeveld, *Ludwig Wittgenstein, Architect,* London1994.

Hubert Chryspolitus Winkler, "Kurze Geschichte der ehem. Hofsilber- und Tafelkammer," in Ilsebill Fliedl and Peter Parenzan, eds., *Ehemalige Hofsilber- und Tafelkammer: Sammlungskatalog Band I,* Vienna 1996, pp. 15–25.

Christian Witt-Dörring, "Die Farbgebung der Möbel am Wiener Hof während der Regierungszeit Maria Theresias," in *alte und moderne kunst,* yr. 23, no. 158, Vienna 1978, pp. 8–12.

Christian Witt-Dörring, "Die Wohnraumgestaltung des Biedermeier: Das Wiener Interieur 1815–1848," in *alte und moderne kunst,* yr. 24, no. 165, Vienna 1979.

Christian Witt-Dörring, "Der differenzierte Konsum: Das Wiener Möbel 1815–1848," in Vienna 1987, pp. 368–384.

Hermine Wittgenstein, *Familienerinnerungen,* unpubl. ms., Vienna 1944.

Ludwig Wittgenstein, *Vermischte Bemerkungen,* Frankfurt am Main 1994.

J. S. Marcus

Ian Buruma, *Anglomania,* New York 1999.

Siegfried Giedion, *Mechanization Takes Command: a Contribution to Anonymous History,* New York 1969.

Brigittte Hamann, *Hitler's Vienna,* transl. by Thomas Thornton, New York 1999.

Claudio Magris, *Danube,* transl. by Patrick Creagh, New York 1986.

John Hope Mason, ed., *The Irresistible Diderot,* London 1992.

Stephen Prickett "Circles and Straight Lines: The Romantic Idea of Tourism," in Hartmut Berghoff, ed., *The Making of Modern Tourism: the Cultural History of the British Experience,* New York 2002.

Howard C. Robbins Landon, *Mozart and Vienna,* London 1991.

Carl Schorske, *Fin-de-siecle Vienna: Politics and Culture,* New York 1990.

Jill Steward, "The Spa Towns of the Austro-Hungarian Empire and the Growth of Tourist Culture: 1860–1914," in Peter Borsay, ed., *New directions in urban history: aspects of European art, health, tourism and leisure since the enlightenment,* Münster et al. 2000.

Geoffrey Trease, *The Grand Tour,* New York 1967.

Elisabeth Schmuttermeier

Gabriele Fabiankowitsch, *Funktion und Wesen des Zeichenunterrichts für Handwerker und seine Auswirkung auf die Möbelentwürfe des Empire und Biedermeier in Wien,* thesis, Salzburg 1989.

Camillo List, "Wiener Goldschmiede und ihre Beziehungen zum Kaiserlichen Hof," in *Jahrbuch der kunsthistorischen Sammlungen des Kaiserhauses,* vol. 17, Vienna 1896.

Gustav Otruba, "Alter, Verbreitung und Zunftorganisation des Goldschmiedehandwerks in Österreich," *Uhren/Juwelen,* 5, 1967.

Walter Wagner, *Die Geschichte der Akademie der bildenden Künste in Wien,* Vienna 1967.

The numbers appearing in italics refer to illustrations.

Abraham, Karl 382
Achleitner, Friedrich 341
Adler, Viktor 384
Albers, Josef *113*
Alberti, Leon Battista 368
Albrecht III, Duke of Austria 372
Albrecht, Thomas *149*, 387
Alt, Rudolf von 254, 347
Alxinger, Johann Baptist 382
Arendt, Hannah 356
Arnstein, Fanny von 357, 381
Arnsteiner, Nathan Adam 357, 382
Artaria, Pasquale 382
Artin, Eugen 345
Asenbaum, Paul 337
Ashbee, Charles R. 182, *215*, 234, *235*
Auersperg, Count Anton Alexander, a.k.a. Anastasius
     Grün 357
Auenbrugger, Leopold 381
Babenberg, Duke of 375
Bachelard, Gaston 336, 340
Baedeker, Karl 356
Bahr, Hermann 188, 234
Barth, Joseph 382
Bazel, Karel Petrus Cornelis de 337
Beardsley, Aubrey 343
Behn, Helga 339
Behrens, Peter 365, 370
Bendavid, Lazarus 54, 70, 74
Berger, Josef 392
Bergmann *170*
Berlage, Hendrik Petrus 337
Berlin, Isaiah 359
Bernini, Gianlorenzo 368
Bertoia, Harry *322*
Biach, Anna 343
Biach, Max 343
Binder (Bindner), Ignaz *47*, 387
Bisanz-Prakken, Marian 337
Blanning, T. C. W. 378
Blaschek, Johann 392
Blasius, Carl *55*, 387
Blumauer, Aloys 382
Blumenbach, W. C. W. *26*, 42, 68
Bock (Beck), Ludwig *123*, 387
Bogner, Dieter 336
Böhm, Adolf 345, 370
Bombelles 378
Bonhomme, Jacques-Antoine 60
Borer, Carlo *174*
Born, Ignaz von 382
Boucher, Juste-François 26
Bougainville, Louis Antoine de 369
Boullée, Étienne-Louis 86, 340, 370
Boulton and Fothergill *54*
Boyer, John W. 383
Brahms, Johannes 347
Brandt, Marianne *108, 114,* 115, *115, 116*
Brecht, Berthold 359
Breuer, Hans *266,* 267
Breuer, Josef *266*
Breuer, Käthy née Mautner *264, 266*
Breuer, Robert *266*
Breunner-Enkevoirth, Count August Ferdinand 378
Brühl, Hanna *266*
Byron, Lord George Gordon 354
Canova, Antonio *72,* 74
Casals, Pablo 347
Chambers, Ephraim 354
Chaplin, Charlie 109
Charles VI, Holy Roman Emperor 368
Charles, Archduke 62
Chigi, Prince 128
Colbert, Jean-Baptiste 368
Cole, Henry *364,* 365
Connor, David *310*
Cook, Thomas 356, 358, 369
Coop Himmelblau 341
Crenneville 378
Curie, Marie 371
Curie, Pierre 371
Czech, Hermann 341
Czech, Josef 393
Czernin, Count Rudolph 377
Czeschka, Carl Otto 254, *276,* 280, 343, 344, *345,*
     347, *347,* 384
Dalberg, Baron Carl 377, 378
Danhauser, Joseph *100*
Dante Alighieri 355
Deffand, Madame du 369
Dell, Christian *112*
Descartes, René 354, 368
Desgodetz, Antoine 368
Desvignes, Peter Hubert 16
Dewald, Jonathan 377
Diderot, Denis 354
Dietrich, Oskar 374
Dietrichstein, Count 372
Doesburg, Theo van *302,* 338
Domanek (Domanöck), Antonius Matthias 19, 387
Dormer, Peter 172
Dresser, Christopher *73,* 96, *96, 98,* 182, 364
Dub (Dubb), Thomas *101,* 387
Duchamp, Marcel 359
Durand, Jean-Nicolas-Louis 370

Dürer, Albrecht 355
Duse, Eleonora 235
Eckermann, Johann Peter 44, 370
Ehrenfels, Christian von 338
Engelmann, Paul *285,* 348
Erbrich, Adolf 393
Erdheim, Mario 384
Ericsson, John 357
Eskeles, Berend Gabriel 376
Evans, Robert J. W. 375
Evelyn, John 368
Fanto, Adolf 346
Fanto, David 345, 346
Fanto, Edmund 346
Fanto, Friedrich 346
Fanto, Lotti (?) née Winterberg 346, *346*
Festetics, Count Georg 382
Figdor, Fanny (see Wittgenstein, Fanny née Figdor)
     212, *212,* 346
Figdor, Wilhelm 344
Fischer von Erlach, Johann Bernhard 368, 369
Flöge, Emilie *258,* 259
Flöge, Helene 259
Foltanek, Primarius 245
Forgatsch (Fergatsch), Georg 56, *57,* 96, *97,* 387
Forster, Georg 382
Foucault, Michel 383
Francis I, Emperor of Austria 62, 357, 372
Francis II, Holy Roman Emperor 62, 357, 372
     (see Francis I, Emperor of Austria)
Francis Joseph I, Emperor of Austria 358, 359, 382
Francis Stephen, of Lorraine, Holy Roman Emperor
     16, 355
Frank, Johann Peter 382
Frank, Josef 340, 341, 374
Frank, Karl 374, 392
Franz, Ida (see Salzer, Ida née Franz) *230*
Franz, Rainald 341
Fréart, Roland Lord of Chambray 368
Frederick III, Holy Roman Emperor 340
Freud, Sigmund 357, 381, 383, 384
Friedmann, Eduard 374
Fries, Count Johann 383
Garnier, Tony 364
Geymüller, Baron Johann Heinrich 377
Giedion, Siegfried 173, 365
Gindle (Gendle), Friedrich *156,* 387
Giovannoni, Stefano *130*
Gladwell, Malcolm 344
Goethe, Johann Wolfgang von 44, *64,* 148, 355, 363,
     370
Gombrich, Ernst H. 339
Gorsen, Peter 340
Grassi, Antonio *24, 34,* 110
Grave, Dirk Evert *56*
Graves, Michael *316*
Gris, Juan 336, 338
Gropius, Walter 109, 188, *306,* 363, 364
Gross, Otto 338
Grün, Anastasius, a.k.a. Count Anton Alexander
     Auersperg 357
Grasmayr, Alois 232
Grasmayr, Magda née Mautner von Markhof 235,
     236, 237, 343
Gschnadt, Joseph 56
Guggenbichler, Franz 392
Guttmann (Gutmann), Johann, Sr. *150,* 373, 387
Guttmann, Johann Jr. *83,* 373, 387
Haas, Caspar 42, *42,* 382
Haber, Fritz 359
Hagenauer, Johann Baptist 33
Haizinger, Amalie *100*
Hann (Han), Johann Georg *79,* 372, 388
Harrod, W. Owen 172
Hartmann, Franz *372*
Harvey, David 380
Hauer, Johann Thomas *33*
Haugwitz, Count Carl 377
Haydn, Joseph 382
Hegel, Georg Wilhelm Friedrich 370
Heine, Heinrich 356
Heinisch (Heintsch), Joseph *37,* 42, *43, 58, 144,* 388
Hellmann, Bernhard 343
Hellmann, Caroline "Lina" *239,* 343
Hellmann, Lili Jeanette (see Waerndorfer, Lili Jeanette
     née Hellmann) 120, 172, *220,* 223, *252, 280,*
     343, 344
Hellmann, Margarethe (see Rémy-Berzenkovich,
     Margarethe von, née Hellmann) 343
Hemingway, Ernest 242
Henneberg, Hugo 343
Henneberg, Marie *219,* 343
Hennebique, François 371
Herder, Johann Gottfried 355
Hesse-Darmstadt, Ernst Ludwig Duke of 370
Hevesi, Ludwig 220, 337, 345
Hildebrandt, Lukas von 268
Hirschwald, H. 255
Hochstetter, Anna (see Schmedes, Anna von, née
     Hochstetter) 346
Hochstetter, Justine (see Wittgenstein, Justine née
     Hochstetter) 212, 346
Hochstetter, Maria 346
Hofbauer, Klemens Maria 357
Hoffmann, Josef 13, 40, 48, *89, 100, 102, 104, 105,*
     106, 108, 109, 122, *135, 136, 137, 138, 139,*
     140, 141, 143, 145, 168, 170, 172, *173, 174,*
     176, 180, 182, *182, 184, 186, 187,* 188, *189,*
     190, 191, 192, 193, 194, *195, 197,* 198, *203,*
     204, 205, 206, 207, 208, *209,* 210, *210, 211,* 212,

     213, 214, 220, *220, 221, 222, 223, 224, 225,*
     226, 227, 228, *228, 230, 233,* 234, 235, 338,
     339, *339,* 340, *340,* 341, 343, *343,* 344, 345,
     346, *346, 347,* 348, *348,* 363, 364, 370, 371,
     373, 374, 384
Holi, Josef 393
Hollein, Hans *341*
Hoppe, Emil 370
Hörmann, Theodor 374
Hoszfeld, Josef *199,* 393
Huber, Bartholomäus *84*
Hughes, Pierre François, Baron d'Hancarville 36, *36*
Hugo, Victor 358
Hukin & Heath 96
Hume, David 369
Husnik, Josef 393
Itten, Johannes 109
Jäger, Gustav 232
Jäger, Herta née Mautner von Markhof 222, 343
Jakobsen, Arne *129*
Jaksch, Joachim *165,* 388
Jaray, Paul 360
Joachim, Joseph 347
Jodl, Friedrich 384
Johnson, Philip 340
Jones, Owen 76, 337
Joseph II, Holy Roman Emperor 13, 16, *16, 19,* 33,
     356, 372, 375, 376, 379, 380, 382, *382,* 383
Jung, Joachim 383
Jünger, Ernst 359
Kain (Kainn), Johann (also Ignaz) *69,* 388
Kallert, Karl 393
Kallmus, Leopoldine "Poldy" (see Wittgenstein,
     Leopoldine "Poldy" née Kallmus) *242,* 254, *254,*
     255, 348
Kandinsky, Vasily 13
Kant, Immanuel 355
Kaplan, Wendy 234
Kaunitz, Prince Wenzel 373
Keesz, Stephan 42, 68
Kern, Joseph Anton *60, 87, 127,* 129, *129, 160,* 388
Kessler, Count Harry 344
Kircher, Father Athanasius 368
Klama, Michael 155, *155,* 388
Klein, A. 96, 345
Klein, Frank 96, 345
Klein, Johann August 355
Kleist, Heinrich von 360
Klima, Johann *28,* 388
Klimt, Gustav 176, 188, *219,* 254, 259, 336, 341,
     343, 344, 347, 370
Klinger, Max 336, 347
Klinkosch (after 1880: Ritter von), Josef Carl *154,* 388
Knips, Anton 343
Knips, Sonja *280,* 343, 344
Knox, Archibald 182, *184,* 248
Koch, Joseph Franz (also Johann) *99,* 389
Kohlmayer (Kollmeier), Georg *59,* 389
Kohn, Felix *197,* 210, 343, 344, 346, *346,*
Kohn, Jacob 194, *210*
Kohn, Josef 194, *210*
Kohn, Maria 194, *194, 197*
Kokoschka, Oskar 188, 345
Köll, Anton, Sr. *81, 113,* 389
Köll (Kell), Franz 92, *93,* 389
Kollowrat-Krakowsky, Count Leopold 382
Kopf, Willi 336
Koppel, Henning *124*
Kornhäusel, Joseph *80*
Kraus, Karl 344, 359, 384
Krauss, Rosalind 67
Krautauer (Krauttauer), Jakob *27, 41, 45,* 50, *50, 58,*
     61, 66, *66,* 67, 208, *364,* 389
Kupka, František 336, *336,* 338
Kuramata, Shiro *322*
Laborde, Alexandre Conte de 31, 95
Lamberg-Sprinzenstein, Count Franz Anton 31
Lanckoroński, Count Karl 378
Lang, Fritz 109
Lang, Marie 382
Latour, Count Vinzenz 235
Laubenbacher, Joseph 48, *48,* 389
Laugier, Marc-Antoine 369
Lauweriks, Johannes Ludovicus Mattheus 337
Le Corbusier, a.k.a. Charles Edouard Jeanneret *304,*
     339, 363, 365
Lebowitz, Fran 62
Ledoux, Claude-Nicolas 48, *48, 82,* 86, *86,* 340
Leitenberger, Johann Joseph 376
Leopold III, Duke of Austria 372
Lessing, Gotthold Ephraim 354
LeWitt, Sol *312*
Liechtenstein, Prince Alois Joseph II 16, 382
Ligne, Prince Charles-Joseph de 40
Ligthowler, Thomas 382
Lilienthal, Otto 146
Lincoln, Abraham 358
Link, Ulrich *372*
Lissitzky, Eliezer 340, 341
Locke, John 354
Löffler, Bertold 384
Loos, Adolf 48, *48,* 96, 122, 194, 206, 207, *284, 330,*
     339, *340,* 341, 342, 344, 346, 359, 364, 365
Louis XIV 368, 369
Louis XV 62, 368, 371
Louis XVI 56
Löwenbach, Emil 122
Lubomirska, Princess 144
Luksch, Richard 180
Luksch-Machowska, Elena 180

Lux, Joseph August 364
Macdonald, Margaret 220, 234, 343
Mackintosh, Charles Rennie 193, 220, 228, 234, 235, 268, 320, 337, 343, 364, 371
Madersperger, Josef 357
Mahler, Alma née Schindler 188, 189, 189, 345
Mahler, Gustav 188, 188, 189, 344, 384
Malaparte, Curzio 251
Malebranche, Nicolas de 354
Maleck, F. 60
Malevich, Kasimir 290, 298, 336, 337, 338, 338, 340
Marcus, Siegfried 357
Maria Christina, Archduchess 72
Maria Ludovica, Empress of Austria, née Princess d'Este 40, 40
Maria Theresa, Empress, Queen of Hungary and Bohemia, and Archduchess of Austria 13, 16, 16, 66, 355, 356
Marx, Karl 358
Mautner von Markhof, Carl Ferdinand 343
Mautner von Markhof, Editha née Baroness Sunstenau von Schützenthal 233, 234
Mautner von Markhof, Editha (see Moser, Editha née Mautner von Markhof) 235, 236, 280, 343, 343, 345
Mautner von Markhof, Herta (see Jäger, Herta née Mautner von Markhof) 222, 343
Mautner von Markhof, Magda (see Grasmayr, Magda née Mautner von Markhof) 235, 236, 237, 343
Mautner, Isidor 266, 323
Mautner, Jenny 264, 266, 267, 343
Mautner, Käthy (see Breuer, Käthy, née Mautner) 264, 266
Maxwell, William 348
Mayer, Alfred 393
Mayerhofer & Klinkosch 136, 160, 161
Mayerhofer, Stefan, Sr. 52, 53, 63, 93, 117, 131, 151, 363, 389
Mayreder, Rosa 384
Mayrhofen, Baroness Anna Maria 375
Mayrhofer, Johann 357
McAdam, Robert 357
Medl, Karl 393
Melies, Georges 359
Mellor, David 122
Mendelssohn-Bartholdy, Felix 347
Metternich, Prince Clemens Wenzel Lothar 60, 86, 357, 377, 378
Metzner, Franz 384
Miethke, H. O. 345
Minne, Georges 343
Mittenzwei, Ingrid 376, 382
Moll, Carl 188, 345
Mondrian, Piet 338
Montesquieu, Charles de 354
Montgolfier, Joseph Michel and Jacques Etienne 356
Morris, William 234, 360, 364, 365, 370
Moser, Koloman 13, 67, 86, 86, 122, 178, 179, 182, 188, 189, 194, 198, 207, 208, 208, 209, 210, 212, 214, 215, 218, 219, 220, 234, 235, 236, 238, 239, 248, 254, 255, 258, 259, 272, 280, 285, 292, 294, 297, 301, 303, 311, 317, 324, 331, 333, 336, 338, 339, 341, 343, 344, 344, 345, 345, 346, 348, 348, 364, 364, 370, 371, 374, 384,
Moser, Editha née Mautner von Markhof 235, 236, 280, 343, 343, 345
Mozart, Wolfgang Amadeus 380, 382
Müller, Karl H. 381
Musil, Robert 359, 360
Myrbach, Felician 384
Nabokov, Vladimir 359
Nákó, Count Alexander 377
Napoleon Bonaparte 28, 62, 96, 354, 377
Natorp, Franz Wilhelm 382
Newton, Sir Isaac 354, 369
Nietzsche, Friedrich 358
Nobile, Peter von 74
Olbrich, Josef Maria 345, 347, 370, 384
Oppenordt, Gilles-Marie 369
Orefelt, Gunnar 310
Ozenfant 365
Palladio, Andrea 368
Paul, Bruno 370
Paul, Jean 355
Parke, Henry 20
Peche, Dagobert 48, 210, 340, 341, 344, 348, 349, 374
Pegge, Samuel 355
Pendias, Rolf 314, 315
Perco, Rudolf 348
Pernerstorfer, Engelbert 384
Perrault, Claude 368, 369
Perret, Auguste 364
Pevsner, Nikolaus 364, 365
Pezzl, Johann 356, 381
Pfeiffer, Johann 372
Plečnik, Jože 272, 370
Plössl, Simon 70
Poiret, Paul 259
Polo, Marco 354
Pompadour, Madame de 371
Poussin, Nicolas 368
Powell-Tuck, Julian 310
Prado, Jeronimo 368, 369
Prandstetter, Martin 382
Prigge, Walter 381
Proudhon, Pierre Joseph 358
Puchberg, Johann Michael 382
Puthon, Johann Baptist 382

Pythagoras 368
Rafael Viñoly Architects 318
Ranninger (Ranniger), Benedikt Nicolaus 31, 31, 33, 59, 75, 365, 386, 389
Ratschky, Johann 382
Reinalter, Helmut 392
Rémy-Berzenkovich, Ladislaus von 343
Rémy-Berzenkovich, Margarethe von 343
Respinger, Marguerite 245
Ressel, Josef 357
Retzer, Joseph von 382
Reuss, Princess 344
Richard Rogers & Partners 308
Riegl, Alois 337, 338
Rietveld, Gerrit 294
Rodchenko, Alexander 286
Rodin, Auguste 246
Roentgen, Konrad 371
Rohan 378
Rohe, Mies van der 363, 365
Roller, Alfred 370, 384
Rossi, Aldo 132, 132, 312
Rudolph I, King of Holy Roman Empire 356
Rukschcio, Burkhardt 344
Ruskin, John 358, 360
Rutherford, Lord 371
Sabattini, Lino 124
Sacher, Franz 60
Saint-Simon, Henri de 358
Salten, Felix 144
Salzer, Helene née Wittgenstein 267, 285
Salzer, Ida née Franz 230
Salzer, Johanna née Wittgenstein 212, 213, 230, 346, 348
Salzer, Johannes "Hans" 212, 213, 230
Sander, Christian 121, 213, 230
Saurau, Count Franz 382
Saxe-Teschen, Albert Duke of 372
Schaefer, Herwin 365
Schaukal, Richard von 347
Scheiger (Schleicher), Carl 158, 390,
Scheinast, Emerich 373
Schiffer, Eduard 161, 390
Schikaneder, Emanuel 382
Schindler, Alma (see Mahler, Alma née Schindler) 188, 189, 189, 345
Schindler, Emil Jakob 188
Schleicher, Jakob 118, 390
Schmedes, Anna von, née Hochstetter 346
Schmedes, Kurt von 346
Schmidt, Friedrich Otto 180
Schmuttermeier, Elisabeth 62, 386
Schmutzer, Jakob Matthias 382
Schneider, Jean Baptist 50
Schnitzler, Arthur 344
Schoenberg, Arnold 359, 383, 384
Schönborn-Buchheim, Count Georg 245
Schorske, Carl 383
Schubert, Franz (composer) 357
Schubert, Franz (silversmith) 125, 152, 380
Schur, Moriz 264, 267
Schwarzenberg, Prince Felix 375
Scott, Sir Walter 356
Sealsfield, Charles a.k.a. Karl Postl 61, 63
Sedelmayer (Sedlmeyer), Karl 77, 123, 132, 132, 390
Seewald, Dr. 343, 344
Sekler, Eduard F. 336
Seymour, Robert 162
Sjögren, Arvid 245
Sjögren, Carl "Talla" 245
Slutzky, Naum 109
Snellmann, Johan Vilhelm 160
Soane, Sir John 84
Soliman, Angelo 382
Sonnenfels, Josef von 356, 359, 382
Sorgenthal, Konrad von 24
Soufflot, Jacques-Germain 76
Spitzweg, Carl 356
Stadion 378
Stalzer, Hans 345, 345
Stamp, Gavin 234
Starobinski, Jean 341
Stein, Gertrude 359
Steiner, Dietmar 341
Stelzer (also Stölzer), Joseph 41, 105, 390
Stifter, Adalbert 357
Stoclet, Adolphe 343, 345
Stoclet, Suzanne 343, 345
Stonborough, Jerome 214, 214, 240, 241, 347, 348
Stonborough, Pierre 348
Stonborough-Wittgenstein, Margaret née Margherita Wittgenstein 176, 214, 215, 240, 241, 241, 245, 246, 254, 267, 267, 285, 347, 347, 348, 348, 349
Strasnitzki, Count 344
Sturm, Alexander 182, 188, 346, 374, 392
Sturm, Maria 346
Sullivan, Louis Henri 339
Sunstenau von Schützenthal, Editha Baroness 233, 234
Suuronen, Matti 174
Swieten, Gottfried van 381, 382
Szeps, Berta (see Zuckerkandl, Berta née Szeps) 188, 207, 280, 344, 345, 382
Taufferer, Baron Siegfried 382
Teltscher, Franz 373
Thonet, Michael 52, 52
Tischbein, Johann Heinrich Wilhelm 355
Trattner, Johann Thomas 382
Trésaguet, Pierre 354
Trollope, Frances 46, 82, 95, 128, 148

Uglow, Jenny 36
Valadier, Luigi 128, 129
Van de Velde, Henry 234, 365
Vantongerloo, Georges 288, 296
Varnhagen, Rahel 355, 357
Venturini, Guido 130
Verne, Jules 359
Verständig, Lorenz 376
Villalpando, Juan Baptista 368, 369
Vitruvius 368
Voigtländer and Son 151
Voltaire 354
Voysey, C. F. A. 364
Waerndorfer (Warndof), Charley 220
Waerndorfer, Adrienne 343
Waerndorfer, August 343
Waerndorfer, Friedrich "Fritz" 40, 120, 172, 198, 208, 220, 220, 223, 235, 239, 266, 285, 343, 343, 364, 371, 384
Waerndorfer, Lili née Hellmann 120, 172, 220, 223, 252, 280, 343, 344
Wagenfeld, Wilhelm 93, 110, 118, 119, 120, 121
Wagenmann & Böttger 164, 390
Wagner, Josef 393
Wagner, Otto 96, 182, 339, 348, 365, 370, 381, 383
Walcher, Joseph 381
Wallnöfer, Carl 112, 115
Wallnöfer (Walnefer, Wallnöffer), Franz, Sr. 390
Wärndofer, Samuel 343
Wärndorfer, Bertha 343
Wastel (Wastl), Johann Michael 167, 391
Watt, James 110, 356
Weckbecker, Johann Peter 376
Wedgwood, Josiah 56
Weinbrenner, Joseph Paul 382
Weirich (Weyrich), Joseph 107, 391
Weiss (Weihs), Jakob 155, 391
Weissenböck (Weisenböck), Franz de Paula Anton 71, 391
Wells, H. G. 359
Wenzel Bachmann & Co. 392
Werfel, Franz 188
Wertnik, Adolf 393
Wetzlar von Planenstein, Raimund 382
Wieninger (Winninger), Joseph 35, 101, 103, 391
Wieninger (Wienninger), Lorenz 356, 386, 391
Wijdeveld, Paul 254
Wilczek, Count Hans 378
Wimmer-Wisgrill, Eduard Josef 208
Winckelmann, Johann Joachim 90, 355, 363, 364, 370
Winterberg, Lotti (see Fanto, Lotti née Winterberg) 346, 346
Wit, Ferdinand Johannes genannt von Dörring 159, 159
Witt-Dörring, Christian 43, 212, 220, 267
Wittelshöfer, Otto 384
Wittgenstein, Anna 212
Wittgenstein, Clara 212
Wittgenstein, Clothilde 212
Wittgenstein, Emilie "Milly" 212
Wittgenstein, Fanny née Figdor 212, 212, 346
Wittgenstein, Franziska "Lydia" 212
Wittgenstein, Friedrich "Fritz" 348
Wittgenstein, Heinz 348
Wittgenstein, Helene (see Salzer, Helene née Wittgenstein) 267, 285
Wittgenstein, Hermann 192, 210, 212, 212, 220, 252, 261, 348
Wittgenstein, Hermann Christian 346
Wittgenstein, Hermine "Fine" 212
Wittgenstein, Hermine "Mining" 212, 214, 215, 267, 347, 348, 349
Wittgenstein, Johanna (see Salzer, Johanna née Wittgenstein) 212, 213, 230, 346, 348
Wittgenstein, Justine née Hochstetter 212, 346
Wittgenstein, Karl 86, 208, 212, 240, 241, 241, 254, 254, 276, 343, 346, 346, 347, 347, 348
Wittgenstein, Leopoldine "Poldy" née Kallmus 242, 254, 254, 255, 348
Wittgenstein, Ludwig "Louis" 212
Wittgenstein, Ludwig 106, 245, 254, 285, 348, 383
Wittgenstein, Margherita (see Stonborough-Wittgenstein, Margaret née Margherita Wittgenstein) 176, 214, 215, 240, 241, 241, 245, 246, 254, 267, 267, 285, 347, 347, 348, 348, 349
Wittgenstein, Marie 212
Wittgenstein, Ottilie "Bertha" 212
Wittgenstein, Paul 184, 212, 246, 247, 344, 346, 347
Wlach, Oskar 341
Worringer, Wilhelm 338
Wren, Sir Christopher 369
Wright, Frank Lloyd 364, 365
Würbel & Czokally 182, 392
Würth (Wirth), Ignatz Franz Joseph 119, 372, 372, 392
Würth (Wirth, after 1827 Edler von), Ignaz Sebastian Joseph (Sebastian Ignaz) 19, 372, 392
Würth (Wirth, after 1827 Edler von), Alois Johann Nepomuk 24, 107, 114, 127, 363, 391
Würth (Wirth, after 1827 Edler von), Franz Joseph Seraphin 110, 111, 363, 391
Zapf, Norman F. 172, 173
Zauner, Franz Anton 382
Zaunschirm, Thomas 336
Zeiller, Franz von 382
Zeppelin, Count 360
Zinzendorf, Count 40
Zuckerkandl, Berta née Szeps 188, 207, 280, 344, 345, 382
Zuckerkandl, Victor 207, 346
Zweig, Stefan 345

PHOTOGRAPHY AND

COPYRIGHT CREDITS

The credits for the black-and-white reproductions in the catalogue are listed with each individual image, except in cases in which owners wished to remain anonymous. The color plate credits (exhibition objects) are as follows:

Asenbaum Photo Archive:
Plate p. 17; cat. nos. 2–100, 103–113, 115–125, 127–133, 135–139, 141–144, 146–150, 152, 156–182

Dirk Bakker, Detroit:
Cat. nos. 114, 134

Kunsthistorisches Museum Vienna, Kunstkammer:
Cat. no. 1

MAK, Vienna:
Cat. nos. 153–155

David Schlegel, New York:
Cat. nos. 126, 140, 145, 151

Technisches Museum mit der Österreichischen Mediathek, Vienna:
Cat. nos. 101, 102